Florida's Lost Galleon

UNIVERSITY PRESS OF FLORIDA

Florida A&M University, Tallahassee
Florida Atlantic University, Boca Raton
Florida Gulf Coast University, Ft. Myers
Florida International University, Miami
Florida State University, Tallahassee
New College of Florida, Sarasota
University of Central Florida, Orlando
University of Florida, Gainesville
University of North Florida, Jacksonville
University of South Florida, Tampa
University of West Florida, Pensacola

FLORIDA'S LOST GALLEON
The Emanuel Point Shipwreck

EDITED BY ROGER C. SMITH

Foreword by Elizabeth D. Benchley

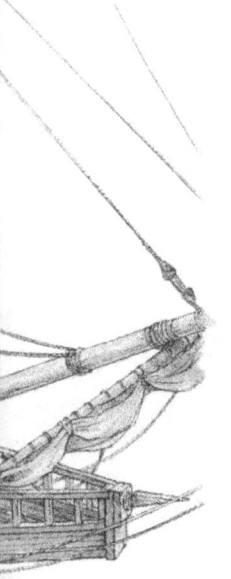

University Press of Florida
Gainesville · Tallahassee · Tampa · Boca Raton
Pensacola · Orlando · Miami · Jacksonville · Ft. Myers · Sarasota

Copyright 2018 by Roger C. Smith
All rights reserved
Published in the United States of America

Frontis: Hypothetical Reconstruction of the Emanuel Point Ship, painting by John LoCastro. Courtesy of the artist.

First cloth printing, 2018
First paperback printing, 2026

31 30 29 28 27 26   6 5 4 3 2 1

Library of Congress Cataloging-in-Publication Data
Names: Smith, Roger C., 1949–2020 editor. | Benchley, Elizabeth D., author of foreword.
Title: Florida's lost galleon : the Emanuel Point Shipwreck / edited by Roger C. Smith ; foreword by Elizabeth D. Benchley.
Description: Gainesville : University Press of Florida, 2018. | Includes bibliographical references and index.
Identifiers: LCCN 2017030451 | ISBN 9780813056760 (cloth) | ISBN 9780813081625 (pbk)
Subjects: LCSH: Underwater archaeology—Florida—Pensacola Bay. | Shipwrecks—Florida—Pensacola Bay. | Pensacola Bay (Fla.)—Antiquities.
Classification: LCC CC77.U5 F59 2018 | DDC 975.9/99—dc23
LC record available at https://lccn.loc.gov/2017030451

The University Press of Florida is the scholarly publishing agency for the State University System of Florida, comprising Florida A&M University, Florida Atlantic University, Florida Gulf Coast University, Florida International University, Florida State University, New College of Florida, University of Central Florida, University of Florida, University of North Florida, University of South Florida, and University of West Florida.

University Press of Florida
PO Box 140239
Gainesville, FL 3261
floridapress.org

GPSR EU Authorized Representative: Mare Nostrum Group B.V, Doelen 72, 4831 GR Breda, The Netherlands, gpsr@mare-nostrum.co.uk

This book is dedicated to Gigi Bertsch-Naggatz (1958–2016), who generously donated her talents and time to the investigation and interpretation of the Emanuel Point Ship.

CONTENTS

List of Figures ix

Foreword xiii
Elizabeth D. Benchley

Acknowledgments xv

1. The Old Spaniard: Introduction 1
   Roger C. Smith

2. Marine Archaeology Comes to Pensacola: Archaeological Background 7
   Roger C. Smith

3. Florida's Forgotten Colony: Historical Background 34
   John E. Worth

4. Nautical Archaeology of a Shipwreck: The Ship's Architecture 68
   James D. Spirek and Joseph Cozzi

5. What They Left Behind: The Artifact Assemblage 122
   John R. Bratten

6. Archaeology in the Laboratory: Artifact Conservation 207
   John R. Bratten

7. Pensacola's Public Participation: Outreach and Engagement 224
   Della A. Scott-Ireton

8. What We Learned: Conclusions 236
   John R. Bratten, Joseph Cozzi, Della A. Scott-Ireton, Roger C. Smith, James D. Spirek, and John E. Worth

9. New Discoveries: Epilogue 254
   Gregory D. Cook, John R. Bratten, and John E. Worth

Appendix 261
References 271
List of Contributors 287
Index 289

FIGURES

1.1. Wooden carving found near the pump well   3
2.1. Small howitzer caught in the dredge *Carolina*   10
2.2. *Pensacola News Journal* article   16
2.3. Cross section of the port side of the shipwreck   19
2.4. Breastplate and rudder as found *in situ*   23
2.5. Jim Spirek preparing the stern site plan   25
2.6. Visiting archaeologists conferring with John Bratten   27
2.7. Staff of the second excavation campaign   29
3.1. Atlas images of Filipina and "Puerto de Nostra Sora de Ochuz"   39
3.2. Painting of Luna's landing by Herbert Rudeen   46
3.3. Planned routes of the Luna expedition   51
3.4. Actual routes of the Luna expedition   54
4.1. Concave opening for the port side pump shaft   71
4.2. Tip of the anchor fluke poking out of the sand   73
4.3. Olive jar rim and shoulder sherd   75
4.4. Distinctive cross carved into the mainmast step   78
4.5. Port side buttresses, showing a broken bilge board   80
4.6. Mast step assembly and associated components   82
4.7. Stern site plan of the Emanuel Point Ship   86
4.8. Surviving lower portions of the ship's rudder   89
4.9. Excavation and recording tools   95
4.10. Dredge spoil being screened, searched, and sorted   96
4.11. Bow plan of the Emanuel Point Ship   100
4.12. Hanging knee that supported a deck beam in the bow   104
4.13. One of two gunport covers   106

4.14. Diagram showing the construction of a gunport cover 107
5.1. Wrought-iron anchor discovered near the ship's bow 124
5.2. Gudgeon that formed a component of the rudder hinge 127
5.3. Square and round fasteners used in the ship's construction 129
5.4. Lead sheathing from the sternpost area 131
5.5. Copper pitcher found in the forward part of the ship 135
5.6. Bruegel engraving (1558) with pitcher 136
5.7. Handle and rim of a copper cooking cauldron #1 138
5.8. Drawing of the entire cooking cauldron #1 139
5.9. Largest of four pieces of cauldron #4 142
5.10. Artist's rendition of likely cauldron #4 shape 142
5.11. Illustration from Scappi (1570) of cauldrons 143
5.12. Largely intact cup recovered from the wreck 145
5.13. Mortar and pestle recovered from the galley area 146
5.14. John Bratten displaying a conserved funnel 147
5.15. Spanish olive jar 151
5.16. Interior of an olive jar coated with pine resin 151
5.17. Chronological framework for olive jar rims 152
5.18. Majolica plate that was found intact 155
5.19. Aztec ceramic sherds with human facial features 157
5.20. Aztec codex showing pottery with human heads 158
5.21. Well-preserved cork, probably an olive jar stopper 161
5.22. Wooden tool handle, probably for an awl or gimlet 162
5.23. Galleon model (1540) and Emanuel Point silhouette carving 164
5.24. Leather sole of a small shoe 165
5.25. Part of a shoe sole broken across the tread 166
5.26. Animal bones, some with butcher marks 168
5.27. Drawing of a rat skeleton showing recovered bones 170
5.28. Remains of cockroaches and beetles 173

5.29. Sapote (*zapote*) seed 178

5.30. A sample of hundreds of recovered olive pits 179

5.31. Limestone cannon balls 183

5.32. Composite lead shot with an iron cube center 185

5.33. Iron and lead shot for a 16th-century wrought-iron cannon 187

5.34. Copper crossbow points 188

5.35. Breastplate reconstructed from CAT scans 193

5.36. Obsidian blades from central Mexico 195

5.37. Copper coin (*blanca*) recovered from the site 197

5.38. Apothecary weights used with a balance scale 199

6.1. Rope segment treated with a freeze dryer 210

6.2. Olive jar sherds with tannin stain 212

6.3. Charles Hughson using an air scribe 213

6.4. Copper funnel in solution while on display 215

6.5. James Hunter III catalogued finds with drawings 221

7.1. Statue of Tristán de Luna, Pensacola 225

7.2. Gigi Bertsch-Naggatz with school children 227

7.3. Fiesta of Five Flags 1994 banner 230

7.4. Spanish king and queen and the Florida governor visiting the wreck exhibit 233

8.1. Final site plan of the Emanuel Point Ship 245

8.2. Chronological chart of Emanuel Point Ship artifacts 251

9.1. UWF archaeology students entering the water 257

9.2. Secretary of State Kurt Browning and Greg Cook diving on Emanuel Point II 258

FOREWORD

It was an incredibly powerful and somewhat eerie feeling to stand on the bluff top of the Luna settlement site in 2016 and look out over the vast expanse of Pensacola Bay. The scene looked just as Tristán de Luna y Arellano had described it in August 1559, except that the ships at anchor were no longer visible. Most of them sank to the bottom of the bay when a hurricane ravaged the Spanish colonial settlement in September 1559. Now only the University of West Florida archaeology program dive barge marked the location of the former anchorage and the ship graveyard.

Luna had brought 1,500 soldiers, sailors, colonists, servants, slaves, and Mexican Indians to this shore from New Spain (Mexico) as part of a Spanish attempt to colonize what is now the Southeast United States. Had the expedition succeeded, the history of the nation would have unfolded very differently! Unfortunately, the hurricane sank six and drove aground one of Luna's twelve ships. The vessels were being used to store the expedition's abundant food supplies while a warehouse and other buildings were being constructed on land. The colonists struggled to survive after the loss of their provisions and searched far inland for Native American groups that might assist them. Eventually the expedition's survivors returned to Veracruz in August 1561 without having accomplished their goals.

The story of the archaeological discovery of the Luna settlement and its shipwrecks began in 1992, when Roger Smith and his team of underwater archaeologists from the Florida Bureau of Archaeological Research, Division of Historical Resources, conducted a magnetometer survey of likely areas in Pensacola Bay that matched Luna's descriptions. Near Emanuel Point the team noted a magnetic target and, diving on it, found indications that it marked an early Spanish shipwreck. This book tells the story of the discovery and years of archaeological research into what we now call the Emanuel Point I Ship. The compilation pulls together information from two field investigations and years of analysis by multiple investigators working under Smith's direction, along with new understandings from recent archival research into the colony. Rather than stressing technical details, the book is carefully written to appeal to the public as well as professional archaeologists.

The Emanuel Point Ship is important to archaeologists for the information it reveals about the construction of mid-16th-century Spanish ships, and about life aboard, and the story it tells about the colonization attempt. But it is also important because it spurred development of a maritime archaeology and public outreach program at the University of West Florida (UWF) that continues decades later. Since 1998 the UWF Archaeology Institute and the Department of Anthropology have regularly conducted surveys and excavations in the area using annual archaeological field schools and occasional multiyear grants from the Florida Division of Historical Resources. In 2007 UWF announced the discovery of a second Luna ship (Emanuel Point II). Soon after, UWF's Florida Public Archaeology Network began to assist in spreading the story of the ships to the public. In 2015 the UWF archaeology program announced the discovery of the Luna settlement site overlooking the shipwrecks. And in 2016 UWF announced the discovery of a third Luna ship, not surprisingly called Emanuel Point III. Over the next several decades, UWF anticipates continuing investigations on the Luna settlement and shipwrecks and enriching the story of North America's first multiyear Spanish colony with both archaeological and archival discoveries.

But it all began with Roger Smith's discovery and investigations of "The Old Spaniard," the Emanuel Point Ship, and the story is shared here for all to enjoy.

Elizabeth D. Benchley
Director, Division of Anthropology and Archaeology
and the Archaeology Institute
University of West Florida

ACKNOWLEDGMENTS

Staff of the Emanuel Point Ship project included John R. Bratten, Joseph "Coz" Cozzi, Charles Hughson, Jeffrey Lockwood, Amy Mitchell, Gigi Bertsch-Naggatz, Keith Plaskett, David Pugh, Della Scott-Ireton, Roger C. Smith, James Spirek, and Michael Williamson. Students who worked on the shipwreck as field school participants or graduate interns included Janet Bancroft, Jason M. Burns, Stuart Derrow, Andrea H. Fossum, Bradley Himour, James W. Hunter III, Sandra Johnson, Sheryl Kennedy, Bill Kerr, Shea McLean, Philip Mitchell, Kyle Mueller, Beth Padgett, David Pugh, Michael Scafuri, Ty Seale, Jinky Smalley, Clifford Smith, Monti Sommer, Lucas Spalding, Brenda Swann, Juliet Tatum, Greg Townsend, Solomon Wahrhaftig, Jenna Watts, Debra Wells, and Sean Williams. Master's theses on topics related to the shipwreck were written by James Collis, Mathew Gifford, Colleen Reese Lawrence, Andrew Marr, David Pugh, Ree Rodgers, Della Scott-Ireton, Jacob Shidner, Clifford Smith, Scott Sorset, and Debra Wells.

The following individuals provided professional input to and voluntary assistance with the project: Redell Akins, Paula Alexander, Christopher Amer, Rick Anuskiewicz, Philip Armitage, J. Barto Arnold III, George Avery, Beth Bader, Barry Baker, Tom Baurley, Robert Bell, Elizabeth D. Benchley, Judith A. Bense, Lt. Sam Black, Marion Blackburn, John Blackie, Marion Bleser, Walter Cardona Bonet, J. Earle Bowden, Dennis A. Bratten, David Breetzke, Robert Brill, Daniel Brimmer, Richard Brosnaham, Shirley and Ted Brown, Gary Bryan, Herb Bump, Frank Cantelas, Miller Caldwell, Worth Carlin, Candy Carlisle, Earl Caudell, Steve Cayona, Ashley Chapman, Tim Chapman, R. Wayne Childers, Sen. W. D. Childers, Carl Clausen, Rebecca Claypoole, Capt. Jeff Clopton, William Coker, James and Irene Coleman, Neal Collier, Annette Cook, David J. Cooper, Robert Corbett, Peg Couch, Alan Craig, Kevin J. Crisman, Caleb Curren, Pat D'Asaro, Denise Dambrackas, David J. Daniels, John Daniels, Ed and Janet Davies, Maria Davis, Kathleen Deagan, Dean DeBolt, John de Bry, Jonathan Decker, Cdr. Jeff Devonchik, Foster

Dickard, Harv Dickey, Calvin Dixon, Richard Doelker, Alan and Amy Drouin, Cullan Duke, Tonya Duke, Jim Dunbar, Lisa Dunbar, Rick Dye, Thomas Dykstra, Mitzi Elliott, Marshall Emerson, Ian Eaves, Jeff Farage, Michael Faught, Gene Ferguson, Richard Fillmore, E. L. "Connie" Franklin, Marianne Franklin, Corey Fulford, Jo Garber, Fred Gaske, Rob Gelhardt, Richard L. Giffin, Jeff Godwin, Don Goggans, Dave Goodwin, Wilton Goynes, Ed Gray, Robert Grenier, Glenn Grimm, Donny Hamilton, John Hann, Kelly J. Hardy, Norma J. Harris, Andy Hemmings, Victor Henry, Daphne Hills, David L. Hilton, Kenneth Hirth, S. Randall Hobgood, Fred Hocker, Paul Hoffman, Charlie Holifield, James Hunter III, John Ireton, Jack Irion, Davis Janowski, Paula Jenkins, Bob Johnson, Dora Johnson, Sandra Johnson, Valerie Joseph, Bill Kaczor, Donald Keith, Alexandra Kiefer, Adm. Robert Kihune, Ann Kirkland, Warren Kirkland, John Kleeberg, Philip Koehler, Hera Konstantinou, James Ladd, Cathy Laird, Denise Lakey, Charles Lambert, Chuck Lapp, Michael Lawton, Alexandra Lee, Anne Lessmann, Roy Lett, James Levy, Brad Loewen, Abraham López, Alessandro López Pérez, Paul Lukkar, Eugene Lyon, Pilar Luna Erreguerena, "Mac" MacDonald, Harold and Pat Marcus, Corey Malcom, Vince and Marion Margiotti, Bonnie Martin, Colin Martin, Duff Martin, Morris Marx, John Maseman, Burl McCoy, Peggy McCready, Keith McIntyre, Lee McKenzie, Dan McLeod, Don McMahon, Dep. Tim McNeil, Chuck Meide, Jennifer Melcher, Ralph Meldahl, Erica Meyer, Jim Miller, Bill Mills Jr., Karen Mims, Steven Mitchell, Lee Monks, Rob Moon, Carolyn Moore, David Moore, Robin Moore, John W. (Billy Ray) Morris III, Bill Muhe, Tom Muir, Deborah R. Mullins, Larry Murphy, Gigi Bertsch-Naggatz, Jeffrey Naggatz, Rhonda New, Lee Newsom, Joseph Neville, Lynette Nore, Sgt. Fred Nye, Thomas Oertling, Robert Overton, Harvey Oyer, J. Mike Palmer, Cathy Parker, Mickey Pate, Jane Peebles, June Peery, George Percy, Brett Phaneuf, John Phillips, Stephen Pollock, Anna Lee Presley, Dawn Printy, Geoffrey Purcell, Betty Rainwater, Pat Regan, Brenda Reid, Margaret Reining, Lucy Rentz, Mable Revell, John Richardson, Al and Martha Riddlehoover, Ryan Robbins, Lynn Robertson, Jerrold Roof, Deanna Roose, Mathew Russell, Sherrie Shaw, Dianne Sherer, Joe Simmons, Dick Smith, KC Smith, John Soule, Alan Stahl, James Stegall, Margo Stringfield, Brenda Swann, June Swann, Charlie Switzer, Robert Taylor, John Joseph Temple,

Sgt. Dale Tharpe, Louis Vallon, Nancy Van Epps, Robert Vickery, Stuart Vine, Rudy Vizsla, Terry Voss, Cheryl Ward, Teresa Ward, Liz Watkins, Janice Watts, Suzanne Weathers, Eri Weinstein, T. J. Weismann, Nico Wienders, Randy Williams, Capt. Bradley Williams, Carrie Williams, Maurice Williams, Mike Williamson, Jacki Wilson, Sandra Windham, Elliot Wright, Bonnie Yates, and Brian Yates.

Funding for research, excavation, analysis, and conservation was provided by the Florida Department of State, Division of Historical Resources; Historic Pensacola Preservation Board; Historic Pensacola Inc.; University of West Florida; Pensacola Maritime Preservation Society; and City of Pensacola. Sub-grants of funds were received from the National Oceanic and Atmospheric Administration (NOAA) through the Florida Coastal Management Program. A legislative appropriation from monies collected by the Florida Department of Commerce from sales of Quincentenary auto tags also was awarded to the project. Sponsorship of twelve graduate student internships and two summer lecture series was generously provided by the Fiesta of Five Flags Association Inc. and the Gulf Breeze Historical Society, Gulf Coast Dive Pros Inc., Gulf Power Company, Pensacola Archaeological Society, Pensacola Historical Society, Pensacola Welcome and Information Center, and Pensacola Yacht Club.

Additional support for the field and laboratory work was generously offered by a number of national and local businesses, including Autodesk Inc., Basic Chemicals Inc., Bell Steel Company, Bogan Supply Company Inc., Brown Marine Services, Building Supply Center, Byfield Marine Supply, Diversified Manufacturing, Cordova Mall, E & B Boat Gear Discount Marine, Emerald Coast X-Ray, Epson of America, First City Paint & Decorating, Florida Drum Company, GTE Wireless Services, Gulf Breeze Dive Pros, Gulf Coast Dive Pros, Gulf Coast Metal Fabrication, Gulf Power Company, Jasco Metal Detectors, Johnson Supply Company, Killinger Marine, Lamar Advertising Company, Licon Inc., Marine Sonic Technology, McMahon and Associates, Monsanto Company, Pensacola Hardware Company, *Pensacola News Journal*, Pensacola Rubber and Gasket Company, Peoples First Community Bank, Pitt Slip Marina, Renfroe Pecan Company, Sacred Heart Hospital, Seville Harbor, Soule Marine Enterprises, Subway Sandwiches & Salads, SunBank of West Florida, T-Square Reprographics, The Boat, WEAR Channel 3, West Marine, W. R. Taylor & Company, and Ye Olde Beef & Ale House.

The authors also would like to acknowledge the involvement and participation of the Bureau of Ocean Energy Management, Escambia County Sheriff's Department, Florida Marine Patrol, Gulf Breeze Rotary Club, Pensacola Archaeological Society, Pensacola Civitan Club, Pensacola Downtown Rotary Club, Pensacola Naval Air Station, Pensacola North Rotary Club, Pensacola Power Squadron, Pensacola Sertoma Club, Ships of Discovery, Washington High School Archaeology Institute, the United States Coast Guard, and the UWF Archaeology Institute for funding much of the later research.

We are also grateful to the external reviewers of the manuscript, Colin J. M. Martin and J. Barto Arnold III, for their careful assessments and useful comments. KC Smith patiently provided preliminary copy edits of the manuscript to make this a better book. We want to thank especially University Press of Florida Director Meredith Morris-Babb, who unflaggingly insisted that we build this book, and her exceptional staff, final copy editor Sally Antrobus, project editor Eleanor Deumens, and book designer Larry Leshan.

Florida's Lost Galleon

1

The Old Spaniard

Introduction

ROGER C. SMITH

As the afternoon diving shift began at the newly discovered shipwreck off Emanuel Point in Pensacola Bay, it was my turn to continue testing the sediments around the mainmast step. I joined the other team members suiting up on the barge and plunged into the water. This immersion ritual, the abrupt transition from air to liquid, is the way in which underwater archaeologists commute to their workplace. However, in this case it took just a few seconds because the site is only 4 m deep. Although the sun was bright, as I approached my work station, visibility decreased in the tea-colored water.

We had begun the excavation by removing some of the ballast stones that had stabilized the ship under sail. We soon discovered pieces of pottery, hemp rope, shoe leather, and olive pits that were surprisingly well preserved in the sediments. We then uncovered the square cavity cut into the keelson to accept the heel of the ship's mainmast, noting a deeper recess on each side for the two bilge pumps. These wells housed the lower ends of the pump shafts, which were fashioned from hollowed-out tree trunks. To protect the wells from becoming clogged with small ballast and other debris, a shallow wooden box had been constructed around the mast and pump shafts. Although these elements were no longer present in the lower hull, remains of the crushed box were evident.

With trowel and paintbrush I began gently exploring layers of silt covering the ship's lower hull. As I fanned the area with my hand, the activity attracted small resident fish hoping that I would uncover something for them to eat. Archaeologists who work underwater become accustomed to the companionship of marine life, especially when their excavations complement the food chain. We normally are tolerant of this company, except when our new friends become impatient and competitive, nipping our fingers to encourage us to work faster. As I swept away the silt with my paintbrush, I saw small carpenter's scraps with adze scars that littered the area around the pump wells. All of a sudden there appeared in my hand a wooden scrap that had a distinctly carved shape; looking at it closely in the dim light, I could discern the outline of a ship. The small, thin piece of waterlogged wood revealed the classic features of a 16th-century galleon—the heavy overhanging beak of the bow, high forecastle and sterncastle, and the balconied gallery at the stern. Whoever fashioned this simple sliver of wood had captured the hallmark characteristics of a ship just like the one we were excavating.

At first I thought this carved ship silhouette might be a child's toy that had become lost in the bilge, but then I realized that it probably had been left behind by the carpenters who constructed the pump well box. I imagined the men taking a lunch break from their work to whittle wood and chat about shipyard experiences. Their "spit and whittle" club was interrupted when the foreman called down the main hatch for them to return to work, and the little ship carving was left behind. As I held the unique, orphaned artifact in my hand, I thought about how many miles and years it had traveled from when the ship was launched until my afternoon shift at the bottom of Pensacola Bay. I wondered whether I had perhaps discovered the "soul" of the ship that wrecked off Emanuel Point.

The shipwreck was discovered in 1992 during a pilot survey of Pensacola Bay conducted by the Florida Bureau of Archaeological Research (BAR) to develop a regional inventory and management model for shipwrecks. The survey sought to locate and assess submerged watercraft in a broad range of aquatic environments and spanning eight periods of Florida's maritime history.[1] Assisted in these explorations by information supplied by local divers and fishermen, the Pensacola Shipwreck Survey also used electronic remote sensing tools to search the waters of the bay. These instruments helped us to find submerged targets, which

Figure 1.1. This small wooden carving was found near the pump well of the ship. Courtesy of the Florida Department of State, Division of Historical Resources.

then were buoyed and dived. When we anchored our boat next to each buoy and quickly swam down the anchor line, we often encountered curious fish inspecting the hook and could follow them to the target, which was their home. During our searches in the bay, we came across construction debris, anchorage refuse, dredging equipment, and "midnight reefs" comprising old auto bodies, appliances, and other rubble dumped at night by fishermen to create secret fishing spots. However, we also discovered the remains of historic watercraft dating from the Spanish, British, and early American occupations of Pensacola.[2] During two years of exploration, more than forty-five sunken vessels were studied; approximately one half were found to have been abandoned rather than wrecked.[3]

In 1992 our survey team included field director Jim Spirek, field supervisor Della Scott-Ireton, and field technicians Chuck Hughson and Mike Williamson. Progressing into the eastern portion of the bay, we encountered an isolated magnetic target in shallow water off the mouth of Bayou Texar, near Emanuel Point. Chuck, Della, and Jim dived to inspect the area and discovered a small, oyster-encrusted mound of ballast stones partially buried in a sandbar. Initial testing of the central portion of the mound revealed that below the stones and sand were the remains of a wooden sailing ship. The source of the magnetic anomaly was found to be a large wrought-iron anchor, buried fluke down at the shoreward edge of the ballast pile.[4] The vessel's mainmast step and its associated architecture revealed distinctive characteristics of early colonial construction.[5] Field specimens of organic materials and botanical remains demonstrated an unusual state of preservation. Sherds of earthenware pottery that appeared to be older than those from other sites in the bay, and fragments of leather and rope from the bilge, suggested the ship might be Spanish, dating from the sixteenth century. The condition of some of the wooden ship remains suggested that it had grounded violently on the sandbar. Broken apart and gradually deteriorating, the ship provided a home to generations of shellfish that lived and died among the timbers and stones, creating a compact matrix of shell and sediments that capped its grave and provided natural protection from storms, occasional fishermen, and modern shrimpers. Our survey work was interrupted by this discovery, which we called "The Old Spaniard," but eventually we renamed it the Emanuel Point Ship for the nearby landform.

Our story begins with how marine archaeology came to Pensacola. A review of early research tied to naval homeport improvement activities is recounted, leading to the state-sponsored Pensacola Shipwreck Survey and its partnerships with the University of West Florida and the Historic Pensacola Preservation Board (now the UWF Historic Trust). Discovery of the Emanuel Point Ship and its characteristics and condition are described, and two campaigns of investigations are outlined, resulting in museum exhibits and a maritime archaeology program at the university.

This is followed by a discussion of Pensacola Bay, its maritime geography as one of the Gulf of Mexico's protected deep harbors, and the early history of European exploration of the Florida panhandle. John Worth traces the voyages of early Spanish navigators who mapped the northern frontiers of New Spain, prompting royal plans for expansion of the colonial territory to the peninsula of Florida. These explorations culminated in the 1559 effort to establish a Spanish colony on the northern rim of the Gulf, at Pensacola, and another on the Atlantic seaboard at a headland called Santa Elena. Commanded by Tristán de Luna y Arellano, twelve ships carrying more than fifteen hundred people embarked from Veracruz, Mexico, on a voyage to Florida. Using official correspondence and archival documents, Worth pieces together the story of this settlement expedition, which ended in disaster because a hurricane struck the colonists only weeks after their arrival in Pensacola Bay.

As a significant element of the well-preserved shipwreck, the Emanuel Point Ship's architecture is discussed in detail by Jim Spirek and Joe Cozzi. Taking the reader with them, they explore the lower hull of the buried wreckage, measuring and recording the parts and pieces of sixteenth-century ship carpentry and explaining how these fit together to form a seagoing vessel of transport. The purpose of this nautical archaeology was to attempt to compile dimensions (scantlings) of the principal timbers to reconstruct the size and cargo capacity of the original ship before it wrecked. Careful observations of construction features provide clues to the age and condition of the ship on its last voyage.

In chapter 5 John Bratten describes the ship's hardware, including its anchor, fastenings, ballast, and lead sheathing. The shipwreck's artifact assemblage is discussed in detail as the material culture of the ship—reflected by the recovery of ceramic and galley wares, cargos and stores, personal possessions, faunal and floral remains, and ordnance and tools—tells the story of a seagoing Spanish galleon.

In chapter 6 Bratten explores the archaeology that was conducted in his conservation laboratories and how he equipped these facilities, used them for analysis and stabilization of waterlogged materials, and adapted them as teaching environments.

Next, Della Scott-Ireton relates the importance of public outreach for the archaeological investigations at Emanuel Point. She details how volunteers were integrated into field and laboratory work, how the project was covered by print and video media, and how presentations, lectures, and reports documented the research in professional and popular arenas.

The authors present their conclusions about the Emanuel Point Ship with discussions about how its wrecking, subsequent salvage by survivors, and evolution as an archaeological site have been reconstructed through excavation and analysis of its contents. Conclusions about the ship's role in Latin American history and archaeology also are offered.

Finally, Greg Cook, Bratten, and Worth present an epilogue that describes UWF's continuing research on shipwrecks in Pensacola Bay. Discovery of two additional vessels from the fleet of Tristán de Luna (Emanuel Point II and III Ships), and the preliminary results of Emanuel Point II's investigation, are discussed in relationship to the first Luna shipwreck. The unearthing of clues to the upland site of Luna's settlement on the bluff at Emanuel Point is also presented. Expectations for the future of research into sixteenth-century Pensacola are outlined to alert readers to further exciting books to come.

Notes

1. Franklin, Morris, and Smith, *Submerged Historical Resources of Pensacola Bay*.
2. Smith, "Pensacola's Colonial Maritime Resources."
3. Spirek et al., "Submerged Historical Resources, Phase Two."
4. Smith, "The Ship at Emanuel Point."
5. Spirek, "Pinned to the Bottom."

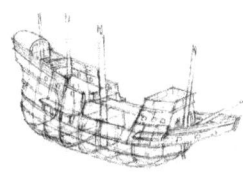

2

Marine Archaeology Comes to Pensacola

Archaeological Background

ROGER C. SMITH

In 1987, shortly after taking my post as Florida's state underwater archaeologist, Bureau of Archaeological Research Chief Jim Miller, my new boss, sent me a newspaper clipping from the *New Orleans Times Picayune*. The article featured a young man named Larry Broussard and artifacts he had collected during weekend dives in Pensacola Bay. A photo showed Broussard, a medical student at Louisiana State University, with an array of iron and other encrusted objects that his research suggested came from a Civil War shipwreck named *Judah* in shallow water at the western portion of the bay. Miller suggested that I contact Norman Simons, then curator of the Pensacola Historical Society Museum, who might shed light on *Judah* and other shipwrecks in the area. I soon learned that for years Simons had carefully collected records of ship losses, old charts and maps, reports of wreck sites, oral histories, and artifacts recovered by divers. He and I contacted Broussard, who agreed to bring the artifacts and meet with us at the museum, housed at Old Christ Church in Pensacola's historic district. I invited Judy Bense, an archaeology professor at the University of West Florida, to attend the Saturday meeting, and she brought her assistant, Caleb Curren. Our discussions soon turned from *Judah* and the artifacts that Broussard had found to the need for an underwater survey of the bay to search for its maritime secrets.

Designation of the Gulf Islands National Seashore in 1971 had prompted an archaeological survey of portions of the new park by Florida State University. With assistance from Simons and others, eight maritime sites were recorded on land and in shallow water.[1] Meanwhile, the National Park Service conducted a brief offshore reconnaissance with a magnetometer near Fort Pickens, but divers encountered no cultural materials.[2] More than a decade later, prior to dredging the Pensacola harbor channel and turning basin for the U.S. Navy's Strategic Homeporting Project, the U.S. Army Corps of Engineers conducted a remote sensing survey in front of the Pensacola Naval Air Station. The two-week survey in 1986 located 173 magnetic targets, of which fifty-six were associated with side-scan sonar images.[3] Twelve were selected for additional investigation, and the following year Tidewater Atlantic Research was contracted to investigate the targets. None were found to be significant, but the scattered remains of *Convoy*, a nearby shipwreck, were recorded.[4] This was the same site from which Broussard had recovered artifacts, thinking that they were from *Judah*. It soon became clear that the Pensacola Bay system was rich with maritime heritage sites. For example, in 1988 local Milton resident Warren Weeks guided me to the site of a well-preserved, two-masted coastal schooner submerged in a back bayou of the Blackwater River. Almost 100 feet in length, the early nineteenth-century vessel was intact from rails to the keel, with its pump and windlass still in place.

In May 1988 Simons and I organized a conference on maritime history and marine archaeology, sponsored jointly by the Florida Division of Historical Resources, Pensacola Historical Society, Historic Pensacola Preservation Board, and University of West Florida. The conference brought together for the first time networks of amateur historians and archaeologists, recreational divers, commercial fishermen, and university and state archaeologists, who began to focus on local maritime history and the potential for marine archaeology in Pensacola Bay. The conference was complemented by the opening of an exhibit of Broussard's artifacts from *Convoy*.

Within months of the conference, UWF archaeologists conducting a terrestrial survey of Deadman's Island for the City of Gulf Breeze were shown the remains of a small colonial ship eroding from the beach in shallow water. Bense invited me and my wife KC to help make a preliminary investigation of the site with students and volunteers, and together we organized a marine archaeology lecture class that was taught in the spring of 1989.[5] The class included fieldwork on a fishing smack buried under the sand at Perdido Key.[6]

Due to the exposed and fragile condition of the wreck at Deadman's Island, a university field school to record the site was undertaken during the summer of 1989. With the co-sponsorship and support of the City of Gulf Breeze, ten undergraduate students from several universities received classroom and field training under supervision by Robert Finegold, Marianne Franklin, and me.[7] We discovered that the small colonial British vessel had been in the process of careening (exposing its hull for cleaning and repair), when she was found to be unseaworthy and apparently was abandoned.[8] A permanent exhibit with artifacts and interpretive materials was installed at the Gulf Breeze Recreation (now Community) Center.

Concurrent with the field school, a team of volunteers under the direction of East Carolina University graduate student David Baumer thoroughly documented the Blackwater schooner, which was placed on the National Register of Historic Places the following year.[9] Loaded with a partial cargo of bricks, the schooner had been abandoned near a local brickyard and forgotten. An eroded name board on its transom was illegible, so the vessel's identity remained a mystery.

Early in 1990, during dredging operations to deepen the entrance channel to Pensacola Bay for the Strategic Homeporting Project, a bronze artillery piece became lodged in the pump of the dredge vessel *Carolina*.[10] A concerned crew member released the news to local media, prompting temporary relocation of dredging activities. Corps of Engineers archaeologist Dorothy Gibbens invited me to inspect the find, and we made our way to the dredge with required hard hats and steel-toed boots. At the head of the boarding ladder, we were greeted by an enormous bulldog named Bud, which eagerly led us across the deck to the bronze cannon. The eighteenth-century howitzer's encounter with the dredge had left a piece of the steel cutter head embedded in the bronze.

Figure 2.1. Small bronze howitzer that became caught in dredge *Carolina*. Courtesy of the Florida Department of State, Division of Historical Resources.

While we were examining the piece, I noticed that Bud seemed to be signaling me to follow him, so I did. He led me to a corner of the barge where a large dumpster contained several splintered ship's timbers and a broken iron anchor, all of which apparently had been retrieved from the pump before it became jammed by the cannon. (Eventually Bud also proudly showed me his overstuffed chair in *Carolina*'s control house alongside the chair of the dredge's cigar-smoking operator.) The state subsequently took charge of the howitzer and asked the Corps to re-survey the area to locate the source of the materials, which appeared to represent a shipwreck. A brief visual and magnetic search, under Corps supervision at the location provided by the dredging contractor, failed to locate any historic materials.[11] After lengthy conservation treatment in the state laboratory, the howitzer was returned to Pensacola, where it remains today in the T. T. Wentworth Jr. Florida State Museum.

Dredging to deepen the navy pier to accommodate the aircraft carrier USS *Forrestal* suddenly stopped one day in 1990. The clamshell operator had noticed that copper-clad wooden beams were being pulled up. He went to his personal vehicle to don his SCUBA gear and investigate the source. With the assistance of navy divers, he determined that the submerged structure was more than 120 feet long and 50 feet wide. Later

Mike Williamson and I made an inspection dive and surfaced to confirm the historical discovery to a crowd of uneasy officials standing on the pier in uniforms and coats and ties. The State Historic Preservation Office requested that the dredging cease until a determination of the object's identity and significance was obtained. Panamerican Consultants Inc. was contracted to assess the site, which was partially excavated to reveal a large wooden container filled with stone, clay, and sand. Concurrent archival research in government records revealed details about a large caisson constructed and intentionally sunk by the navy in the early 1830s. It was agreed that after sufficient documentation and additional historical research, the structure could be removed, which occurred early in 1991. The project was completed after extensive recording of the caisson remains, collection and conservation of artifacts, and the construction of a scale model of the structure for public exhibit.[12]

Reported by local and regional media, these discoveries prompted a growing and intense curiosity about what else might be at the bottom of the bay. In a region of Florida noted for its active promotion of historic preservation, a new awareness about tangible relics of the area's maritime heritage began to emerge along the Pensacola waterfront. The time had come to begin a systematic survey and inventory of the bay's submerged cultural resources.

A Bathtub of Sunken Relics

In 1990 the Florida Bureau of Archaeological Research (BAR) received the first of a series of federal grants through the Florida Coastal Management Program to begin a pilot study of Pensacola Bay shipwrecks and to prepare a regional model for their management and protection. The Pensacola Shipwreck Survey was launched with staff members Marianne Franklin, John "Billy Ray" Morris, and me working with volunteers, including Broussard and Williamson. The project was housed in the city's historic waterfront district at the Tivoli High House in conjunction with the Historic Pensacola Preservation Board. Based on information collected by Simons at the historical society and reports supplied by local divers and fishermen, the first phase of the survey located, recorded, and assessed thirty-three sites of wrecked or abandoned vessels, ranging from colonial to modern times. The Bureau of Archaeological Research published a survey report with classifications of sites and recommendations for further work.[13] The recommendations included, among other things, remote sensing surveys and a formal survey of USS *Massachusetts*, the nation's oldest surviving battleship, which is lying offshore of Pensacola Pass and had been nominated by Broussard to become Florida's fourth Underwater Archaeological Preserve.[14]

The second phase of the Pensacola Shipwreck Survey began in 1992 with a new staff consisting of Jim Spirek, Della Scott-Ireton, Chuck Hughson, and Mike Williamson. The survey was headquartered at the Old Christ Church Parish School House in the historic district. Offshore, systematic mapping of USS *Massachusetts* produced site plans to compare with 1910 refit construction drawings of the ship. These archaeological data, combined with historical and archival materials, helped us to produce a formal proposal for the new preserve, which we presented to the public in May 1992 during a second conference on maritime history and archaeology.[15] The preserve officially opened the following year, on the hundredth anniversary of the battleship's launching.

A primary goal of the second phase was to conduct remote sensing operations in the bay to locate and record additional colonial vessels. As we planned our electronic survey operations, emphasis was placed on identifying areas of the bay associated with colonial maritime activities in Pensacola, especially those relating to the First Spanish (1513–1763) and Second Spanish (1781–1821) periods. The prospect of locating remains of the lost ships of the 1559 Tristán de Luna expedition prompted us to design a survey strategy toward that end.[16] We gathered historical, geographical, and local knowledge to determine which areas of the bay should be prioritized for electronic scrutiny that might turn up sites dating to the targeted time periods. Areas selected were the northwest and southwest shores of Pensacola Bay near its entrance, the northwest and southwest extremities of the Gulf Breeze peninsula, and Emanuel Point near the mouth of Bayou Texar.[17]

We used a marine magnetometer, which measures specific changes in the earth's magnetic field created by ferrous objects such as cannons and anchors; a LORAN-C position finder; and a marine fathometer. Alan Drouin and David Marsh came to help with their side-scan sonar dual track recorder and new global positioning system to search for acoustical reflections of man-made objects protruding from the bay floor. The survey was carried out using two veteran (read: old) state boats—a 21-foot cuddy-cabin recreational vessel to deploy the survey instruments and a 22-foot open fisherman to dive on targets. The 21-foot boat worked well until we noticed a strong smell of gasoline coming from the cabin and discovered a serious leak in the old galvanized fuel tank. After finally admitting that it was a floating bomb, we managed to fit a smaller fiberglass tank in the cabin space and continued the work. The 22-foot vessel had been a confiscated drug-smuggling boat (with a hidden compartment below deck) that we had convinced the Marine Patrol to transfer to BAR for one dollar. After a refit with a new transom and outboard engine, the boat was put back into service for a different purpose. An opportunity to purchase a new boat came in 1992 when we contracted with a Florida company to build a proper 21-foot dive boat to our specifications.

Casting a wide survey net over selected portions of the bay yielded many man-made targets; however, the majority that could be verified turned out to be modern, ranging from metal cables, pizza ovens, car bodies, and construction debris to dumped military and commercial trash. Traditional anchorages contained layers of discarded materials built up over time as ships swung at anchor in the tides and currents. These anchorage sites are the maritime equivalent of refuse middens located near prehistoric camps and historic homesteads on land. Other targets included ballast dumps created when sailing ships came to port "in ballast" to take on cargo. To accommodate the added weight of cargo, ballast stones were jettisoned prior to docking and loading. Many of the targets we explored were artificial reefs intentionally deposited by fishermen to attract fish. One day Chuck and I dived to investigate a promising sonar target with hard and soft acoustical reflections above the floor of the bay. As we pulled our way down the anchor line, we became engulfed by a cloud of bright red reflections moving around us wherever we shone our dive lights. It took us a while to penetrate the schooling snappers and discern the rusted truck bodies they called home. On another day Della and I descended on a boat-shaped sonar target that we estimated from the acoustical recording to be 25 feet long and 6 feet wide. What we found in the murky water was a curious object in the shape of a fat cigar. Its surface was fibrous and covered with brownish-green algae. There was no resistance as I repeatedly stuck my aluminum probe into it; although the strange mass was quite heavy, it was soft and pliant. Della and I exchanged looks that confirmed how spooky our discovery seemed and decided to leave this "alien cocoon" to itself. We later imagined this object rolling back and forth with the tides across the bottom of the bay, over time collecting and incorporating bits of rope, plastic, rotting organic debris, and malevolence to form its cylindrical shape.

Along with these byproducts of modern industrial Pensacola, we found that the bay also contains the remains of its earlier maritime past—a virtual bathtub of sunken relics. Both electronic tools—the magnetometer and side-scan sonar—detected older shipwrecks. At one location near anchorages on the north side of Santa Rosa Island, sonar images led us to the site of an early colonial Spanish ship that had wrecked along the shore.[18] Later field and archival investigations by UWF students identified the ship as a forty-six-gun Spanish frigate that sank during a storm in 1705.[19]

The Ship That Wrecked on a Sand Bar

In late 1992 our remote sensing operations shifted to the shallow waters off Emanuel Point, one of the suspected Luna colony landfall locations in the bay. In October Jim, Chuck, and Della visually inspected three primary anomalies in the survey area and discovered a tubular-steel tower for shrimp net rigging and a metal cable. Chuck and Della descended on the third anomaly, with Della paying out the circle-search line from the buoy anchor to Chuck, who swam in a series of concentric circles. Chuck eventually swam to the end of the line but noticed fish swimming away from him. He followed the fish to a low mound of ballast stones that was their home. The mound was situated in 3–4 m of turbid water on a sand bar that extends westward from Emanuel Point to the mouth of Bayou Texar. The exposed stones consisted of river cobbles and some quarried rock overgrown with large oysters. It appeared that the ballast had become incorporated into the bottom over a long period of time, providing a substrate for generations of shellfish to find a home. On a second dive Jim removed several stones along the edge of the ballast pile and discovered an eroded wooden timber that appeared to be a ship's plank, a clue that told us we were dealing with a shipwreck and not just a pile of jettisoned ballast stones. To control our investigation of the site, we laid a baseline along the longitudinal axis of the mound, which measured 16 m long and 8 m wide. We then opened up three test units that yielded animal bones, ceramics, shoe leather, rope, and the central portion of the ship's structure where the mainmast had been stepped. Given their situation in the shallow, warm water of the bay, we were astonished to find these materials well preserved.

To find the source of the 400-gamma magnetic anomaly that had led us to the wreck, we began a systematic metal detector search across the site. At the shoreward end of the ballast pile we discovered an iron knob sticking out of the sand. Removal of sediments around it revealed a large wrought-iron anchor, buried fluke down; its shank had been twisted and broken off, just below the lugs that would have held the wooden stock in place. We noticed that the shape and construction were very similar to those of anchors found at the sites of Spanish ships wrecked off Padre Island, Texas, in 1554.[20] These initial glimpses of the Emanuel Point Ship's hull structure, hardware, and associated artifacts offered a tentative time period and cultural affiliation for the shipwreck. Features of the central architecture (keelson, mast step, and pump wells) closely resembled examples recorded on sixteenth-century shipwreck sites at Highborn Cay, Bahamas; Western Ledge, Bermuda; and Red Bay, Labrador.[21] Ceramic sherds provided additional diagnostic clues—tin-enameled majolica and coarse, unglazed earthenware sherds of early colonial Spanish olive jars.

These preliminary investigations led to several conclusions. The well-preserved shipwreck appeared to be the earliest yet found in Florida's waters. Dating from the First Spanish Period (1513–1763), the site could be associated with the first European attempts to colonize Florida, perhaps even the remains of a vessel lost during the Luna expedition of 1559. Located near shore in a region of the state noted for its historical attractions, the shipwreck site and its contents could be developed and interpreted in a cooperative effort for the public benefit. Opportunities for research and publication in conjunction with a long-term project would attract scholars and students from numerous academic disciplines.

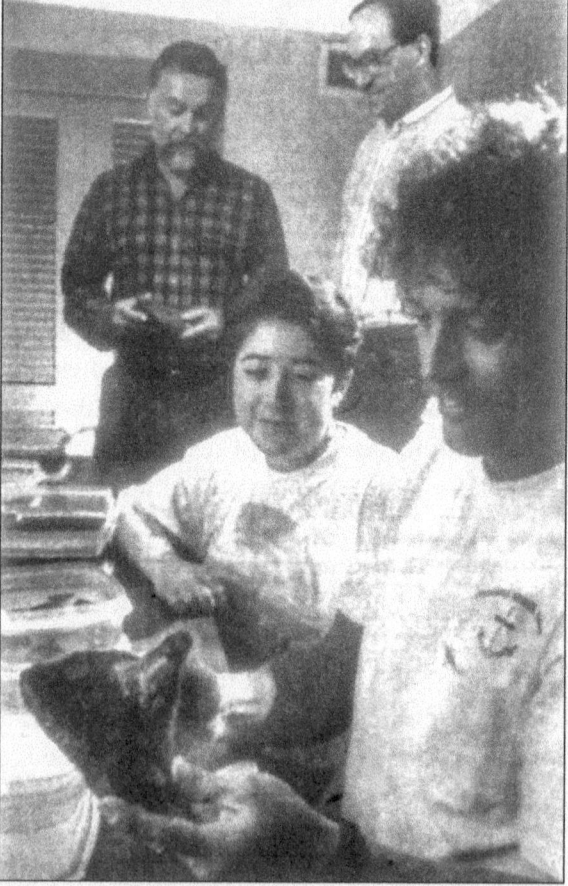

PENSACOLA News Journal

A Gannett Newspaper   Wednesday, March 3, 1993   Pensacola, Florida

Wreck could be de Luna's

Clues don't refute, confirm possibility

By Dave Goodwin
News Journal

Early evidence from the 16th-century Spanish shipwreck in Pensacola Bay neither quashes nor confirms speculation that it was part of Tristan de Luna's doomed fleet of 1559.

But the sunken remains indicate the vessel, like de Luna's fleet, might have met a violent end, said state underwater archaeologist Dr. Roger C. Smith:

■ The heel of the mainmast is sheared off — although it could have been broken off by man.

■ The anchor's shank is twisted and broken, although Spanish iron anchors of the era were not strong and often are found broken.

■ "It appears as though this ship came up on a sandbank and stayed there. The people were unable to refloat it, so it stayed right where it ran aground," Smith said.

The ship was found in August 1992 by the Pensacola Shipwreck Survey, which is charting shipwrecks in the bay. Over the next few months, evidence began to point researchers toward the 16th century, which would make it the state's oldest shipwreck and one of the oldest in the Americas.

The team is not disclosing its location for fear of vandals.

De Luna made the first attempt at settlement of Pensacola when he landed in the bay on Aug. 15, 1559, and allowed

See SUNKEN, back of section

Bruce Graner/News Journal
Chuck Hughson holds a relic — perhaps part of a cooking brazier — found on what might be a 16th-century shipwreck. Survey team members include Della Scott, left, Dr. Roger Smith, back left, and Jim Spirek, back right.

Figure 2.2. *Pensacola News Journal* article featuring the shipwreck investigations. Reproduced with permission, Pensacola News Journal/pnj.com

Early in 1993 Bureau Chief Miller and I met with Division of Historical Resources Director George Percy in Tallahassee to brief him on the importance of the site and show him a preliminary site plan. Percy expressed his strong support for a state-sponsored program to investigate, develop, and interpret the Emanuel Point Ship. The secretary of state was briefed on the new discovery, as were members of the West Florida legislative delegation. I prepared a five-year plan and preliminary budget that included the continued investigation of the shipwreck, conservation and display of its recovered remains in a public exhibit, and the gradual development of a university program in marine archaeology.

The Historic Pensacola Preservation Board, under the direction of John Daniels, agreed to become an active partner in the project. Plans were formalized to establish a conservation laboratory in the historic district for treating the wreck's waterlogged materials and to prepare a major public exhibit of the conserved artifacts for Pensacola's citizens and visitors. The University of West Florida agreed to become an academic partner in the multiyear project, which was seen as a way to increase its academic capabilities in marine and terrestrial archaeology. Public impact of the shipwreck discovery on Pensacola immediately was demonstrated by expressions of intense interest, support, and involvement. The shipwreck soon became a favorite topic of media coverage and public attention. In response to continuous requests, we began to provide lectures to the local historical and archaeological societies, civic and business groups, and schools, creating an enthusiastic network of volunteers and sponsors.

The joint project began in May 1993 with a field school composed of eleven graduate and undergraduate students from several universities, supervised by my staff, which now included Amy Mitchell and Jeffrey Lockwood.[22] Based at the project headquarters in the historic district, the six-week field school began systematic test excavations at the site that uncovered more of the ship's central architecture and portions of the galley (kitchen). We invited marine archaeologists familiar with other early Spanish shipwrecks to come and examine the site, lecture to students, and give presentations to the Pensacola public in a formal summer lecture series, which was sponsored by the Fiesta of Five Flags Association.

The First Underwater Dig

We fixed a series of underwater datums to orient our investigations, record site features, and provide provenience for the materials we expected to encounter. We drove eight steel rods into the sand bar to serve as primary datums for a 30 × 40 m grid system that was aligned with the ship's keelson. The grid then was subdivided into four quadrants, and subdatums were placed in the center of each quadrant. Because onsite visibility was limited, we connected the eight primary datums with bright yellow polypropylene rope, providing an underwater pathway around the site and a boundary line to contain lost divers.

To control our wreck site excavations, we constructed 1 m and 2 m square frames of one-inch diameter PVC pipe graduated in 10 cm intervals that were secured over the areas to be worked. Each unit frame was positioned horizontally in relation to northing and easting from the southwest corner of the site perimeter. We leveled each frame vertically in relation to the tip of the ship's exposed anchor fluke, which represented a zero vertical datum from which to record the depth of deposition for features and artifacts as they became exposed. We then divided each excavation unit into four quadrants that were identified by compass directions (northwest, northeast, southeast, or southwest). One quadrant at a time was excavated in 10 cm levels to expose the wreck deposit.

As we carefully dug into the shipwreck, we began to understand why its contents were so amazingly well preserved. The present-day surface of the sandbar is composed of loose coarse sand and fine silt that migrates along the bottom with seasonal tides and occasional storms. The top of the ballast mound protrudes above this surface, providing a base for oyster growth and a home for stone crabs and fish. Below the sand is a second layer of dense oyster, clam, and mussel shells bound together in compacted silt, which is the result of gradual accumulation of generations of mollusks that lived and died on this ancient artificial reef.[23] The dense stratum of shells effectively has capped the upper portion of the site, protecting it over the centuries from erosion by waves and currents. Below this shell cap is a complex layer of loose silt and shell that represents the original deposition of marine sediments that entered the ship's hull as it wrecked on the sand bar and disintegrated. Artifacts and

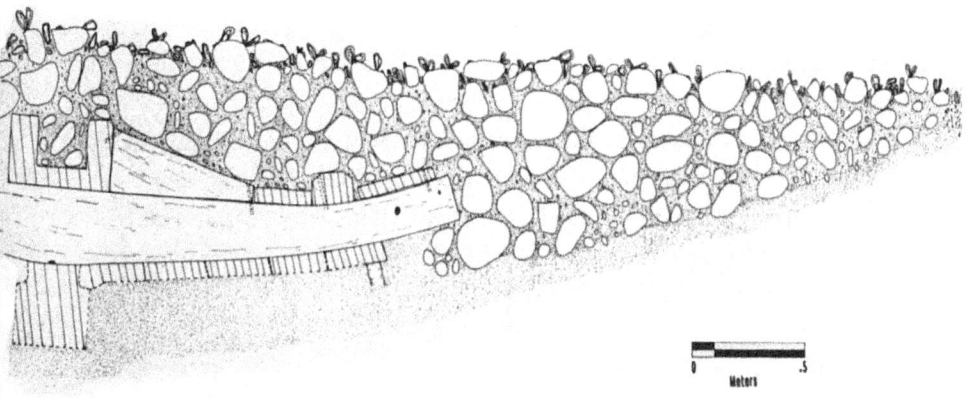

Figure 2.3. Stratigraphic cross section of the port side of the shipwreck amidships. Drawing by James Spirek. Courtesy of the Florida Department of State, Division of Historical Resources.

other remains associated with these events are found within this layer, while those that had migrated to the bottom of the ship during its sailing career are trapped in a dense but soft organic deposit between the ship's frames and in its bilge.[24] When we reached this layer, we discovered a surprising array of botanical and animal remains and other organic debris. Below the ship's hull are sediments of clean, gray sand and remnants of ancient shells and worms that represent the original sand bar upon which the ship broke its back and came to rest.

To excavate, we used the common tools of archaeology—trowels, paintbrushes, metric tapes and folding rules, carpenter's levels, and plumb bobs. They were modified for use underwater, usually with a string lanyard around our wrists, so that they did not float away or get lost during each dive. An electronic carpenter's rule encased in an underwater housing (called a goniometer) helped us to measure and record angles of the hull timbers quickly. Depths of the hull and elevations of artifacts were recorded with a simple clear plastic hose, which served as a long bubble level when we blew air into it and stretched it from the anchor fluke tip to the desired object. Data and notes were written with a pencil tied with string to a slate faced with Mylar sheets. After exposing and mapping artifacts, we placed them in sealable plastic bags with sequentially numbered plastic tags that remained with each find throughout recovery, conservation, analysis, and interpretation. Larger artifacts were collected and transported in a variety of plastic containers and tubs.[25]

We found that it was quite difficult and time-consuming to dig through the shell layer beneath the ballast stones because the shells were densely compacted and had sharp edges. After many cuts and scrapes, we learned that wearing gloves helped, although the glove fingers wore out quickly unless reinforced with duct tape. We collected the larger shells and bagged them onsite. Sediments in suspension and small shells were lifted from the excavation units with water-induction dredges that discharged into topside screening stations. The dredges were powered by high-pressure, low-volume pumps connected to couple-jet venturi heads with flexible suction hoses. Because onsite visibility averaged about one meter depending on rainfall and tides, the suction hoses kept the units clear of sediments and improved water clarity. Often we could see only our immediate work area but not the entire excavation unit ("dark-aeology"). For this reason, all dredge spoil was screened, and bags of shells collected on the bottom were searched topside. Two levels of screens, an upper quarter-inch and a lower eighth-inch, trapped shells and any finds that had escaped our sight on the bottom. Topside screeners sorted through the spoil by hand, working quadrant by quadrant from each unit. As we completed each quadrant, we came to the surface to tell the screeners, who then emptied the remaining spoil onto trays for additional sorting. Whether we were using SCUBA or surface-supplied compressed air, the site's shallow depth allowed us plenty of bottom time to excavate carefully and methodically through the compacted layers of shell and silt.

Pensacola has long been a home to shrimpers, who continue to pull their nets along the bottom of the bay. At night, one can see their lights as the boats methodically run their fishing patterns. Once our primary and secondary datums and grid had been put in place, we became concerned that shrimpers might drag their nets over our underwater framework, so we printed fliers that explained the project, provided a detailed map and coordinates, and included our contact information. These fliers were distributed along the commercial fishing docks in town and handed out to shrimp boat captains and crews. Many of the recipients had heard about the shipwreck in the news and agreed to pass the word and fliers along to others. We also put a buoy with a radar reflector above the site to mark its location.

Shortly afterward, we arrived at the shipwreck one morning and found that our grid system had been pulled off site. Clearly, it had been impacted by a shrimper's net. We went back to the shrimping community to explain what had happened, and several boat captains suggested that we talk with the small group of Vietnamese shrimpers who, they said, did not use radar. We did this and managed to pass the word to them about our project and its location in the bay. Once they understood, they promised to avoid the area. We re-rigged our grid system, which remained intact from then onward, but just to be sure, we fixed a night light on the marker buoy over the site.

Initially we made all our dives from the boats, which limited the amount of people and equipment we could use at the shipwreck. Fortunately, a local marine contractor loaned us a 12x30-foot wooden barge to anchor on site, which then served as our work platform. We adapted an old pontoon boat to house the dredge pump and a small sailing catamaran to serve as a floating dredge screen, both of which were tied to the barge. This arrangement allowed us to work from a stable platform with more divers and equipment, although we still ferried everything from shore to site and back every day. This was a good thing, because at least twice we arrived on site in the morning to discover that the barge had sunk overnight on top of the shipwreck. Each time, we refloated it with large, inflated truck inner tubes, pumped it out, and continued work. We hoped to secure the loan of a larger, more stable barge from the Naval Air Station, or to lease one from the local marine construction industry, but these negotiations were unsuccessful. Eventually, for the second campaign of excavations we contracted a metal fabricator to construct a custom 36 × 16-foot steel platform with three watertight compartments. The contractor allowed us to assist with cutting, welding, and painting the new barge, which reduced its cost considerably. We christened our new work platform *Nautilus*, after the university's official logo.[26]

During the 1993 field season seven excavation units exposed central features of the ship's lower hull (mainmast step assembly, pump sumps) and a wide variety of artifacts and floral and faunal specimens.[27] Forward of these features we found a metal pitcher, partially buried in the sediments. One day as Chuck and I were exploring this area, he suddenly swam up to me through the gloom and with wide eyes yelled something though his regulator. I did not understand him at first, so he took hold of me and in my ear slowly garbled what sounded like, "Can you say copper?" I followed him to a gleaming bright metal object that turned out to be the handle of a large copper cauldron embedded in the silt. This wasn't the first time that Chuck was drawn to the site's hidden features; we already knew that he had a knack for finding things underwater. Later in the season he discovered a concreted iron gudgeon (rudder fitting) and the lower remnants of the ship's wooden sternpost aft of the ballast mound.

We were fortunate to convince conservator John Bratten to join our staff; he quickly established a proper conservation laboratory in 1994 in the basement of the T. T. Wentworth State Museum, near the project headquarters. With surplus appliances and equipment, John and volunteer Gigi Bertsch-Naggatz assembled a facility for research and analysis that included a donated dental X-ray unit and electrolytic treatment tanks. Equipped to stabilize and treat our waterlogged recoveries, the laboratory became a staging point between the shipwreck and its eventual public interpretation at the museum.

Continued work at the site called for uncovering the stern of the ship and recording the architectural features that might help to explain the ship's wrecking process. Between June 1994 and February 1995 we opened eleven 2 m^2 units, revealing the ship's tail frames that narrowed toward the sternpost and additional gudgeon straps that had fallen from it.[28] Between the tail frames was a fine, compacted muddy silt that contained a variety of organic materials. Ammunition crudely fashioned from stone, lead, and iron suggested that the ship had been armed with various types of cannon. Near the sternpost we discovered the lower portion of the ship's rudder, made of two enormous wood planks through-bolted together, lying flat on the seabed. And then, between the sternpost and rudder, Chuck encountered a round metal object that we at first thought might be a bell. Closer inspection revealed it to be corroded iron, rather than bell metal. As I carefully fanned away the sediments, it took the

Figure 2.4. Iron breastplate and edge of rudder as found *in situ* at the stern of the shipwreck. Courtesy of the Florida Department of State, Division of Historical Resources.

shape of a breastplate lying face up on the seabed. I wondered how this piece of body armor had come to rest outside the ship near the rudder. It crossed my mind that it might contain the still-buried remains of its owner, because it would have been impossible to swim while wearing the breastplate. But after slowly removing the piece from its context, we found no evidence of its owner.

Our progress in exploring the shipwreck was followed eagerly by the media. We learned how to respond to the inevitable questions—"Have you found any gold?" "Aren't you worried about sharks?" "What's the most valuable artifact you've found so far?" News exposure in print and audio-visual outlets gave us the opportunity to share what we had discovered with the public and to explain the process of archaeology in the water and in the lab. Of course, coverage of the project was provided continuously by the *Pensacola News Journal*, and the local Associated Press bureau ensured that the story reached the wider world.[29] Once we developed a working relationship with the press, we became comfortable with journalists who wanted more than just a quick headline and sought to follow the unfolding story of the shipwreck. One intrepid young reporter managed to land a special assignment from the *News Journal* and dived with us on the site for two days, recounting his adventure in a multipage spread.[30] The *Journal* also published numerous editorials supporting our work that helped to increase awareness of its relevance to Pensacola's history.[31] The inevitable question of the shipwreck's association with Tristán de Luna's fleet always came up, as reporters hoped we would pronounce it so. I repeatedly explained that the ship would tell its own story if we did our archaeology work carefully, collecting and analyzing the clues it gave us.

Perhaps the most unusual media episode began in the winter of 1994 with an urgent phone call from FX cable television channel, requesting that we work with them to produce a live underwater interview at the Emanuel Point Ship. The channel's flagship show, *Breakfast Time*, was aired every morning from an apartment in New York City, featuring unique places around the United States. Intrigued by the idea, we assembled at the dock on the scheduled December day at four o'clock in the morning, since the live interview was to air at breakfast time. The television crew arrived with its satellite truck and connected to New York, where the show was broadcasting live jazzercises. We joined in the exercises on the dock in our warm clothing and then cruised in the darkness to the excavation barge. The show's "roving reporter" and I donned dry suits and full face masks with hard-wire communications. The reporter, Phil Keoghan, was an excited, energetic fellow who told me that his previous assignment a few days earlier had been to interview an electrician who was changing the lightbulbs at the top of the Golden Gate Bridge. Now, he was anxious to add another "stunt" to his repertoire of live broadcasts.[32] As the sun came up, Phil, his cameraman, and I descended to the site and made a chatty roving tour of the wreckage, which appeared live between a segment about New York City high school cheerleaders and Christmas shopping clips.

We discontinued fieldwork in late summer 1995, just prior to hurricanes Erin and Opal, which struck Pensacola back to back but without damaging the shipwreck site. Our explorations had revealed preliminary clues to the ship's original size and shape, and the articulated structure appeared to be much larger than we anticipated. Thousands of objects

Figure 2.5. James Spirek preparing the stern site plan from field drawings. Courtesy of the Florida Department of State, Division of Historical Resources.

and specimens had been collected from inside and outside the hull, including the remains of insects and rodents that inhabited the bilge during the vessel's sailing career.[33] As Della was excavating her unit one day, she uncovered a curious ceramic piece with what looked like a human eyeball staring at her from the sediments. Soon another piece turned up with a grimacing mouth and teeth. These unusual molded and painted Aztec ceramics were identified with the help of Mexican archaeologists. Jim and John began to notice small droplets of shining liquid mercury between the stern frames in the bilge, evidence that our ship had carried quicksilver, which was imported from Spain to Mexico beginning in 1556. These finds increased our growing awareness that the shipwreck may have been part of the Tristán de Luna expedition, which arrived in Pensacola from Mexico in 1559. At the conclusion of the first campaign of investigations, we realized that we had explored only a fraction of the site; that more investigations in the forward part of the ship, including the galley, could finally reveal its original size and much more about shipboard life; and that to continue we would need additional funding and support.[34]

Our survey activities in Pensacola Bay initially had been supported in part by a grant of federal NOAA funds administered by the Florida Coastal Management Program of the Department of Community Affairs. With the discovery of the Emanuel Point Ship, increased state support was made available from our agency, a Historic Preservation Grant was awarded to Historic Pensacola Inc., and a legislative appropriation of monies collected by the Florida Department of Commerce from sales of Quincentennial automobile license plates was made to the project for fiscal year 1994–95. Meanwhile, support from Pensacola's private sector grew in direct proportion to the project's public exposure. More than twenty-five local businesses became corporate sponsors of the research, providing cash, goods, and in-kind services. These sponsors included hardware and lumber outlets, marine supply vendors, chemical suppliers, dive shops, advertising companies, and banking firms.[35]

At the same time, we established a graduate student internship program to provide field and laboratory opportunities for promising students from universities nationwide. Sponsored jointly by the Bureau of Archaeological Research and Fiesta of Five Flags Association, the program eventually involved twelve graduate interns, each of whom worked on the project for twelve weeks in return for a modest stipend.[36] Fiesta of Five Flags also hosted two summer lecture series, which allowed other archaeologists familiar with sixteenth-century shipwrecks to visit the project, work with staff and students, and share their professional perspectives with the public at large.[37]

To address its partnership role in the project, the University of West Florida established an Archaeology Steering Committee, which was charged with seeking public and private funding to enhance the university's archaeology program with marine capabilities and to support continuing investigation of the shipwreck. Appointed by President Morris Marx, committee members included prominent local business leaders and community patrons, university administrators and foundation officers, and archaeologists.[38] Aside from soliciting local support through the university foundation, a plan was announced to seek additional state legislative appropriations with the help of local delegates. Between January 1994 and May 1995 the committee met on numerous occasions. One offshoot of the meetings was the decision by several committee members

Figure 2.6. Visiting archaeologists (*left to right*) Abraham López (Cuba), Corey Malcom (*seated*) (Key West), Juan Vera (Puerto Rico), and Donald Keith (Texas) conferring with John Bratten. Courtesy of the Florida Department of State, Division of Historical Resources.

to create the Pensacola Maritime Preservation Society, an independent, nonprofit entity with the intention of raising funds for the shipwreck and eventually a maritime museum.[39]

Fortunately, with the help of the Historic Pensacola Preservation Board and the Pensacola Maritime Preservation Society, we received funding to continue treatment and analysis of the shipwreck collection in the laboratory for an additional year. We nominated the Emanuel Point Ship to the National Register of Historic Places, and it was listed officially in 1995. This recognition resulted from our demonstration of the site's distinction in the national historical and archaeological record. Shortly thereafter, the first formal report of investigations at the Emanuel Point Ship was released by the Bureau of Archaeological Research.[40] Meanwhile, a major search for archival documents about the Luna expedition in Spanish archives was completed.[41] Sponsored by the City of Pensacola, copies of more than 160 documents were collected, catalogued, partially transcribed, and translated. In addition a major display of artifacts from the Emanuel Point Ship became the centerpiece of a new exhibit about Pensacola's history and archaeology, which opened to the public in the fall of 1996 at the J. Earle Bowden Building in the city's historic district.

The Second Underwater Dig

As recurring funding was granted to UWF by the Florida legislature to enhance archaeological research and training, the prospect of a program in maritime archaeology became a reality. Plans for new campus facilities devoted to archaeology included a permanent conservation laboratory, which would be equipped for the treatment of waterlogged objects. Meanwhile, the Division of Historical Resources received funding from the Florida Legislature for the continuation of fieldwork at the Emanuel Point Ship. The division subsequently awarded the funds to the University of West Florida in 1996 for a second campaign of excavations. The award agreement authorized UWF, in cooperation with the division's Bureau of Archaeological Research, to continue excavations at the wreck site. This work began in early 1997 with the establishment of another field headquarters at the Christie House in Pensacola's historic district.

Our staff now consisted of J. "Coz" Cozzi, field director; John Bratten, laboratory director; Keith Plaskett, equipment manager and diving safety officer; and David Pugh, field technician. Over the course of the second campaign, six graduate student interns were selected from various universities to assist with all aspects of the project. Each intern was given a modest stipend in return for a twelve-week internship and the opportunity to learn the process of underwater archaeology. In addition, five UWF students were introduced to underwater archaeological activities during a six-week field school taught by project staff.[42] An active volunteer program, consisting of interested people of all ages, augmented daily work activities in the field and in the lab.[43] Meanwhile, as a UWF adjunct professor, I continued to teach graduate seminars in maritime archaeology.

At the conclusion of the first campaign of investigations, we attempted to estimate the size of our ship based on explorations of the vessel's

Figure 2.7. Staff of the second excavation campaign: (*left to right*) David Pugh, Keith Plaskett, Roger Smith, "Coz" Cozzi, John Bratten, and Rudy Vizsla. Courtesy of the Florida Department of State, Division of Historical Resources.

midship architecture and stern structure, including the rudder. Measurements of principal timbers and proportional relationships between features such as the sternpost, mainmast step, and anchor produced a figure of more than 400 *toneladas* (tons) for the ship's cargo capacity. Its length was estimated to have been 29.5 m, beam 9.5 m, and depth of hold 4.5 m.[44] To refine the dimensions further, we needed to excavate in the bow of the vessel to search for the forward end of the keel and any remaining portion of the stem. A precise determination of the length of keel—a principal dimension of any wooden sailing vessel—would help to reconstruct the size of the Emanuel Point Ship more accurately.

Discovery of the metal pitcher and copper cooking cauldron during preliminary investigations forward of the mainmast step led us to think that the location of these features might represent the ship's galley area. The pitcher had been fashioned of copper lined with tin and was designed to heat liquids and stand upright without capsizing at sea.[45] The nearby cauldron, exposed only partially to reveal its rim, shoulder, riveted lugs, and heavy bale, appeared to be well preserved. These artifacts made us excited about the possibility of finding additional cooking and dining implements and related foodstuff remains. Exploration of the ship's galley area thus became a major objective of the second campaign.

Early in 1997 we returned to the site, relocated the anchor fluke, and found the datum stakes that had been installed around the periphery of the shipwreck during the previous excavation campaign. We then began a metal-detector survey of the forward section of the site to locate, mark, and map buried metallic objects in the area we planned to excavate. Detected anomalies were marked with numbered pin flags, and their locations were recorded and plotted on the site plan. Our initial efforts were directed toward uncovering the copper cauldron to devise a strategy for its recovery. However, when we removed the surrounding sediments, the more deeply buried portions of the container proved to be in a poor state of preservation, with most of the body converted into brittle copper sulfide.

The galley area forward of the mainmast produced a variety of cooking vessels of different sizes and shapes, as well as other related implements, all essential for food preparation aboard a sixteenth-century Spanish ship at sea.[46] Recovery of ceramics during this campaign more than doubled the number previously collected—totaling some 2,000 individual sherds. The majority of these represented the common Spanish olive jar, used at sea to transport all manner of products; we found olive pits, almond shells, and pitch in association with the pieces of these jars.[47] Hand-painted and glazed earthenwares also were recovered in this portion of the ship.

As we uncovered the bow area of the shipwreck, we found that the port side of the hull had been broken away violently, while the starboard side had collapsed almost intact, perhaps under the weight of the anchor. Two gunport covers were found in association with the starboard side. Discovery of elements of the stempost assembly, connected to the keel, allowed us finally to determine the original length of the ship, which was a large vessel compared to other known sixteenth-century Spanish shipwrecks.[48]

Working through the winter of 1997–98 required us to use dry diving suits to keep warm underwater. Our Canadian colleagues laughed when they learned we were wearing dry suits in Florida, but hours of kneeling in our excavation units without much movement sucked the heat from our bodies. Besides, we learned that "dry" suits are really not that dry, as the bay water inevitably trickled down the backs of our necks, starting shivers up and down our spines. We returned the Canadians' jests about our winter apparel by pointing out that they had to work in suits heated with hot water during their summer excavation of a similar Spanish shipwreck in Labrador.

In late October 1997 the ship's anchor and copper cauldron were raised amid much public fanfare during a well-attended offshore ceremony officiated by UWF President Morris Marx and Judy Bense, now UWF Archaeology Institute director. Brown Marine Services towed a barge with a crane to the site to make the lift. Keith and the students had wrapped the cauldron like a mummy with yards of athletic bandages, placed it in a steel tub filled with sand, and rigged a sling for lifting. Coz descended to the site, guided the crane's hook through lifting straps, and surfaced to signal for the 950-pound anchor to be raised. Next the fragile cauldron was raised, and both artifacts were taken to the laboratory. Aside from the lower hull, the anchor and cauldron were the largest of more than 5,000 artifacts and field specimens recovered from the Emanuel Point Ship.

The second underwater dig came to conclusion in March 1998 with the final reburial of the shipwreck site. We estimated that not more than 40 percent of the site had been explored, but we had conclusively answered all our research questions about the size of the ship, its construction and subsequent life at sea, its role in history, and its place in Florida's maritime heritage.[49] We decided that the remainder of the shipwreck should rest undisturbed where we found it; perhaps it can serve to answer additional questions in the future for archaeologists with better tools and techniques. Meanwhile, the shipwreck's focal point in Pensacola's affairs led to a new UWF program in maritime archaeology, with John and Coz as faculty, Keith as diving supervisor, and a growing group of graduate students who had exciting new underwater research opportunities. We hoped this new program would continue the survey of Pensacola's shipwrecks and perhaps turn up remains of other ships from the Luna fleet. We have not been disappointed.

Notes

1. Tesar, "Survey and Testing of Gulf Islands."
2. Lenihan, "Survey of the Offshore Lands of Gulf Islands."
3. U.S. Army Corps of Engineers, "Underwater Remote Sensing Survey."
4. Tidewater Atlantic Research, "Underwater Archaeological Investigations."
5. Bense, *Deadman's Shipwreck.*
6. Williamson (ed.), "Jack's Wreck."
7. Students in the field school included Jane Barkley, Scott Ceier, Cecily Fruchey, Keene Heywood, Josh McDaniel, Amy Mitchell, Rich Parmelee, Della Scott, Peg Smith, and Teri Stark. Volunteers included Ruth Grant, GiGi Bertsch, Larry Broussard, and Mike Williamson.
8. Smith, "Marine Archaeology Comes of Age in Florida"; Finegold, "Deadman's Island Sloop."
9. Baumer, *Bethune Blackwater Schooner.*
10. DiPaulo and Clausen, "Cannon Brought Ashore."
11. U.S. Army Corps of Engineers, "Underwater Archaeological Investigation."
12. Mistovich, Agranat, and James, *Brodie's Wharf.*
13. Franklin, Morris, and Smith, *Submerged Historical Resources of Pensacola Bay.*
14. Smith, "Florida's Underwater Archaeological Preserves"; Florida Bureau of Archaeological Research, "Proposal to Establish USS *Massachusetts.*"
15. Florida Bureau of Archaeological Research, "Proposal to Establish USS *Massachusetts.*"
16. Pensacola's awareness of Tristán de Luna came primarily from the work of local historian John Appleyard, who wrote a historical novel about the expedition: *De Luna, Founder of North America's First Colony.*
17. Spirek et al., *Submerged Historical Resources, Phase Two.*
18. Ibid.
19. Hunter, Bratten, and Cozzi, *Santa Rosa Island Wreck*; Hunter, "A Broken Lifeline of Commerce."
20. Arnold and Weddle, *Nautical Archaeology of Padre Island.*
21. Oertling (ed.), "Highborn Cay Wreck: Limited Excavations"; Watts, "Western Ledge Reef Wreck"; Grenier, "Basque Whalers in the New World."
22. Field school students included Janet Bancroft, Stuart Derrow, Sandra Johnson, Sheryl Kennedy, Bill Kerr, Shea McLean, Kyle Mueller, Beth Padgett, Monti Sommer, Greg Townsend, and Debra Wells.
23. Clifford Smith, "Site-Formation Process."
24. Smith et al., *The Emanuel Point Ship, 1992–1995.*
25. Cozzi, "Techniques on the Emanuel Point Ship Excavation."
26. Cozzi, "Hull Remains of the Emanuel Point Ship."
27. Smith, "Ship at Emanuel Point."
28. Spirek, "Pinned to the Bottom."
29. Goodwin, "Wreck Could Be De Luna's"; Goodwin, "Treasures from the Deep"; Kaczor, "Spanish Shipwreck Dates to 16th Century"; Kaczor, "Wreck Believed to Be Immigrants' Galleon."

30. Janowski, "Clues to the Past."

31. *Pensacola News Journal*, "Fort, Shipwreck Bring Past Alive"; "Shipwreck Gets Research Reprieve"; "Ship's Excavation a Gold Mine Chance."

32. "According to his book, *No Opportunity Wasted*, Phil Keoghan set out to live his life to the fullest by accomplishing exotic goals and taking risks after a near-death experience at the age of 19. Since then, he's broken a world bungee jumping record, gone diving in the world's longest underwater caves, eaten a meal on top of an erupting volcano, and renewed his vows underwater while feeding sharks." https://en.wikipedia.org/wiki/Phil_Keoghan.

33. Bratten, "Olive Pits"; Scott-Ireton, "Unique Artifacts"; Wells, "Examples of Ceramics."

34. Smith, "Emanuel Point Ship."

35. Scott-Ireton, "Role of Historic Preservation."

36. Student interns during the first field campaign included Stewart Derrow, David Pugh, Michael Scafuri, Jinkey Smalley, Clifford Smith, and Debra Wells. Interns during the second campaign included Brad Himour, Philip Mitchell, Ty Seale, Juliet Tatum, Solomon Wahrhaftig, and Jenna Watts.

37. We invited the following archaeologists, who have worked on sixteenth-century Spanish shipwreck sites, to visit the site, examine our finds, and lecture to students and the general public: Christopher Amer, J. Barto Arnold, Carl Clausen, Donald Keith, Denise Lakey, Abraham López, Corey Malcom, Joe Simmons, and Juan Vera.

38. The UWF Archaeology Steering Committee included Judy Bense, Earle Bowden, Ted Brown, Miller Caldwell, Peg Couch, John Daniels, Pat D'Asaro, Rick Dye, Harold Marcus, Pat Marcus, Don McMahon, Lucy Rentz, John Soule, Roger Smith, Margo Stringfield, Randy Williams, and Sandra Windham.

39. Founding members of the Pensacola Maritime Preservation Society included Ted Brown, Don McMahon, and John Soule.

40. Smith et al., *The Emanuel Point Ship, 1992–1995*.

41. Lakey, "Don Tristán de Luna y Arellano"; Lakey, "Don Tristán de Luna y Arellano: Addendum."

42. Field school students included Jason Burns, Andrea Fossum, James Hunter, Lucas Spalding, Sean Williams, and directed study student Brenda Swann.

43. Volunteers included Gigi Bertsch-Naggatz, Harv Dickey, Cullan Duke, Connie Franklin, Corey Fulford, Norma Harris, James Hunter, Bob Johnson, Ann Kirkland, Hera Konstantinou, Michael Lawton, "Mac" MacDonald, Chuck Meide, Deana Roose, Dianne Sherer, Nancy Van Epps, Suzanne Weathers, and Mike Williamson.

44. Smith et al., *The Emanuel Point Ship, 1992–1995*.

45. Smith, "The Ship at Emanuel Point."

46. Moore, "Emanuel Point Galley Ware"; Rodgers, "Stale Bread and Moldy Cheese."

47. Meyer, "The Spanish Olive Jar"; Williams, "Analysis of Tin-glazed Ceramics"; Wells, "Examples of Ceramics."

48. Cozzi, "Ship's Architecture."

49. Smith, "Luna's Fleet and the Discovery of the First Emanuel Point Shipwreck."

3

Florida's Forgotten Colony

Historical Background

JOHN E. WORTH

On June 11, 1559, the fleet of Tristán de Luna set sail from Veracruz, Mexico, with 1,500 colonists destined for the northern coast of the Gulf of Mexico. Following orders from King Phillip II and Viceroy of New Spain Luís de Velasco, and building on intelligence gathered from previous failed expeditions to southeastern North America, Luna's expedition had specific objectives. It was to establish a first colony at Pensacola Bay in western Florida, march inland to settle a second colony at the native province of Coosa in what is now northwestern Georgia, and travel to the Atlantic coast to found a third colony at Port Royal Sound, which is in southeastern South Carolina. Not only would these outposts impede anticipated French intrusions along the margins of the Spanish colonial empire, but they also would provide an overland route to the Atlantic from Mexico, avoiding the treacherous Bahama Channel off south Florida.[1] Had the expedition succeeded in annexing Florida as an extension of New Spain (Mexico), the colonial history of southeastern North America would have turned out very differently.

Luna's *entrada* was the third settlement effort by the Spanish in the southeastern United States, by then known as *La Florida* following its 1513 discovery by Juan Ponce de León. Prior to Luna, at least eleven Spanish expeditions are documented to have reached the southeastern coast, including two that penetrated the interior. However, despite these explorations and colonial attempts, as of 1559 Spain still had no foothold in the region. The Luna expedition was intended to solve this problem.

Tracking the historical and archaeological traces of sixteenth-century Spanish expeditions in the southeastern United States is an avocation with a long history itself and has been pursued on various occasions by armchair enthusiasts and professional scholars alike for well over century. My own introduction to the subject came about as I began my undergraduate studies at the University of Georgia in the mid-1980s. This happened to coincide with the height of an ongoing long-term research project led by anthropologist Professor Charles Hudson, who with his many colleagues aimed to bridge what he sometimes called "the great black hole of southern history." By exploring the social geography of the late prehistoric Southeast using new and more accurate reconstructions of the routes of sixteenth-century Spanish explorers, they planned to establish a geographical and cultural benchmark against which much later ethnohistoric accounts of the eighteenth century could be compared.

Although I had originally intended to pursue prehistoric archaeology, Charlie's inspiring enthusiasm and amazingly broad vision of linking archaeological and documentary sources of evidence in studying the cultural transformation of the Southeast during the European colonial era quickly drew me in. After my master's thesis fieldwork along the route of Hernando de Soto in middle Georgia, I expanded and deepened my combined archaeological and documentary skills at the University of Florida while studying the seventeenth-century Spanish mission system. Beginning with the rich microfilm collections of the P. K. Yonge Library of Florida History, followed by a three-month trip to the Archivo General de Indias (AGI) in Seville, Spain, I came to realize the pivotal importance of working directly with the primary historical sources in concert with my archaeological research.

While the material traces of past human activity provide a direct link to what people actually did, archaeology can only attain indirect and ambiguous access to what people thought. And while documents offer us direct access to the mind of the writer, they can only provide indirect evidence of what actually happened. Separately, archaeology and history lend only incomplete access to the people and events of the past, filtered through the mind of writers in the past or researchers in the present. Used together, however, archaeological and documentary evidence can provide a far more robust and complete portrait of the past. And over the course of my professional career, I have found this to be particularly important for tracking Spanish explorers and colonists on the sixteenth-century landscape of the North American Southeast.

The first Spanish documented expedition to reach Florida was led by Juan Ponce de León in 1513.[2] Sent from Puerto Rico to search for the fabled island of Bimini, it resulted instead in the discovery of the landmass that Ponce named *La Florida* in honor of its sighting on Easter, or *Pascua Florida*. The expedition explored the middle and lower Atlantic coast of Florida, rounded the Florida Keys, then sailed the Gulf coast to the Charlotte Harbor vicinity of southwest Florida before returning to Puerto Rico.

Not long after Florida's discovery, slavers who were gradually depopulating the Caribbean and Bahamas islands took notice of the newfound landmass. Sometime between 1514 and 1516 Pedro de Salazar sailed north from Hispaniola to search for American Indian slaves. Landing on the lower Atlantic coast, he captured as many as five hundred native residents on an island later called the "Island of Giants."[3] Although few of the slaves survived long after reaching Hispaniola, information gathered on this voyage set the stage for later Atlantic exploration. About 1516 Diego de Miruelo launched an expedition, perhaps from Cuba, to search for slaves along Florida's western coast. The outcome of this raid may have been documented the following year in a lawsuit by Ponce de León against Cuban governor Diego Velázquez del Cuellar for having allowed three hundred Florida Indians to be captured and brought illegally to Cuba. The expedition also documented and named the large Bay of Miruelo on the northern Gulf coast, although later expeditions had difficulty identifying it.

In 1519 Jamaica Governor Francisco de Garay launched an expedition under Alonso Alvarez de Pineda to explore the region between Ponce de León's Florida and Hernán Cortés's recently discovered New Spain.[4] The four-ship exploratory flotilla charted the entire northern Gulf of Mexico, resulting in the first map of this region. Although Garay's 1523 colonizing expedition only succeeded in discovering the Río de las Palmas (the modern river Soto la Marina) in the western Gulf, information gathered on this trip foreshadowed the later voyage of Pánfilo de Narváez.

In 1521 Ponce de León finally organized his long-promised venture to colonize Florida, setting sail from Puerto Rico with two ships and two hundred colonists.[5] The expedition landed in the vicinity of modern Fort Myers but soon was repulsed by a Calusa Indian attack. After receiving a serious wound, Ponce withdrew his forces and sailed to Cuba, where his death in Havana ended the enterprise. In the same year two slaving ships from Hispaniola under Francisco Gordillo and Pedro de Quejo joined forces after meeting in the Bahamas and sailed north to find the land that Pedro de Salazar had discovered on his earlier slave raid.[6] They captured some sixty slaves from the lower Atlantic coast before returning to Hispaniola. Among the captives was an Indian later called "Francisco el Chicorano," whose descriptions of his homeland not only fueled the sometimes fanciful and exaggerated stories reported in Europe by Pietro Martire d'Anghiera (Peter Martyr) but also spurred the colonial interests of Hispaniola judge Lúcas Vázquez de Ayllón.

In 1523 Ayllón obtained a contract to establish a colony along the Atlantic coast and sent Pedro de Quejo in 1525 to reconnoiter the area of his colonial plans. Quejo sailed along much of eastern North America before returning with extensive intelligence about the region.[7] In 1526 Ayllón mounted Spain's second formal attempt to settle southeastern North America, leading six ships with six hundred colonists.[8] In late September the expedition established the town of San Miguel de Gualdape, possibly along the middle Georgia coastline, but Ayllón's death and internal and external disputes doomed the colony to failure. The survivors fled by the end of October, although only a quarter of them made it back to the Caribbean.

In 1528 a fleet of ships led by Pánfilo de Narváez sailed from Cuba under royal contract to settle the region explored under Francisco de Garay's direction between 1519 and 1528.[9] Destined for the Río de las Palmas north of Cortés's New Spain colony, the ships were driven ashore by severe storms at Tampa Bay on Florida's west coast. Expedition members tried in vain to find Diego de Miruelo's bay and eventually marched overland to the land of the Apalachee Indians at modern Tallahassee. Ill and exhausted, they constructed improvised barges and attempted to skirt the Gulf coast toward northern New Spain, but most men died along the way. Eight years later Álvar Núñez Cabeza de Vaca and three companions finally reached Mexico City after wandering in an epic journey across the interior of Texas and northern Mexico.

Several years later veteran conquistador Hernando de Soto launched his own expedition with a royal contract to explore the territories visited by Ayllón and Narváez and to discover suitable locations for colonies along about two hundred leagues of coastline.[10] In 1539 a flotilla of nine ships and about six hundred people, mostly soldiers, sailed from Cuba and landed at Tampa Bay. Soto's expedition pushed inland rapidly, hoping to find a mountainous region with riches on the same scale as he and Francisco Pizarro had experienced in Peru. The expedition seems to have followed Narváez's trajectory, marching inland and northward toward Apalachee at modern Tallahassee, where it spent the winter. From there, it pushed deep into the interior Southeast, wandering for more than three years across much of eastern North America. Only half of the expedition members survived to sail down the Mississippi River and along the Gulf coast to Mexico; among them was a handful of men who would return with Tristán de Luna in 1559.

Of importance to the later Luna expedition, while at Apalachee, Soto sent Francisco de Maldonado west with two brigantines to explore the coast until he discovered a town, province, and port called Ochuse, now known as Pensacola Bay.[11] Deciding to use Ochuse as his principal port and rendezvous point, Soto dispatched Maldonado and Gómez Arias Dávila to Havana to gather supplies and return with three ships to Ochuse, where Soto's army would return in October after exploring the interior. Maldonado and Arias sailed for Ochuse with a caravel and two brigantines in the fall and winter of 1540–41; finding no word of Soto's army, they explored the coast for news and finally returned to Havana.[12] Subsequent rescue missions were made in the summers of 1541 and 1542 and spring of 1543, after which word was received in Veracruz about the return of the expedition's survivors at Pánuco in New Spain.

The total failure of Soto's massive expedition led to the adoption of a new proposal by Dominican missionary Luís Cancer de Barbastro. The friar was granted royal permission and financial support to lead an expedition from Veracruz in 1549, consisting of four Dominican priests

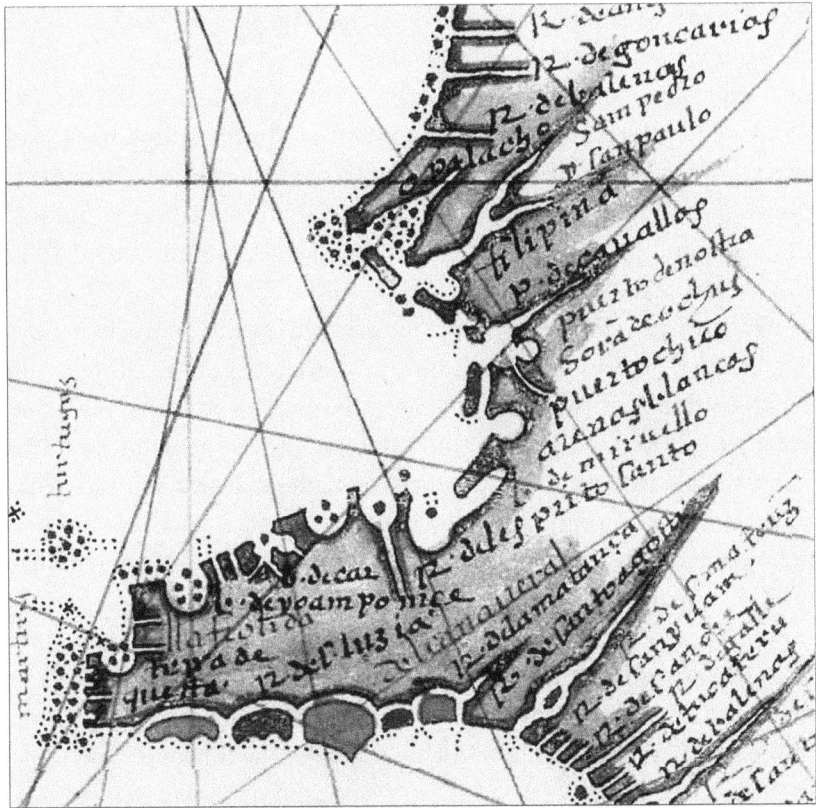

Figure 3.1. A portion of a portolan atlas by Sebastião Lopes dated 1590 that shows Filipina and "Puerto de Nostra Sora de Ochuz." Bibliothèque Nationale, Paris, from the collection of John Worth.

and one farmer, to establish a religious settlement along the Florida Gulf coast with the goal of spiritual conversion rather than military conquest.[13] Although he cautioned the ship's pilot not to take him near any place where Spaniards already had landed, the vessel arrived precisely where Narváez and Soto had made landfall in the vicinity of Tampa Bay and where anti-Spanish sentiment ran high. Following the capture and murder of one priest and the farmer, Cancer was clubbed to death on the shore in sight of the ship, and the expedition withdrew in failure.

By the 1550s the coveted region called Florida had claimed the lives of hundreds of explorers and colonists, including expedition leaders Juan Ponce de León, Lúcas Vázquez de Ayllón, Pánfilo de Narváez, Hernando de Soto, and Luís Cancer. Nonetheless, the Spanish crown maintained a strong interest in claiming Florida as its own. In addition, increasingly bold incursions into Spain's growing New World empire by French explorers and pirates made the colonization of Florida a high priority—one that King Phillip II was willing to finance with considerable expenditure of royal funds. As such, the expedition by Tristán de Luna became the most ambitious state-sponsored colonial venture yet attempted in southeastern North America.

Until recently the Luna story has escaped public awareness about Spanish exploration and settlement in the United States, in part because historians of colonial-era Spanish Florida barely noted the failed Luna expedition and because only one published firsthand narrative was available between 1596 and the twentieth century.[14] With the 1928 publication by Herbert Priestley of a two-volume compilation of primary sources relating to the expedition, called *The Luna Papers*, Luna's failed colonial effort saw a resurgence in scholarly and popular attention.[15] Several overviews and analyses subsequently appeared, including scholarly reevaluation in the 1980s of the terrestrial routes of Luna's and Soto's expeditions in light of all sixteenth-century Spanish exploration in the southeastern interior.[16] The discovery of the Emanuel Point Ship in 1992 was a catalyst for research into maritime and financial aspects of the Luna expedition.[17] The recent identification of the colony's 1559–61 settlement doubtless holds similar promise for renewed research and insight.[18]

My first direct involvement in studying Tristán de Luna's expedition came about between 1998 and 2001 while I worked at the Coosawattee Foundation based in Calhoun, Georgia, just downriver from the cluster of archaeological sites thought to be the core of the Coosa chiefdom visited by Spaniards during the expeditions of both Soto and Luna. While conducting archaeological fieldwork at one of the village sites likely visited during both expeditions, I made two month-long trips to the Archivo General de Indias in Seville, during which I obtained microfilm copies of most of the original documents in Herbert Priestley's *The Luna Papers*, along with the Veracruz account audits of Luna's expedition as well as a previously unrecognized 1575 military service record from a Luna expedition member that included independent proof of the raid by Luna's men against the Napochies (described later). Although in 2001 I left Coosa country to move to southwest Florida to manage a Calusa mound site for the Florida Museum of Natural History, little did I know then that these Luna documents would again prove useful when my career path ultimately led me to the University of West Florida in 2007.

Beginning even before my arrival in Pensacola, I began poring through the microfilms in search of details about Luna's colonial fleet, knowing that ongoing maritime archaeological fieldwork at a wreck site discovered the previous summer was likely to demonstrate that UWF had discovered a second ship in Luna's 1559 fleet. By the time I had settled in to my new faculty position that fall, the Emanuel Point II wreck had been announced to the public, and I began my long-term collaboration with John Bratten and Greg Cook and the rest of the UWF maritime archaeology program. Although nautical archaeology was new to me at the time, the documentary record of not just Luna's expedition but the entire Spanish maritime culture of the colonial era proved to be an amazing and fascinating new resource for scholarly research. Just as I had found to be the case with terrestrial archaeology, the concurrent use of archaeological and documentary lines of evidence provides far greater potential for meaningful insights than either is capable of alone. Moreover, with particular focus on the Luna expedition, combining both maritime and terrestrial research with a broad geographic scope gives us the ability to situate the shipwrecks of the Luna fleet in the broader context of Luna's expedition on both land and sea. This affords us a much deeper understanding of the connections between the artifacts we study and the people who used them. For example, the connection between the remnants of olive jars scattered around the ballast piles on the floor of Pensacola Bay and the small assortment of glass beads and other trade goods found in Native American villages in northwest Georgia helps to bring to life the people of Luna's expedition, each of whom had a name and a personal history, and all of whom were products of the culture of colonial Mexico. And as my mentor Charles Hudson asserted on many occasions, it is this ability to navigate between the individuals and the broader social and geographic landscape in which they lived that makes our research compelling. Illuminating the world of Tristán de Luna's colonial endeavor adds relevance and importance to the underwater investigations of the Emanuel Point wrecks, and to that end let us turn to a detailed overview of the expedition.

The royal order directing the viceroy of New Spain to establish a colony at Punta de Santa Elena was dated December 29, 1557.[19] It followed earlier requests by Franciscan friar Andrés de Olmos to establish one of several proposed missions along the Gulf coast at Ochuse, an idea supported by Soto expedition veteran Rodrigo Rangel, who had written in April that Ochuse was "the best entrance into Florida."[20] In July 1558 Viceroy Luís de Velasco ordered royal officials in Veracruz to arrange for a maritime reconnaissance of the Florida coast.[21] In August orders were dispatched to begin cutting wood for new sailing vessels for the Luna expedition, to be launched the following year.[22] Official instructions were issued to Luna on October 30, followed by a public ceremony in the cathedral of Mexico City to confer his title on November 1.[23] After many of the preparations already had been made, Velasco's selection of Luna was confirmed officially by the Spanish Crown in a royal order conveyed to Luna in Mexico City on March 30, 1559.[24] In that order Luna was appointed governor of all Spaniards who accompanied him then or afterward, as well all Indian inhabitants, in a region defined as extending eastward from a north-south line drawn fifty leagues west of the mouth of the Mississippi River—basically the entire eastern half of North America.

Preparations to launch the expedition in mid-1559 had been under way in New Spain for months. Expenditures for a reconnaissance expedition had begun in August 1558, including the outfitting of three small sailing vessels—a bark (*barca*), a foist (*fusta*), and a shallop (*chalupa*)—to carry about sixty soldiers and sailors.[25] Led by Guido de Lavezaris, the fleet departed the port of San Juan de Ulúa on September 3, sailed north to the Texas coast, then headed southeast across the Gulf to shoals north of the Yucatan peninsula known as Los Alacranes to take aim at the Florida coast. The full Luna fleet would repeat the same maneuver the following summer.[26] Due to contrary weather, the expedition reached shore on the Mississippi coast south of Pascagoula and traveled ten leagues east to Mobile Bay, which they explored and named Bahía Filipina. Unable to push eastward due to winds, the fleet returned to San

Juan de Ulúa, arriving on December 14. In February, Lavezaris and his pilots made a formal declaration about their discoveries to the viceroy in Mexico City.

A second, poorly documented reconnaissance apparently was dispatched in 1558, consisting of a single ship under captain Juan de Rentería and pilot Gonzalo Gayón. They arrived in Havana from New Spain and sailed north "to discover the ports of the said coast of Florida."[27] Gayón and his witnesses attested that the ship "discovered the port of Polonça [Ochuse, or Pensacola Bay], which is in the said coast, and the port of Filipina [Mobile Bay], and the coast of Apalache and coast of Médanos, which is in the said land of Florida and the coast of New Spain." This suggests that the ship scoured the northern Gulf coast from south of present-day Tallahassee to the Texas coast.

Financial accounts of the Luna *entrada* indicate that the cutting of wood for new ships for the main expedition began in mid-October. The viceroy originally described plans to construct:

> six large barks of 100 tons each, each one of which can carry forty horses and a hundred men and four pieces of artillery, and will be made so that when loaded they will be able to navigate in four palms [about 2.74 ft.] of water, because this is suitable to enter and leave from the rivers and bays that there are on the coast of Florida, and for defense from the canoes of the Indians who they tell me gather together in great numbers for the defense of the rivers and ports.[28]

However, subsequent records detail the actual construction of just four vessels, including a new galleon (*San Juan de Ulúa*), two barks (*San Luís Aragón* and *La Salvadora*), and an unnamed frigate.[29] They were built in a shipyard on the mainland opposite the island port of San Juan de Ulúa, alongside the modern city of Veracruz. In early 1559 eight additional ships were purchased or leased, including another bark (*Corpus Christi*), four cargo ships (*Santa María de Ayuda, San Amaro, Santi Espiritu*, and *San Andrés*), a caravel (also *Santi Espiritu*), and serving as flagship and vice-flagship, respectively, an *urca* (*Jesús*) and another galleon (also called *San Juan de Ulúa*).[30] Not only did the Spanish Crown finance the construction, purchase, and lease of Luna's fleet, but it also paid the more than two hundred officers and sailors who crewed the ships and assisted in unloading the vessels after arrival.

As initially planned by Velasco and reported to the king in fall 1558, the Florida expedition was to have 500 Spaniards, including 400 soldiers divided evenly between cavalry and infantry; 100 craftsmen to construct the new towns and fortifications; several appointed royal treasury officials; and six Dominican missionaries.[31] By the following spring the military component had expanded to some 500–550 soldiers divided equally between infantry and cavalry, with the likelihood of the same number of servants.[32] A month before their departure, Velasco complained to Luna about the "mob of mestizos, mulattos, and Indians" who were said to be accompanying the expedition and who he projected would "serve only to place the camp in confusion and eat up the supplies."[33] Later accounts indicate that 800 to 1,000 colonists departed with the soldiers, bringing the total to about 1,500 people on the expedition.[34]

Before leaving Mexico City for the coast, the soldiers were given advance salaries of 150 gold pesos for cavalry and 100 for infantry, in addition to an equal amount of in-kind assistance.[35] They were recruited from Mexico City, Puebla, Oaxaca, and Zacatecas.[36] Documents indicate that high-ranking recruits included Soto expedition survivors, including the expedition's royal factor, Luis Daza; two company captains, Alvaro Nieto and Juan de Porras; and the head bailiff, Rodrigo Vázquez.[37] The names of the captains and other principal officials on the expedition can be reconstructed from various documentary sources, but the original muster roll with a list of all paid soldiers and their place of origin has not been found, although it was sent to the king by the viceroy prior to the voyage.[38]

Only limited documentation exists about other members of the expedition. The diverse group of individuals was described by one participant as including "married Spanish women, black men and black women of service and other servants, and some friendly Indians." Some documents refer to wives and children of at least thirty-six soldiers and to personal servants and African slaves.[39] Perhaps the most unusual group to accompany Luna's expedition were Aztec Indians ("Mexica Tenochca") native to Mexico City and neighboring Santiago Tlatelolco. They included

100 warriors described in the Spanish text of the Codex Osuna as "principal Indians with their weapons, which they made at their cost" (and described elsewhere as "principal Indians" and "Indian soldiers") and a group of "Indians of service" or "craftsmen," presumably part of the 100 originally projected Spanish craftsmen.[40]

When Luna's fleet sailed on June 11, 1559, the 1,500 colonists were furnished with the equipment, supplies, and armament they would need to establish a settlement on Pensacola Bay and more than a year's worth of food packed into the large merchant vessels of the fleet.[41] Unlike earlier *entradas* such as Soto's that suffered because they relied on food bartered or taken from native communities, the Luna expedition was designed to avoid potential tensions and provide enough food for colonists to survive until a colonial town was built and crops were planted and harvested. This had been the most important advice provided by four Indian women captured by Soto and kept as advisors and interpreters.[42] According to records, the stores included more than a million pounds of solid food, including more than 600,000 pounds of corn, 300,000 pounds of hardtack, 130,000 pounds of beef, as well as beans, wheat flour, rice, chickpeas, pork, fish, cheese, and salt, and 8,300 gallons of olive oil, wine, and vinegar.[43] The Dávila Padilla narrative of the expedition later claimed that "in these ships there was food enough for more than a year, even if the fifteen hundred persons who were there had eaten amply."[44]

The Best Bay in the Indies

After departing from port, Luna's fleet followed the same course as Lavezaris's reconnaissance vessels, sailing a month in good weather before making landfall on the Florida coast about eight leagues west of the Bay of Miruelo and east of their intended destination.[45] After taking on water, firewood, and fodder for the horses, the fleet departed July 17 in search of the bay of Ochuse, but overshot its destination when the pilot of the lead frigate missed the entrance in poor weather, arriving instead at Mobile Bay. While waiting for the frigate to backtrack and find Ochuse, Luna offloaded the 130 to 140 horses that remained of 240 originally put on board and sent the cavalry companies eastward by land.[46]

Figure 3.2. Painting of Luna's landing by Herbert Rudeen (1888–1985). Courtesy of University of West Florida Historic Trust.

When the frigate returned with news that Ochuse was twenty leagues to the east, the fleet departed on August 9 and entered Pensacola Bay on August 14 or 15, 1559.[47]

Initial reports indicate that the colonists regarded the bay favorably, and scouting by land and water along the shore resulted in the selection of a site for the new port settlement of Santa María de Ochuse (now known to have been about ten miles from the entrance on a high bluff overlooking the bay).[48] Based on Luna's early reports, the viceroy effused confidence in the site:

> It is one of the best ports that there is among what has been discovered in the Indies . . . and it is a very spacious port, which has three leagues in width in front of where the Spaniards are now . . . and the naos can be anchored in 4 or 5 fathoms at one crossbow-shot from land, and the port is so secure that no wind can do them any damage.[49]

Luna himself wrote: "Seamen say that it is the best [bay] that there is in the Indies, and the site that has been taken in order to establish the town is no less, because it is a point of high land that overlooks the bay where the ships arrive to anchor."[50] Luna's August 25 letter to the viceroy evidently indicated that the fleet would remain in Ochuse "until seeing the disposition of the land and where the first settlement and fort is being made, and understanding the remaining particulars and qualities that they can." Account records state that many of the ships did not complete offloading and discharge their crews until September 9–13, with the rest apparently still in the process as of September 19.[51] Progress clearing brush and laying out the new town seems to have proceeded gradually over the first five weeks, and although people and equipment evidently were offloaded promptly, the all-important food stores were kept on the ships, since as yet "on land there was neither house nor shelter to go home to."[52]

A few weeks before the fleet's departure, the viceroy submitted a plan view drawing for the Ochuse pueblo that showed "one hundred and forty house lots, and forty of them comprise a plaza, monastery and church, and royal house where the governor resides, and where the weapons, artillery, munitions, and provisions are well kept" with "one hundred houses for one hundred residents that seem to be sufficient for the defense of the pueblo."[53] He further specified that "the four gates that the town should have should be visible from the plaza"; the town "should be sufficient to gather all the people"; and the royal house (clearly the warehouse) "should be sufficient for everything, and free-standing, and should have its defenses and manner of a stronghouse." This overview was supplemented by the lengthy formal instructions issued to Luna in April, which included mandates to construct "an assigned house where you will make your *cabildo* and *ayuntamiento* (town council) . . . on the principal public plaza" containing an "archive and chest" for documentation, as well as a "butcher shop, slaughterhouse, granary, jail, and inns."[54]

In similar drawings dating to the late sixteenth century, house lots (*solares*) normally are grouped in blocks of four, arranged within a rectangular grid of streets, with public plazas being located in the center of the town layout. The 1573 royal ordinances also codified the practice that "the principal plaza where the settlement should be begun, being on the coast of the sea, should be made at the landing of the port, and being in the middle of the land, in the middle of the settlement" and "should be in an extended square which is in length at least one and a half times its width, because this shape is the best for the fiestas with horses, and whichever others that are to be done," and the plaza "should not be less than two hundred feet in width and three hundred in length, nor greater than eight hundred feet in length."[55] Given this, it seems likely that the layout for Luna's first settlement would have consisted of a 5 × 7 rectangular configuration of four-lot blocks, with a central area containing a plaza bordered by all major public buildings. Implementing this design likely would have been a focus of considerable work during the first weeks after the settlement site was chosen, although as we will see, any progress in this direction was soon to be delivered a near-fatal blow.

The new galleon was sent back to San Juan de Ulúa on August 25 with the expedition's royal factor, Luis Daza, and news of the successful landfall. Luna also had two ships prepared to travel directly to Spain to carry the same news as well as one of the friars to request additional missionaries.[56] As the offloading of ships and construction of the settlement proceeded during September, Luna dispatched one hundred men to explore inland and northward; they apparently traveled up the modern Escambia River valley in two companies, one by land, one by boat, and each accompanied by a missionary.[57] Finding only one small Indian village about ten leagues upriver, the group continued another ten leagues without discovering other populations or food and returned to the bay with only a single Indian woman named Lacsohe as a prospective interpreter. The viceroy later inferred from Luna's correspondence about the river that "it seems that it was not of importance, by the river being very sinuous and narrow, and the land not being well populated."[58]

However, before the exploratory party actually returned to Ochuse, the settlement was struck by disaster. With the ships at anchor offshore, including the two fully crewed ships destined for Spain, storm winds began to blow during the night of September 19, heralding the arrival of a massive hurricane that already had done severe damage to Spanish settlements in Puerto Rico a week before.[59] Caught completely by surprise, the settlers could do little but hold on as the storm wrought near-total devastation on the fleet. Winds coming from all directions over the course of twenty-four hours tore the ships loose from their anchors, drove them aground, and broke them to pieces. In the end only the caravel *Santi Espiritu*, the barks *Corpus Christi* and *San Luís Aragón,* and the frigate remained afloat.[60] Six ships, including the largest vessels, the flagship *Jesús* and vice-flagship *San Juan de Ulúa*, were driven aground and sunk. A seventh vessel, probably the bark *La Salvadora*, was driven ashore and settled undamaged in a dense grove of trees just an arquebus-shot (*arcabuco*) from the settlement, where its entire contents were able to be recovered "without losing even a pin."[61] No figures for the loss of life are listed; Luna referred to the "losses by many seamen and passengers, both of their lives and their possessions," and in his subsequent letter to Luna, the viceroy thanked God "that it happened at a time that Your Lordship had yourself and your army on land."[62] Names are known for only a few who drowned, including Dominican Bartolomé Matheos, Diego López, captain of *Jesús*, and a soldier who was on it. The difference between the number of original colonists (1,500) and the number who had moved inland by the following February (1,150–1,200) might account for many of the casualties, but these numbers were only estimates and may not include the more than 200 sailors also present during the hurricane.

Despite the recovery of some food on the miraculously preserved vessel, which they "distributed like relics," Luna's colonists otherwise "walked along the shore, hoping that the waves would make some restitution of what the sea had robbed from them."[63] Hunger began to set in almost immediately, and *Corpus Christi*, commanded by Felipe Boquín, a master of one of the lost ships, was dispatched on September 29 with word of the calamity and requests for aid. The bark arrived in Veracruz on October 5, and the news was on the viceroy's desk in Mexico City on October 13.[64] From that moment onward, Viceroy Luís de Velasco's energy and time increasingly became focused on arranging for the replacement of provisions, supplies, and equipment for the stranded colonists, a process that would extend for the next year and a half.

Luna's focus also turned immediately to the situation at hand. To the governor and his men, the native inhabitants of the coast generally were "of little use by being idle, and if they are pressed, given their few possessions and roots they have, it would be cause for them to exile themselves from their native lands and go away to other places."[65] Consequently, just days after the storm, the governor dispatched 150–200 men under four captains to push farther northward into the interior in search of native populations and food, where he hoped he eventually could move most of the colonists.⁶⁶ Led by Sergeant Major Mateo del Sauz and accompanied by other officers and frays Domingo de la Anunciación and Domingo de Salazar, the detachment marched inland at least forty leagues across "vast unpopulated regions, hills, and woods, across never-used roads, with extraordinary difficulty" until reaching a "very large and deep river" (presumably the modern Alabama River), along which they discovered a number of small Indian settlements. One of these, called Nanipacana, was notably larger than the rest, with eighty houses, some of which appeared ruined.⁶⁷ Although the inhabitants fled across the river on the approach of Luna's men, the Spaniards attracted them back with gifts and were told that "that city had been famous, both in the number of people and in sumptuous houses by their standards, and that the Spaniards who had arrived there in other times had seen it as it was."⁶⁸ Despite this, in return for their good treatment and gifts of ribbons and glass beads, Luna's men were fed well and decided to remain in the town, sending a detachment back to Ochuse that arrived in mid-November with the good news.

Luna also sent expedition treasurer Alonso Velázquez and apparently "several sick Spaniards and Indians" to Havana for provisions.⁶⁹ The treasurer's service record later included the testimony of other expedition survivors that "he went in the fury of winter at great risk to his person to the villa of Havana, and brought from there two ships loaded with provisions and horses."⁷⁰ Velázquez presumably employed the caravel *Santi Espiritu* and remaining bark *San Luís Aragón* on this voyage.

Meanwhile, the viceroy had organized an initial relief expedition of two ships—*San Antón* (alias *El Francesillo*) and the new galleon *San Juan de Ulúa*—that departed the port of San Juan de Ulúa in mid-November, arrived in Ochuse in December, and returned by the end of January.⁷¹ Along with provisions, supplies, and equipment, the viceroy enclosed a letter to Luna, lamenting his bad fortune but making abundantly clear that he expected the project to continue forward.⁷² The viceroy concurred with Luna's decision to move most of the colonists inland, except for a detachment of up to sixty soldiers under Captain Juan Xaramillo, but he emphasized the importance of holding the port: "I charge him not to abandon the port, and that he hold it with the guard that is entrusted to his person, given that it has to be and is the principal stronghold of

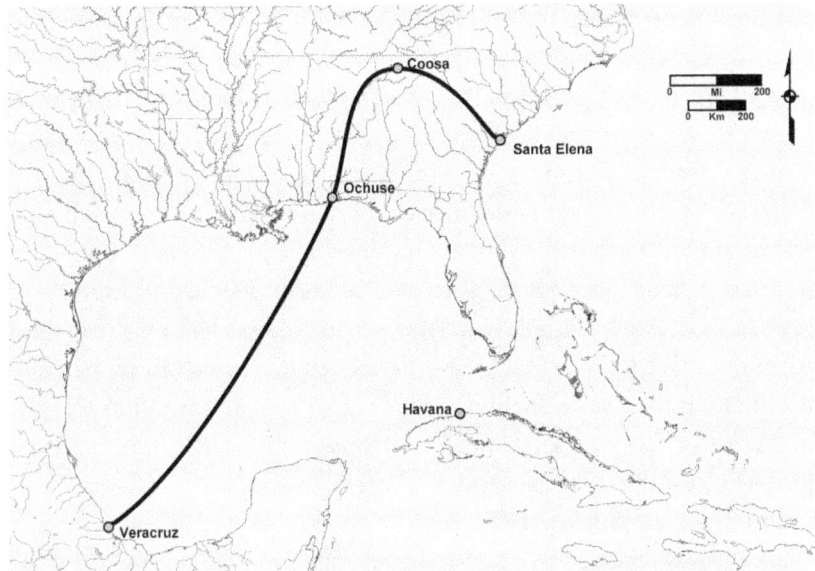

Figure 3.3. Planned routes of the Tristán de Luna expedition. Drawing by John Worth.

those kingdoms, and that which is most important." He specifically enjoined Luna to guard the ships in port and those that would go there, so Indians in the area could not burn or damage them and unauthorized individuals could not use them to leave without permission.[73] To this end, he ordered "the sails, oars, masts, and rudder" of all vessels to be held under lock and key in the royal warehouse. Luna later wrote in response that "he does not intend to give any license to a single person except those that think they are dying."[74] To facilitate transport and communication between Florida and New Spain, the viceroy also ordered Luna to construct two new vessels, a frigate and a small foist, from the wood and nails of the wrecked ships and to try to recover the anchors of wrecked ships to secure ships at Luna's port settlement.

Move to Nanipacana

When the first relief fleet arrived at Ochuse in December, Luna had yet to initiate the move inland to Nanipacana, and subsequent testimony asserts that despite the pleas of his officers, the governor staunchly refused to leave the port until the relief ships' provisions had begun to run out after the New Year. About the same time, he reportedly became feverish and crazed, calling out for his deceased wife.[75] Luna eventually consented to move inland, dispatching soldiers under two captains to clear a road between Ochuse and Nanipacana before initiating the move. In the meantime, his men had constructed two brigantines—presumably with materials salvaged from the wrecked ships, but also new timber cut from around the bay.[76] Both were used to carry people and supplies to Mobile Bay (Bahía Filipina) and upriver to Nanipacana on the central Alabama River (Río de Piachi), while the rest of the colonists marched north along the newly opened road.[77] Captain Juan Xaramillo was left in charge of the port settlement at Ochuse with at least one hundred people, including fifty to seventy soldiers and some African slaves.[78] Descriptions of the journeys to Nanipacana paint a picture of severe hunger along the way and frequent dispatches of corn from the pueblo to aid the travelers as they approached. Luna continued to be plagued by illness and increasingly was considered "indisposed" to continue his leadership, a circumstance that eventually would result in several lengthy legal disputes between the governor and his officers.

In the end more than one thousand colonists reportedly reached the abandoned town of eighty houses, which they christened Santa Cruz de Nanipacana, and settled in for a stay that would last four months.[79] However, on arrival they discovered that the Indians who previously had gathered on the other side of the river had departed and taken their food stores, leaving the Spaniards in increasingly dire straits. By early March the governor's illness was of renewed concern, and by common consent, Field Marshal Jorge Cerón Saavedra was appointed to govern temporarily in Luna's place. However, shortly thereafter Luna requested Cerón to lead 100 men upriver in the two brigantines and two smaller boats. They traveled 60 to 70 leagues along the river before returning three to four weeks later, reporting recently abandoned fields and houses for the first half of the trek and an unpopulated zone beyond that.[80] The depopulated zone likely corresponds to an area later called the "Province of Upiache" that generally was thought to be suitable for Spanish settlement.[81] Undeterred, a few days after the return of the first detachment, the Spaniards dispatched an expedition of about 200 people, including 100 infantry and 50 cavalry, under the leadership of Sergeant Major Mateo del Sauz. Their mission was to push north to the fabled province of Coosa (Coça in all the documents) in present-day northwest Georgia, hoping finally to find food.[82]

A full account of Sauz's seven-month expedition to Coosa and back is beyond the scope of this chapter; however, the journey's extensive documentation warrants a few comments.[83] The expedition spent more than three months reaching the main town of Coosa, and the first forty or fifty days were through an abandoned zone without food or Indian populations. They found corn at an isolated location called Caxiti and sent thirty-five to forty *fanegas* (about 3,500–4,000 pounds) downriver on rafts with Juan de Porras and a few men. The detachment then marched another ten to twelve days through an unpopulated zone before reaching a town called Onachiqui at the edge of the Coosa province, which they estimated to be about 100 leagues from Nanipacana and 35 leagues from Coosa itself through a densely populated river valley. From this point northward, the Indians were said to be more tolerant of the Spaniards, allowing them to camp adjacent to their villages. Resting and provisioning there for a week, the group continued about fifteen leagues upriver to Apica, where they penned a series of letters to Luna and the viceroy in early July, although they waited to send them until reaching Coosa, twenty leagues farther, in mid-July. The letters were dispatched to Nanipacana on August 1 via Captain Christóbal Ramírez de Arellano and a dozen men on horseback. For the next two months, the rest of the Sauz detachment remained in Coosa with the goodwill of its chief, even volunteering to accompany Coosa's chief in late August on a successful military raid to the nearby province of Napochín (aka the Napochies) to reestablish the tributary status of the province.[84]

Back at Nanipacana, food resources had dwindled rapidly. Despite scouring the nearby countryside and fields along the Tombigbee River (Río Tome) to the west, all of which were devoid of the crops that natives had pulled and burned, the colonists at Nanipacana were reduced to processing and consuming the abundant acorns and a range of unfamiliar leaves, herbs, and roots, some of which were poisonous and resulted in deaths.[85] By early June, even these starvation foods had run out. On June 11 thirty-six married soldiers submitted a formal petition to the

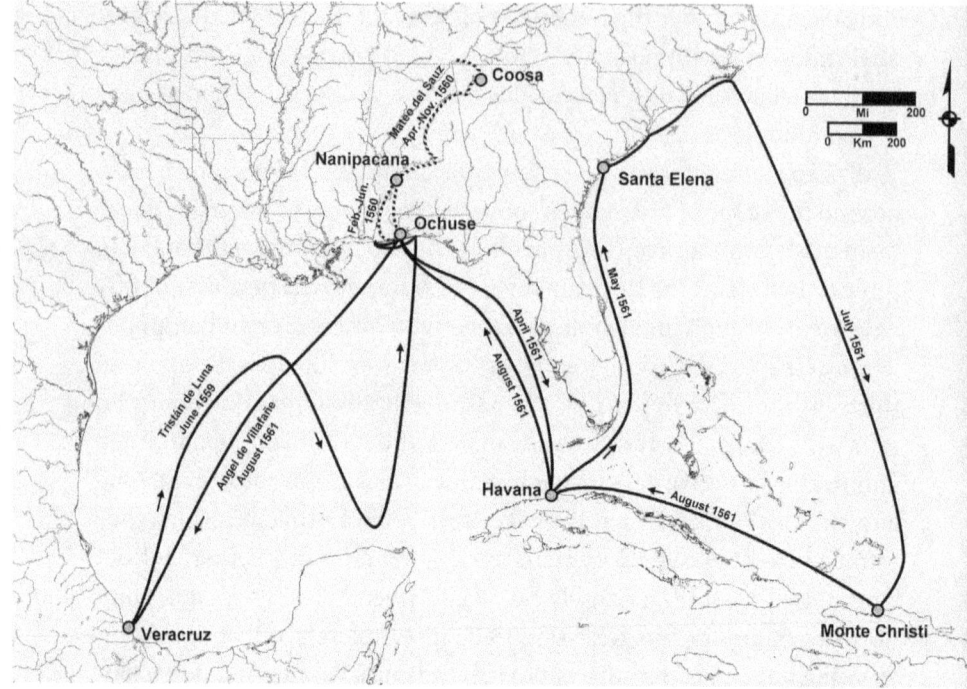

Figure 3.4. Actual routes of the Tristán de Luna expedition. Drawing by John Worth.

governor to permit them to return to New Spain with their families—a proposal that initially was denied but that was reiterated six days later, supported by similar requests from Aztec warriors and craftsmen on June 23.[86] Digging in his heels, Luna not only denied their request during a meeting on June 19 but also communicated his decision to move the colonists inland to Coosa, despite not yet having had word from the Sauz detachment beyond the arrival of Juan de Porras.[87] Field Marshal Jorge Cerón and the expedition's royal officials and remaining captains immediately protested, arguing that moving to Coosa was unwise and that the camp instead should move downriver to Bahía Filipina (Mobile Bay), "where the people could sustain themselves with the abundant oysters and crabs, and with the fish that are there, and with the great quantity of hearts of palm that are near there, and beyond this there is a great quantity of deer."[88] In the face of universal resistance, Luna relented and ordered Nanipacana to be abandoned on June 24. The entire camp relocated downriver, leaving a letter in a pot buried beneath a tree with a note pinned to it in case any of the Coosa detachment should arrive.[89]

While the colonists were at Mobile Bay, the governor's fitness for command again was challenged formally by the royal officials, officers, and soldiers, who requested that an investigation be conducted in front of Field Marshal Jorge Cerón. Paperwork for this action later was cited by several company captains requesting Luna's removal from office.[90] According to Cerón, in the midst of the investigation, the governor suddenly decided to leave Bahía Filipina and return to the port at Ochuse (also referred to as Polonza). Everyone who could fit in the brigantines came with him willingly, leaving Cerón to follow later. Soon after their arrival at Pensacola Bay in July, Luna dispatched one of the new brigantines to take letters to the viceroy as well as taking the ailing Juan Xaramillo and several others.[91] The little ship was driven off course to Havana and delayed two weeks, but eventually reached New Spain, bringing word to the viceroy. Three days after Xaramillo's departure, the second relief fleet arrived at Ochuse, including the galleon *San Juan de Ulúa*, *San Antón*, the patache *Santiago*, and a new frigate, loaded with provisions and other supplies and equipment.[92]

Among the letters brought by the fleet was a copy of a royal decree dated December 18, 1559, insisting that Luna should proceed immediately by sea to occupy Punta de Santa Elena—the original goal of the entire expedition—but also commanding that the settlement at Ochuse not be abandoned.[93] The governor quickly organized an expedition to sail to Santa Elena via Havana, taking fifty-five men and assorted supplies aboard the galleon *San Juan*, two frigates, and a bark, led by Luna's nephew Martín Doz and including the newly arrived captain Diego de Biedma and fray Gregorio de Beteta, the latter a survivor of the 1549 Luís Cancer expedition.[94] After the fleet's departure on August 10, bad weather once again intervened. The galleon was unable to make port in Havana and sailed back to San Juan de Ulúa, arriving on September 5, with the other vessels reaching El Marién (present day Mariél) in Cuba. The viceroy used these vessels for the same purpose the following year. After delivering supplies, *San Antón* was dispatched back to New Spain with fray Pedro de Feria and an unspecified number of returning colonists, while the patache *Santiago* remained at Ochuse at the governor's insistence.[95]

Meanwhile, the situation at Santa María de Ochuse was about to get worse. The simmering tension between Luna and his officers reached boiling point after Christóbal Ramírez de Arellano's detachment from Coosa returned to Ochuse on August 27, having discovered the governor's note in the buried jar at Nanipacana.[96] Now in possession of several detailed letters from the sergeant major and other officers and the Dominicans in Coosa, the governor called his own staff together at Santa María and declared his intent for the army to move inland to Coosa. The reaction was immediate, and the next few days witnessed an intense flurry of legal proceedings back and forth between an increasingly intransigent Luna and his equally resistant officers and soldiers.[97] Caught in the middle was second-in-command Field Marshal Jorge Cerón, to whom all of Luna's opponents flocked to resist the governor's demands. Cerón was unsure of the extent to which the opposition would support him in the long term and was well aware of the potential consequences of deposing a royally appointed governor without full justification. The paperwork for the lawsuit was voluminous, consisting of sixty-five folios of paper, front and back, when transcribed the following January by notary Juan de Vargas. While a full retelling is not within the purview of this chapter, several details are important to the story of the expedition.

Apart from revealing the continued and very real concerns about food, documentation from the lawsuit includes the only accurate count of the exact number of colonists still living in Santa María at that time:

> At the present there are in this camp and port three hundred sixty two souls who eat, and among all of them there are no more than fifty useful and necessary soldiers, because the rest are sick men, women, children, Indian men and women, and other unfit people who serve for nothing other than eating, apart from those who are in the interior, who are two hundred persons, not counting those who are on the patache and ship *San Juan*, which is expected from Havana, which will be another thirty, that in all will be five hundred souls.[98]

Thus by the end of its first year Luna's expedition had decreased from 1,500 original colonists to fewer than 500. The difference is attributable not only to deaths due to the hurricane and subsequent starvation but also includes an unknown number of colonists evacuated during the first and second relief voyages.

The lawsuit papers incidentally provide important clues about the structures and layout of the settlement at Santa María de Ochuse as it stood nearly a year after the hurricane. There are numerous specific mentions of the structure known as the royal warehouse, where food, other supplies, and equipment were kept under lock and key, presumably including the relief supplies delivered to the settlement and carefully rationed out to the starving colonists during the two years after the 1559 hurricane.[99] Also noted was a church administered by the Dominican missionaries (called a *ramada* in the Dávila Padilla account).[100] Other documents mention the private houses of Luna and several of his officers.[101]

A "Notable Indisposition"

An intense legal struggle ensued over whether the colonists should go to Coosa or the Coosa detachment should return to Ochuse and, most important, who should be allowed to make that decision. The governor withdrew from further involvement in the matter and issued a formal order condemning his officers to death (pending confirmation by the viceroy).[102] Field Marshal Cerón and the other officials dispatched Juan de Porras back into the interior on September 9 with a letter for Sergeant Major Sauz, explaining the situation and ordering him to return to Ochuse.[103] Also on September 9, Cerón's faction overrode the governor's wishes and dispatched one hundred of the "sick, married, and unfit persons" on the patache *Santiago*, accompanied by the ailing Captain Pedro de Acuña, to provide a report and letters to the viceroy.[104] When the Coosa detachment arrived in early November, only about one hundred soldiers were said to remain in camp, presumably not counting other remaining colonists.[105]

When *Santiago* arrived in New Spain and Luna's letters, written in the heat of the dispute with his officers, reached the viceroy on September

30, Velasco immediately had Acuña thrown in jail for insubordination. In a letter on October 2 he threatened to do the same to those who had opposed Luna at Ochuse.[106] However, by October 4, following a meeting with his governing council (*audiencia*) in Mexico City, the viceroy seems to have had a complete change of heart. He wrote to Luna and suggested that since he obviously was suffering from "such a notable indisposition," perhaps he should step aside and leave Florida to heal himself.[107] Overtly recommending that Field Marshal (and reluctant head of the anti-Luna faction) Jorge Cerón was the best choice to replace him, Velasco warned Luna that he should not return to New Spain, where this "would not be conducive to your life, honor, nor estate," but instead should go to Havana to await a fleet traveling to Spain to give account of his actions to the king.

In the meantime, the promised third relief fleet arrived in December 1560, comprising the returning galleon *San Juan* and a caravel named *San Marcos*, both loaded with supplies.[108] When the ships departed in January 1561, not only did they carry more evacuees back to New Spain—possibly including the remaining Aztec Indians, about whom the viceroy had noted in September, "here their relatives whine for them"—but they also carried letters from the remaining officers and Dominicans asserting that Luna was no longer fit to govern and should be replaced.[109] Luna's own reply about transferring power to Cerón seems to have been a petulant statement that the viceroy was doing him a grave injustice by not sending an outside replacement who could investigate the disobedience of the officers.[110] Combined with the disappointing news that Luna no longer had a detachment deep in the interior, these letters doubtless contributed to the viceroy's decision at the end of January to send the mayor of Veracruz, Angel de Villafañe, as Luna's replacement.

In early April, when newly appointed Florida governor Villafañe arrived with forty to sixty men aboard the fourth and final relief fleet to Ochuse, he promptly signed a formal license for Luna to take the next ship to Havana and then Spain.[111] Carrying a bundle of paperwork, including many original letters and a full transcription of the drawn-out lawsuit from the previous August and September, Luna sailed to Havana in one of the frigates. He evidently caught a ride to Spain in a fleet under Pedro Menéndez de Avilés, who, ironically, would return to Florida four years later and found Spain's first successful colony at St. Augustine. His appeals denied in Spain, Luna eventually returned to New Spain, where he lived the rest of his life in relative obscurity and austerity, dying in Mexico City on September 16, 1573, unable even to pay his own burial expenses.[112]

Villafañe's fleet included the galleon *San Juan de Ulúa*, on its fifth voyage to Ochuse; a caravel named *San Juan*; the frigates *Trinidad* and *San Juan*; and a patache, also named *San Juan*.[113] After taking possession of the governorship and accepting an oath of allegiance from all but a handful of the officers, he embarked on the next phase of his expedition—sailing to Punta de Santa Elena. Leaving behind Captain Diego de Biedma and 50 to 60 men to hold Ochuse until he returned, he sailed to Havana with 160–200 men to take on supplies.[114] Designating about ninety of the men in Havana to accompany him, he sailed through the Bahama Channel and up along the Atlantic coast in good weather. The fleet made several landfalls, beginning with the long-awaited Santa Elena on May 27, and although they took possession of several locations, leaving crosses marked on trees, none was deemed suitable for settlement. After exploring northward as far as the Cape of Trafalgar (Cape Hatteras), the galleon and caravel became separated, and both frigates and all hands were lost in a storm on June 14. On the homeward voyage, the caravel rejoined the galleon before reaching the port of Monte Cristi on Hispaniola on July 9. After refitting the remaining ships for nearly a month, Villafañe sailed for Ochuse via Havana, evacuated the remaining soldiers, and returned to New Spain. Luna's settlement had been occupied for slightly more than two years, making Santa María de Ochuse the longest-lived European colony in the continental United States to date.

The failure of Luna and Villafañe to fulfill the Spanish Crown's desire to settle Santa Elena on the modern South Carolina coast set the stage for French colonists under Jean Ribault to establish the short-lived Charlesfort settlement there in 1562, along with a second French colony at Fort Caroline near modern Jacksonville.[115] However, the arrival of a Spanish expedition under Pedro Menéndez in 1565 succeeded not only in eliminating the French presence and founding the first permanent European settlement in Florida but also in establishing a Spanish colony on the ruins of Charlesfort at Santa Elena in 1566.[116] During the next two years,

Menéndez sent several expeditions under captain Juan Pardo to reach Coosa from the coast, essentially backtracking Luna's intended route to the Atlantic. However, he also failed to establish a land route across the Appalachian summit and westward to New Spain.[117] Luna's Pensacola Bay faded into obscurity as Spanish Florida grew from St. Augustine, and 137 years passed before Spaniards finally established a permanent presence there in 1698—initiated and supplied out of San Juan de Ulúa, like Luna's *entrada* before them. Although Tristán de Luna's expedition was an unmitigated failure, it nonetheless represents a significant and unique episode in the history of early European colonialism in North America, making it an important target for continued historical and archaeological research.

Notes

1. See four letters in Priestley, *The Luna Papers 1559-1961* (2010, ed. John E. Worth), hereafter cited as Priestley (2010) with volume and page numbers: Luís de Velasco to Tristán de Luna y Arellano, May 6, 1560, in Priestley (2010), 1:102–5; Velasco to the Spanish Crown, May 25, 1559, in Priestley (2010), 2:224–25; Velasco to the Spanish Crown, September 30, 1558, in Priestley (2010), 2:256–59; Pedro de Feria to Dominican superior, March 3, 1559, in Priestley (2010), 2:324–25.

2. Davis, "Juan Ponce de León's Voyages"; Lawson, *Discovery of Florida*; Peck, "1513 Discovery Voyage"; Weddle, *Spanish Sea*, 38–54; Worth, *Discovering Florida*, 8–19, 43–86.

3. Hoffman, "New Voyage of North American Discovery."

4. Weddle, *Spanish Sea*, 95–108.

5. Davis, "Juan Ponce de León's Voyages," 52–64; Lawson, *Discovery of Florida*, 51–56; Peck, "1513 Discovery Voyage," 65–67; Weddle, *Spanish Sea*, 47–48; Worth, *Discovering Florida*, 19, 61–63, 82–86.

6. Hoffman, *New Andalucia*; Hoffman, "Lúcas Vázquez de Ayllón."

7. Hoffman, *New Andalucia*, 50–59.

8. Ibid., 60–83.

9. Hoffman, "Narváez and Cabeza de Vaca in Florida," 50–73.

10. Spanish Crown, Asiento with Hernando de Soto; Hudson, *Knights of Spain*.

11. Clayton, Knight, and Moore, *The De Soto Chronicles*, 1:73–74, 227–28, 268; 2:244–45.

12. Ibid., 2:550–52.

13. Lowery, *The Spanish Settlements*, 411–27; Weddle, *Spanish Sea*, 234–46; Worth, *Discovering Florida*, 23–28, 154–89.

14. Padilla, *Historia*, 189–229, translated in Swanton, *Early History of the Creek Indians*, 231–19. Despite its authorship and late date, Padilla's account probably represents in

part a firsthand recollection. The relevant portion originally may have been written by Luna expedition participant Fray Domingo de la Anunciación, who is listed by Padilla among the prior authors and reviewers of sections of his final edited manuscript; "Ancient Florida," in Winsor, *Narrative and Critical History of America*, 256–260; Lowery, *The Spanish Settlements*, 351–77.

15. Priestley, *Luna Papers*; Priestley, *Tristán de Luna*.

16. Priestley, *Luna Papers*; Priestley (2010), Arnade, "Tristán de Luna and Ochuse"; Weddle, *Spanish Sea*, 251–84; Hudson, "A Spanish-Coosa Alliance"; Hudson et al., "Tristán de Luna Expedition"; "The Tristán de Luna Expedition, 1559–1561," in Milanich and Milbrath, *First Encounters*, 119–34; Hoffman, *New Andalucia*, 144–81; Galloway, *Choctaw Genesis*, 143–60.

17. Smith et al., *The Emanuel Point Ship, 1992–1995*; Scott-Ireton, "Analysis of Spanish Colonization Fleets." During the early 1990s diverse work was carried out in Spain, Mexico, Florida, and other archival repositories by a number of researchers. Selected reports, inventories, and translations include Lakey, "Don Tristán de Luna y Arellano"; Lakey "Addendum to the Catalog"; Hann, "Report on Contaduría 877"; Hann, "Summary on Research for Luna Project"; Hann, "Report on Trip to Gainesville"; Lyon, "Abstracts and Translations: Luna Fleet Documents"; Childers, Translation of Pedro de Yebra, Translation of Alonso Ortíz de Urrutia.

18. Worth, "Preliminary Observations."

19. Luís de Velasco, Issuance of December 29, 1557, Royal Provision to Tristán de Luna y Arellano, March 30, 1559, transcribed by Juan de Vargas, 1561, in Priestley (2010), 1:42–47.

20. Pedro Rodríguez Canillas and Rodrigo Rangel to the Spanish Crown, April 25, 1557, in Priestley (2010), 2:262–67.

21. Childers, Audit by Martín de Yugoyen, 129.

22. Ibid., 137.

23. Luís de Velasco, Commission to Tristán de Luna y Arellano, October 30, 1558, in Priestley (2010), 1:14–17; Luís de Velasco, Licenciado Zorita, Doctor Bravo, Doctor Villalobos, Instructions to Tristán de Luna y Arellano, April 3, 1559, in Priestley (2010), 1:18–33; Oath administered to Tristán de Luna y Arellano, November 1, 1558, in Priestley (2010), 1:32–43.

24. Velasco, March 30, 1559, in Priestley (2010), 1:46–53.

25. Smith, "Ships in the Exploration of La Florida"; Childers, Audit by Yugoyen, March 21, 1554–January 31, 1559, accounts of Alonso Ortíz de Urrutia, deputy treasurer of Veracruz, 1569; Guido de Lavezaris, Testimony regarding the Florida expedition, February 1, 1559, in Priestley (2010), 2:330–37; Hernán Pérez, Constantino Oreja de San Remo, and Bernaldo Peloso, Testimony regarding the Florida expedition, February 1, 1559, in Priestley (2010), 2:336–39. Lavezaris's name was rendered as Labazares in the Luna documentation.

26. Los Alacranes appear both as aids to navigation and hazards to ships in many colonial-era documents. During the sixteenth century they were described as being an area about fifteen by ten leagues east-west and centered some twenty leagues north of the Rio Lagartos on the northern coast of Yucatán.

27. Gonzalo Gayón, Interrogatory regarding service of Gonzalo Gayón, Havana, July 13–17, 1564, in Gayón, Gonzalo, Petition and service record, 1567, Archivo General de Indias (AGI) Santo Domingo 11, no. 41.

28. Velasco, Letter, September 30, 1558, in Priestley (2010), 2:256–57.

29. Childers, Audit by Yugoyen, 1569; Worth, "Documenting Tristán de Luna's Fleet." Based principally on the absence of any subsequent pay records for crew belonging to the new frigate, I previously concluded that this vessel did not make the original voyage. However, a recent detailed review and organization of the Childers translations of these accounts by University of West Florida graduate student Charles Bendig, combined with other documentation, suggests that the frigate was likely towed uncrewed along with the other eleven ships in Luna's fleet and actually survived the hurricane that destroyed seven additional vessels.

30. Smith, "Early Spanish Shipping in Pensacola."

31. Velasco, Letter, September 30, 1558, in Priestley (2010), 2:254–61.

32. Velasco, Letter, May 25, 1559, in Priestley (2010), 2:223; Account of what happened in the City of Mexico on March 8, 1559, in Priestley (2010), 2:238–39; Tristán de Luna y Arellano, Report to the Spanish Crown, 1561, in Priestley (2010), 1:4–5; Luna, Letter to the Spanish Crown, [May 1, 1559], in Priestley (2010), 2:210–13. Luna's May 1 letter clearly is written in his hand, but the date (May 1) and the place (Tlaxcala) are erroneous because it describes events shortly after the fleet's arrival in August. It seems to be a copy he made for inclusion in his 1561 petition and service record, which he misdated.

33. Luís de Velasco to Tristán de Luna y Arellano, May 12, 1559, in Priestley (2010), 1:54–55.

34. Luna, Letter, [May 1, 1559]; Alonso de Montalván, Testimony, August 11, 1561, in Priestley (2010), 2:284–85; Padilla, *Historia*, 190.

35. Velasco, Letter, May 25, 1559, in Priestley (2010), 2:223; Montalván, Testimony, August 11, 1561, in Priestley (2010), 2:284–85; Christóbal Velázquez, Testimony, August 11, 1561, in Priestley (2010), 2:300–3; Miguel Sánchez Serrano, Testimony, August 12, 1561, in Priestley (2010), 2:312–13.

36. Velasco, Account, March 8, 1559, in Priestley (2010), 2:238–39.

37. Avellaneda, *Sobrevivientes de la Florida*. Padilla states that eight Soto veterans were sent, including two captains and six soldiers; Padilla, *Historia*, 190.

38. Velasco, Letter, May 25, 1559, in Priestley (2010), 2:222–23, 226–27.

39. Montalván, Testimony, August 11, 1561, in Priestley (2010), 2:284–85; Married Soldiers, Petition to Tristán de Luna y Arellano, June 11–17, 1560, in Priestley (2010), 1:132–43.

40. Indios Principales, Petition to Tristán de Luna y Arellano, June 23, 1560, in Priestley (2010), 1:142–45; Indios Oficiales, Petition to Tristán de Luna y Arellano, June 23, 1560, in Priestley (2010), 1:144–47; Luís de Velasco to Tristán de Luna y Arellano, September 13, 1560, in Priestley (2010), 2:150–51; Childers, Audit by Hortuño de Ybarra of the November 4, 1559 to August 31, 1563, accounts of Pedro de Yebra, deputy treasurer of Veracruz, 1564.

41. Padilla, *Historia*, 194; Childers, Audit by Yugoyen, 1569.

42. Pedro de Feria, Domingo de la Anunciación, and Domingo de Salazar to the Spanish Crown, May 4, 1559, AGI Mexico 280; Alonso Ortíz de Urrutia, Payment to Hernán Crespo, May 2, 1558, in Childers, Audit by Yugoyen, 1569.

43. Worth and Bratten, "The Materials of Colonization."

44. Padilla, *Historia*, 194. Luna's erroneously dated copy of a letter that likely was written after the fleet's landfall in August paints a different picture in requesting help from the viceroy, stating that he intended to move all but 80–100 of his people into the interior because "here there is no way to be able to sustain so many people . . . there remains no more than eighty days of food," Luna, Letter, [May 1, 1559]. However, even though the lack of any reference to the loss of the fleet in the hurricane suggests it was written before September 19, it may instead post-date the destruction of the food (or even the arrival of the first relief fleet in December), which would perhaps account for the limited rations.

45. Luís de Velasco to the Spanish Crown, September 24, 1559, in Priestley (2010), 2:268–77.

46. Ibid; Luna, Letter, [May 1, 1559].

47. Although both Luna and the viceroy state that the fleet entered on the feast day of the Assumption of Mary, which was August 15, Padilla's account (a firsthand account by Fray Domingo de la Anunciación) specified that the fleet arrived on August 14, the vigil of the feast day for which the bay was named (Santa María Filipina, or "La Bahía Filipina del Puerto de Santa María). Tristán de Luna y Arellano to the Spanish Crown, September 24, 1559, in Priestley (2010), 2:242–47; Luna, Letter, [May 1, 1559]; Velasco, Letter, September 24, 1559, in Priestley (2010), 2:268–77.

48. Padilla, *Historia*, 192–93.

49. Velasco, Letter, September 24, 1559, in Priestley (2010), 2:268–77.

50. Ibid; Luna, Letter, [May 1, 1559], in Priestley (2010), 2:210–13.

51. Worth, "Documenting Tristán de Luna's Fleet," 85.

52. Padilla, *Historia*, 194.

53. Velasco, Letter, May 25, 1559, in Priestley (2010), 2:224–25.

54. Velasco et al., Instructions, April 3, 1559, in Priestley (2010), 1:18–33.

55. Translations by the author from transcriptions in Nuttall, "Royal Ordinances."

56. Luís de Velasco to Tristán de Luna y Arellano, October 25, 1559, in Priestley (2010), 1:56–57; Padilla, *Historia*, 193–94.

57. Padilla, *Historia*, 193–94; Velázquez, Testimony, in Priestley (2010), 2:303–4; Velasco, Letter, October 25, 1559, in Priestley (2010), 1:65–67.

58. Velasco, Letter, May 6, 1560, in Priestley (2010), 1:96–97.

59. Worth, "Documenting Tristán de Luna's Fleet," 88–90. Priestley relied on Padilla's erroneous date of August 20, but Luna's own letter dated just a few days later confirms the September date, as does the Montalván testimony regarding the passage of time between first landfall and the storm; Priestley (2010), 1:xxxvi; Padilla, *Historia*, 194; Luna, Letter, September 24, 1559, in Priestley (2010), 2:244–45; Montalván, in Priestley (2010), 2:284–85.

60. Although no name is provided for the frigate noted in Montalván's testimony about "two barks and a caravel and a frigate" surviving the storm, it may be the *San Juan*

that accompanied the frigate *Trinidad* (newly built for the second relief fleet) in Villafaña's 1561 fleet. Worth, "Documenting Tristán de Luna's Fleet," 84–87; Luna, Letter, September 24, 1559, in Priestley (2010), 2:244–45; Montalván, in Priestley (2010), 2:284–85.

61. Here I am explicitly discounting Padilla's statement that the miraculously preserved vessel found in a grove of trees near the settlement was a caravel, since the only documented caravel (*Santi Espiritu*) is well documented elsewhere to have survived afloat. Padilla's description seems to preclude the vessel somehow having been refloated, noting that "the grove was encircled by very dense trees, and even if that ship had not been blocked and broken on them, it would have been in the grove itself." Moreover, Padilla later erroneously used the term caravel to describe the brigantines built at Ochuse and sent to Nanipacana. Padilla, *Historia*, 194–95, 200.

62. Luna, Letter, September 24, 1559, in Priestley (2010), 2:244–45; Velasco, Letter, October 25, 1559, in Priestley (2010), 1:76–77.

63. Padilla, *Historia*, 194–95.

64. Velasco, Letter, October 25, 1559, in Priestley (2010), 1:56–57.

65. Velasco, Letter, May 6, 1560, in Priestley (2010), 1:116–19.

66. Padilla, *Historia*, 199–200; Luna, Letter, September 24, 1559, in Priestley (2010), 2:244–45; Montalván, in Priestley (2010), 2:286–87; Velázquez, in Priestley (2010), 2:302–5.

67. The name appears commonly as Ypacana and also as Nypacana as well as Nanipacna, as used by Padilla.

68. Padilla, *Historia*, 199; Velasco, Letter, May 6, 1560, in Priestley (2010), 1:93–95.

69. Velasco, Letter, May 6, 1560, in Priestley (2010), 1:94–95, 106–7.

70. Alonso Velázquez, Petition and service record, 1562, in Priestley (2010), 2:304–5.

71. Velasco, Letter, May 6, 1560, in Priestley (2010) 1:92–93; Childers, Audit by Ybarra.

72. Velasco, Letter, October 25, 1559, in Priestley (2010), 1:56–79, 80–81.

73. Ibid., 1:70–73.

74. Velasco, Letter, May 6, 1560, in Priestley (2010), 1:116–17.

75. Montalván, in Priestley (2010), 2:286–89; Velázquez, in Priestley (2010), 2:304–5.

76. Velasco, Letter, May 6, 1560, in Priestley (2010), 1:94–95.

77. Padilla, *Historia*, 200; Montalván, in Priestley (2010), 2:288–89; Velázquez, in Priestley (2010), 2:304–5; Sánchez Serrano, in Priestley (2010), 2:314–5.

78. Montalván, in Priestley (2010), 2:288–89; Velázquez, in Priestley (2010), 2:306–7; Sánchez Serrano, in Priestley (2010), 2:314–15.

79. Padilla, *Historia*, 200–1.

80. Montalván, in Priestley (2010), 2:290–91; Velázquez, in Priestley (2010), 2:304–5; Jorge Cerón Saavedra, Reply to the petition of the captains, August 30, 1560, in Priestley (2010), 2:32–33.

81. Jorge Cerón Saavedra, Reply to Tristán de Luna y Arellano, June 19, 1560, in Priestley (2010), 1:152–59; Alonso Velázquez Rodríguez and Alonso Pérez, Petition to Tristán de Luna y Arellano, June 19, 1560, in Priestley (2010), 1:170–79; Mateo del Sauz to Tristán de Luna y Arellano, July 6, 1560, in Priestley (2010), 1:218–23; Domingo de la Anunciación, Mateo del Sauz, Christóbal Ramírez de Arellano, Alonso de Castilla, Gonzalo

Sánchez de Aguilar, Alvaro Nieto, and Rodrigo Vázquez to Tristán de Luna y Arellano, August 1, 1560, in Priestley (2010), 1:222–33.

82. The town and chiefdom of Coosa during the mid-sixteenth century is well established to have been located at the Little Egypt site, based on extensive research by Charles Hudson and his colleagues in the 1980s, despite earlier (and some later) claims of its location downriver in northeast Alabama, where the eighteenth-century Creek town of Coosa was located; see Hudson et al., "Tristán de Luna Expedition," and Marvin Smith, *Coosa*; also see Swanton, *Final Report of the United States De Soto Expedition Commission*, and Galloway, *Choctaw Genesis*, 143–60.

83. Important sources include Padilla, *Historia*, 201–22; Sauz, Letter, July 6, 1560; Anunciación et al., Letter, August 1, 1560; Domingo de la Anunciación, Mateo del Sauz, Christóbal Ramírez de Arellano, Alonso de Castilla, Gonzalo Sánchez de Aguilar, Alvaro Nieto, and Rodrigo Vázquez, to Luís de Velasco, August 1, 1560, in Priestley (2010), 1:232–43; Domingo Salazar to Francisco Navarro, July 31, 1560, in Priestley (2010), 1:244–47; Jorge Cerón Saavedra, Alonso Velázquez Rodríguez, Alonso Pérez, Baltasar de Sotelo, Diego Tellez, Juan de Porras, Pedro de Acuña, and Julián de Acuña to Mateo del Sauz, September 9, 1560, in Priestley (2010), 2:118–25; Jorge Cerón Saavedra, Instructions to Juan de Porras, September 9, 1560, in Priestley (2010), 2:124–29; Christóbal de Luna, Declaration regarding service of Luis de Soto, February 1, 1575, AGI Mexico 213, no. 1, ff. 1r–v.

84. Galloway suggested that the entire Napochies incident, as reported in great detail by Padilla in his 1596 text, was fictional; however, the independent attestation of the same raid in 1575 testimony by Christóbal de Luna seems to confirm it as fact; for details on the raid, see Hudson, "A Spanish-Coosa Alliance."

85. Cerón Saavedra, Reply, June 19, 1560, in Priestley (2010), 1:152–59.

86. Married Soldiers, in Priestley (2010), 1:132–43; Indios Principales, in Priestley (2010), 1:142–45; Indios Oficiales, in Priestley (2010), 1:144–47.

87. Tristán de Luna y Arellano, Declaration regarding going to Coosa, June 19, 1560, in Priestley (2010), 1:146–53.

88. Pedro de Acuña, Baltasar de Sotelo, Antonio Ortíz de Matienzo, Diego Tellez, Juan de Porras, and Pedro López de Nava, Reply to Tristán de Luna y Arellano, June 19, 1560, in Priestley (2010), 1:162–65; Cerón Saavedra, Reply to Tristán de Luna y Arellano, June 19, 1560, in Priestley (2010), 1:152–59; Alonso Fajardo, Reply to Tristán de Luna y Arellano, June 19, 1560, in Priestley (2010), 1:166–69; Martín Doz and Julián de Acuña, Reply to Tristán de Luna y Arellano, June 19, 1560, in Priestley (2010), 1:170–71; Velázquez Rodríguez and Pérez, Petition, June 19, 1560, in Priestley (2010), 1:170–79.

89. Padilla, *Historia*, 217.

90. Pedro de Acuña, Baltasar de Sotelo, Diego Tellez, Juan de Porras, and Julián de Acuña, Petition to Jorge Cerón Saavedra, August 30, 1560, in Priestley (2010), 2:28–31; Jorge Cerón Saavedra, Reply to the petition of the captains, August 30, 1560, in Priestley (2010), 2:36–37.

91. Luís de Velasco to Tristán de Luna y Arellano, August 20, 1560, in Priestley (2010), 1:180–95; Velasco, Letter, September 13, 1560, in Priestley (2010), 2:146–47.

92. Velasco, Letter, September 13, 1560, ff. 162r, in Priestley (2010), 2:136–37; Childers, Audit by Ybarra, 1564; Velasco, Letter, May 6, 1560, in Priestley (2010), 1:94–97; Velasco, Letter, August 20, 1560, in Priestley (2010), 1:182–83.

93. Spanish Crown, Cédula to Tristán de Luna y Arellano, December 18, 1559, in Priestley (2010), 2:174–75.

94. Montalván, in Priestley (2010), 2:298–301; Velázquez, in Priestley (2010), 2:310–11; Sánchez Serrano, in Priestley (2010), 2:318–19; Velasco, Letter, September 13, 1560, in Priestley (2010), 2:136–41; Luís de Velasco to Tristán de Luna y Arellano, September 15, 1560, in Priestley (2010), 2:156–59; Luís de Velasco to Tristán de Luna y Arellano, September 23, 1560, in Priestley (2010), 2:175; Luís de Velasco to Tristán de Luna y Arellano, October 1, 1560, in Priestley (2010), 2:168–71.

95. Luís de Velasco to Gonzalo Gayón, September 15, 1560, in Gonzalo Gayón, Petition and service record, 1567, AGI Santo Domingo 11, no. 41, ff. 9r–v.

96. Padilla, *Historia*, 219–20; Tristán de Luna y Arellano, Declaration of intent to go inland, August 27, 1560, in Priestley (2010), 1:198–201.

97. Tristán de Luna y Arellano, Lawsuit between Tristán de Luna y Arellano and his officers, August 27–September 13, 1560, in Priestley (2010), 1:198–253, 2:2–137.

98. Jorge Cerón Saavedra, Petition for meeting with Tristán de Luna y Arellano, September 9, 1560, in Priestley (2010), 2:94–95.

99. For example, Alonso Velázquez Rodríguez and Alonso Pérez, Petition to Jorge Cerón Saavedra, August 31, 1560, in Priestley (2010), 2:64–65; Juan de Vargas, Declaration to Tristán de Luna y Arellano regarding the refusal to issue rations, September 2, 1560, in Priestley (2010), 2:68–71; Company Officers, Petition to Jorge Cerón Saavedra, September 2, 1560, in Priestley (2010), 2:80–83; Tristán de Luna y Arellano, Order to send the patache *Santiago* to New Spain, September 9, 1560, in Priestley (2010), 2:98–99; Jorge Cerón Saavedra, Petition for meeting with Tristán de Luna y Arellano, September 9, 1560, in Priestley (2010), 2:106–7; Jorge Cerón Saavedra, Jorge, Alonso Velázquez Rodríguez, Alonso Pérez, Baltasar de Sotelo, Pedro de Acuña, Diego Tellez, Christóbal Ramírez de Arellano, and Julián de Acuña, Meeting and decision to dispatch the patache *Santiago* to New Spain, September 9, 1560, in Priestley (2010), 2:132–33.

100. For example, Padilla, *Historia*, 224; Gonzalo Suárez, Declaration regarding an incident at the church at Santa María de Ochuse, March 8, 1561, in Priestley (2010), 1:86–91.

101. For example, Suárez, in Priestley (2010), 1:86–91; Tristán de Luna y Arellano, Reply to petition by Jorge Cerón Saavedra, September 9, 1560, in Priestley (2010), 2:94–97.

102. Tristán de Luna y Arellano, Condemnations against the captains and royal officials, September 2, 1560, in Priestley (2010), 2:70–73.

103. Cerón Saavedra et al., Letter, September 9, 1560, in Priestley (2010), 2:118–25; Cerón Saavedra, Instructions, September 9, 1560, in Priestley (2010), 2:124–29; Padilla, *Historia*, 222.

104. Cerón Saavedra et al., Meeting, September 9, 1560, in Priestley (2010), 2:130–35.

105. Montalván, in Priestley (2010), 2:292–93.

106. Velasco, Letter, October 1, 1560, in Priestley (2010), 2:168–71; Luís de Velasco to Tristán de Luna y Arellano, October 2, 1560, in Priestley (2010), 2:174–77.

107. Luís de Velasco to Tristán de Luna y Arellano, October 4, 1560, in Priestley (2010), 1:80–83.

108. Childers, Audit by Ybarra, 1564.

109. Montalván, in Priestley (2010), 2:292–93; Velázquez, in Priestley (2010), 2:306–7; Sánchez Serrano, in Priestley (2010), 2:314–17; Velasco, Letter, September 13, 1560, in Priestley (2010), 2:150–51.

110. Luís de Velasco to Tristán de Luna y Arellano, January 30, 1561, in Priestley (2010), 1:8–15.

111. Angel de Villafañe, License for Tristán de Luna y Arellano to go to Spain, April 9, 1561, in Priestley (2010), 1:8–9. Before this, Villafañe was a co-captain of the salvage expedition to the *flota* wrecked at Padre Island, Texas, in 1554.

112. Priestley (2010), 2:lxvi–lxvii; Priestley, *Tristán de Luna*, 186–92.

113. Childers, Audit by Ybarra, 1564.

114. Francisco de Aguilar, Testimony regarding the expedition of Angel de Villafañe, July 10, 1561, AGI Patronato 19, Ramo 11; Montalván, f. 3v–4r, in Priestley (2010), 2:294–99; Velázquez, ff. 5v–6r, in Priestley (2010), 2:306–11; Sánchez Serrano, ff. 7r–v, in Priestley (2010), 2:316–19.

115. Laudonnière, *Three Voyages*; Bennett, *Laudonnière and Fort Caroline*.

116. Lyon, *The Enterprise of Florida*.

117. Hudson, *The Juan Pardo Expeditions*.

4

Nautical Archaeology of a Shipwreck

The Ship's Architecture

JAMES D. SPIREK AND JOSEPH COZZI

In late October 1992 the Pensacola Shipwreck Survey team returned to Emanuel Point to investigate the sources of several anomalies detected during a magnetometer survey conducted in August that year.[1] Three of the anomalies proved promising, having a signal that lasted for several seconds and an intensity that was recorded over several adjacent survey lanes. Inclement weather had prevented an earlier side-scan sonar survey over these targets to aid in identifying their potential archaeological or historical significance. Inspection of the first target, located in soft mud, failed to reveal the source of the anomaly. Subsequent inspection of the anomaly later determined the source as a car. The second target also proved of a modern vintage—a section of an outrigger from a shrimp trawler.

Pinpointing the third magnetic target with the magnetometer and dropping a buoy to mark the site, Della Scott-Ireton and Chuck Hughson dived 10 feet (3 m) to the bottom to conduct a circle-search to locate the source of the anomaly. Chuck, the searching diver, after several widening passes and reaching the end of the 50-foot line, encountered a school of fish making for structure. Chuck dropped the end of the line and followed the fish as best he could in the opaque water. Moving in the direction of the darting fish, he soon encountered a compact concentration of ballast stones covered with oyster shells and shell hash and level with the adjacent sandy bottom. Chuck crawled around the rock mound looking for other features, such as fasteners, ceramics, or wood, to suggest the presence of a shipwreck. After making a cursory inspection of the site, Chuck and Della returned to the boat to announce their discovery.

To determine if the ballast mound represented a shipwreck, I (Jim Spirek) descended on the site to see if there were any wood or ship structure buried beneath the stones. We had during the course of the survey encountered several other similar sites, which proved on further investigation to be simply ballast dump sites, so we remained cautious about supposing the rock mound signified a shipwreck. I made another inspection over the length and breadth of the site and again found no visible or diagnostic features on or around the ballast mound, or the cause of the magnetic anomaly. Selecting an area along the northern periphery of the ballast mound at the rock and sand interface, I began to remove small stones, shells, shell hash, and sand. Digging several inches down revealed the presence of a flat wood board, perhaps a piece of planking. The presence of the wood buried beneath the rock mound suggested the wreck of a sailing vessel. Excited by the find, we returned to the office and planned the next steps to investigate the shipwreck further in an effort to determine its age, origin, and the source of the magnetic anomaly.

Discovery at Emanuel Point: The First Field Campaign

The team returned to the site over the course of several weeks in November and December to undertake preliminary testing at the shipwreck site. The ballast mound, barely rising above the surrounding sediments, lay in a northwest to southeast orientation with the visible portion of the mound measuring approximately 40 feet long by 23 feet wide (12 × 7 m). We strung a baseline along the longitudinal axis of the ballast to guide test excavations in the central portion of the site, the presumed site of the mainmast step, a major diagnostic architectural feature of a sailing vessel that would assist in identifying the age and origin of the shipwreck.

Digging at Test Unit A, situated slightly offset to the south of the baseline, required removal of a number of stones varying in size and shape, some large requiring two hands to remove and others hand-sized or smaller, and some angular and others rounded in shape. Interspersed between the rocks were small wood fragments, most likely dunnage (packing material) used to cushion and stabilize the ship's cargo. Digging downward through the rocks, wood fragments, and sediments revealed well-preserved ship structure. The wooden timbers included a beveled footwale (an interior longitudinal timber used to strengthen the hull) and a ceiling plank (placed over the frames to protect those timbers and the exterior hull planks from the ballast and cargo). Beneath these two timbers lay two frames, just visible outboard of the footwale, but with no visible sign of any exterior hull planks. Interestingly, several fastening holes, both treenail (wooden dowel) and iron spike holes, did not align with the frames below. In addition to the dunnage, we found several glazed and unglazed pottery sherds and a fragment of an animal rib.

Selecting a location just north of the baseline and parallel to first test unit, we began digging at Test Unit B and encountered below the surface of the mound another footwale. Artifacts recovered from this test unit included several coarse earthenware pottery sherds, a leather sole of a shoe, and the vertebrae of an animal. Locating these port and starboard footwales revealed that the centerline of the shipwreck was situated directly underneath our baseline. Excavation of Test Unit C, located along the centerline and between Test Units A and B, uncovered the aft section of the diagnostic mainmast step, part of the ship's keelson (a longitudinal timber fitted over the frames above the keel). This expanded section of the keelson, fashioned to accept the foot of the mainmast, also featured a carved concave opening for a bilge pump shaft, which allowed us to see several lower exterior hull planks and the molded surface of the ship's frames. A soupy matrix of organics and sediments lay within this area between the frames and contained a number of ceramic sherds. On the other side of the pump sump was an athwart timber, or buttress, placed against the expanded keelson.

Following these initial exploratory test units we closed the site for the season and prepared a preliminary report detailing the findings from this shipwreck. Results from the initial investigations hinted at the presence of a well-preserved shipwreck that featured hallmarks of sixteenth-century Spanish ship construction, such as an enlarged and buttressed mainmast step, similar to that in a small contemporary Spanish

Figure 4.1. Concave opening in the keelson for the port side pump shaft. Courtesy of the Florida Department of State, Division of Historical Resources.

shipwreck in Bermuda that I had worked on while a graduate student. Intriguingly, the wreck showed evidence of violently shattering on the shoal off Emanuel Point. Of course, we discussed privately its potential to be associated with the Luna fleet lost in 1559. In fact, every time the magnetometer detected a large magnetic anomaly during the course of our survey operations, Chuck exclaimed, "Luna!" Visual inspection of the source often found it to be a car, wire, a washing machine, or other modern debris, but perhaps this time he was right. Despite the uncertainty of the shipwreck's identity at this phase of the project, all the findings so far suggested that this site offered a unique and rare opportunity to explore Pensacola's and Florida's maritime heritage. During the next several months Roger made arguments to his superiors in Tallahassee for continued investigations of the site to explore it more fully and tell the story of the shipwreck lying off Emanuel Point.

At this stage in the shipwreck investigations, there had been no diagnostic artifact with which to corroborate the sixteenth-century hallmarks of ship construction. The abundance of earthenware ceramic sherds appeared to be from olive jars, common to all Spanish colonial sites, but were composed solely of body fragments. We had found no well-preserved rim sherds, the shape of which would assist in pinpointing a date range of their manufacture. There was, however, one interesting glazed coarse earthenware sherd recovered deep in one of the test units. This piece was the bottom of a round ceramic container with an interior apparently coated in black glaze. Della noted that the glaze coating the paste suggested to her a tin-glaze. She took the sherd for consultation with UWF archaeologists, who, being familiar with eighteenth-century Spanish pottery, identified the piece as black lead glaze common during that century. The dating of the piece to the eighteenth century contra-indicated the ship's architecture that pointed to the sixteenth century. Della persisted in believing the glaze was tin and not lead. Roger then took the piece and several olive jar sherds to noted archaeologist Kathleen Deagan, professor and curator at the Florida Museum of Natural History in Gainesville, who had excavated at sixteenth-century Spanish settlements including St. Augustine and in the Caribbean. Deagan examined the black-glazed earthenware piece, pronounced it dirty, and then proceeded to wipe away the dark stain to reveal a light-blue tin majolica glaze. She identified the sherd as a fragment of *bacín*, a bowl-shaped ware used by the Spanish for various functions, from the sixteenth century. We now had another temporal marker indicating a sixteenth-century date for the shipwreck and its contents.

First Field Campaign

After receiving institutional and financial support from Tallahassee to conduct further study at the site, we planned for more extensive excavations at key sections of the shipwreck, namely amidships, stern, and forward, to answer specific research questions about its cultural and temporal connection, site preservation, and spatial distribution. Additional partners joined us for this phase of the project, including the Historic Pensacola Preservation Board and the University of West Florida, which co-sponsored with the Bureau of Archaeological Research a field school to launch the excavations. The original staff of the Pensacola Shipwreck Survey team was also increased with the hiring of Amy Mitchell to conserve the recovered artifacts and Jeffrey Lockwood to photograph the work and to assist as an archaeological technician. A local marine

Figure 4.2. Tip of the anchor fluke poking out of the sand. Courtesy of the Florida Department of State, Division of Historical Resources.

contractor generously loaned us a large wooden barge from which to support the field operations. As will be seen, the barge proved both a blessing and an albatross around our necks.

Prior to continuing excavations at the amidships area we set up a series of datum stakes strung together with polypropylene line to form a rectangular shaped 30 × 40 m grid that encompassed the site. The grid not only acted as a reference for all the subsequent work at the site but also served as a physical barrier to corral any errant divers from losing their way in the turbid waters. Second, to learn more about the buried features at the site we undertook a controlled metal detector survey within the grid, marking and mapping metal targets buried beneath the sand. A number of shallow targets were identified, usually metal fasteners, while others were buried deeper in the sediments. We found that the metal objects formed a narrow halo around the ballast mound in the forward and midship areas but became wider in the stern area. We also located the tip of an anchor fluke poking out of the sand at the forward edge of the ballast mound. Review of the metal detector data suggested that the anchor was the primary source of the 400-gamma magnetic anomaly detected during our initial magnetometer survey off Emanuel Point. Discovery of an iron gudgeon strap, used on the sternpost of the ship to affix the rudder, confirmed the orientation of the shipwreck, with the bow pointing westward and the stern toward the east.

After establishing the means to control overall recording of the site, we worked to resume and enlarge our initial excavations in the amidships area. In order to control the excavations at the mainmast assembly we placed six 2 × 2 m grids created from PVC pipes over the ballast mound. These grid units would control the horizontal documentation of the shipwreck and artifacts encountered during the excavations. To record the depth of the buried hull and artifacts, a vertical datum was established on the anchor fluke, the highest point of the shipwreck. Teams of staff and students began the process of removing and suctioning away the overburden of ballast rocks, shells, and sediments covering the wooden structure of the ship.

Eroded and *teredo*-worm riddled boards just below the top layer of stones were encountered and recorded. As the excavations continued, other similar boards were recorded close to the keelson. These deteriorated wooden pieces suggested the presence of the pump well box created by the ship builders to keep ballast, cargo, and trash from clogging the pumps. As with the preliminary test units, we uncovered a number of artifacts, mostly olive jar body sherds. And, as noted previously, one important and singular find was the carved silhouette of a galleon found by Roger in the pump sump among scraps left behind by the ship's carpenters.

Some of the interiors of the recovered sherds were covered with a black organic layer, later found to be pine resin used to seal the jar for transporting liquids, such as wines or olive oil. These along with other artifacts were recorded and then bagged for recovery. Up until this point, we had encountered no diagnostic olive jar rims to corroborate the age and origin of the shipwreck as suggested by the ship's architecture or the majolica *bacín* sherd. Spanish potters had developed over time the shapes of the rims or openings of these containers in a chronologically identifiable sequence. Then, while digging around the mainmast mortise, one of our visiting scholars, Christopher F. Amer of the South

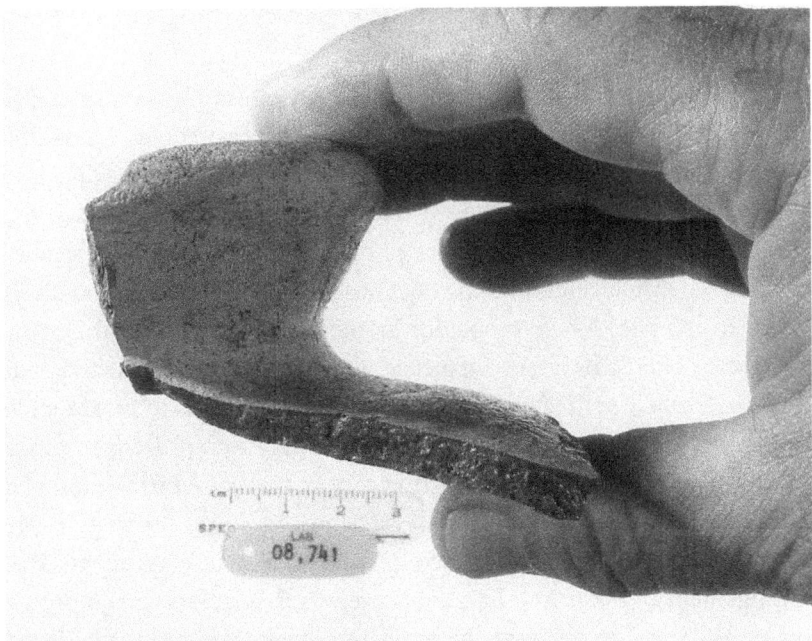

Figure 4.3. Olive jar rim and shoulder sherd. Courtesy of the Florida Department of State, Division of Historical Resources.

Carolina Institute of Archaeology and Anthropology and former excavator of the whaling galleon at Red Bay, Labrador, finally uncovered an olive jar rimsherd with part of the shoulder attached. The profile of the sherd compared favorably to the Middle Style of olive jars featuring an inverted tear-drop style rim that dated to the mid-1500s. We also located a portion of an olive jar's contents—a cache of olive pits that I found interspersed between the ballast stones.

As I began to extract the pits by hand into a specimen bag, some delicate, dark looking objects swirled into the water column. At first they looked like small helicopter seeds from a maple tree. Careful scrutiny revealed that instead of seeds they were in fact the wings of cockroaches that had apparently been dining on a last meal of olives. Later analysis determined the presence of many other parts and pieces of cockroaches (see chapter 5). While these particular insects did not survive the journey, no doubt others did and in all likelihood formed the genesis of subsequent generations of roaches that continue to scurry about Pensacola.

Royal Visitors

Project headquarters was located in the Old School House at the Historic Pensacola Village. Our two project boats operated out of a nearby marina, Pitt Slip, which had graciously offered us convenient dockage. Personnel and equipment moved out daily from headquarters to the marina and then a short commute by boat to the wreck site. In the beginning we simply anchored the boat near the ballast mound and dived down to the site. As we prepared for the field school, a local marine contractor offered us the use of a 20 × 30-foot wooden barge with about 2 feet of freeboard. This larger work platform allowed us to increase the number of people for dive teams and the operation of dredge pumps and air compressors. Another marine contractor offered us the use of a burned-down pontoon boat, which we converted into a floating dredge screen with additional deck space for personnel and equipment. This arrangement of boats and barges allowed us to keep some equipment out on the water to decrease the setup and breakdown time each day at the site.

In the beginning the barge was a blessing, but after a while we could not wait to get it off our hands. One off-day while going to lunch, Chuck and I drove along the Emanuel Point bluff and noticed the barge lying low in the water. At first we thought it was an optical illusion caused by the fog and mist that day. We continued to the restaurant to join the rest of the team. After lunch, we decided to check on the barge again, but this time only the tall tower used to raise and lower pier pilings was standing above the water. The barge had sunk. In fact, it sank two more times, one time with us on it valiantly fighting to keep it afloat, but to no avail. Each time it sank, we refloated it using a combination of truck inner tubes and beer keg tubs filled with air to lift it off the bay bottom. Then we put the dredge intake hose into the barge and slowly pumped out the water. After the third and final time, we thanked the marine contractor and asked him to take back his barge.

For the remainder of the project we relied on the boats and the dredge-screen pontoon to continue the excavations. Although we had reduced the topside work area by giving up the barge, the pontoon served us well, as we were able to leave it lighted and anchored on the site, which like the large barge permitted quick setup and breakdown each day. Then as fall turned into winter our pontoon became the preferred overnight roosting and pooping platform for a flock of royal terns, which lasted for several months. Each morning before setting foot on the pontoon, one of us would hop aboard with the discharge end of the dredge hose, and another would fire up the dredge pump so that we could wash down the deck from the previous night's mess of bird feces, feathers, and on one occasion a lifeless bird. We tried a number of tricks and devices to deter the terns, including laying out string on the deck, leaving stuff scattered about, and installing a fake owl, only to return each morning to clean the deck from the terns' nightly deposits. Adding insult to injury, on the first morning after the fake owl took its station on the pontoon, it had a trickle of poop running down its head and body. Eventually the birds migrated away, finally leaving us with a clean deck on which to start our mornings.

Midships Architecture (at the "Pelvis" of the Ship)

Our excavations had uncovered a large section of the keelson at the mainmast assembly, probably one of the most important sections of the wreck, since it supported the mainmast as the principal propulsion of the ship and contained the pumps to remove water in the event of a leak. The mainmast step (*carlinga*) is an area in the center of the hull that housed the heel of the largest mast, which was stepped into the keelson (*contraquilla*). To create a sturdy base, the shipwrights carefully shaped the longitudinal timber so that it was larger and thicker than the rest of the keelson. This critical architectural feature displays fine workmanship, especially at the flaring transition point from keelson to mast step and in the carving of the sunken rectangular mortise into which the mast was stepped. Notched to fit over the floor frames, the keelson was fastened to the keel with iron bolts. An adze or broad ax gouge mark was noted on the port side of the step, possibly indicating the midpoint of the vessel.[2] The mainmast mortise contained a distinctive cross gouged into the wood. While the meaning of this mark is unclear, it may have had religious significance, much like the secular practice of depositing a coin in the step for good luck. It also is located at the ship's point of maximum

Figure 4.4. A distinctive cross was carved into the mainmast step mortice. Courtesy of the Florida Department of State, Division of Historical Resources.

breadth, since the master couple (the widest) frame lies directly below the carving. At either end of the mortise were lodged two wood pieces, a shim and a chock, once used to wedge the mast heel firmly in place.

Two smaller mortises in the mast step may have housed tenons for vertical timbers supporting the lower deck or pump well assembly. Just forward of the mast step mortise shim is the remnant of a tenoned stub still in its mortise. The stub may represent the remains of a pillar, or stanchion, used to support a lower deck beam. Aft of the mainmast step, there is a smaller mortise let into the keelson, perhaps intended for a framing timber for the pump well housing.

Aft of the mainmast mortise and on either side of the step are two carved-out pump shaft receptacles leading into the bilge. Since every wooden ship leaks, especially at sea, functional pumps (*bombas*) to clear water from the lower hull are a critical part of seafaring and require constant attention and care. The pump sumps extend between two floor frames to the garboard strake (*traca de aparadura*, lowermost run of planking). Only the port sump was excavated; the starboard was left undisturbed. Each sump once held a pump shaft (*mangueta*), fashioned from the hollowed-out trunk of a tree to form a tube. Water in the bilge was manually forced up the shafts by various types of piston rods and valves to the main deck, where it was allowed to run overboard. Pumping the bilge (*achicar la bomba*) was a routine chore aboard a ship; on older vessels continual leakage had to be monitored carefully for the sake of cargo below and the safety of the ship. Crewmen on the first daylight watch took a keen interest in the color of water coming up from the bilge. If it was dark and foul, they were glad—the hull was sound; if it was clear and green, they began to worry—the hull was leaky.

Although no remnants of pump shafts or hardware were found, a small square board, with a nail at each corner, was discovered lying on the garboard strake. This board may have provided a bed on which a pump foot valve (*morterete*) rested. The lack of pressure marks on the Emanuel Point board suggests that perhaps the pump tube did not rest on the board against the hull but rather was braced on the exposed floors on either side of the pump shaft.[3] A smaller section of the tube could have extended the pump bore into the sump and onto the valve and its board. Arranged in this fashion, stress created by downward tube pressure would have been taken by the floors, instead of the board or exterior plank. To protect the pump sumps from becoming clogged by ballast stones or bilge debris, a pump well (*arca*), or wooden enclosure, was constructed around the pump shafts. Several disarticulated structural remnants discovered around the sump probably represent baseboards from the pump well.

The mainmast step is supported laterally by buttresses, four of which were uncovered on the port side of the keelson. These buttresses were intended to brace the step, preventing its lateral movement as the ship sailed on various tacks or rolled from side to side. Timbers partially visible on the unexcavated starboard side of the keelson revealed the same arrangement as on the port side. The thicker ends of buttresses are toe-nailed in place to the mast step, while the outboard ends are let into the adjacent internal plank, which has been sawn with cutouts to accept them, thus preventing the assembly from shifting under stress.[4] Removable bilge boards (*tablas de la canal*) are let into the spaces between the buttresses to protect this area from trash that might clog the bilge and subsequently the pump. Rabbets (grooves) were cut on the interior and upper edge of the buttresses to allow bilge boards to fit between and flush

Figure 4.5. Port side buttresses, showing a broken removable bilge board. Courtesy of the Florida Department of State, Division of Historical Resources.

with the tops of the four timbers; they were fashioned so that they could easily be removed to inspect the lower bilge area.

Runs of internal ceiling planks (*amuradas*) were fastened to frames on the interior of wooden ships' hulls to prevent ballast stones, or shifting cargo, from damaging the integrity of the outer hull planks. Midships ceiling uncovered on the port side of the mast step consisted of seven common planks, totaling four strakes (continuous longitudinal runs of planks). Ceiling widths and thicknesses were fairly uniform, except for one extremely narrow board, noted running along the outboard side of the pump sump; it may have been inserted after the wider planks were laid. Three small square iron fasteners attached the two outermost planks to the frames below. Inner ceiling runs lie unfastened on the frames. Additionally, two large knots were noted on the upper two ceiling planks, suggesting that a lower grade of wood was utilized in this area. Outboard of the third run of ceiling planks is a chamfered footwale (a thicker ceiling plank), which served to strengthen the hull where elements of the framing (floors and futtocks) are joined. The top of the footwale is beveled on both inboard and outboard edges. Two fasteners in squared recesses secured the footwale to frames.

Midships framing is composed of alternating floor timbers (*varengas*) and first futtocks (*genoles*), which represent the "ribs" (*ligaçon*) of the ship's skeleton. Floors are laid at intervals across the top of the keel. Central waterways, or limber holes (*groeras*), were cut through the bottom edge of the floors and run parallel to the keel. The waterways allowed circulation of bilge water through the hull to the pump sump. Outboard and between each floor are fastened futtocks to form an interlocking and alternating band of timbers that curve outward and upward from the keel to form the framework of the hull. Each outboard end of the floor timbers was notched out where small iron fasteners were driven into the first futtock. The main connection point between floors and futtocks, however, was obscured by ceiling and bottom planking. Interlocking dovetail scarfs (joints) were a common method of connecting floors and futtocks on ships of the sixteenth century; although their presence is suspected here, dovetail scarfs could not be confirmed without disassembling the ceiling planking.[5]

The point at which the direction of the notches in the floors changed (from facing aft to facing forward) is the ship's main frame (*quaderna maestre*). Located at the broadest part of the hull (below the forward end of the mainmast step mortise), the main frame is distinguished by a master couple, where the main floor has two futtocks attached to it, instead of one. At this point, futtock placement changes, i.e., forward of the main frame, futtocks are fastened to the forward edge of each floor, and abaft the main frame, they are attached to the after edge of each floor. In this way the ship's interlocking framework was given uniform integrity and strength. Deadrise (the amount of elevation above the horizontal plane) in the midship floor, from centerline to the outboard edge of the port footwale, is flat, rising at around one degree. Beyond the footwale, the floors curved upward to begin the turn of the bilge.[6]

On the port side of the mainmast step the after futtock of the master couple was found to be splintered; its outboard end terminated abruptly, along with the ceiling planking. Excavations in this area encountered no additional ship's hull structure. Instead, only loose ballast stones,

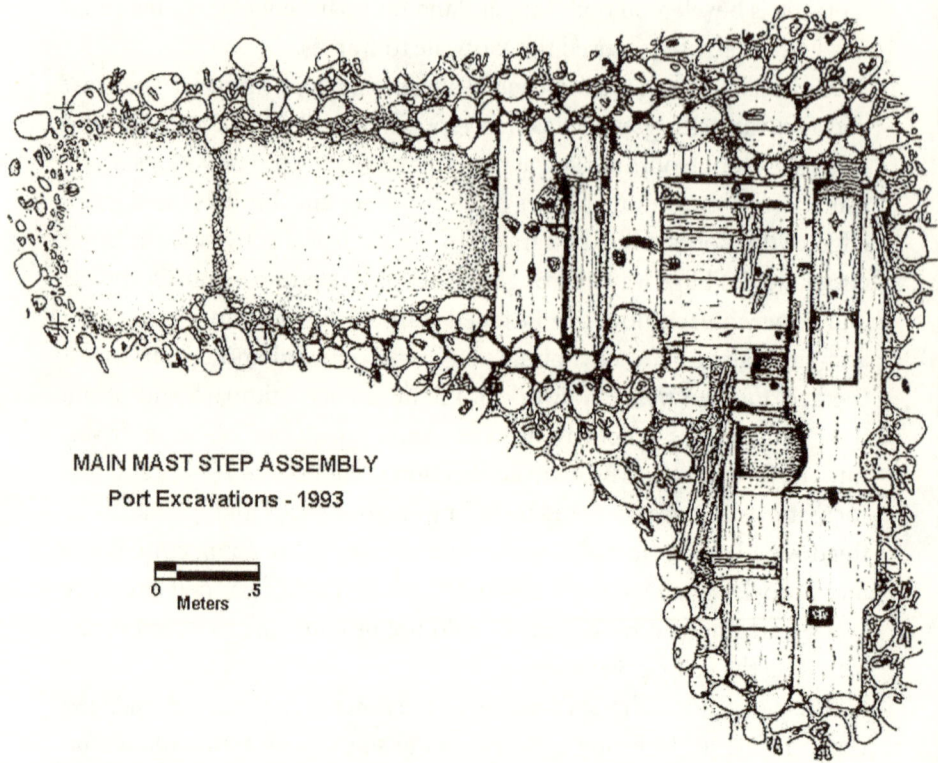

Figure 4.6. Mast step assembly, showing the keelson, pump wells, buttresses, and missing hull structure on the port side. Drawing by James Spirek. Courtesy of the Florida Department of State, Division of Historical Resources.

ceramic sherds, and a single length of heavy rope, running parallel to the hull, were found. Below, there was only sterile sand. Apparently the ship had suffered from a violent pounding on the sand bar, which caused severe damage to this portion of the hull. Although hull structure was absent on the port side beyond the outer ceiling plank, removal of sediment underneath the broken frames revealed a hull plank, heavily concreted with barnacles and corrosion. Pillars composed of iron corrosion and sand, reminiscent of *Titanic*'s "rusticles," extend downward from fastener heads into the sterile sediments below the hull.[7]

Excavations during the field school had revealed well-preserved and articulated lower hull remains that are quite similar to the architecture of other sixteenth-century Spanish shipwrecks that have been studied:

an expanded keelson, with mortise and chock to house the foot of the mainmast; a pump well and sump to house the shaft of the ship's bilge pump; and four perpendicular buttresses on each side of the mast step to support this critical area of the hull laterally. A similar number of buttresses and bilge boards were found on the Basque whaler *San Juan* that sank in Red Bay, Labrador, in 1565.[8] An early sixteenth-century Spanish wreck at Highborn Cay, Bahamas, had a mast step that was supported by only three buttresses per side.[9] One unique feature and important aspect of construction was the juxtaposition of the notched ceiling plank between the buttress and footwale. Typically, the outboard end of the buttress was butted to the wale, and the difference may perhaps represent a regional or individual preference for shoring up this critical mainmast step assembly.[10]

Aft and on either side of the mainmast step were the half-moon cutouts for the pump sumps. *San Juan* at Red Bay had only one pump, while another galleon nearby had a dual pump arrangement.[11] The Highborn Cay Wreck had two pump sumps; however, both were situated on the port side of the step, and the aftermost one appeared to be unfinished or aborted.[12] To improve safety at sea, one of the many maritime edicts of Philip II required in 1552 that newly constructed ships were to have two pumps.[13] Enforcement of this requirement may have taken time to become widespread. Unlike the single pump sump in *San Juan*, which was found to be rather crudely fashioned, the sumps in the Emanuel Point Ship appear to have been carefully carved with forethought and finished with care.[14] A small board found in the pump sump resembled one that was found in the bilge of the Fuxa Wreck in Cuba, thought to be *Nuestra Señora de Rosario*, which ran aground in 1590. That board displayed a distinctive circular impression of the foot valve base on one side.[15]

After the field school ended and the test units had been backfilled with clean sand, we continued limited exploratory testing. Investigation of a metal target located 10 m forward of amidships revealed a concreted metal pitcher and a portion of the ship's starboard bow structure. The structure consisted of three cant frames (*forcazes*, frames that are canted forward), and associated hull planking. Fastener concretions protruding through the timbers indicate that first futtocks, which are no longer present, were mated to the forward edge of these frames. Well-preserved exterior hull planks were also noted in the unit. A large copper cauldron located nearby suggested that the ship's galley may have been situated in this area of the ship.

Investigation of another metal target in the stern area uncovered an object shaped like a donut, which turned out to be a disarticulated gudgeon strap (the female part of the rudder hinge), which had become detached from the sternpost above. The discovery of the sternpost allowed us to obtain a critical measurement—the distance between the main frame and the sternpost—which measured 12 m. With another field season planned for the following year, this measurement would help to determine the overall size of the ship.

Stern Architecture (at the "Tail" of the Ship)

Investigations at the shipwreck resumed in August 1994 and continued until June 1995. We lost team members Della, Mike, Amy, and Jeff but recruited John Bratten, who constructed a conservation laboratory in the basement of the T. T. Wentworth Museum near project headquarters, to treat the diverse assortment of floral, faunal, organic, and metallic artifacts. To augment our staff we offered several internships throughout the field season to graduate students, who, along with a number of volunteers, worked onsite and in the laboratory.

At the stern of the shipwreck a total of eleven 2 × 2m excavation units were opened, revealing articulated and disarticulated ship structure, rudder and associated fittings, lead sheathing, and iron fastener concretions.[16] We removed stones and sediments to expose the tail frames of the ship; between them we encountered a layer of fine, matted organic materials that later proved to be rat and mice bones, insect parts, and floral remains. Working between one frameset, I noticed several disparate seeds in a grouping and imagined that perhaps these were a rat's cache stored for later consumption. When excavating, we used a flexible, clear, corrugated plastic tube, about 4 inches in diameter, to vacuum the sediments between the frames. We often placed a fine mesh screen over the mouth of the dredge pipe to prevent the destruction of any fragile floral or faunal remains, and we gathered seeds and other small organics by hand.

On one particular day the dredge was not operating at its usual strength, and I went back to check along the clear hose to diagnose the issue, typically a clog of shells or sediment in the line. Moving along the hose I did not find any obstruction, but I noticed a mirror-like liquid pooled up in the bottom of the tube. I surfaced, ordered the pump shut down, and asked for any available container at hand. Given a plastic bag, I went back down and carefully corralled the shiny liquid toward the mouth of the hose and into the bag. The shiny liquid was quicksilver. Peering closely with a light between the frames, I began to see tiny reflective drops of quicksilver intermixed in the organic and sediment matrix. As excavation continued we attempted to gather up larger concentrations of the quicksilver, about dime-sized, with an eyedropper, but that proved tedious. So we opted simply to continue using suction and to recover any quicksilver in the dredge tube into a sample bag at the end of the day. By these means we recovered several pounds of quicksilver.

Excavations outboard of the ship structure revealed a number of diagnostic and interesting artifacts strewn about the stern of the ship. These included hand-chiseled stone cannonballs, iron shot, an iron breastplate, anthropomorphized pottery, and a severely degraded coin. The coin was found at the lowest level of the archaeological deposit. When working in the northern stern excavation units, I removed a piece of lead sheathing and spied a roundish wafer-like object lying on the hard gray sand. I immediately knew it was a coin, the first such object found during the course of the project. Subsequent X-ray images and numismatic research identified the coin as a *blanca*, made of silver heavily debased with copper, the lowest denomination of currency in the Spanish kingdom, minted between 1471 and 1474. Whenever people find out what I do for a living they invariably ask me if I have ever found treasure and I always mention this coin and reply, "Yes, I once found a silver coin, but it was heavily debased with copper." What the "silver" coin lacked in monetary value, however, was offset by the mystery of why this small, worthless item was on the ship, as described in the next chapter.

Excavations between the ballast mound and the partially exposed gudgeon revealed the articulated remains of the tail of the ship, from the after end of the keelson to the sternpost. This portion of the lower hull was the narrowest part of the vessel, which ran aft below the waterline

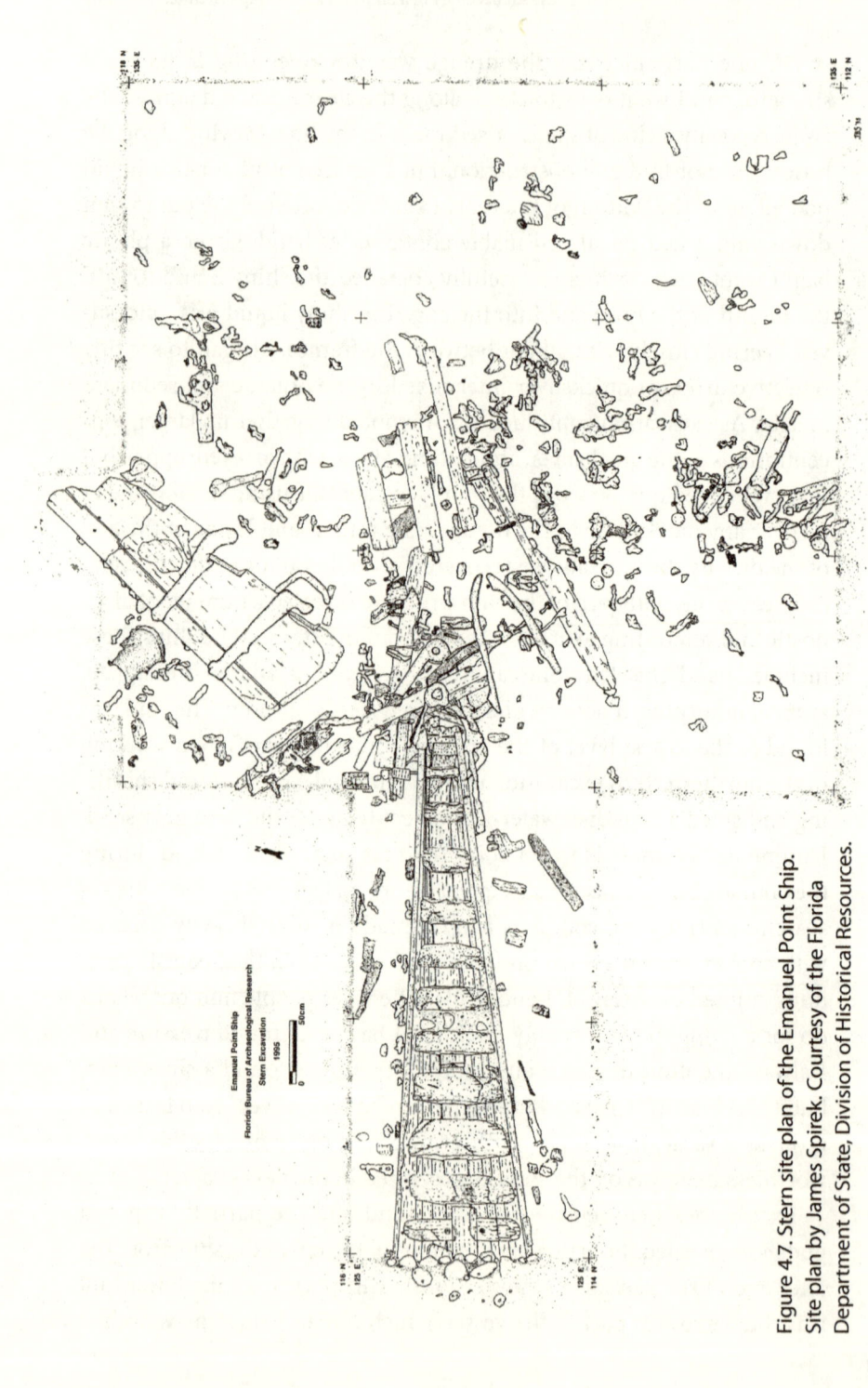

Figure 4.7. Stern site plan of the Emanuel Point Ship. Site plan by James Spirek. Courtesy of the Florida Department of State, Division of Historical Resources.

toward the rudder. The stern architecture of the ship was exposed over a distance of 4.5 m and included the after end of the keelson, eleven tail frames, lower hull planking, and the sternpost and stern knee. In addition the rudder was encountered, along with its fittings. The surviving height of the stern structure is estimated to be 1.4 m, from the bottom of the keel to the eroded tops of the frames. The whole structure lists to port some 4 to 7 degrees, which corresponds to the port list measured amidships.

The sternpost (*codaste*) is the principal backbone at the stern of a ship, where the planking terminates, and on which the rudder is hung. This straight timber, originally tapered at the after edge, had rabbets cut into the forward face to let in ends of the hull planks and to provide a backing on which to fasten them with square-shanked iron spikes. The sternpost has an estimated rake (*lançamiento*) of 60 degrees of arc, measured upward from an imaginary horizontal extension of the keel (or, 30 degrees aft of vertical). A stern knee served both as a brace between the sternpost and keel and as a base for the after-most frames. Fayed (fitted smoothly) to both the sternpost and keel, the stern knee was fabricated from a naturally curved timber and fastened to the keel by an iron fastener and a wooden treenail (*cabilla de palo*).

Eleven frames were recorded in the tail section. The frames were given numbers from 1 to 11 for recording purposes. Frame 1 is located forward of the sternpost and upper limb of the stern knee, while Frame 11 is located at the aft end of the keelson. All the frames in this section are made of compass timbers (naturally curved pieces) to shape the concave after end of the ship. The first ten frames in this section of the hull were originally Y-shaped, while Frame 11 is V-shaped in appearance. Only Frame 10 retained the original worked crook between the two frame arms. Environmental factors—that is, natural decay and shipworm (*Teredo navalis*) activity—have degraded the crooks of the other frames and subsequently the rising line (gradual longitudinal rise in height of the frames to effect a narrow stern) aft from Frame 11 to Frame 1.

Frame widths varied, and surviving height of the frames also varied, depending on location. Each frame except Frame 1 has a dome-shaped limber hole through its base. The position of the limber holes varies from directly on-center to those favoring the port side. Several fissures along the grain of the forward side of one frame suggest that this particular timber, unlike the others, was seasoned, or dried, before use in the construction of the ship. The other frames were most likely shaped from green timbers and retained a high moisture content due to their position below the waterline. This practice helped to prevent the wood from splitting.[17] All the compass timbers or frames were fashioned from the naturally occurring crooks of limbs and boughs of a tree.

Both starboard and port sides of the ship's tail section have four runs of surviving outer hull planks. No stealers (short planks inserted between strakes) were observed. Curiously, no treenails have been encountered in the stern planking; these wooden dowels typically were used to fasten planks to frames below the waterline, since they were non-corrosive and swelled to make a tight fastening connection. Rather, iron fasteners were recorded in a pattern of two or three round-headed, square-shanked planking nails aligned vertically to fasten planks to frames.

Outboard of the stern section were found disarticulated ship structure and artifacts. One substantial find was the ship's rudder lying behind and to starboard of the sternpost. It appears to have pirouetted from the sternpost and then fallen onto its port side sometime during the wrecking incident. Three pintles, the pins that hung in gudgeons on the sternpost to form hinges, are still fastened to the rudder. A more detailed discussion of the rudder hardware and the information it contains about the shape of the stern is presented in the following chapter.

By the fifteenth century the axial, or stern, rudder had become a key component in the development of seagoing sailing ships. Made from dry beams of straight timber bolted together, the rudder (*timón*) hung from the sternpost on iron hinges and was operated by a long tiller (*caña*) that ran inboard to the main deck. To protect the rudder from accidentally becoming unshipped if the vessel ran aground, shipwrights sometimes fashioned the after-most end of the keel into a skeg that sloped back to the forward edge of the rudder, which was curved accordingly. If the rudder did become unshipped due to unforeseen circumstances, it was saved from becoming lost by a rudder pendant (*barón del timón*) consisting of chains or ropes attached to the hull on each side of the rudder, or by a piece of rope that passed through a hole in the rudder and was made fast to the ship.

Nautical Archaeology of a Shipwreck: The Ship's Architecture · 89

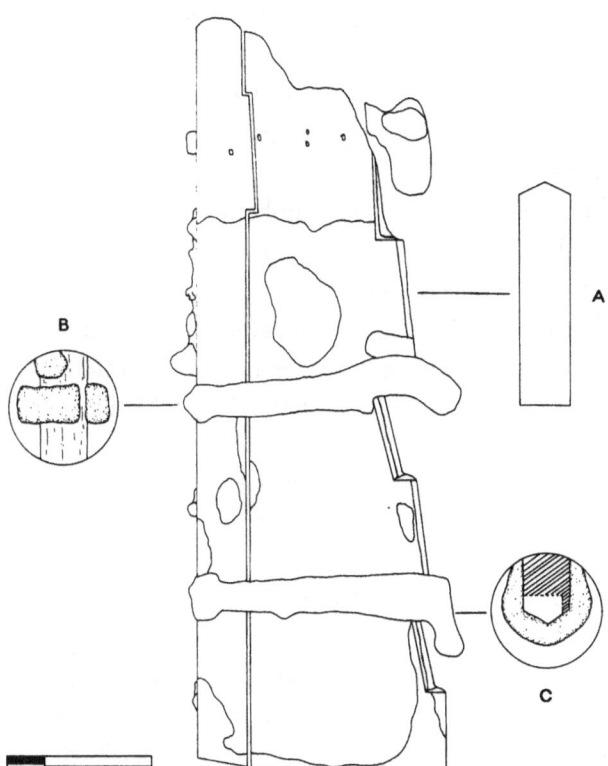

Figure 4.8. Surviving lower portions of the ship's rudder. Courtesy of the Florida Department of State, Division of Historical Resources.

The rudder was constructed from two thick planks of wood edge-joined with at least three large wrought-iron drift pins driven in from the aft edge of the after plank to join the forward plank. The forward plank (called the main piece) represents the principal structure of the rudder, tapering in width from the lower forward edge to the uppermost surviving portion. The forward edge of this plank has been beveled to a sharp point. The after plank (called the after piece) is much narrower than the main piece. The aft end of the main piece is recessed to let in the forward end of the after piece. A preliminary reconstruction of the rudder's juxtaposition with the sternpost suggests that when the rudder was shipped (hung) to the 60-degree-raked sternpost, it descended below the longitudinal axis of the keel. Although the forward edge of the rudder base has been diagonally sawn to fit on top of a skeg at the after end of the keel, the presence of a skeg was not verified during excavations, due to the large amount of corrosion products adhering to the lower portion of the sternpost and keel.

The stern of the shipwreck provided a number of elements for comparative analysis with other contemporary shipwrecks. The tail frames were saddled over the keel or stern knee in a similar arrangement to that noted on the whaler *San Juan*, although most of the frames have a tab on one side only.[18] The rake of the sternpost of the Emanuel Point Ship was 60 degrees, the same sternpost rake as on *San Diego*, a Manila galleon lost off the Philippines in 1600.[19]

The remarkable degree of preservation of the rudder permitted its comparison to several contemporary and documented rudders. The two-plank construction of the Emanuel Point Ship rudder is similar to the rudder of *Mary Rose*, flagship of Henry VIII that sank in 1545.[20] Other rudders from the sixteenth century, such as from the Villefranche wreck, an early Genoese carrack that sank in the French Mediterranean, had at least four composite pieces.[21] *San Diego*'s rudder was constructed from three timbers, and *San Juan*'s was built from one timber.[22] The after timber of the Emanuel Point rudder was let in to the main forward piece, whereas the main forward piece of *Mary Rose*'s rudder was let into the after piece.[23] The Emanuel Point pintle positions were hollowed out on the starboard side, sharing a similar arrangement with *San Diego*'s rudder at its pintle positions.[24]

Remnants of surviving rudders from this period on the *Mary Rose*, *San Diego*, and *San Juan* reveal that they were constructed of straight timbers, which when joined together assumed the rake of the sternpost. In comparison, the rudder of *San Juan* is safely situated level with the keel and protected by its skeg; however, the rudders of both *San Diego* and the Dramont "H" wreck, an eighteenth-century vessel located off France, descended below the plane of the keel and skeg.[25] A possible explanation for the design of the low-slung rudder is that its drag through the water and vulnerability to unshipping were offset by the additional steering capabilities provided by an extra "bite" into water below the hull. Such a rudder is depicted on a contemporary drawing of a typical sixteenth-century Italian galley, in which quick and responsive maneuvering was necessary.[26]

Following the stern excavations the decision was made to discontinue work at the site for the time being. Stabilization and conservation of the recovered artifacts continued in partnership with the museum and UWF. Several months were spent preparing the first archaeological report detailing the findings, as well as archiving field notes, drawings, photographs, videos, and other materials associated with the project. Our investigations had revealed a shipwreck with a well-preserved ship structure and artifact assemblage. Excavations at the selected areas of the site uncovered the ship's lower hull, extending from the bow to the stern and athwartships to just below the turn of the bilge. Surviving hull length was estimated to be around 28 m, with a breadth of 1.8 m on the port side, and a breadth of about 2.8 m on the starboard side. The wreck lay on the sand bar at a slight list of 4 to 7 degrees to port.[27] Scattered timbers and fasteners—remnants of the ship's upper structure that had disintegrated over time—were found buried around the periphery of the ballast mound. Throughout the process of recording the vessel's architectural remains, fine craftsmanship was noted in the construction of the hull, especially at the mast step assembly, and also in the general finished appearance of the ship's timbers.

BARGE *NAUTILUS* IS BORN: THE SECOND FIELD CAMPAIGN

May 27, 1997, was a glaringly bright, sunny day at the Pensacola Shipyard when the Emanuel Point Ship excavation team launched a purpose-built steel work barge into the murky waters of Bayou Chico. The day was full of promise for a successful field project to continue the investigation of the oldest shipwreck discovered in Florida. This was the beginning of the second field campaign at the Emanuel Point Ship. The first campaign had revealed much about the site, and the second campaign was no less ambitious.

Christened *Nautilus* after the UWF logo, the new barge was launched after the customary breaking of a champagne bottle on her bow. In attendance were the university's dean of the College of Arts and Sciences, Dr. Richard Doelker, the director of the university's Archaeology Institute, Dr. Judith Bense, and the 1997 field crew: Principal Investigator Dr. Roger Smith, Laboratory Director John Bratten, Field Director Joe "Coz" Cozzi, Equipment Manager and Dive Safety Officer Capt. Keith Plaskett, and Field Technician David Pugh, as well as student interns Juliet Tatem and Solomon Wahrhaftig. As field director I ("Coz" Cozzi) felt proud to have a suitable platform from which to conduct our upcoming underwater work. Was this how a Spanish shipwright or captain felt when the Emanuel Point Ship was launched? Did he wonder what adventures lay ahead for the vessel?

As earlier described, the previous field campaign had used an old wooden barge that tended to sink unexpectedly—not a great way to start your work day. In January we began trying to find a better work platform. Our first thoughts were that we might make good use of an old shrimp boat or perhaps a more seaworthy commercial barge. The university's purchasing department agreed to assist in this search. We located one fishing boat, but it was quite old and in need of considerable work. We had seen worse and were desperate to get going, but in view of the repairs this boat needed, we decided to pursue leasing a barge. However, we could not find anything we could act upon. The problem was twofold. First, our grant-sponsored funding did not allow us to make any "capital" purchases for more than five hundred dollars. We also ran into difficulty leasing a barge as owners did not want to assume any liability for a vessel not under their supervision and required a letter of indemnification for a lease agreement.

I had just come to Florida from the LaSalle Shipwreck Project for the Texas Historical Commission, which had received a generous offer from a marine contractor to loan the project a 100-foot-long steel barge. All the commission had to do was to sign a letter of indemnification, holding the owner harmless should they lose control of the barge and create some unintended damage. It turned out that employees of state agencies are precluded from signing such letters as the State is self-insured, meaning it does not really have any insurance. It was frustrating to lose such a generous donation, but hours of time in meetings with lawyers did not resolve the issue to anyone's satisfaction. We faced this same dilemma in Florida.

John ran into the conundrum when trying to buy a computer for use on the Emanuel Point project. Our funding, however, did allow us to purchase "supplies" without any price limitation, so John bought the components of a computer and built one himself. This became a brilliant solution to our barge dilemma as well. Prior to graduate school, I had worked as a commercial diver and underwater welder. Keith also had considerable experience in metal fabrication. So we purchased ¼-inch plate steel, C-channel, and angle iron, and contracted with a local welding shop to build a barge. They put a welder on the project at night, and we worked on it during the daytime.

This was a marvelous solution because it allowed us to design a barge to suit our needs. We had all served on projects before where an odd assortment of vessels had been pressed into service with varying degrees of success. We designed a 36 × 16-foot (11 × 5 m) box with a raked bow. We knew we needed plenty of deck space from which to work and a shed in which to stow our gear. We also designed racks at the bow to hold sets of nested screens and the dredge heads that powered our primary excavation tool. There were some size limitations because we would need to transport the barge from the welding shop to the shipyard for launching, and anything more than 5 m wide required expensive permitting to move by road. As it was, we used a crane and tractor trailer rig to haul the completed barge to the water. In addition, we wanted to be able to move the barge offsite and into nearby Bayou Texar in the event that a hurricane threatened the area. The entrance to the bayou is bridged by a railroad line, and the trestle has a span of only 7.5 m through which watercraft can pass.

After the barge's launch, the diving unit from Pensacola Naval Air Station arrived to tow *Nautilus* out to the site. Listening on the marine radio for the navy's arrival, we heard the exchange between the navy launch pilot and the operator of the Bayou Chico drawbridge. The navy boat called out, "Bayou Chico Bridge, can we get an opening?" The bridge operator responded, "Captain, can you identify your vessel?" "This is the United States Navy." "Come on through Navy." The navy launch towed our barge through some fairly heavy chop in Pensacola Bay out to Emanuel Point and moored it over the shipwreck site with four 35 kg anchors. Our field season was off to an excellent start.

Fauna Non Grata

We first focused on relocating the datum markers from the initial field campaign and conducted a metal detector survey of the site, especially the area of the bow, where Roger asked us to focus our attention. Our goal was to determine the forward extent of the site's hull remains and to see if there was any evidence of a galley. We began our excavations in the area from which a tin-washed copper pitcher had previously been recovered. In this first unit we also rediscovered the copper cooking cauldron. I had volunteered several times during the previous campaign and remembered that the hull remains on the port side had been violently wrenched away by pounding on the sandbar. We planned our strategy in the bow to focus on what should be a better-preserved starboard side, and we were not disappointed. As the tops of centerline timbers and starboard framing timbers appeared, we began to realize that the anchor had pinned a large section of the starboard bow to the bay floor, where it had silted over and was preserved for us to find.

Often shallow-water wooden shipwrecks in the Gulf of Mexico are not very well preserved because the warm salt water and wave action have caused a major deterioration of hull remains over the centuries. At the 1554 Spanish shipwreck *San Estéban*, contemporary with the ship at Emanuel Point, researchers found only a small piece of the keel and sternpost with a stern knee joining them.[28] In the shallow waters off Padre Island, Texas, the remainder of the hull had disappeared over centuries, leaving mainly large iron objects such as cannons and anchors and the material that had concreted to them. The protected bay of Pensacola does not experience large rolling ocean waves. To be sure, the storm that sank Luna's fleet was a powerful gale that created rough water on the bay, but this hurricane was primarily a wind event for the ships trapped in the harbor. It was likely violent enough to wrench the port side of the vessel free, as evidenced by the fractured port timbers encountered first amidships and later in the bow. This, and subsequent storms over the centuries, did not repeatedly churn up the bay bottom. Instead we see evidence that only the top 25 cm of sand are oxygenated by water movement and that below this level there is an anaerobic environment that protected the lower hull after the initial wrecking event.

Uncovering the articulated architecture of the ship's starboard bow created a great deal of excitement. Each dive offered an opportunity to discover and learn more about the construction of early Spanish ships. Since very few of these have been explored by archaeologists, we felt privileged to record details of construction so familiar to the shipwrights who built the ship but generally unknown to modern students of sixteenth-century Iberian shipbuilding.

We began each day with a morning briefing at our headquarters in the Christie House in the Historic District to plan the day's tasks. We loaded the project truck and drove to Pitt Slip Marina to take our boat out to the site; usually a five-minute trip. Upon arrival we unloaded the barge shed and set up diving compressors and their hoses along with dredge pumps and their hoses.[29] Using the suction dredge like a vacuum cleaner to clear sediments in suspension, we excavated in 1 × 1 m quadrants within 2 × 2 m grid units. Within each quadrant we dug by hand fanning and

Figure 4.9. Excavation and recording tools. Courtesy of the Florida Department of State, Division of Historical Resources.

Figure 4.10. Keith Plaskett screening, searching, and sorting the dredge spoil. Courtesy of the Florida Department of State, Division of Historical Resources.

trowel at 10 cm intervals. Dredge spoil was collected in nested screens on the barge. Finds made underwater or from sorting dredge spoil were tagged and bagged with their provenience logged according to quadrant and unit. We employed folding rules, reel tape measures, clipboards with mylar sheets for recording notes underwater, and video and still cameras.[30] I asked all crew members to copy their underwater notes to the excavation data sheets the same day they were taken, so that they could include things that they remembered from the dive but did not have time to write under water.

Every morning we looked forward to new discoveries and anxiously anticipated what we would learn in this underwater classroom. One morning, however, we encountered interlopers in our inner sanctum. Whenever one excavates and alters the bottom environment, even when it seems like a desolate moonscape, a flourish of activity is created as a variety of fishes and bottom dwellers arrive to see if any new food sources have been uncovered. We befriended most of the small fish that watched intently as we dug; they nipped at the hairs on our arms to see if these were edible. However, the new intruders quickly became *fauna non grata*. Stone crabs had found our cave-like excavations and timber structures and had set up homes. They proved more destructive than the sheepshead fish that crunched on the worm-eaten ends of timbers hoping to release hidden worms. The stone crabs tore through perfectly preserved timbers to make their dens, an alarming situation that we turned into a disarming situation. Every morning we sent down divers to relocate these denizens of the deep far away from our site and to relieve them of their offending claws.

The opportunity to work with a well-preserved sixteenth-century hull comes along so rarely that one never wants it to end. Once underwater, recording hull structure with its myriad subtleties, there is little reason to come up. Diving in Florida in the summer on hookah in such shallow water allowed us to spend as much time underwater as we liked. Consequently I dropped about fifteen pounds from an already slender frame. My wife, Hera, began to call the project cell phone at midday to instruct our crew to shut down the diving compressor to make her husband come up and eat lunch.

Bow Architecture (at the "Head" of the Ship)

Our excavations during the second field campaign revealed well-preserved and articulated forward hull remains with centerline timbers and starboard bow structure below the ship's waterline. We began in the area where the cauldron and pitcher had previously been found. From there we proceeded forward and to each side until the hull remains played out as well as aft into the forward end of the ballast pile. Hull timbers were uncovered almost immediately and represent framing and hull planking and the vessel's centerline timbers. Further exploration soon revealed extensive remains of the starboard side of the lower hull, with scant remains on the port side. The bow excavation uncovered an area more than 10 m long following the centerline of the vessel and 6 m wide. Hull remains were detected in as little as 15 cm of sediments, while the deepest timber was buried 1.8 m deep. The vessel's bow lies on the sand bar in 3.3 m of water with a 5-degree list to port.

"Between the Devil and the Deep Blue Sea"

The lower bow excavation revealed seven well-preserved floor frames and the lower portion of eight starboard first futtocks, seven starboard hull planks, three port hull planks, four starboard ceiling planks and a footwale as well as a port ceiling plank and a footwale. Several disarticulated planks and timbers were also encountered. Centerline timbers included the ship's keel, keelson, stem, and stemson.[31] The keel (backbone of the ship), upon which floor frames are laid was scarfed (joined) at the forward end to the first of two curved timbers representing the stem assembly. The stem is the forward-most vertical member of the ship, to which the port and starboard sides of the hull are attached. A length of stemson, an internal supporting timber bolted to the stem and keel at their juncture, was found resting on the scarf between the two. At least two separate elements of the stem are preserved on the Emanuel Point Ship. Both pieces are fashioned with similar dimensions, a curved shape, and leading edges that have been rounded to present less resistance when passing through the water. These timbers were joined in sequence by vertical scarfs. They are both rabbeted (grooved) along each side to accept the forward ends of the hull planks and were caulked with rope fibers and resin and extensively patched with lead sheathing. This sheathing was found both in place and scattered in the deposit and is also indicated by distinctive blue staining on the surface of the timber and by the presence of tack holes in the timbers.

The first section of the stem assembly was still joined to the keel, but the second section was found disconnected from the first; it originated higher up in the ship's structure and has evidence of a repair along the rabbet where port side planking ends had likely deteriorated over time. A filler piece was fastened by two countersunk, square iron nails. This repair suggests planking deterioration over the life of an older vessel around the ship's waterline.

At the waterline the hull timbers were subject to being alternately wet and dry, depending on the load the ship was carrying and the rise and fall of the vessel as it cut through the water under sail. This area, referred to by modern sailors as "the splash zone," is most susceptible to rot. The phrase "between the devil and the deep blue sea" refers to the devil line on a ship where these conditions cause caulking to become dislodged and water to leak into the vessel. This necessitated repair while underway, which meant a sailor had to hang over the side in a bo'sun's chair and drive new caulking into these planking seams. The sailor was therefore in a precarious position between the devil line of caulking and the deep blue sea.

Collapsed Starboard Side

At the edge of the excavation units containing the lower bow were frames and planks that had broken away from the rest of the hull, near the turn of the bilge, and collapsed to the bay floor, becoming buried and preserved in sediment levels between 20 cm and 1 m deep. This collapsed starboard side consists of twenty-six framing timbers, nineteen of which were articulated, while seven were scattered farther forward.[32] Some frames had completely deteriorated, but there were fastener openings that spoke to where the missing frames had been. The pattern of fastener holes was like a puzzle to be unraveled in order to understand how the shipwright had framed and fastened his vessel to withstand the forces that the sea exerts on the hull.

Framing

Each framing station consists of a floor frame and a series of futtocks that rise up the side of the vessel. First futtocks only survive on the starboard side of the lower bow excavation and alternate with floor timbers as they rise up the vessel's side, canting forward from the centerline. No first futtocks are complete, although some survive at their lower and upper ends with missing central portions, while others have significant runs along the hull although one end or both ends may be missing. Seven floor frames and ten first futtocks were documented in the lower starboard bow. Fastener evidence in the upper face of stem timber indicates two additional floor timbers that did not survive. The collapsed starboard side has the remains of eleven first futtocks, and a single second futtock, with fastener evidence in the planking that indicates the location of another four second futtocks.

The extant bow floor frames sat on the keel, with their bases square to the centerline and leaning forward, while their arms cant forward. The

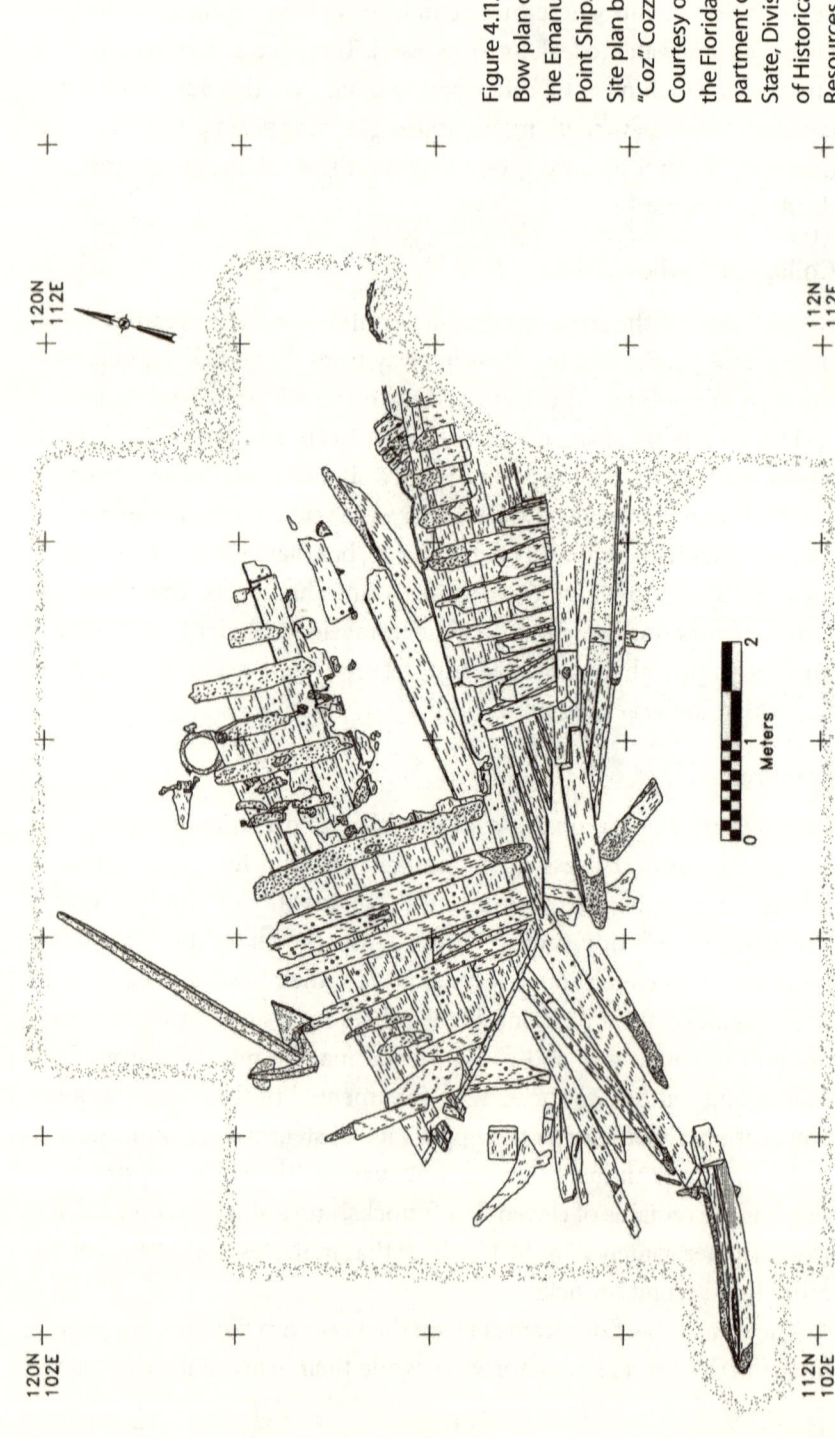

Figure 4.11. Bow plan of the Emanuel Point Ship. Site plan by "Coz" Cozzi. Courtesy of the Florida Department of State, Division of Historical Resources.

floors are spaced 40 cm on center. Each of the seven floors has a square limber hole cut through the center of the timber's base. One floor has a hole drilled for a bolt that attached it to the keel, but the bolt passed through a limber hole, which would have hindered the flow of water to the bilge pumps. The starboard sides of the floors are well preserved; only one floor survives on the port side, making it the only complete floor uncovered in the bow. Portside arms of other floors appear to have been broken off at their base by a violent action. One floor was made from a crook (naturally curved timber) of slighter dimension than the adjacent floors. Where this timber meets the centerline, the shipbuilder simply removed the bark and slipped the timber into place. The other bow floors were made from much larger pieces of wood and are all squared off where they cross the centerline. The use of wood of slight dimension indicates economies by the builder. It is important to point out that these economies do not mean that the ship was poorly made, since the timbers are of sufficient dimension to serve their purpose of attaching the two sides of the vessel together at the centerline. It simply means the builder did not go to the effort of finding timbers large enough that they could be squared off along their entire length.

First futtocks alternate with floor timbers and rise up the vessel's starboard side, canting forward from the centerline. A total of fourteen first futtocks were uncovered; none are complete, although their remains represent all portions of a futtock. Nine examples in the lower bow are complete from the centerline to the seventh starboard strake. Remains of the lower ends of four first futtocks were brought to the surface for detailed recording and to facilitate measurement of the hull's "lines" underwater in the bow with the aid of a goniometer (a digital carpenter's level in an underwater housing). Lines are taken at the interface of the outer edge of the frames and the inner surface of the hull planking. Archaeologists use these lines to reconstruct the shape of the hull. The Emanuel Point Ship was found to have an extremely fine or sharp entry to cut through the water. A hollow in the bow begins at the scarf between the stem and the keel and proceeds aft to the limit of excavation.

Second futtocks overlap first futtocks and extend farther up the side of the vessel. Only one second futtock was preserved to the extent that dimensions could be obtained. Fastener holes in the hull planking indicate the location of four more second futtocks, which also were placed against the forward face of corresponding first futtocks. No nails or bolts were used to fasten floors to first futtocks or first to second futtocks. The only fastenings are between planking and framing. This means that futtocks were inserted into the hull following installation of some planking, and that the frames were not free-standing or pre-erected.

Planking

Hull planking remains begin at the keel with what is believed to be the garboard strake (the lower-most run of planking let into the keel). Planking continues outboard uninterrupted on the starboard side for the first through sixteenth strakes. On the port side three strakes were uncovered, and more are likely present under the unexcavated deposit.

A key problem with wooden sailing ships is that the hull is narrowed down at the bow to cut through the water, and at the stern for water to flow over the rudder, so the ends of the ship do not provide as much buoyancy as the more fully shaped center of the hull. The bow and stern of vessels from this period, especially galleons, had large castles that bore down with great weight on this limited buoyancy. This led to a condition called "hogging," where the ends of the vessel droop, causing planking seams to open, caulking to be dislodged, and water to be admitted. To combat this tendency the shipwright provided longitudinal stiffening in the form of timbers that run fore-and-aft to help support the vessel's heavy ends. On our shipwreck we saw evidence of this in the fastening pattern of the starboard bow. The hull planking was routinely fastened to the frames by square iron nails, but there was a line of circular fastener holes running fore-and-aft that indicate a longitudinal timber (wale) that stiffened the hull.

Planking on the interior of the framing is called ceiling. Four ceiling planks and a thicker footwale are preserved on the starboard side. The order of construction from the centerline was to install two ceiling planks, then a footwale, followed by two more ceiling planks. The ceiling was fastened to first futtocks by iron nails, with one nail at each intersection with a futtock. The uppermost ceiling plank is notched on its upper face at intervals between frames to accommodate filling pieces that prevented debris from falling down into the bilge, where small objects could clog limber holes and interfere with the operation of the bilge pumps. Eight filling pieces were encountered, five of which were still in place. The filling pieces are beveled on both ends to fit against the inner surface of the hull planks and to follow the contour of the inboard surface of the ceiling. They are fastened with a single iron nail, toe-nailed either into an abutting frame or into a hull plank.

Fasteners

Iron and wooden fasteners were utilized in combinations to attach planking to frames. Each plank at a frame intersection on the collapsed starboard bow where a determination could be made is fastened by at least one square iron and one round wooden fastener (treenail, pronounced "trunnel"). The most common pattern is a treenail through the center of a plank and iron nails slightly in from the plank seams. Two treenails, and in one case three treenails, at a plank on frame intersection were noted. This may reflect misplacement of the first fasteners by the builders, a concern for sturdiness in the bow, or a repair after treenails loosened up. Wooden wedges driven into the inboard ends of treenails to lock the fastener in place were noted in three instances.

At six framing stations in the bow, small round holes were noted along starboard planks. No fasteners remained, although all had iron concretions around the holes, indicating the use of iron bolts at these locations. Two holes of this smaller diameter were also noted on a plank quite high up on the starboard side. These bolt holes indicate the shipbuilder's concern to strengthen the attachment of the hull planking at this point. Since this is where the higher portion of the starboard side broke off and collapsed to the bay floor under the weight of the anchor, it may represent the forward ends of strakes at the turn of the bilge, which had to be bent considerably to meet the stem, therefore requiring stronger fasteners. It may also provide evidence of the order of construction, whereby free-floating futtocks were placed after the erection of hull planking in the lower bow but before planking was placed on the portion that collapsed to the bay floor.

Knees

The arms of two hanging knees were uncovered in the bow timber scatter. The knees are L-shaped timbers that supported the ends of deck beams on the interior of each side of the hull. At the breech of each knee is a partially preserved notch to allow the knee to fit over a clamp. The angle of the surfaces that sat against the clamp indicate that the knees came from opposite sides of the vessel. These partially preserved notches indicate dimensions for the clamps that no longer survive. Both knees broke where a bolt hole pierced the breech and throat just beneath the clamp for the attachment of the knee to the hull. The knees were otherwise devoid of fasteners with the exception of one square-sectioned

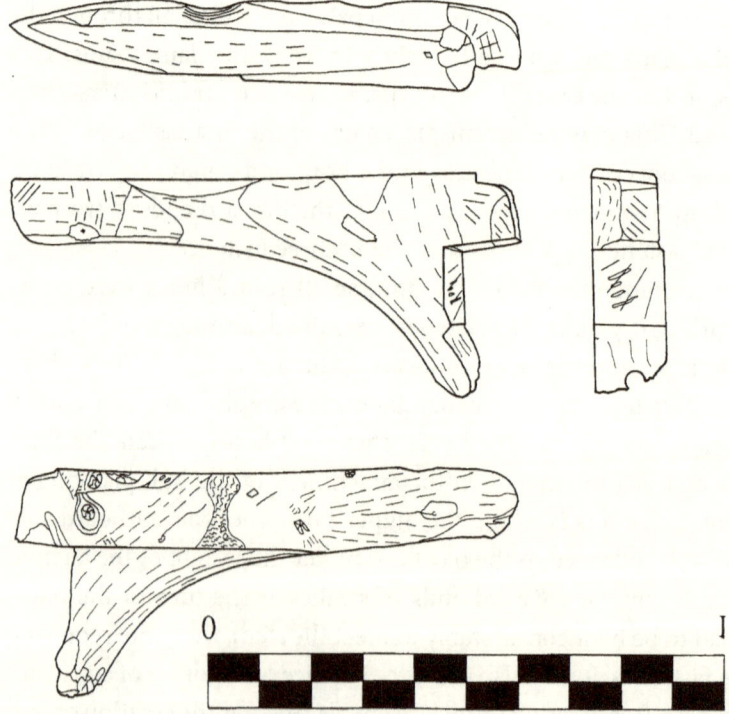

Figure 4.12. This hanging knee supported one of the deck beams in the bow of the ship. Drawing by Harv Dickey. Courtesy of the Florida Department of State, Division of Historical Resources.

hole noted on the top surface of one knee and running not through to the bottom but out at the side. The after face of the starboard knee arm was recessed, indicating that the arm was fashioned to accommodate an adjacent deck beam. The knees, therefore, were placed alongside the deck beams and not underneath them. The placement of the notch for the clamp also supports the interpretation that the deck beams were set beside the knees and atop the clamps.

Port Covers

Two extremely rare finds were made in the bow excavation. The remains of two port covers were found buried beneath the lower part of the starboard bow. These covers shielded openings (ports) in the sides of the upper hull above the waterline. Hinged at the top, the covers opened when guns were to be fired through the ports but otherwise remained closed to prevent spray and water from entering the ship. Both covers were recovered and carefully recorded. The larger of the two was returned to the site following disassembly and recording; the smaller port cover was selected for conservation and display. Each is constructed from two sets of five planks arranged perpendicular to each other and fastened together with square iron nails. Each port cover was attached to the hull by a pair of iron strap hinges, which survived only as concretions on and imprints in the planks of each port cover's outer surface. Discovery of these port covers was surprising since elements of the upper hull above the waterline do not usually survive on shallow-water shipwrecks.

When the second campaign of excavations at the Emanuel Point Ship concluded at the end of 1997, some 64 m^2 of the forward portion of the shipwreck had been exposed, approximately 50 m^2 of shell and sediments had been moved, and more than 2,500 objects had been tagged, bagged, and delivered to the laboratory. The site was closed by placing donated cloth bank bags filled with sand in and around the exposed hull remains to hold them in place, then backfilled with sand to restore it to its original contour.

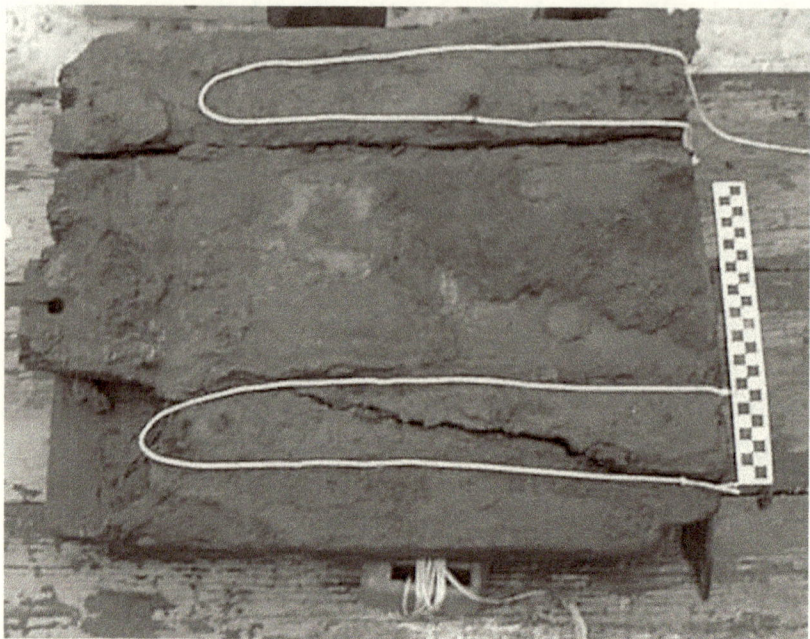

Figure 4.13. One of two gunport covers found under the collapsed starboard bow. White string indicates where the iron hinge straps were located. Courtesy of the Florida Department of State, Division of Historical Resources.

Discussion

Based on the architectural components studied during both campaigns of work on the Emanuel Point Ship, we concluded that it was a large vessel, especially in comparison with other sixteenth-century Iberian wrecks investigated by archaeologists. The estimated 20.14 m keel length is substantially greater than that of the Basque whaler *San Juan*, which at 14.75 m is the only other complete keel from a contemporary site.[33] Timbers uncovered amidships during the first campaign of excavations indicate larger frames and planks than those reported for the Molasses Reef Wreck, the site at Highborn Cay, and the Western Ledge Wreck.[34] Bow timbers uncovered during the second campaign proved to be similarly substantial, although of the sites mentioned, only *San Juan* has extensively preserved bow remains. Consequently the projected overall

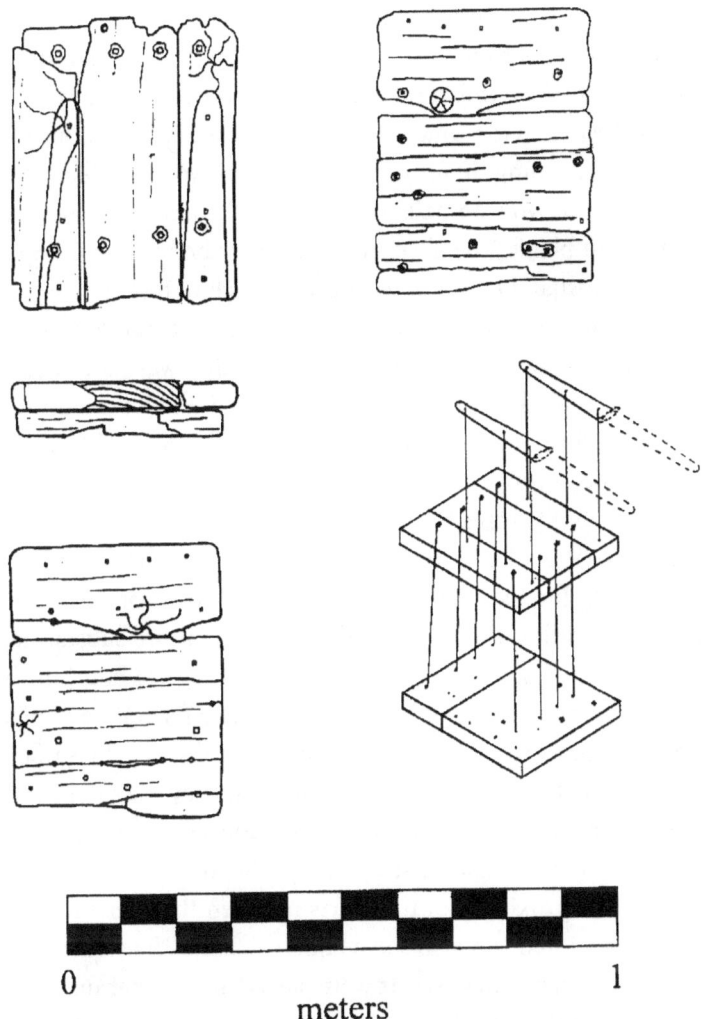

Figure 4.14. Diagram of one of the two port covers showing its construction. Drawing by "Coz" Cozzi. Courtesy of the Florida Department of State, Division of Historical Resources.

dimensions of the shipwreck at Emanuel Point suggested to us that it was one of the larger ships in the Luna fleet.

The ship appears to have been quite well built, although old at the time of sinking. The number of fasteners indicate concern by the builder that planks be joined to frames by more than the customary one wooden and one iron fastening. In numerous instances two treenails were noted side by side, and two iron nails were frequently used at the intersection of a frame and plank. The absence of fasteners between framing members is not unusual. On *San Juan* the same lack of fasteners was noted, indicating that the vessel was built of free-standing frames.[35] The lower frames were first set up, and then some planking was placed on them. Next the first futtocks were inserted. At this point more planking could be installed before the second futtocks were positioned. Although not as systematic as erecting all frames prior to planking, this does not make for a less well-built vessel.

There is some evidence for economy in construction. One floor timber that was fashioned from a limb of small dimension simply had its bark removed rather than the builder finding a more substantial timber from which to shape this frame. There are several butt joins in the starboard hull planking, and we found evidence for only one planking scarf. Scarfed joins would be sturdier, but their absence does not necessarily reflect anything other than the fact that they may not have been required. There seem to have been errors made, as in the example of the floor with a bolt hole that passed through the limber hole, rendering it ineffective. The proximity of the scarfs between the keel and stem and the keelson and stemson also seems questionable. The structure would have been stronger if these scarfs were placed at a greater distance from one another. Yet these are the only examples found on a large vessel, and it therefore appears that the ship was sturdily built overall.

The vessel was quite old at the time it sank. There was extensive use of lead sheathing in both the bow and stern. The repair to the joint between the port hooding ends and the stem—a juncture where water-tightness is extremely important—indicates that enough time had passed for wood to deteriorate and require replacement.

In an attempt to reconstruct dimensions and the type of ship, several natural and cultural factors limit the analysis of the remains. These factors include the shipwreck event itself, salvage operations, and environmental preservation. To account for the limitations imposed by these factors, consulting other shipwrecks and contemporary shipbuilding treatises can help fill in the architectural gaps. But in the end, understanding the shipwreck relies on a blend of empirical information, theoretical work, and a little conjectural imagination to reconstruct the ship from the archaeological remains lying on the Emanuel Point shoal.

The ship struck the shoal, apparently with terrific force during a storm. The port side along the entire length of the site is less well preserved than the starboard site. Portside timbers are broken off, as opposed to those on the opposite side, which are worm eaten and eroded and are preserved farther up the side of the vessel. Aside from massive damage to the lower hull, the ship most likely suffered destruction of the more lightly constructed upperworks, which may have included separation of the poop deck and the forecastle from the lower hull, and perhaps the tumbling overboard of the main and other masts. These elements and others would have floated away or perhaps remained tenuously attached to the hull by the rigging.

The next sequence in the breakdown occurred with the purposeful salvage of materials by the expedition survivors. After the storm colonists began the process of recovering not only foodstuffs but also any useful materials from the shipwreck, namely wood, fasteners, rigging, and other elements. The hull rests in shallow water and consequently offered a substantial amount of recoverable materials. The presence of stone cannon balls and other projectiles indicates that the ship was armed, but her cannons and other ordnance were removed from the sunken vessel. It is possible that portions of the vessel's starboard side were also salvaged. The presence of so much material underneath the starboard hull suggests that these objects fell down to the bay floor early on in the site's deformation. If portions of the hull were broken up and recycled, then the port covers and hanging knees from higher up in the ship, together with an olive jar, a cask hoop, and an intact earthenware plate that were found beneath portions of the hull, could have fallen down at this time. The presence of a broken anchor on site suggests that it may have been on deck. The more deeply buried forward framing ends of the collapsed starboard bow support this interpretation. Aside from this evidence, we know that Viceroy Velasco ordered Luna to rebuild two small vessels using timbers and other components recovered from the shipwrecks.[36]

Afterward, the natural processes of biological, chemical, and elemental forces began reducing and leveling the exposed structure to become completely buried under the shoal. In a matter of weeks, the insatiable shipworm, *Teredo navalis*, began to bore into and weaken the wooden hull. As shipworms worked in the wood, oysters and barnacles found footholds on the hull. In addition to the biological assault on the wooden components, chemical decomposition of the iron fasteners caused by immersion in the salt water served to weaken the structure. Constantly working was the bay itself, with wind, waves, and currents providing a relentless battering on the exposed hull. All these factors—the invisible borings of the shipworm, weight of the biofouling, corroding fasteners, and the forces of the water, eventually reduced the hull to the bay floor, with only a shallow pile of ballast stones and the tip of the anchor visible to mark the site of this shipwreck.

Nonetheless, a substantial amount of the Emanuel Point Ship has survived. This can be attributed to several factors. Its location in the bay rather than in the open waters of the Gulf of Mexico has protected the site from strong tidal surges and shoreline erosion. The fact that winds do not have a chance to build substantial waves in the bay has also helped. The low salinity of the bay water has played a role in site preservation as well. The ship's location at the mouth of a bayou and adjacent to the Escambia River delta would seem to be factors likely to cause sediments to be deposited on the site, but the shallowness of the wreck's burial does not bear this out. Instead, the ship seems to have served as an artificial reef, attracting sea life for generations. This resulted in a densely packed layer of shell that has shielded the site, especially against more recent threats, such as the activities of the local shrimping fleet.

The more deeply buried portions of the site have been preserved by sand that accumulated alongside the hull early in the deformation process. When the port side broke away, the ballast rocks spilled outboard and pinned the floor of the vessel in place, while the interstices between the rocks filled with sand, sediments, and shell hash. The fineness of sand and sediment deposited on the site has also helped to create an anaerobic environment at a relatively shallow depth in the deposit, providing excellent organic preservation. Hull timbers that quickly became buried have survived better than those that were exposed for an extended period. Timbers of the collapsed starboard side, while in good shape on the surface, proved to be completely worm eaten in the interior. More deeply buried timbers of the lower bow, however, were substantial enough to provide samples for wood identification. This indicates that these timbers were not exposed for very long, otherwise they too would have been riddled with worm holes.

The protective shell layer and the fine sand presented a considerable challenge to the excavation of the site. The tightly packed shells and their matrix could only be removed by hand, and sand from the perimeter of the excavation had a tendency to slump in as the units became deeper. This was satisfactorily addressed by continually placing sand bags around the edges of the excavations.

After careful excavation and recording of the preserved shipwreck, we developed a list of timber dimensions (scantlings), as shown in table 1 of the appendix, with which to approach estimations of the ship's size and cargo capacity (tonnage). We then turned to the historical and archaeological record to guide us and to account for the missing elements in reconstructing the ship. A number of sixteenth-century shipbuilding treatises can assist in developing a conjectural model of the Emanuel Point Ship. Their authors sought to codify ancient shipbuilding techniques to form rules and principles for shipbuilders. One of the first published treatises on Spanish shipbuilding was Diego García de Palacio's *Instrucción Náutica Para Navegar*, published in Mexico in 1587.[37] Palacio's discussion covers the principal architectural dimensions required to build a *nao* of 400 tons. A second source is from the Portuguese author Fernando Oliveira, titled *Livro da Fabrica das Naos* (1580).[38] Another Portuguese tome is João Baptista Lavanha's *Livro Primeiro da Architectura Naval*, ca. 1615.[39] In Venice, Pre Theodoro de Nicolò, a shipbuilder employed at the Venetian Arsenal in the mid-sixteenth century, wrote *Instructione sul modo di fabricare gelere*.[40] This manuscript provided instructions for building armed warships and smaller merchant vessels for which Nicolò had personally overseen construction activities. An important concept in all these sixteenth-century shipbuilding treatises is the relationships or ratios of important structural elements, primarily the length of the keel, which then determined the width and height, and the narrowing of the hull to create a hydrodynamic yet stable watercraft. Referring to these tomes provided useful templates of dimensions and ratios with which to guide a hypothetical reconstruction of the Emanuel Point Ship.

An additional source of information is a comparative analysis of contemporary shipwrecks described in archaeological reports. Several shipwrecks provided architectural features to compare and contrast with those of the Emanuel Point Ship. The remains of the Basque whaler *San Juan* at Red Bay, Labrador, the best preserved Spanish shipwreck found in the New World, offers many insights into Iberian shipbuilding techniques.[41] Other examples studied include the Molasses Reef Wreck, a Spanish shipwreck in the Turks and Caicos Islands dated to the early 1500s; the Western Ledge Reef Wreck, a presumed dispatch vessel from the late 1500s in Bermuda; the Highborn Cay Wreck, a ship dating from the early 1500s wrecked in the Bahamas; and others distributed throughout the Caribbean and Old World.[42] Each of these wrecks helped to fill in gaps in the archaeological record of the Emanuel Point Ship.

To begin reconstructing a hypothetical model of the ship that wrecked at Emanuel Point requires several key measurements—keel length, beam, and depth of hold. The full length of the keel was not uncovered during excavations; the beam terminated abruptly on the port side; and the upper portions of the ship had been swept away centuries before. Without these primary measurements, estimating the vessel's overall length and tonnage is purely conjectural. Our only solid archaeological measurement is the distance from the aft keel terminus to the known master couple, a distance of 11.2 m. The only other firm measurement is from the extant sternpost to the forward-most extant bow strake, which appears structurally integral, a distance of approximately 28 m. This distance gives us a minimum overall vessel length. With this scant information, a preliminary estimation of the ship's original size and cargo capacity can be hypothesized by comparing available data from the hull remains with contemporary sixteenth-century sources on naval architecture and recent studies of the topic. While any resulting conclusions can, at this point, be considered only preliminary, the exercise offers a glimpse of the size and volume of what once was a large sailing ship that carried people, arms, and supplies to Pensacola.

The basic unit of measurement used by medieval Spanish shipwrights was the *codo*, or cubit. Depending on regional usage through time, the value of the *codo* varied somewhat, causing a certain amount of confusion among modern students of maritime history. Standardization of weights and measures was periodically attempted by the government of Spain, but traditional (as well as colonial) values often persisted far from central authority. According to one scholar (Phillips), the modern value of the official shipbuilding *codo* (*codo real*, or royal cubit) is 56.5 cm.[43] Another scholar (Casado Soto) defines two kinds of *codos*: the *codo real* (also known as the *codo cantabrico*, or Cantabrian cubit) of 57.5 cm, and the *codo castellano* (Castilian cubit) of 55.7 cm.[44] These differences in values, while slight, can become compounded to create diverging dimensional estimates, unless a standard unit is used for computation. For the purpose of this discussion, the *codo* value of 56.5 cm is used (it falls almost exactly between the values of *codos cantabricos* and *castellanos*).

For mariners, the most important conceptualization of a ship's size is its tonnage, expressed in tons. Medieval tonnage referred not to a ship's weight, or the amount of water its hull displaced, but to the internal volume of the hold; that is, the ship's cargo carrying capacity. Therefore a ton (from the wooden container called tun) was a unit of volume, rather than weight, and a vessel's tonnage represented the hypothetical number of containers it could ship at sea. The Spanish unit of volume measurement, *tonel*, was the equivalent of two pipes (*pipas*) of wine, or eight cubic *codos*. Another unit, *tonelada*, originally was a unit of accounting, which was obtained by adding 20 percent to 25 percent to the estimated tonnage in *toneles* of a ship to increase its rate of pay when hired by the Spanish Crown. By the mid-sixteenth century the distinction between the two gradually became blurred; fraudulent abuses of customs fees and royal subsidies prompted a royal decree in 1590 that required the *tonel macho* to be used to measure gross cargo tonnage.[45] Hence calculation of cargo space (*arqueamiento*) in the complex and irregular shape of a ship's hull was subject to varying interpretations and also was dependent mainly on whether a vessel was outfitted for merchant or naval use. Basically, tonnage calculation evolved to become expressed in arithmetical formulas based on principal dimensions of ships' constructional components, such as length of keel, maximum breadth or beam, width of the floor, depth of hold, and overall length. These dimensions were also useful in characterizing the general shape of a ship's hull by expressing ratios between them; for example, the ratio between overall length and beam.

García de Palacio's discussion of the principal architectural dimensions required to build a *nao* of 400 tons is a useful template with which to approach a hypothetical reconstruction of the Emanuel Point Ship. The first step is to determine the keel length (*quilla*). Palacio stated that the midship frame should be placed two *codos* forward of the midpoint of the keel.[46] The site plan of another Spanish shipwreck, *San Diego*, indicates that the position of this 300-ton galleon's main frame on the keel was close to Palacio's recommendation.[47] On the Emanuel Point hull the distance between the center of the main frame and the estimated point of the keel's aft terminus is calculated at 11.2 m (19.82 *codos*). Moving two *codos*, or 1.13 m, aft from the center of the main frame gives a keel midpoint of 17.82 *codos*, or 10.07 m. Adding the two halves of the keel together brings the total length of the keel to 20.14 m, or 35.65 *codos*.

According to Palacio, the beam (*manga*) of the ship, measured between the outer sides of the main frame without hull planking, should be almost half the keel length.[48] A keel length to beam ratio of 2.125:1 (for every 2.125 *codos* of keel length there is a corresponding *codo* of beam), figured from Palacio, produces a beam of 16.77 *codos*, or 9.48 m. A check on the relative accuracy of this measurement is the floor dimension (*plan*), or the distance along the flat part of the midship floor to the bottom of the curve signaling the turn of the bilge. Palacio recommended that this distance should be about one third of the ship's beam, or 0.32 *codos* for every one of beam.[49] Fortunately, the floor dimension is available on the Emanuel Point Ship. It was determined by recording a cross section of the port side of the hull at the main frame, which measured 1.5 m. When doubled to include the starboard side, the floor equals 3 m, or 5.31 *codos*, which is just under a third of the ship's estimated beam. This value provides a ratio of 0.31 *codos* of beam to every one *codo* of floor. A Spanish shipbuilder of the time may have obtained a greater or smaller value depending on his rule-of-thumb. Depth of hold (*puntal*), according to Palacio and reinterpreted by Phillips, puts forth a ratio of 0.48 *codos* to one *codo* of beam.[50] This equals 8.05 *codos*, or 4.55 m, for depth of hold, and was measured from the top of the floors to the top of the lower deck planks.

To the Spanish shipwright, the overall length (*esloria*) of the vessel was expressed as the distance from the stem to sternpost along the lowermost deck, or the deck above the hold. This measurement was crucial in calculating the tonnage of the vessel. Palacio explained that to extend the hull beyond the keel, the stempost should rake forward one-third the distance of the keel length, while the sternpost should rake aft one-sixth the length of keel. Another source on contemporary shipbuilding, Fernando de Oliveira, illustrated how the stempost and sternpost rakes could be obtained.[51] According to Oliveira, the height of the stem, as well as the stern, should equal one-third of the keel's length, which corresponds with Palacio's estimation of the stempost's rake. To obtain the bow shape, a height of 11.9 *codos*, or 6.72 m, is measured from the bottom of the keel upward. A compass is then placed at this point, and an arc is drawn from the bottom of the keel to a height equal to the above-mentioned height. Excavations revealed that the shipwreck's sternpost has a rake of 60 degrees, which was documented by an electronic leveling machine device. By extending a line aft from the proposed end of the keel upward to the height suggested by Oliveira, the basic outline of the hull begins to take shape.

At this point, the overall length of the ship can now be estimated. The estimated depth of hold is 4.55 m, or 8.05 *codos*, which, when measured from the top of the floors, provides a point from which to draw a level line to the bow and to the stern. The distance equals 29.5 m, or 52.21 *codos*. This estimated length compares favorably to the 28 m of the extant archaeological remains, which suggests that the preserved hull represents a substantial portion of the vessel, at least on the starboard side.

These computations, based on actual measurements of the Emanuel Point hull remains and the extrapolated dimensions of timbers that could not be measured, and when guided by contemporary sixteenth-century shipbuilding proportions, appear to harmonize with those of Palacio's 400-ton model. Palacio wrote that a ship of 400 tons should have 34 *codos* of keel and 16 *codos* of beam, 11.5 *codos* depth of hold (which is a third of said keel), and a length of 51.33 *codos*.[52] The Emanuel Point Ship is estimated to have had 35.65 *codos* of keel and 16.77 *codos* of beam, 8.05 *codos* depth of hold, and a length of 52.21 *codos*. The shallower estimated depth of hold compared to that listed by Palacio may be due to his depth measurement of all the enclosed area of the hull, including the upper deck, which was 3 *codos* above the lower deck.[53]

Given these calculations of the basic hull dimensions (length of keel, beam, depth of hold, and overall length), the tonnage of the Emanuel Point hull can be estimated. Four different methods produced a range from 417 *toneles machos* to 502 *toneladas,* as follows:

One formula common in Spain during the sixteenth and seventeenth centuries gives a tonnage of 441 *toneladas*—depth of hold times beam, the result divided by 2, times length on deck, the result divided by 8.[54]

A Cantabrian formula prevalent from 1520 to 1590 in northern Spain gives a tonnage of 417 *toneladas*—length on deck times (beam divided by 2, plus depth of hold, the result divided by 2)^2, the result divided by 8, and converting the metric hull dimensions to the *codo cantabrico*.[55]

A formula used in Seville and Cadiz around 1560 produces a tonnage of 419 *toneles*—length of keel times beam times depth of hold, times two-thirds, the result divided by 8, and converting the metric into *codo castellano*.

Using an official formula for warships, the Emanuel Point Ship's tonnage is estimated at 418 *toneladas,* increased by 84 to become 502 *toneladas*—depth times beam, divided by 2; the result times length on deck; minus 5%; the result divided by 8, plus 20% (which subtracted 5% to account for reduced cargo capacity due to heavier internal bracing, but added 20% to account for increased weight of men and munitions).[56]

A carefully and thoroughly researched thesis by UWF graduate student James D. Collis addressed the task of combining the results of our excavations of the Emanuel Point Ship with historical ship construction treatises and archaeological examples to suggest other probable dimensions of the ship.[57] Rather than relying solely on Palacio to reconstruct the shipwreck remains, he analyzed the aforementioned shipbuilding treatises with the key surviving measurements to prepare a set of dimensions and corresponding lines depicting a hypothetical reconstruction of the hull. He estimated the overall length of the vessel at 34.8 m, with a breadth of 8 m, depth of hold 2.7 m, and height to the top deck of 6.3 m.[58] Plugging these numbers into several standard Spanish military and commercial tonnage formulae resulted in tonnages ranging from 297 tons for a warship to 260 tons for a cargo ship.[59] Collis also provided a few more thoughts on the number of decks and general shape of the hull. Guided by the extant sections of the lower hull at the tail-frames and bow-frames suggested a vessel with a sharp entry at the bow and a fine sweep at the rudder below the waterline. Evidence seemed to indicate that the Emanuel Point builder used a circle by which to derive the bow height, and guided by the theorists, this produced a height of the hull, or to the hawse pipes, of 5.75 m. The preferred number of decks by each of the theorists was three. Evidence of the existence of upper decks is found in the loose knees and the cannon port covers at the bow.[60]

Whether the ship had a rounded stern or a flat transom is unclear. The shapes of the four lower gudgeon arms expand outward from their base at the pintle ring, but not nearly to the point of flatness as is required to affix the rudder to a square transom.[61] Iberian *naos* were originally built with a round-tuck stern, a form related to the round ships of the previous century, but this evidence suggests that early galleons also sometimes employed this type of stern.[62] Last, the vessel would have had tumblehome, or turning in of the hull above the waterline, to provide stability by limiting the size of the main deck where heavy guns, supplies, and gun crews operated. A vessel of this size no doubt had at least three masts; that is the mainmast, mizzen, and foremast, with a bowsprit, and perhaps a boomkin over the stern.

Having conjectured the dimensions of the ship, the concluding step is to determine a likely candidate for this vessel in the Luna fleet. Historical records indicate that the fleet consisted of eleven vessels that were specifically built, leased, or purchased for the expedition. The assembled fleet comprised an *urca*, two galleons, two *naos*, two *navios*, three *barcas*, and one caravel. Reporting on the disaster to Velasco, Luna stated the hurricane had destroyed five ships, the galleon *San Juan* of Andonasgui, and one bark, or seven vessels in all.⁶³ By the process of elimination, several vessels that survived or returned to Veracruz can be struck off the list, leaving those believed destroyed by the hurricane as potential candidates for the Emanuel Point Ship.

Of the twelve vessels, a new galleon *San Juan de Ulúa* and two *barcas* of 100 tons were specifically built for the expedition using wood local to the Medellin River, just south of Veracruz.⁶⁴ Wood analysis of the shipwreck determined that the hull contained very limited New World species of trees, except in the bow area, which suggested a hasty repair, perhaps completed prior to embarking on the voyage. Historical documents indicate that the new galleon *San Juan* was sent back to Veracruz to report the fleet's safe arrival. This galleon and one of the *barcas* survived the hurricane. Another newly built *barca* that succumbed to the hurricane can be discounted, not only because of its limited size and construction with New World species of wood but also because evidence suggested that the Emanuel Point Ship remains were those of a vessel that had seen substantial service before the 1559 expedition. Therefore her remains would have to be one of the vessels purchased or leased by Velasco's agents.

Of these, several can be discounted due to their small documented tonnages of less than 200 tons and because they are known to have survived the storm. That leaves three viable candidates reported to have sunk during the hurricane—the 492-ton *nao San Andres*; the 570-ton *urca Jesús*, the flagship of the expedition; and the galleon *San Juan de Ulúa*, master Pedro Andonasgui, the vice-flagship. John Worth has estimated the undocumented tonnages of the vessels composing the fleet using the known sizes of the crews or the probable sizes of crews through the payment of wages.⁶⁵ By these means he projected the tonnage for the galleon *San Juan de Ulúa*, master Andonasgui, at 500 to 600 tons.⁶⁶ Collis estimated the tonnage of the galleon at values of 297 tons for a warship and 260 tons for a cargo ship. These figures compared favorably with a listing of ships that accompanied the 1558 fleet from Spain to the New World, which records that Andonasgui's *San Juan* had a capacity of 220 tons.⁶⁷ Interestingly, the vessel was listed as a *nao* on the voyage from Spain to New Spain but was called a galleon for the Luna expedition. Similarly, *Jesús*, reportedly sailed over with *San Juan* in 1558 and was listed as a *nao*, 220 tons, but for the Luna expedition *Jesús* was listed as an *urca* of 570 tons.⁶⁸ This may also be the case with *San Juan*, documented with a smaller tonnage from Spain to the New World, but actually a larger vessel as estimated by the crew's wages for the Luna expedition. The discrepancies between the dimensions, both documented and estimated, and even the type of vessel, serve as a caution to researchers when conjecturing tonnages and ship types during this time period.

Archaeological analysis of the shipwreck provides some evidence, but not conclusive evidence, for the ship's identity. Relying on Palacio to derive the ship's tonnage, we calculated a range from 417 to 441 tons, and 502 tons for a warship. The small amount of ballast suggests that the vessel had been heavily loaded with cargo and supplies at the time of its sinking. The presence of cannonballs and other projectiles, and gunport covers, indicate that the vessel was armed, but all Luna's vessels may have carried some ordnance to protect the fleet crossing the Gulf and provide protection for the fledgling colony. Excavations at the stern encountered only gudgeons fashioned for a round-tuck stern, rather than gudgeons for a flat-panel stern. While the presence of these round-tuck gudgeons may suggest a *nao*, or perhaps an *urca* (rather than being the flat panels associated with a galleon), only four were found, and they may represent those that were located at and below the waterline where the bottom planking joined the sternpost. At the time of this writing, comparison of the architectural components or artifactual contents with the historical documents has not provided conclusive evidence to determine the identity of the Emanuel Point Ship.

From its initial assessment to determine if the ballast mound was a shipwreck to the systematic and extensive excavations at the bow, midships, and stern, we hoped the archaeological investigations would answer specific research questions centered on determining the cultural and temporal connection, site preservation, and spatial distribution of the shipwreck found wrecked on the Emanuel Point shoal. Ultimately, excavations undertaken at the Emanuel Point shipwreck uncovered approximately 40 percent of the shipwreck, revealing the remains of what was once a relatively large, well-made ship of the sixteenth century. The most likely candidates for its identity are the *San Andres,* Luna's flagship *Jesús*, or the vice-flagship *San Juan de Ulúa*. Further excavations may reveal additional information about the ship remains buried under the ballast and shoal, but the key aspects of the ship's architecture have been recorded, and most likely further digging will only serve to refine our observations and conclusions. For now, the architectural elements of the shipwreck have been carefully studied not only for their role in the Iberian Atlantic shipbuilding tradition but as parts of a wooden container that carried other cultural materials for the colonization of North America, as described in the following chapters.

Notes

1. Hughson, "Remote Sensing in Pensacola Bay."
2. Spirek, "Pinned to the Bottom," 46.
3. Thomas Oertling, personal communication, 1993.
4. Spirek, "Ship's Architecture," 31.
5. Oertling, "Few Remaining Clues," 101.
6. Spirek, "Ship's Architecture," 34.
7. Ballard, *Discovery of the Titanic*, 208.
8. Stevens, *Underwater Research at Red Bay: 1981 Season*, fig. 1.
9. Smith, *Vanguard of Empire*, 68–69, figs. 3.7, 3.8.
10. Spirek, "Pinned to the Bottom," 47.
11. Grenier, "Basque Whalers in the New World," 76, fig. 14.
12. Smith, *Vanguard of Empire*, 71.
13. Casado Soto, "Atlantic Shipping in Sixteenth-Century Spain," 99.
14. Waddell, "Pump and Pump Well of a 16th-Century Galleon," 257.
15. López Pérez, "Estructura del Pecio de Fuxa," 12.
16. Spirek, "Ship's Architecture," 35.
17. McGrail, *Ancient Boats in N.W. Europe*, 28.
18. Robert Grenier, personal communication, 1995.
19. Carré, Desroches, and Goddio, *San Diego*, 148.
20. Rule, *Mary Rose*, 71.
21. Guérout, Rieth, and Gassend, *Navire Génois de Villefranche*, 33–34.
22. Carré, Desroches, and Goddio, *San Diego*, 148; Robert Grenier, personal communication, 1995.
23. Friel, "Carrack," 90.
24. Carré, Desroches, and Goddio, *San Diego*, 140; Parks Canada, personal communication, 1995.
25. Robert Grenier, personal communication, 1995; Carré, Desroches, and Goddio, *San Diego*, 141; Michel L'Hour, personal communication, 1995.
26. Dotson, "Treatises on Shipbuilding Before 1650," 160.
27. Spirek, "Pinned to the Bottom," 44.
28. Rosloff and Arnold, "Keel of the San Estéban."

29. Plaskett, "Logistics and Equipment," 13.
30. Cozzi, "Techniques on the Emanuel Point Ship Excavation."
31. Cozzi, "Ship's Architecture," 28.
32. Ibid., 31.
33. Steffy, *Wooden Shipbuilding*, 140.
34. Oertling, "Molasses Reef Wreck Hull Analysis"; Oertling, "Highborn Cay Wreck: 1986 Field Season"; Watts, "Western Ledge Reef Wreck."
35. Grenier, "Basque Whalers in the New World," 75.
36. Priestley, *Luna Papers, 1559–1561*, 1:79.
37. Palacio, *Instrucción Náutica*.
38. Oliveira, *Livro da Fabrica das Naos*.
39. Lavanha, *Livro Primeiro da Architectura Naval*.
40. Lane, "Venetian Naval Architecture about 1550."
41. Grenier, Bernier, and Stevens, *Underwater Archaeology of Red Bay*.
42. Oertling, "Molasses Reef Wreck Hull Analysis"; Morris, "Western Ledge Reef Wreck"; Watts et al., "Sixteenth-Century Spanish Wreck off Bermuda"; Smith, Keith, and Lakey, "Highborn Cay Wreck."
43. Phillips, "Sizes and Configurations of Spanish Ships in the Age of Discovery," 72.
44. Casado Soto, "Atlantic Shipping in Sixteenth-Century Spain," 105.
45. Ibid., 103.
46. Palacio, *Instrucción Náutica*, fols. 92–92v.
47. Carré, Desroches, and Goddio, *Le San Diego*, 147.
48. Palacio, *Instrucción Náutica*, fol. 90v.
49. Ibid., fol. 91.
50. Phillips, "The Evolution of Spanish Ship Design," 295.
51. Smith, *Vanguard of Empire*, 58.
52. Palacio, *Instrucción Náutica*, fols. 90–91v.
53. Phillips, "Spanish Ship Measurements Reconsidered," 294.
54. Phillips, "The Evolution of Spanish Ship Design," 236.
55. Casado Soto, "Atlantic Shipping in Sixteenth-Century Spain," 106, table 2.
56. Phillips, *Los Tres Reyes 1628–1634*, 68.
57. Collis, "Empire's Reach."
58. Ibid., 124, 125.
59. Ibid., 128.
60. Ibid., 122.
61. Smith et al., *The Emanuel Point Ship, Archaeological Investigations 1992–1995*, 57.
62. Phillips, "Iberian Ships and Shipbuilding," 228.
63. Priestley, *Luna Papers, 1559–1561*, 1:xxxiv.
64. Childers, Alonso Ortíz de Urrutia Account Audit by Martín de Yugoyen, 1569, 336.
65. Worth, "Documenting Tristán de Luna's Fleet."
66. Ibid., table 3, 87.
67. Chaunu and Chaunu, *Seville et l'Atlantique (1504–1650)*, 2:552, 553.
68. Ibid., 2:552; Worth, "Documenting Tristán de Luna's Fleet," 87.

5

What They Left Behind
The Artifact Assemblage

JOHN R. BRATTEN

Pottery fragments, olive pits, encrusted spikes, and an iron anchor were among the first artifacts we encountered at the Emanuel Point Ship site. Following these initial discoveries, more than 5,300 additional artifacts were collected underwater, recovered from the surface screens while sorting dredge spoil, or identified by microscope in the laboratory. The collection and analysis of these artifacts eventually answered many of our questions about the vessel's nationality, date, and sailing route. Although survivors obviously had salvaged the ship soon after its sinking, items that were lost to them provided us with clues that reflected the lifeways and diet of the sailors, soldiers, and colonists. These items also allowed inferences to be made about how these people defended themselves on the ship and on land. Other artifacts aided in the interpretation of the ship's construction. At this writing, our analysis of the collection is ongoing, and new discoveries still are being made in the conservation laboratory.[1]

Upon recovery, artifacts were kept wet, given an identification number, and transferred to holding areas in the conservation laboratory. The various conservation treatments that we applied to them are discussed in chapter 6. Table 2 in the appendix is an overview of the artifact assemblage separated into five major categories—organic, ceramic, metal, glass, and stone. These categories are divided further into subcategories. Notably, and not surprisingly, the largest single subcategory of artifact is

Spanish olive jar, followed by encrusted iron objects (mostly spikes and tacks). Olive jars are ubiquitous on colonial Spanish archaeological sites from this period, and the iron spikes and tacks all are associated with the Emanuel Point Ship's construction. The remainder of the assemblage is the most interesting. We received help from many individuals in identifying some of these remains, and others were analyzed thoroughly by graduate students in a variety of thesis research projects. An overview of these analyses is provided in this chapter.

Ship's Hardware

Anchor

A broken wrought-iron anchor (*ancla*) was found buried fluke down on the shoreward side of the wreckage, just to starboard of the vessel's axis. The overall length of the anchor's shank is 3.14 m, from crown (where the arms are attached) to the broken end, which appears to have been twisted under heavy stress. The missing portion of the shank would have included stock lugs, around which a two-piece wooden stock would have been fastened, and an iron anchor ring. The shank is square in cross section, tapering from where it joins the crown to the broken end.[2] Despite the break, dimensions and proportions of the remainder of the anchor are of diagnostic importance. The lengths of the arms are approximately the same measurement as the distance from fluke tip to fluke tip, forming an equilateral triangle from tip to crown to tip. Similarly, the flukes' palms are shaped in equilateral triangles. The palms are welded to the upper surfaces of the arms, occupying roughly one-third of their extremity, but are slightly set back from their pointed tips.

Of ten anchors associated with the 1554 Spanish fleet wrecked on Padre Island, Texas, three were found to have been broken at the shank, similar to the Emanuel Point Ship anchor, and the shanks of several others had been bent at least twice under stress of use.[3] The dimensions and proportions of these anchors are quite similar to those of the Emanuel Point anchor. Another close parallel is the sheet anchor (the largest of a ship's anchors) found on an early sixteenth-century Spanish shipwreck at Molasses Reef in the Turks and Caicos Islands.[4] The Molasses Reef

Figure 5.1. This wrought-iron anchor was discovered buried near the ship's bow. Courtesy of the Florida Department of State, Division of Historical Resources.

and Emanuel Point anchors both have a chip broken from one of their flukes—another example of the brittleness of the iron used by blacksmiths of the time to forge ship anchors.

The anchor's location on the site suggests that it may have been a starboard bower anchor, secured to the forward gunwale. Although its situation on the bottom—one fluke dug into the sand bar—is the normal position for an anchor intentionally deployed from the ship, its proximity to the vessel's remains suggests otherwise, because a longer scope of cable would have been required if it had been in use, even in shallow water. In addition, the anchor shank appears to have been broken previously below the wooden stock, rendering it non-functional for securing the ship. And had the anchor been deployed without its wooden stock, the arms would have lain flat on the bottom, instead of digging into it. Perhaps the anchor was fast in the sand bar and broke just before the ship came to wreck and settle near it. Alternatively, the anchor may have been deployed and broken in an attempt to kedge the vessel off the sand bar after it wrecked; however, its position close to the starboard bow, rather than offshore in deeper water, does not support this conclusion. The presence of the remains of a bow frame in association with the anchor further confounds the question. Perhaps future discovery of the missing anchor segment, with its ring and stock remains, can help to reconstruct the role of the anchor in the ship's demise.

Rudder Fittings

Pairs of wrought-iron pintles and gudgeons were bolted to the rudder and sternpost to act as attachment points and hinges for the rudder's movement from side to side. The Portuguese called these assemblages *machefemeas* due to their male-female relationship.[5] The female gudgeons (*hembras del timón*) were long iron straps embracing the sternpost, each with an eye to receive a male pintle (*macho del timón*), which had a vertical pin attached to the leading edge of the rudder. The rudder was fashioned with its several pintles to be hung into corresponding sternpost gudgeons, but was left unsecured so that it could be unshipped for repairs by hoisting it upward.

We found four pairs of rudder pintles and gudgeons during excavation of the stern. Three concreted pintles were discovered fastened to the surviving portion of the rudder, although the strap of the uppermost pintle had deteriorated, while those of the lower two are still extant. The ends of the straps appear to have been designed to extend completely around the after edge of the rudder, where they were joined together.

An example of the fastening pattern of the pintle straps was observed on the top pintle, due to the absence of the starboard strap—a series of four or five square-shanked fasteners was used to fasten the strap to the rudder. The fasteners are not in line with each other but alternate up and down. A fourth pintle was found abaft the sternpost on the port side of the ship. This pintle appears to be smaller and different in construction than those on the rudder and most likely is an uppermost pintle on the ship.

Four rudder gudgeons were found in association with the sternpost, although only one remains attached to the ship's hull. Two others appear to have fallen downward onto each other as the sternpost deteriorated after the wrecking event. A fourth gudgeon may have become disarticulated from the sternpost along with the rudder, because it was found behind the hull broken in two. The lower-most gudgeon remains fastened to the hull, with four round-headed, square-shanked fasteners that were driven through both planking and frames. Gudgeon arms slope diagonally downward toward the ring. The forward extremities of the arms appear to have been hammered to a round, flat shape to provide larger attachment surfaces at their ends.

A second gudgeon was situated just above the lower articulated one, but free of the sternpost, from which it appears to have fallen. Since the angle of its arms is much wider than that of the lowermost gudgeon (and wider than a third gudgeon found on top of it), this second gudgeon may have been the third from the bottom fitting on the sternpost. We left it *in situ*, concreted to the sternpost assembly.

The third gudgeon from the bottom actually was the first to be discovered; it was located just below the sand during a preliminary metal detector survey of the site. Remnants of lead and cloth were discovered on the starboard arm, which was broken, and stress cracks were noted on the arms on either side of the gudgeon ring.

What They Left Behind: The Artifact Assemblage · 127

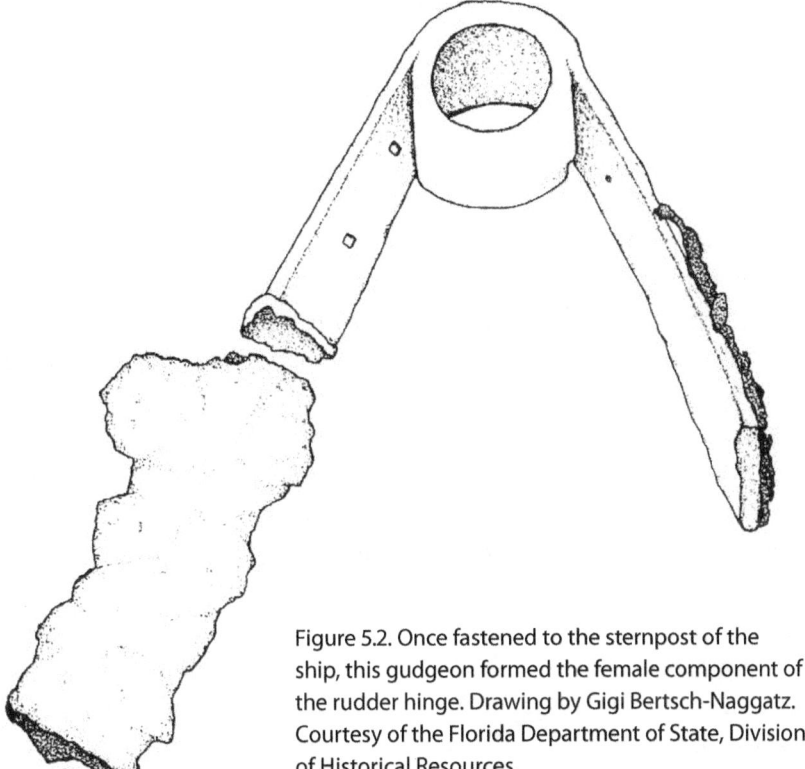

Figure 5.2. Once fastened to the sternpost of the ship, this gudgeon formed the female component of the rudder hinge. Drawing by Gigi Bertsch-Naggatz. Courtesy of the Florida Department of State, Division of Historical Resources.

A fourth gudgeon was found to port abaft the sternpost assembly. The angle of its arms cannot be determined because the arms are broken and missing their ring. Both arms are concreted with corrosion products and the remains of lead sheathing. This fitting could have been the third or fourth gudgeon from the bottom of the sternpost.

No gudgeons were found that would fit a flat stern transom. The arms of the gudgeons do not angle away to fit flush against a flat surface; rather, they appear to have been fastened to a narrow and rounded stern. In comparison, gudgeon shapes from the Padre Island and Molasses Reef shipwrecks indicate that those ships had a square-tuck, flat transom.[6] The Basque ship *San Juan*, which had five sets of rudder fittings, also had a flat transom; however, the uppermost gudgeon is an eyebolt fastened to the sternpost.[7] This raises the question of whether the four pairs of rudder pintles and gudgeons found on the Emanuel Point Ship represent a complete set for the vessel, or only those that were located at and below the waterline, where the ship narrowed toward the rudder.

Fastenings

One of the largest single artifact categories in the Emanuel Point collection is iron fasteners (*clavazón*), with more than five hundred examples. Some are whole but show stress and distortion caused by the ship's wrecking and subsequent disarticulation; others, including many of the smaller fasteners, are broken and fragmentary.

All fasteners are heavily encrusted with corrosion products, and most have lost their original metal composition. After more than four centuries of submersion in salt water, the iron has converted to a black iron-sulfide slush. However, in most cases, the original shape of the fastener, whether whole or broken, has been preserved in its concretion, which can serve as a mold to cast an epoxy replica for study and display.

Spanish shipwrights employed a number of standardized iron fasteners in their trade. A study of Basque shipbuilding contracts indicates that iron fasteners were sold by weight, according to the number it took to make a pound, and that estimates of the total weight of fasteners required to build a ship of a certain tonnage were used in the purchasing negotiations of a shipyard.[8] For example, mid-sixteenth-century shipwrights understood by rule-of-thumb that a ship of 200 tons would require 50 *quintals* (hundredweights) of iron fasteners, which was the case when fasteners were purchased for the construction of a vessel named *Santa María* in 1559.[9]

The Basque contracts specified twelve different types of fasteners that were used for shipbuilding. Four of these were round (*clavo redondo*) and referred to as bolts (*pernos*), while the other eight were square (*clavo cuadrado*) and referred to as spikes (*pregos*).[10] García de Palacio wrote in 1587 that fasteners used to build ships were classified as *pernos de punta* (pointed drift bolts), *pernos de chaveta* (forelock bolts), *clavos de barrote* (scantling nails), *clavos de escora* (bottom nails) and *medio escora* (medium bottom nails), and *clavos de costado* (nails for the ship's sides).[11] A study of Spanish ship construction contracts and an eighteenth-century

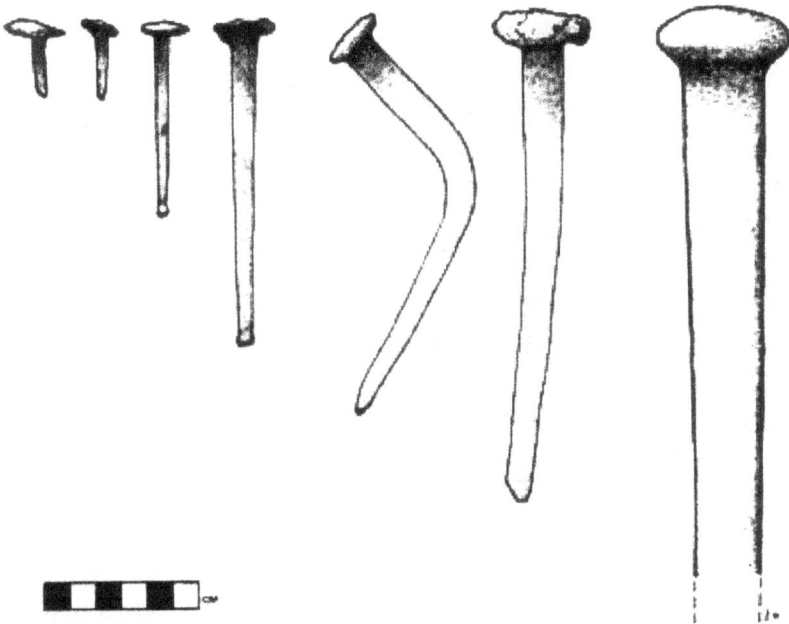

Figure 5.3. Square and round fasteners of different shank sizes were used in the construction of the ship. Drawing by James Hunter III. Courtesy of the Florida Department of State, Division of Historical Resources.

illustrated naval dictionary has shown that spikes and nails were also classified as *clavos de peso*, as opposed to bolts and wooden treenails (*cabillas*).[12]

Among the *clavos*, larger fasteners are distinguished with the names *encolamiento, cinta, costado*, and *escora*. Each came in varying sizes from the largest (*major*) to the smallest (*quarto*). Aside from *clavos de peso*, there were smaller fasteners, such as *barrotes, tillados*, and *estoperoles* (tacks).

A preliminary study of more than a thousand fasteners from the Molasses Reef Wreck was the first to attempt to catalogue actual fastener remains from a sixteenth-century shipwreck. Each example was categorized by differences in head shape and diameter, shank length, shank cross-section shape and diameter, and point configuration.[13]

Rather than attempting to assign contemporary sixteenth-century nomenclature to the different fastener types, the Molasses Reef study divided examples into bolts (large, long, round-shanked fasteners with added-on heads), drift pins (long, square-shanked, peen-headed fasteners with beveled ends), nails (slender, headed, square- or octagonal-shanked fasteners with fine drawn or flat points), and tacks (small, short-shanked, sharp-pointed nails with broad flat heads).[14]

Recovery of numerous examples of iron fasteners from the sixteenth-century Spanish terrestrial sites of Santa Elena and Fort San Felipe in South Carolina, excavated by Stanley South and colleagues, has resulted in the formulation of a hypothetical model for the classification and typology of Spanish nails. Analysis of field specimens was compared with documentation of eighteenth-century ship fasteners to see whether a pattern of colonial nails by type and size emerged that could be useful to archaeologists.[15] The model differentiates between nails used by a ship's carpenter (*carpintero de ribera*) and those used by a joiner or building carpenter (*carpintero de blanco*). Although both kinds of nails were known by the same names and had similar dimensions, nails used in joining had flatter heads than those used in shipbuilding.

Measurement of fastener casts of whole nails recovered in concretions from the Emanuel Point Ship suggests that they can be readily applied to South's Spanish nail model. Those chosen for study by graduate student David Pugh were measured in overall length from the peak of the head to the end of the point; cross-sectional dimensions of the shank were taken at the base of the head and at the point.[16] Each example has a square shank and generally can be classified as a ship's nail. Since the Emanuel Point examples are epoxy casts, their weights are not applicable to the model. Table 3 in the appendix shows a comparison of reconstructed fasteners based on South's Spanish nail model.

Lead Sheathing

European wooden sailing ships plying the South Atlantic and the Americas were subject to predations of the shipworm (*Teredo navalis*), which quickly devoured outer hull planking below the waterline. To combat this marine borer and prevent fouling of ships' hulls by other organisms,

Figure 5.4. Lead sheathing from the sternpost area. Courtesy of the Florida Department of State, Division of Historical Resources.

shipyard workers devised several methods of coating and sheathing exposed planks. One relatively inexpensive method employed an outer layer of fir planking, backed by felt and caulking, nailed to a ship's hull to serve as sacrificial sheathing, which was replaced when consumed. A more permanent method used thin lead sheets to cover vulnerable portions of the hull, including the seams between planks and around through-hull fittings such as rudder gudgeons. This method appears to have been used on sixteenth-century Spanish ships and is evidenced by the remains of lead sheathing found on the 1554 Texas wreck of *San Estéban*, the Molasses Reef Wreck, and the Emanuel Point Ship.[17]

A large number of pieces of drawn lead sheets (*planchas de plombo tirado*) or patching material have been recovered from the shipwreck. All have holes left by sheathing tacks (*estoperoles*), most have tack head impressions, and a few have impressions of caulking fabric. Most of the lead was recovered loose in sediments outside the hull; other pieces were found still attached to the hull and were left in place. From shapes and sizes of the lead, the number and arrangement of fastener holes, and preserved impressions, a general pattern of sheathing can be deduced.

All intact pieces have regular rows of sheathing tack holes; many have two distinct rows, and others have three. Spacing between these rows varies according to the widths of the lead strips, but all have a row along the upper and the lower edge, and others have a third row along the middle of the strip. The strips apparently were used to cover the seams (*comentos*) between hull planks and keep the caulking (*estopa*) from working out of the seams. One piece was observed in place, covering the ends of planks where they joined the sternpost. The outer rows of tacks were driven into the wooden planks, while the center row was driven into the caulked seam between the planks. Varying widths of the strips reflect differing widths of planks. Lead strips for seam sheathing reported on *San Estéban* were much narrower, covering only the seams between the planking with one row of fasteners rather than three.[18]

Lead sheathing from the sternpost area demonstrates a typical fastening pattern (three rows with tack head impressions). Spacing between tacks on a row varied; on some rows it was quite regular, while on others it was irregular, giving the impression of neat and sloppy—possibly the work of different individuals or work carried out under different conditions or time constraints. However, in no case were fastener holes close enough together for the heads to touch, as observed on examples of seam sheathing on *San Estéban*.[19]

Three additional diagnostic lead sheets that have no clear pattern of tack holes may have been used as patching materials. García de Palacio listed lead and sheathing nails as necessary repair stores taken to sea aboard a ship. He also described the process of patching a warship that has just received a shot below the waterline and is leaking. He advised the captain to "break away from the battle, and . . . put the ship on the opposite tack, and with that, the ship will heel to the other side, and the leak will remain above water. . . . The hole being covered, caulked, and a sheet of lead, lined with canvas . . . applied over it the ship will be able to navigate and return to fight, if such is agreeable."[20]

Examination of lead sheathing and patching materials from the stern of the Emanuel Point Ship suggests that use of lead on this vessel's hull was more extensive than on other sixteenth-century ships excavated so far. The English-built Woolwich ship, dated to the first half of the century, was kept watertight by wooden seam ribbands and had lead sheathing only on the butt of the garboard strake.[21] Another early site, the Cattewater wreck, yielded one piece identified as lead sheet.[22] On

San Estéban somewhat more lead was used. Narrow strips, only slightly wider than the diameter of the fastener heads, were used only to cover the edges of the gudgeon arm and the seams between deadwood timbers of the keel.[23] Larger amounts of lead were found on the Molasses Reef Wreck; some were apparently forced into seams between strakes, rather than fastened over them, while others may represent patching materials.[24]

The amounts of lead thus far observed on the Emanuel Point Ship suggest extensive, though not total, sheathing of the hull, primarily to protect planking seams and areas where the rudder hardware was fastened to the stern. Widths of lead sheets were more than sufficient to cover seams, but not to overlap adjacent pieces of lead sheathing. This practice may have been a practical compromise between protection against loss of caulking and shipworm attack and the expense and weight of total sheathing. The irregularity of strip and tack dimensions may indicate that partial resheathing of seams was necessary after an initial application. Last, the ship was in use long enough to require at least some patching of leaks that developed over its sailing career.

Andrew Marr, conducting research for his master's thesis, arranged to have fifteen samples of the Emanuel Point Ship's lead tested for lead isotope ratios. Using multiple-collector inductively coupled plasma mass spectrometry, Marr confirmed that all samples originated from Mina La Sultana in southern Spain. As outlined in his thesis, Marr further investigated the practice of using iron tacks to attach the lead to the hull. He designed an experimental archaeology project that confirmed this method of attachment as one that would allow the metal to remain attached to the hull during a complete transatlantic voyage.[25]

Ballast

A preliminary study of ballast stones was undertaken by field school student Janet Bancroft.[26] Stephen Pollock and Dennis Bratten of the University of Southern Maine's Geology Department slabbed and visually examined forty-six stones randomly picked from the shipwreck's ballast mound.[27] A small number of stones initially was chosen as a good starting point to determine preliminary rock classes and types. Table

4 in the appendix lists the rock classes and identified types. The most common ballast encountered in the sample consists of a quartzite-like mineral known as arenite (39.12%); followed by the sedimentary rock micrite (19.55%); and the igneous rock basalt (13.03%). Other types in the sample include quartz (8.68%), tuff (4.34%), and single examples of aphanite, granite, calcarenite, jasper, and one unidentified specimen. Based on this suite of types, the sample is not inconsistent with rocks and minerals associated with the Caribbean basin or a Mediterranean region. Specifically, Bratten suggested Veracruz, Hispaniola, and northwestern Spain as probable sources. Further analysis of the ballast was conducted by UWF graduate student Matthew Gifford.[28] Using thin-section geochemical analysis, Gifford determined that the samples he selected for testing were basalt. With the use of Argon-Argon dating, he determined the age of ballast to be 1049.9 ± 1.5 million years, an age that geographically matches the coast of Brazil near Salvador.

Galley Wares

Limited testing of metallic targets in the forward portion of the ballast mound in line with the keel revealed two associated artifact deposits that are thought to represent the location and contents of the ship's galley.

Copper Pitcher

A one-meter test pit was excavated through coarse sand, shell hash, and compacted silt. The feature ultimately revealed a large encrusted metal container, a small brass ring, fragments of hemp rope and other organic debris, and small ballast stones that apparently fell down between the worm-eaten remains of two starboard bow frames. Except for the wooden remains, all materials were recovered for analysis.

The metal container is a crudely fashioned pitcher with a heavy handle and thickened rim, which appears to have been soldered as one piece to a thinner cone of metal. The rim expands to an extremely wide base, to which a concave disk of metal has been lap-soldered. The lower end of the handle may have been riveted to the body of the pitcher; the

Figure 5.5. A large copper pitcher, found in the forward part of the ship, was probably used for cooking or for heating liquids. Courtesy of the Florida Department of State, Division of Historical Resources.

doughnut-shaped mouth has a subtle indentation to serve as a pouring spout.

After recovering the pitcher, we sifted its contents (silt, mud, and shell), but no evidence of foodstuffs could be identified. Pinholes in the wall of the vessel were noted, as were cracks and a larger hole in the bottom. Dark coloration visible throughout the metal's encrustation initially suggested that the pitcher may have been made of tin or pewter. A

Figure 5.6. A container with features similar to the copper pitcher (fig. 5.5) is shown at the lower left in this engraving by Peter Breugel the Elder, titled *The Alchemist*, dated 1558 (from Klein, *Graphic Worlds*, 171). Courtesy of the Florida Department of State, Division of Historical Resources.

radiograph of the entire object revealed that little parent metal is left; the majority of the pitcher's fabric consists of corrosion products.

To determine the composition of the original metal, we sent a sample to the Western Australia Maritime Museum (WAMM) Chemistry Centre for analysis using a scanning electron microscope. Test results concluded that the pitcher was made of copper. Additional testing by WAMM found traces of sulfur, tin, and iron, which would be consistent with contamination from nearby objects.[29] The Winterthur Museum Analytical Laboratory tested another sample of the pitcher's outer fabric using X-ray fluorescence and confirmed that the vessel was made of copper with less than 1 percent of such trace metals as tin, antimony, silver, and lead. However, an analyzed sample from the vessel's interior revealed concentrations of tin up to three times as high as those found in the exterior samples.[30] This suggests that the interior of the container may have been coated or lined with tin.

Fashioned with a relatively small mouth and large flared base, the pitcher probably was used to heat liquids. Its thin, concave bottom would have collected heat without burning, and its wide base would have lowered the center of gravity to enhance stability and to prevent the pitcher from capsizing at sea. To date, no parallels for this artifact have been found on contemporaneous sites or in museum collections consulted. However, two similarly shaped containers appear in a 1558 engraving by Peter Bruegel the Elder depicting an alchemist's laboratory.[31]

Brass Ring

A small copper alloy ring was found in association with the pitcher. The ring and the pitcher were resting on what probably are forward starboard frames of the vessel. The ring is in pristine condition and, when first recovered, was shiny. A similar but smaller brass ring of unknown usage was recovered from *San Estéban* off Padre Island.[32] The function of the ring has not been determined, although it may be associated with galley wares. Iron and copper alloy rings were found at excavations of La Isabela in the Dominican Republic and may have been horse bridle hardware.[33]

Copper Cauldrons

In the forward part of the ship we recovered four cauldrons that varied in size, shape, and degree of preservation. Each was fashioned with rivets that were punched from the inside out and then covered on the inside with a small, flat copper "cap." The caps were soldered to the body of the cauldrons with what has been described as an amalgam, probably of tin, lead, and pitch.[34]

Cauldron #1

A large copper cauldron was discovered near the copper pitcher and ring. Although it was not completely exposed during testing, we noted

Figure 5.7. The handle and rim of a copper cooking cauldron (cauldron #1), photographed *in situ*, appear as shiny and new as on the day the pot was lost more than 450 years ago. Courtesy of the Florida Department of State, Division of Historical Resources.

certain of its attributes. The thin-walled container has a built-up rim, and two heavy lugs are attached to thick straps at opposite sides of the shoulder, each fastened to the body of the cauldron with two copper rivets. The lugs support the tapered ends of a heavy, solid copper handle, which pass through the eyes of the lugs but are bent back in opposing directions. The cauldron appears to have been mashed on the port outboard side, perhaps by the ship's wrecking process. Although the metal is in good condition, we noted several holes and tears in the thin body of the container. After measuring and documenting the upper portion of the cauldron, we reburied the feature for the time being. The close proximity of the pitcher and this cauldron, both of which are cooking ware, suggests that this area of the bow was the location of the galley.

In 1997 the cauldron was excavated again with the goal of recovery. Upon complete excavation, it became apparent that parent metal survived in the rim and bail, but the body had been entirely converted into brittle copper sulfide. To raise the object in one piece, we wrapped the

What They Left Behind: The Artifact Assemblage · 139

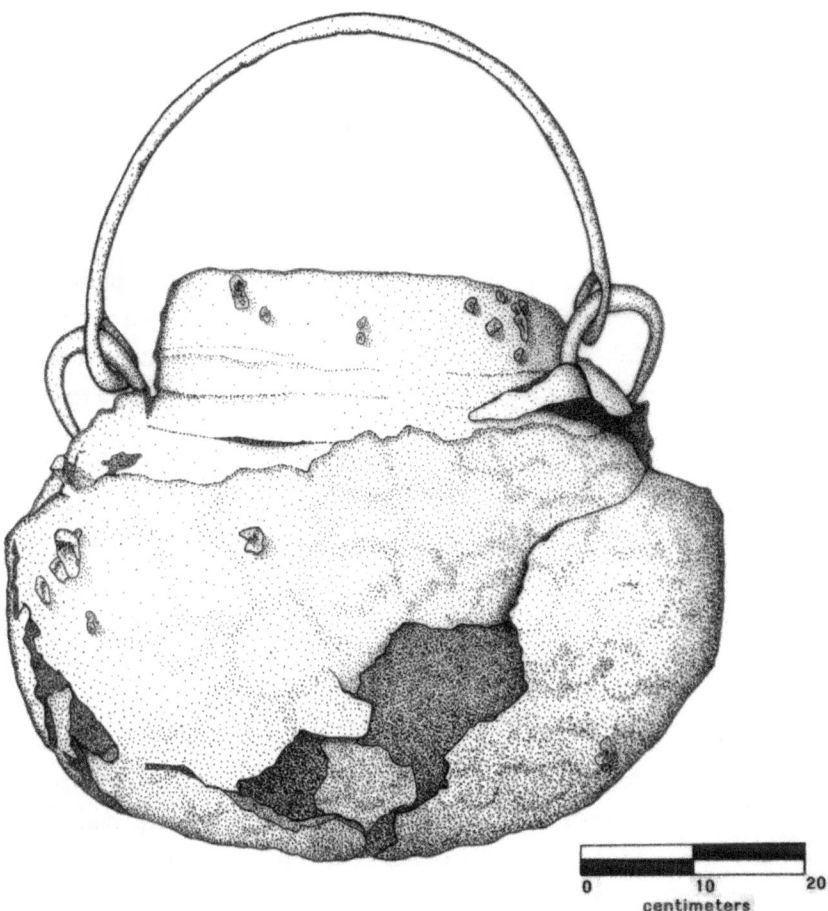

Figure 5.8. Upon complete excavation of cauldron #1, it became apparent that parent metal survived in the rim and bail, but the body had been converted entirely into brittle copper sulfide. Drawing by James Hunter III. Courtesy of the Florida Department of State, Division of Historical Resources.

cauldron with elastic bandages and carefully lifted it to the surface in a separate container so that its contents could be searched for cultural remains. During a "second excavation" in the lab, the cauldron was found to be filled with a mixture of sand, mud, fragmented oyster shells, giant clams, an iron fastener concretion, olive jar sherds, and a few animal bones.

Cauldron #2

We located remnants of a second, smaller copper cauldron a few meters away from the first. This vessel also was found in a very shallow position on the site, resting upside down. In this example the surviving parts consist of a fairly flat neck area with two riveted lugs on each side and a thin bail connected to the lugs. The upper rim is gone, but one rivet hole located in the highest part of the neck area suggests that the cauldron's rim may have been reinforced with a riveted outer band. Small portions of the body are still connected to the intact neck piece and flare out dramatically from it, but not enough of the container remains to determine how wide or deep the body was.

This cauldron appears to have been a smaller cooking container with the body, neck, and rim fashioned from one piece of metal. The base probably also was a singular piece with the body and rim. The lugs were separate pieces riveted to the neck and body of the cauldron at the three points of a Y-shaped design. The design of these handles suggests that their purpose was not solely attachment lugs for a bail but was also designed for lifting.

The supporting bail does not appear to have been made with the same degree of precision as the rest of the cauldron. Its width is uneven, and the ends are curled crudely to hold at the vessel handles. The bail may not have been made specifically for this particular container, since its curled ends are open and could have fit on others as well.

Cauldron #3

In the same area but at a much deeper level we discovered a third cooking container. Because this cauldron was buried deeply, it was found in an extremely deteriorated and fragmented condition. The surviving metal has been transformed into copper sulfide, and the detail along the rim is much harder to discern than on the other cauldrons. Its bail is rectangular in cross section and exceptionally heavy, suggesting that the vessel was designed to hold a considerable weight. Unlike the other cauldrons, the side attachments are not handles but circular pieces with holes made specifically to hold the bail, which would have been fitted into the lugs before they were attached to the cauldron. The lugs appear to have been riveted to the body of the cauldron at the reinforced rim, but the degree of corrosion at these contact points obscures this detail. The reinforced rim consists of two wide bands riveted around the body rim and overlapping at their ends. Metal thickness of the bands is much heavier than the thickness of the body rim.

This cauldron was a large container that could only be carried with the bail and probably was used for a specific purpose rather than being a multiuse container like the smaller cauldrons may have been. Its shape is impossible to determine because of the absence of any main body sections. The entire rim was recovered in badly bent pieces, but it does not appear to have angles that suggest a rectangular shape.

Cauldron #4

Another large copper container may not have been associated with food preparation. Originally composed of four side panels riveted together with vertical seams, the container was found broken apart and scattered across the site, perhaps by a modern shrimper's net chain. The panels had been inserted into and riveted to a connecting strap, which in turn was riveted into a round bottom. Two horseshoe-shaped handles originally were located at the top. Additional strength was added to the rim and handles by another riveted band of copper.

A hard residue was found in the bottom of this cauldron. The substance is not a corrosion product and is extremely heavy, suggesting a high metallic content, such as lead or mercury, and also suggesting the cauldron was not used as a cooking vessel. The 1587 manual *Instrucción Náutica* for Spanish shipping in Mexico lists the necessary implements needed on board a ship. One implement is "a cauldron for tar."[35] The riveted cauldron may have been put to such use, but further analysis will be required to determine the composition of the deposits. Figure 5.10 shows an artist's rendition of what the cauldron probably looked like when it was intact.

Cauldrons (*caldari*) with similar neck and body (shoulder) shapes are depicted in Bartolomeo Scappi's Venetian cookbook of 1570.[36] A vessel of comparable size to Cauldron #4 with a band encircling the rim and similar bail and lugs is labeled *caldaro da sei some* (cauldron of six *somas*, *soma* = ca. 26.4 gal). The pictured cauldron is pear-shaped and consists

Above: Figure 5.9. Originally composed of four side panels riveted together with vertical seams, cauldron #4 was found broken apart and scattered over the site, perhaps by a modern shrimper's net chain. Courtesy of the Florida Department of State, Division of Historical Resources.

Right: Figure 5.10. An artist's rendition of what cauldron #4 probably looked like when it was intact. Drawing by James Hunter III. Courtesy of the Florida Department of State, Division of Historical Resources.

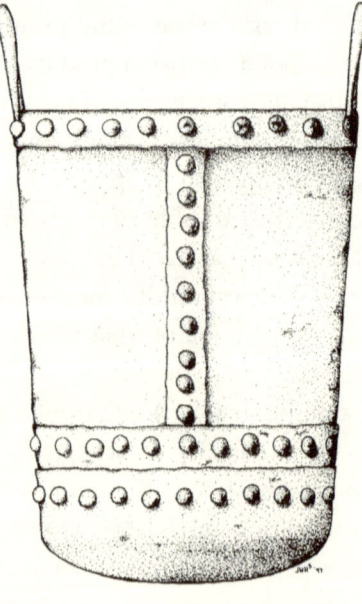

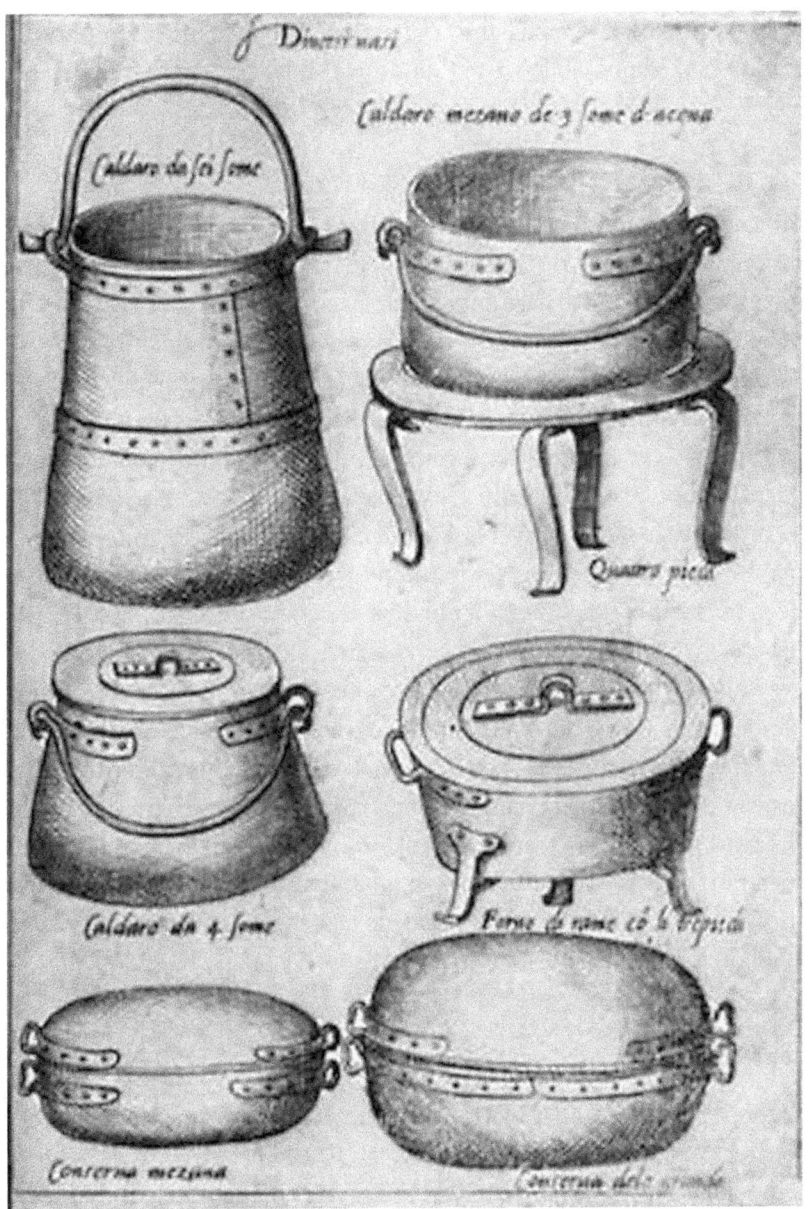

Figure 5.11. Cauldrons depicted in Scappi's *Opera* (1570). The vessel at the upper left is labeled "*caldaro da sei some*" and appears similar to cauldron #4; the cauldron at the middle left appears similar to cauldron #1. Courtesy of the Florida Department of State, Division of Historical Resources.

of riveted body segments in the upper half of the vessel and a singular, large base below a riveted band connecting the upper and lower parts. A cauldron of comparable size to Cauldron #1 is labeled *caldaro da 4 some*.

Skillet

The bottom to another copper utensil was recovered in fairly good condition, although the rim and any handles that may have been attached are missing. The sides flare out and arc back inward as they rise, but the height of the utensil cannot be determined because of the missing rim. Two holes along the side appear to be rivet holes that probably held the rivets of a handle. The metal of the base is much thicker than the sides, and the base is slightly raised in the center interior. This container appears to have been a skillet or frying pan.

A copper band with rivet holes and an extended socket into which a handle could be inserted was found near the pan. This piece may have been the handle attachment because its design obviously is made for being attached to a wide, rounded surface such as a pot or pan. Scappi's engravings show such band and socket pieces in use with wooden rods for handles. It is worth noting that none of the cooking pans shown in the Venetian cookbook uses a band and socket piece for attaching a handle; instead they have metal handles that are all of one piece. They attach to the pans with similar shaped bands, but the bands are part of the same metal piece as the actual handle. If a band and socket attachment was used with the pan, then perhaps a detachable wooden handle may have been preferred on ships for storage purposes.

Sauce Pan or Cup

A copper utensil, similar in shape to a sauce pan or a large, handled cup, was recovered intact from the shipwreck. The cup is structurally sound, although one side has been bent. The fabric is much thicker than that of the cauldrons. The sides do not flare out but rise straight up from the base. A thick, rounded handle is riveted to the upper portion of the cup with two rivets on each side.

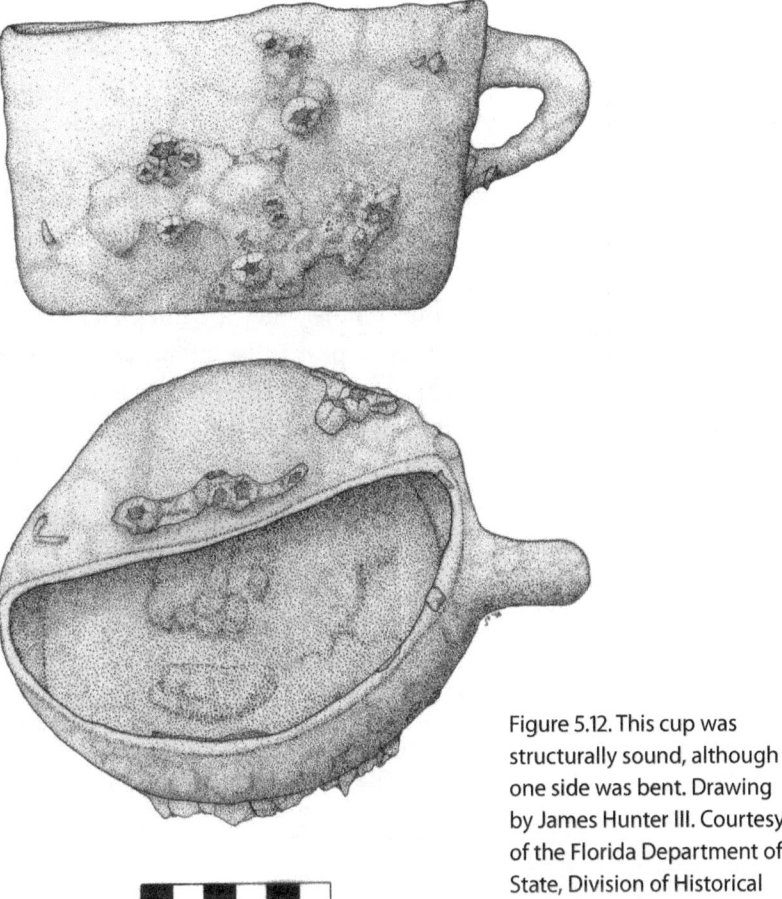

Figure 5.12. This cup was structurally sound, although one side was bent. Drawing by James Hunter III. Courtesy of the Florida Department of State, Division of Historical Resources.

A small amount of corroded deposits are concreted to the interior of the cup. The appearance of the cup's interior compares favorably with the interior of the large copper pitcher had that been washed with tin, suggesting a similar treatment. Copper serving and dining wares commonly were lined with tin in the sixteenth century because the copper imparted an unsavory taste to drink or food. Garcia de Palacio refers to such wares as "tin-plate . . . dishes for the service of the crew."[37] This cup may have been used in many capacities for dining and cooking.

Bronze Mortar and Pestle

A heavy bronze mortar was recovered from the galley area of the shipwreck. A pestle also was recovered, but its size seems to be too large for the mortar. The base and sides of the mortar are octagonal, and the mortar is slightly deformed from its base up through the sides. Its rim narrows and curves outward from the sides into a slightly circular shape. Four appendages are located at equal heights along the upper part of the sides. Evenly spaced from one another, they are thick rectangular pieces with center holes. The pieces appear to be utilitarian additions to the mortar and not just ornate appendages. They possibly were used to secure the mortar to some type of stand. The interior of the mortar

Figure 5.13. A heavy bronze mortar and pestle were recovered from the galley area of the shipwreck. Courtesy of the Florida Department of State, Division of Historical Resources.

Figure 5.14. John Bratten displaying a large funnel that was found in two pieces: the conical body and the cylindrical spout. Courtesy of the Florida Department of State, Division of Historical Resources.

rounds out smoothly at the bottom, and the body metal along the upper sides gets thicker toward the bottom.

The mortar and pestle are the only galley ware objects that likely were cast as opposed to being hammered (see discussion following). The symmetry of the appendages and side panels and the solidity of the appendages where they are attached to the body support the supposition of the mortar being mold cast.

Funnel

A funnel was found in two pieces consisting of the conical body and a cylindrical "spout" that originally was attached to the main cone. With the exception of a small missing piece of body and rim, all parts of the funnel are intact. The funnel rim is folded inward along its entire circumference. No seams or rivets are visible on the body of the funnel or on the cylinder. The rim on the end part of the cylinder is folded in the same manner as the rim on the body. This is a curious design because an inward fold of the rim would tend to catch any substance being funneled.

This funnel is a big implement that was designed to transfer a large amount of (presumably) liquid. The cylinder opening is fairly wide and could not have been used to pour into a small opening accurately. The list of "small items necessary to the ship and its provision" from the *Instrucción Náutica* of 1587 includes "a funnel of copper and another of wood." The book also mentions that the *fonil* was used to transfer water or wine into storage vessels.[38] The document lists no other use for funnels.

Discussion

According to Biringuccio (1540), "a great labor, surely, is that of the coppersmith, since every work must be hewn from the mass of copper by force of the hammer."[39] All the recovered copper ware would have been painstakingly heated, hammered, reheated, and hammered again and again. That copper wares were hand-wrought and not molded gives one a certain appreciation for the cauldrons, pans, and other copper implements that were so commonly used. The only items in this assemblage that were not hammered into shape were the mold-cast bronze mortar and pestle. Interestingly, the process by which the mortar was cast is the exact process used in the sixteenth century for bell founding, in which cores were an essential element of the molding process.

Garcia de Palacio's list of essential implements to have on board includes all that was recovered from the Emanuel Point Ship except for the mortar. His list of cuprous provisions includes "a cauldron for tar; two cauldrons for the hearth; . . . a funnel of copper . . . copper pans; [and] tin-plate . . . dishes."[40] In addition, comparison of artifacts recovered from other sixteenth-century Spanish shipwrecks reveals interesting similarities and attests to the common occurrence of such items. For example, copper cauldrons and a bronze mortar of similar size and design were recovered from the wreck of *Santa María de la Rosa*, a Spanish

Armada ship sunk in 1588.[41] The mortar has four appendages along its sides, as does the Emanuel Point Ship mortar. Are such similarities in the mortar design purely stylistic, or was there a practical purpose for the appendages? The holes in the appendages of the mortar recovered from Pensacola Bay suggest a utilitarian usage such as attachment to a stand.

Copper cauldrons are probably the most common type of galley ware to be recovered from older shipwrecks. However, stylistic changes among the vessels are not well chronicled, and it is a "rare occasion when a stylistic chronology exists for European domestic articles (e.g., knives, axes, cauldrons)."[42] For this reason, Bartolomeo Scappi's depictions of cookware were relied upon heavily for speculative interpretations of the Emanuel Point cauldrons.

However, as with the mortar, similarities among the cookware and other items found on different shipwrecks are useful for establishing the common usage of such implements. Excavation of the seventeenth-century Spanish treasure ship *Nuestra Señora de Atocha* produced a rounded base very similar to the base of the riveted cauldron from the Emanuel Point Ship, and the wreck of a sixteenth-century St. John's Bahamas Spanish shipwreck (thought to be *Santa Clara*) produced a body panel with rivet holes similar to those on the same cauldron.[43] Both of these wrecks suggest the common occurrence of such a cauldron aboard Spanish ships.

UWF graduate student Ree Rodgers examined the ship's galley ware assemblage and compared it to contemporary Spanish dietary practices in Spain and at sea.[44] Rodgers concluded that the numerous galley-related artifacts offer insights into the daily meals that colonists consumed during their time at sea between Veracruz and Pensacola Bay. Her study of both archaeological remains and historical documents revealed that a European diet remained intact on the journey with only a few substitutions. She further noted that "mealtime refuse indicates opportunities for displays of wealth and status, and for reinforcement of conventional European attitudes about privileged classes." The collection of galley ware recovered from the Emanuel Point Ship is a good representative sample of the domestic implements used aboard a sixteenth-century Spanish ship.

Ceramics

The ceramic assemblage recovered from the Emanuel Point Ship includes coarse earthenwares of the olive jar variety, lead-glazed earthenwares, tin enamelwares, and colonial Aztec wares. In addition, brick or galley tiles and what may be a portion of a cooking brazier were found. Most ceramic artifacts recovered during excavations were stained by the dark tannin-bearing water and sediments. However, they slowly became identifiable after soaking in a solution of hydrogen peroxide. A study of the collection by graduate student Debra Wells typed the ceramics by attributes (color, paste, temper, coatings, shape, and thickness) and compared them with similar examples from other archaeological sites to suggest a chronological range for the wrecking of the ship.[45]

Olive Jars

The ceramic assemblage is characterized predominantly by fragments of Spanish coarse earthenware of the olive jar variety. Descending from Mediterranean wine amphorae, olive jars (known as *botijas, botijuelas,* and *botijas peruleras*) were used as containers for wine, olive oil, vinegar, honey, and other foodstuffs. They frequently are found on Spanish colonial sites and are especially common on Spanish shipwrecks. Depletion of wood resources in southern Europe, caused by centuries of shipbuilding and domestic usage, required an equally stable and versatile alternative to the wooden cask or barrel. Highly portable and shaped in such a way that they could easily be stacked in the hold of a ship, olive jars had the benefits of strength and reusability. On transoceanic voyages these storage vessels served a dual function of cargo and ballast; once the voyage was complete, the jars could be emptied, washed, and refilled for a return voyage.

Storing liquids in earthenware containers could result in seepage because the coarse, low-fired wares tended to absorb their contents. One method of solving this problem was to coat the inside of the vessel with a waterproof substance. Many olive jar sherds from the Emanuel Point Ship were coated on the interior with two different kinds of sealant—a clay slip on some and pine pitch on others.[46] Most of the sherds exhibit

Figure 5.15. The Spanish olive jar was a common form of ceramic container for olive oil, wine, and other foodstuffs. Courtesy of the Florida Department of State, Division of Historical Resources.

Figure 5.16. Olive jar interiors frequently were coated with pine resin to prevent liquids from seeping out of these porous ceramic containers. Courtesy of the Florida Department of State, Division of Historical Resources.

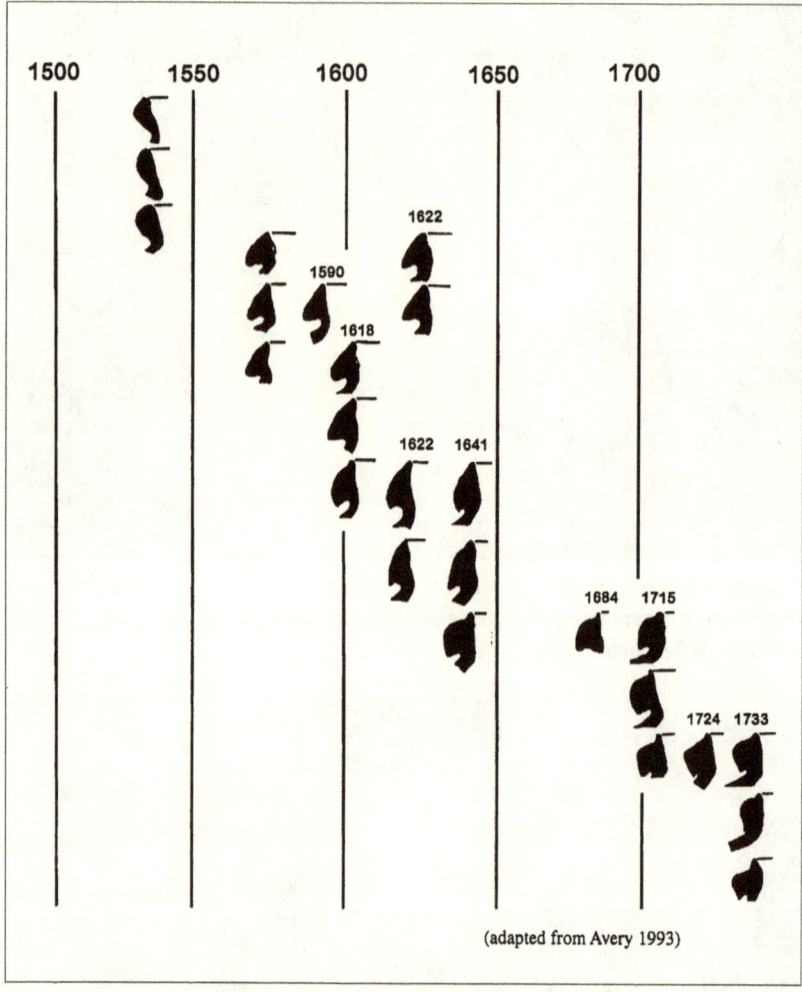

Figure 5.17. Chronological framework for Shape A Middle Style Olive Jar rims. Courtesy of the Florida Department of State, Division of Historical Resources.

a white efflourescence on the exterior surface, which may have resulted from the unfired vessel having been washed with a saltwater slurry and then fired, causing the calcium within the clay to rise to the surface.

The traditional typology of olive jars is the work of Goggin (1960), who divided the containers into three distinct styles (early, middle, and late) based on vessel form and rim shape.[47] Goggin was able to establish separate date ranges for the different styles. Based on paste characteristics and sherd thickness, most of the Emanuel Point olive jar sherds fit within Goggin's Middle Style; however, based on rim style, they appear to be of an early variety that has since been noted by more recent researchers of mid-sixteenth-century shipwrecks.[48] The rim shapes correspond to what Marken has defined as Type 2, examples of which have been found on the St. John's Bahamas wreck (1564) and at Padre Island, Texas (1554).[49]

A comparative study by George Avery of olive jar rim shapes from shipwrecks that are securely dated because their year of sinking is known documents a gradual change in rim styles over time.[50] Avery used rim sherd examples from the St. John's wreck (1564); Padre Island wrecks (1554); Spanish Armada wrecks (1588); *Rosario* (1590); *San Martín* (1618); an unidentified wreck believed to be from the 1622 fleet; *Concepción* (1641); the 1715 fleet wrecks; *Tolosa* and *Guadalupe* (1724); and the 1733 fleet wrecks. He recorded the transition from an early to mid-sixteenth-century inverted teardrop rim shape to a curved, triangular-in-profile rim shape that begins in the 1580s and evolves through the seventeenth century to an elongated "question-mark" shape, culminating in a fat, donut-shaped rim profile.

Compared with Avery's chronological outline, the Emanuel Point rim sherds are unlike those from sites dated 1588 and later; rather, they are similar in profile to examples from the St. John's and Padre Island sites, which date from the middle of the sixteenth century. This shape (Marken's Type 2) has turned up on the Spanish Armada wrecks, but this represents an isolated example among the predominance of Marken Type 3 Middle Style rims.[51] In turn, some examples of thicker, Middle Style rims are in the Padre Island collection, aside from the Type 2 shape.[52] Based on his research, Avery suggested that the date for the Middle Style olive jar can be pushed back to 1554; he also proposed a possible connection between rim shape and container usage.[53]

Analysis of body sherds in the Emanuel Point collection indicates that in addition to early Middle Style jars, the ship carried another variety of container with thinner body walls. The thin-walled sherds have a reddish paste, large quartz inclusions, clay slip on the interior, and efflorescence on the exterior. They are probably from an Early Style vessel, since vertical rather than horizontal rilling patterns (the impressions left by a potter's fingers or tools) are evident on several partially reconstructed sherds. However, no handle remnants or breakage scars appear on the portions thus far recovered. Avery suggests that the Early Style container defined by Goggin is not of the olive jar variety but rather a form of cantina.[54] Known as a *cantimplora*, an early style ceramic vessel with handles descended from the Near Eastern pilgrim bottle, this portable container fell into disuse in mid-sixteenth century.[55]

Lead-Glazed Earthenwares

The second group of ceramics recovered from Emanuel Point is lead-glazed coarse earthenware. Sherds of this group include two diagnostic types, Melado and El Morro. Date ranges of usage for these two types have been established in archaeological contexts at St. Augustine and Santa Elena as well as other colonial sites within the Caribbean area.[56] Melado ware (1490–1550), a lead-glazed pottery with a white underslip, is distinctively honey colored and is associated with Spanish colonial sites from the early to mid-sixteenth century. Seven Melado sherds are represented in the collection; a handle fragment with an apple-green glaze variant compares favorably with a similar sherd in the Lister type collection at the Florida Museum of Natural History. El Morro ware (1550–1770) is characterized by a thick, shiny green or rust colored glaze and has some temper inclusions in the ceramic paste.[57] Thirteen sherds of this type are represented in the collection.

Tin Enamelwares

The third group of ceramics found at Emanuel Point consists of tin-glazed enamelware, which was introduced during the fifteenth century in Italy and which became vastly popular throughout Europe. Referred to as maiolica (Italian) or majolica (Iberian), faience (French), and delft (Dutch and British), the original Italian form had a thick white tin slip, was hand painted (usually with a floral or geometric design), and was overglazed with a clear glossy finish (*coperta*), then fired.

Several varieties of majolica are represented in the collection, nearly all of which were heavily stained dark gray or black in color. This discoloration results from a chemical infusion of sulfur and iron compounds

What They Left Behind: The Artifact Assemblage · 155

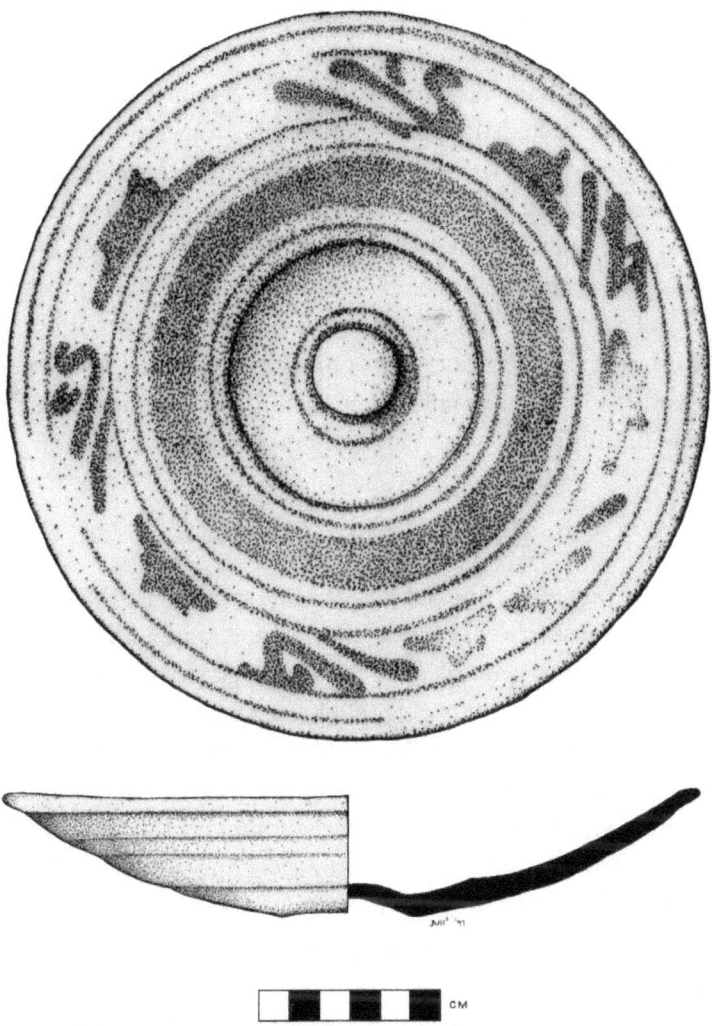

Figure 5.18. This majolica plate was found intact beneath the ship's anchor. Drawing by James Hunter III. Courtesy of the Florida Department of State, Division of Historical Resources.

in the reduced oxygen environment found in portions of the site. Their natural colors are easily restored by a short immersion in a solution of 3 percent hydrogen peroxide. Several examples of Columbia Plain *platos* (plates) were recovered. Although each saucer-like plate is slightly different in size and shape, each has a raised dimple in the center and a raised ring circling the interior surface roughly midway between the center of the plate and rim. Yayal Blue on White majolica is present in the *plato*, *escudilla* (bowl), and *bacín* (utility basin or chamber pot) forms. Each features the characteristic cobalt blue banding. Other *escudillas* are present in the Columbia Plain variety, and all examples have foot rings.

Another example is of a style known as Sevilla Blue on White or Blue on Blue, with a light gray background color, a dark blue sprig and flower design, and dating from between 1492 and 1600.[58] Quite surprisingly, the only whole, intact ceramic vessel recovered from the site is a majolica plate discovered under the crown of the ship's anchor. The pattern of the design and its manganese color are similar to the ceramic type known as Isabela Polychrome, but only one color is present.

Aztec Ware

A unique group of ceramics collected close together in the stern of the ship consists of six sherds of Post Classic Aztec wares. The type is called *negro grafitto sobre rojo Pulido* and is characterized by a buff paste with a highly burnished red-to-orange slipped exterior, frequently seen with graphite-based paint applied in geometric patterns.[59] The type also is called Aztec IV to mark its sequence in the progression of Mesoamerican pottery traditions.[60] The first sherd found on the shipwreck has a geometric design consisting of black zigzag lines and dots. This motif occurs in various Aztec art forms, but to date no pottery parallels have been found to suggest the size, shape, or function of the container represented by this sherd.

Two curious molded effigy sherds—one with a downward grimacing mouth filled with outlined teeth and surrounding facial decoration the other with a molded left eye and cheek with facial decorations—also appear to be of the Aztec IV tradition. Photographs of the sherds were sent to Pilar Luna Erreguerena of the National Institute of Anthropology and History in Mexico City, who showed them to her colleague, John Joseph Temple. According to Temple, the molded facial forms, burnished on one side with red-to-orange color and unburnished (black) on the interior, were described by Barlow in relation to a codex made by sixteenth-century Indian potters from Cuauhtitlán in the Central Valley

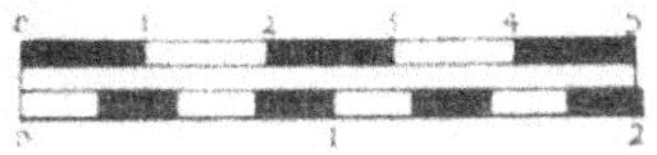

Figure 5.19. These remarkable ceramic sherds, depicting a human eye with cheekbone in relief and a grimacing mouth, were made by Aztec potters. Courtesy of the Florida Department of State, Division of Historical Resources.

of Mexico.[61] Among their wares, the potters fabricated examples that showed the faces of Africans and Spaniards. Barlow found the codex in the Aubin-Goupil collection of the Bibliothèque Nationale in Paris. His interpretation was that the codex represented a legal plea for reimbursement by four potters (who were Chicimecan refugees) in 1564 to the resident Spanish judge because their wares had not been paid for by the local *alcalde* (mayor), who had ordered them. On the codex, the potters illustrated in color the forms and numbers of ceramics in

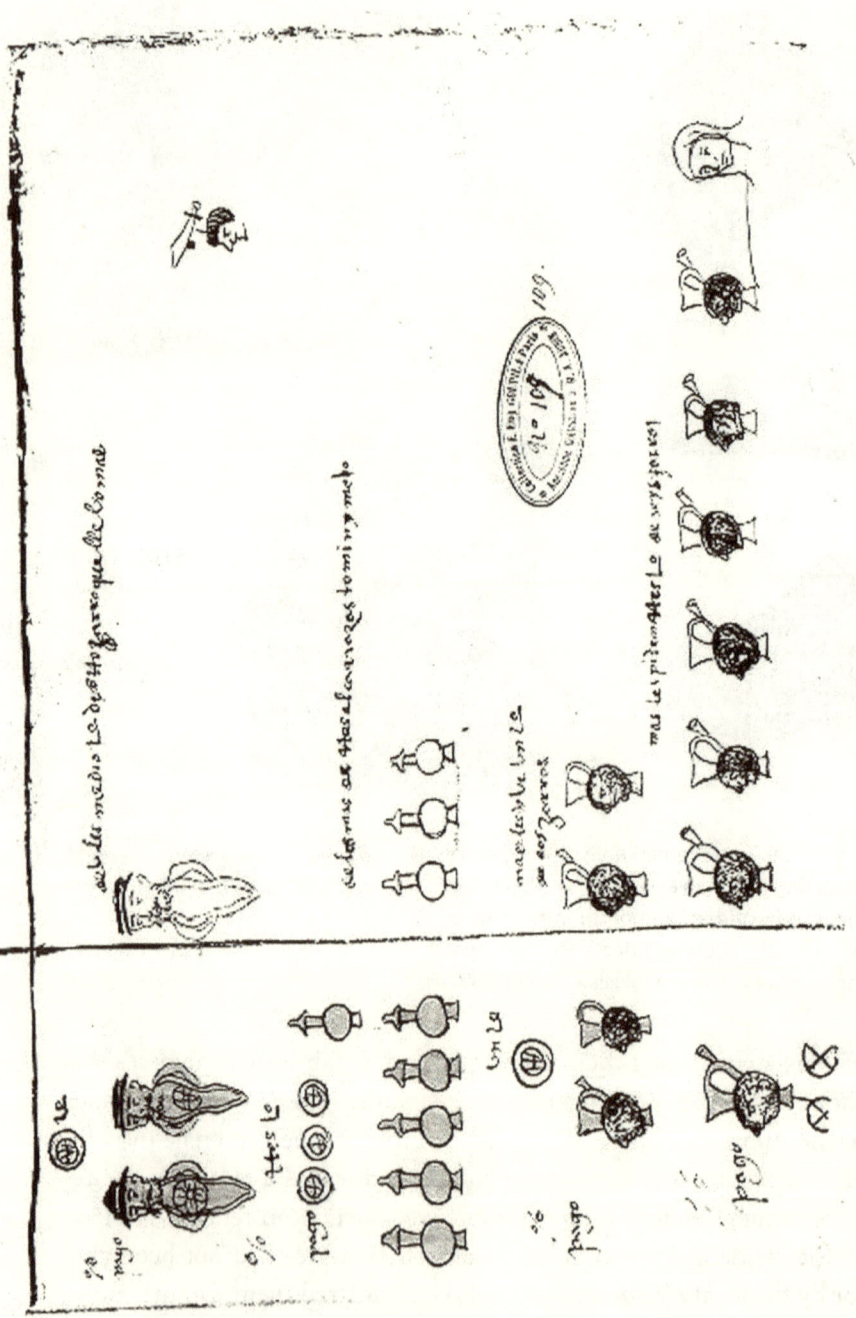

Figure 5.20. This 1564 Aztec codex from the Central Valley of Mexico depicts pottery in the shape of human heads. From *El Códice de los Alfareros de Cuauhtitlán*. Courtesy of Bibliothèque Nationale, Paris.

question, along with their value in *pesos* and *tomines*, and completed the document with iconographic portraits of themselves as signatures. Apparently the Cuauhtitlán potters stopped making pottery after a massive epidemic of *cocoliztli* (plague) occurred in 1576. This information was relayed to historian John de Bry, who happened to be working in the Bibliothèque Nationale. De Bry found the codex and was able to copy portions containing illustrations of pottery decorated in the shapes of human heads.

Three additional Aztec pottery fragments were subsequently found in excavations at the stern. One is a small fragment that joins the earlier sherd with a grimacing mouth. Whether these examples of colonial native Aztec wares are from Cuauhtitlán or whether they represent the faces of Africans, as shown on the codex, is not certain. Their enigmatic discovery in the stern of the vessel suggests that the ceramics were not cargo but belonged to a high-ranking occupant of the ship. According to one Aztec ceramic specialist, wares of this type were often used for ceremonial purposes, as in the consumption of pulque, a fermented Mexican beverage.[62]

Other Ceramics

A single sherd of Brown Cologne Stoneware was present on the Emanuel Point Ship. This fragment comes from a Beardman jug and exhibits a floral pattern situated between two raised bands and part of a medallion with the profile of a helmeted soldier. Similar examples of these non-Spanish, salt-glazed sherds were recovered from the Padre Island wrecks, Western Ledge Reef Wreck, and in sixteenth-century context at St. Augustine.[63]

Finally, a single ceramic fragment of unknown type was recovered during early testing of the ballast mound. Of thick, soft paste, this poorly tempered piece at first was thought to be a portion of a lug handle for a large earthenware storage jar. Alternately, it could represent a portion of one of the legs of a cooking brazier. Its provenience among the ballast raises the possibility that it may have been introduced as debris, perhaps along with a load of ballast stones, sometime during the sailing career of the Emanuel Point Ship.

Discussion

Analysis of the Emanuel Point Ship ceramic assemblage and its comparison to collections from other dated archaeological sites indicate that the shipwreck occurred between 1550 and 1580, thus corresponding to the time of the Luna expedition. However, ceramics can be used for other purposes than to establish a chronology for the site. In the case of the Emanuel Point ceramics, an interesting result of attempts to mend olive jar sherds has demonstrated the potential of shedding light on the ship's wrecking process. A trend seemed to occur with one particular vessel as olive jar sherds from various proveniences were cross-mended. A partial rim and shoulder were recovered from the outer port footwale, upper body sherds were found inboard, and middle body sherds came from above the keel. Tracking the positions of the cross mends suggests that the jar fell toward the port and broke, depositing sherds in a linear pattern.[64] Table 5 in the appendix shows a summary of ceramics recovered from the Emanuel Point Ship.

Organic Debris

Below midships ballast and between frames in the stern, the ship's bilge sediments preserved a surprising array of organic debris that had accumulated throughout the vessel's sailing career. Materials recovered in these deposits include wooden packing materials (dunnage), rope and cordage, animal remains, and botanical specimens such as leaves, nuts, and seeds.

Examples of each of these materials are discussed in following sections. In addition to botanical specimens, other organic artifacts such as wooden objects and the remains of leather shoes also were recovered.

Cork

We found two cork stoppers in association with several olive jar sherds. The most complete cork is tapered to fit the mouth of a jar; it has a resinous deposit adhering to its upper surface with a color and odor very similar to pine pitch. Additionally, two smaller corks were recovered.

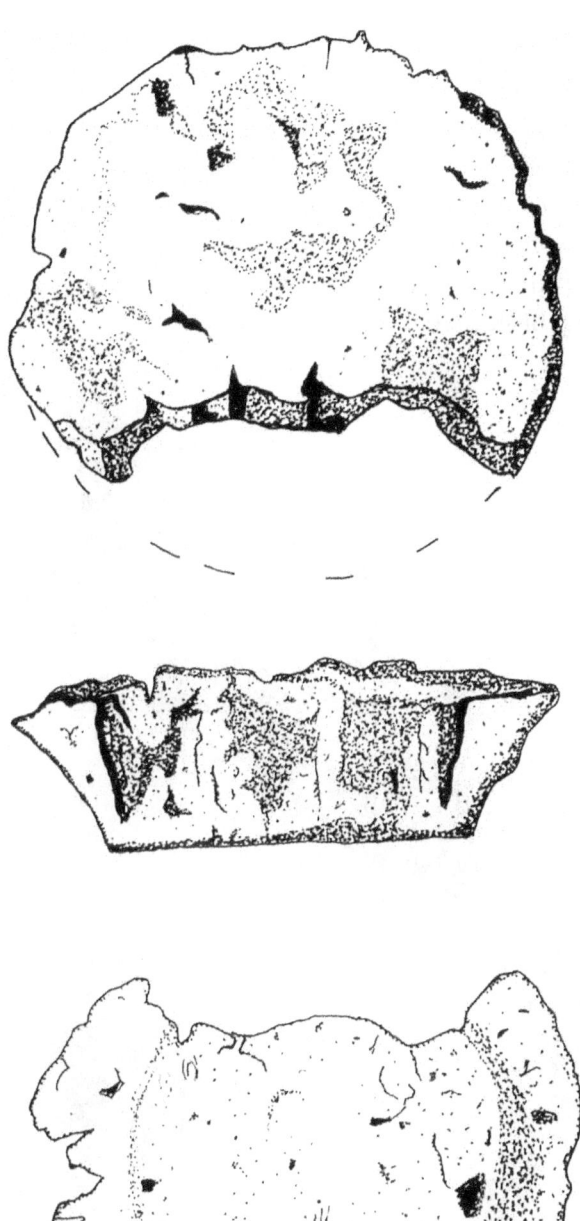

Figure 5.21. Remarkably preserved in the waters of Pensacola Bay, this cork is undoubtedly a stopper for an olive jar. Drawing by James Hunter III. Courtesy of the Florida Department of State, Division of Historical Resources.

Wooden Implements

A small, tapered wooden tool handle with a square hole and associated iron concretion was found on top of the port bilge boards at the mainmast step. The handle is circular in cross section and tapers at each end. A hole at one end once held the iron tool, probably a small auger or shipwright's gimlet, which may have been discarded in the bilge, perhaps at the time of the ship's construction.

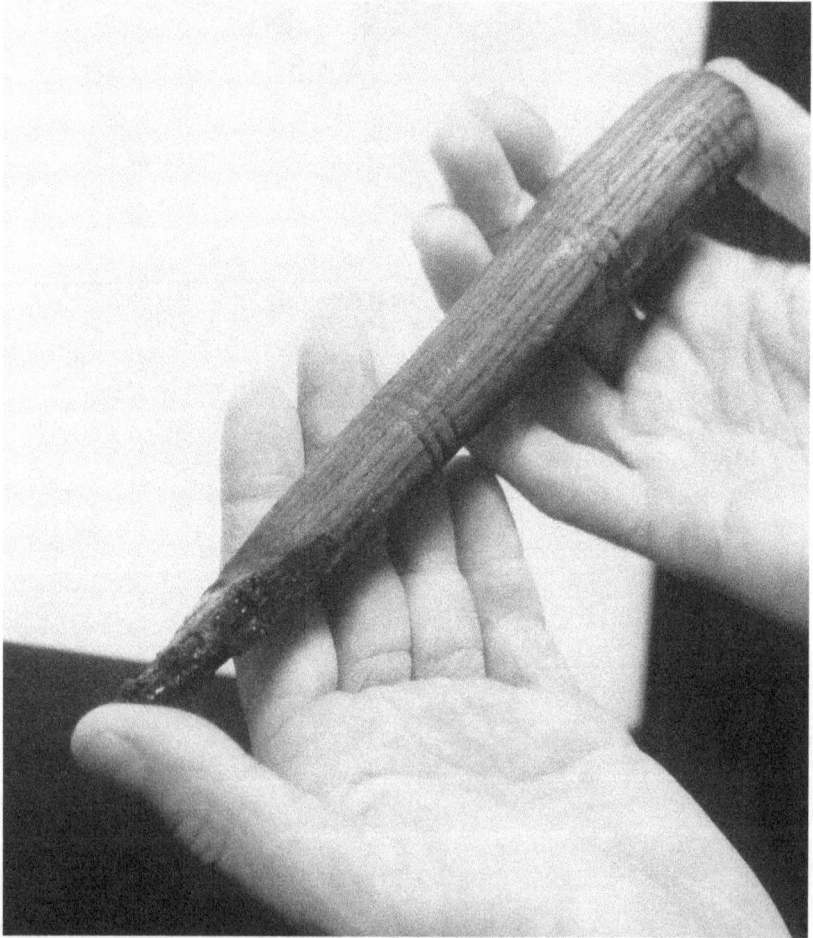

Figure 5.22. A wooden tool handle, probably for an awl or gimlet, was found in the ship's bilge. Courtesy of the Florida Department of State, Division of Historical Resources.

A smaller piece of worked wood also may have been associated with the ship's construction. The object is a carved stick, circular in cross section and with a notched end that may have been an attachment point for a string or other implement. Speculation as to this artifact's function includes as a line level or plumb bob handle; however, it could have been the product of idle whittling. We also found three wooden stoppers or plugs. One of these is similar to a wooden plug recovered from the English Tudor warship *Mary Rose*, sunk in 1545, that had been used to stopper a leather flask.[65] The other plug-like objects may have served as bottle or flask stoppers, or a type of closure peg for a cabinet or storage box, or possibly as cannon touch hole stoppers.

A fourth wooden artifact is a softwood peg that resembles a "tinker toy" or a tuning knob for a musical instrument. The lower end of the piece is a small dowel, terminating into a rectangular "nut." At the top of the nut-like portion a mortise has been carved and a small remnant of a tenon has been inserted. The function of this artifact is unknown.

Ship Silhouette Carving

Deep in the bilge among scraps of wood and other carpenters' debris just abaft the port pump sump, a curious and unique object was discovered: the small carved silhouette of a ship. Stained dark from the sediments in which it was buried, the miniature carving, fashioned from fir, bears the classic features of a typical sixteenth-century Spanish galleon—a heavy beakhead in the bow, a pronounced forecastle, high freeboard, and towering sterncastle and gallery. The silhouette had been faithfully reproduced by someone who was quite familiar with the contemporary hallmarks of naval architecture.

The carving's discovery beneath ballast and bilge sediments suggests that it probably was deposited in the ship at the time of its construction, perhaps inadvertently left behind by an apprentice shipwright as he resumed his work. The only other known image of a Spanish galleon found in the New World is a graffiti-like rendering on a plank discovered on the Basque vessel *San Juan*, which sank in Red Bay, Labrador, in 1565.[66]

Figure 5.23. Galleon model dated 1540 in the Museo Naval in Madrid (*top*) and the Emanuel Point silhouette carving shown at same size (*bottom*). Courtesy of the Florida Department of State, Division of Historical Resources.

Leather

We recovered eight fragments of leather during excavation of the mainmast step. The three largest pieces are the remains of shoes; each piece exhibits stitching holes along its outer edge, and many of the holes retain traces of the original thread that secured parts of the shoe.[67] According to a study by David Breetzke, the leather fragments are cow hide that probably was tannin treated.[68]

Shoes represented by these three fragments were either of turnshoe or turn-welt construction. The former is one of the oldest methods of shoemaking. The shoe is made wrong side out; after stitching, the shoe is turned right side out and reshaped for finishing. Turn-welt construction was a transitional point between the turnshoe and the welted shoe. The turnshoe is made with an extra wide rand (strip of leather) sewn in the seam, which becomes a welt to which a first sole, or later repair sole, can be stitched.

One shoe fragment is the sole of a small shoe or mule, with four stitches per centimeter. The number of stitches per centimeter can indicate the quality of craftsmanship and the price of the shoemaker's product.[69] Lacking a heel, the sole is comparable in size to a modern woman's 5½ to 6½ shoe (U.S. sizing). According to June Swann, a consultant on the history of shoes and shoemaking, the sole may have been part of a woman's or girl's platform shoe known as a *chapin*, of typical Spanish style.[70]

Another fragment is part of a shoe sole broken across the tread (the area of greatest wear). At the other end, the sole has been cut just in front of the seat (rear end of the sole where the heel rests). The straight cut suggests a repair to the shoe. Two of the outer edges of the sole seam are turned over, with what appears to be a fragment of the rand surviving. The sole has three to four stitches per centimeter.

The third fragment is from a larger shoe or boot, either part of a vamp (front upper section) that originally was square with rounded corners, or part of a heel. Wear marks suggest that it was worn on the left foot. This fragment has four to five stitches per centimeter.

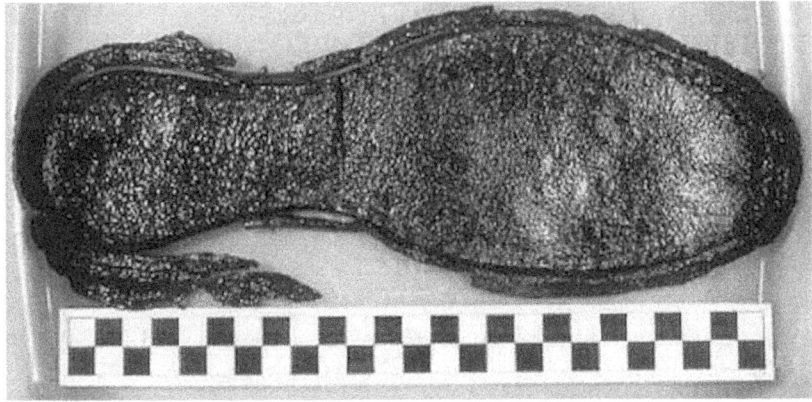

Figure 5.24. This leather sole of a small shoe, possibly a woman's platform shoe called a *chapin*, is typical of Spanish-style footwear popular in the 1540s. Courtesy of the Florida Department of State, Division of Historical Resources.

Figure 5.25. Part of a shoe sole broken across the tread. This straight cut may indicate a repair. Courtesy of the Florida Department of State, Division of Historical Resources.

Prior to the discovery of these shoe fragments, the earliest recorded European footwear found in North America was represented by the shoe remains recovered from the Basque ship *San Juan*, excavated in Red Bay, Labrador.[71]

The remaining leather fragments consist of small pieces of various thickness and texture. One fragment appears to be felt, and another, recovered from the port pump well, may be a remnant of the sump pump's flapper valve.[72]

Vertebrate Faunal Remains

When test excavations began on the Emanuel Point Ship in 1992 we encountered faunal remains in all units. All samples were collected directly from the excavation units or from a quarter-inch screen situated at the outflow of a water-induction dredge. Testing with floatation procedures or smaller mesh-screen sorting of bilge sediments provided no substantial increase in recovery over the quarter-inch screen. Preservation of faunal materials generally was very good, perhaps because of effluents (silts and tannin) from a nearby bayou and the general compactness of the overlying sand, ballast pile, and built-up mound of oyster shells. Materials were recovered from within and without the surviving ship structure.

All obvious rodent materials were sent to Philip L. Armitage for identification and analysis. Non-rodent faunal specimens were examined by Barry W. Baker and Anna Lee Presley, physical anthropology department, Texas A&M University. Identification of the remains was aided by that department's Zooarchaeological Research Collection and by Armitage's personal collection of rat skeletons. One fish vertebra also was identified in materials sent for botanical identification.[73] Analysis of the vertebrate material was accomplished using standard zooarchaeological procedures. Specimens were identified as precisely as possible based on structural features, animal biogeography, and the temporal setting of the site.[74] Information such as sex, age, and taphonomic processes (burning, cut marks, rodent gnawing, and breakage) was noted for all materials along with limited morphometric data.[75]

A total of 339 complete or fragmented bones and teeth were identified from this phase of excavation. Faunal specimens from the ship's bilge appear to represent deposits of discarded bones from shipboard provisions as well as the remains of organisms that died in or near the ship. These include the bones of domestic pig, cow, even-toed ungulates (cloven-hoofed mammals, e.g., sheep and goat), and chicken, which undoubtedly were used as food aboard the ship. Fragments of various fish are present in the faunal assemblage and are believed to be intrusive, having been deposited after the ship ran aground. Similarly, a beak fragment from a shore bird (sandpiper family) may have found its own way aboard the ship. The largest collection of faunal remains is that of stowaway rats, which both bred and died in the ship during its career at sea.

Condition of the Samples

Vertebrate samples from the Emanuel Point Ship allow several observations. In general, they are well preserved with little degradation apart from a few specimens that exhibit abrasion.[76] Slight exfoliation was expected and is typical of artifacts that require extensive soaking then dehydration to remove water and salts. Several specimens were stained brown, presumably from marine sediments, and in a few cases required cleaning with a 3 percent solution of hydrogen peroxide. Other specimens exhibited a light bluish-gray discoloration sometimes associated with burning.[77] Only one specimen clearly was identified as burned because of its charred black color.

Six specimens exhibited cut marks; of these, five were from mammals. One specimen, a pig bone, was completely sawed through. The other specimens appear to have been cut with a metal knife. Seven specimens exhibited rodent gnawing.

Sixty-eight of the bones show some type of breakage, and most of the broken elements exhibit angular fractures, which occur after the bone has dried. Sixteen specimens have spiral fractures, which suggests that they were broken while they had a relatively high degree of collagen; in other words, they were still fresh.

Figure 5.26. Animal bones, some with butcher marks, indicate food sources available on the ship. Courtesy of the Florida Department of State, Division of Historical Resources.

Although the non-rodent sample size is small (135), a few subsistence observations can be made. Bones from animals apparently serving as food sources include domestic chicken (8), cow (8), and domestic pig (6). One chicken bone shows a transverse cut mark on its shaft. Two additional large bird elements also may represent chicken, and the majority of the mammal bones very likely are cow.[78] In fact, the presence of vertebrae and vertebral ends of left ribs of a subadult cow may represent a rib cut from a left side of beef. None of these specimens are sawed, though many show green bone fractures that may have resulted from butchering. Pig bones exhibit cut marks and spiral fractures characteristic of food remains. Many of the other specimens probably also are food items, but a medium-sized mammal (dog-sized) rib remains difficult to interpret. A subadult goat-sized lower limb also is present in the sample.

In contrast, none of the fish elements exhibit cut marks, spiral fractures, or rodent gnawing. Most of these remains show very little degradation, and most appear very recent, suggesting that they are intrusive.

Rats and Mice

A total of 206 bone specimens were recognized as black rat, and two small bones were identified as belonging to the common house mouse. Analysis of the rat bones revealed population size and makeup, evidence of cannibalism, and abnormal skeletal pathology. As with the other faunal material, preservation of the rodent material is very good, though some of the more fragile specimens (skull and vertebrae) suffered some damage in antiquity. Identification of rodent specimens was undertaken using Armitage's modern comparative collections of rat skeletons and those of the Natural History Museum in London and Booth Museum of Natural History in Brighton, England.[79]

Based on the stages of fusion seen in the rat bone specimens, a range of age classes was recognized: newborn, very young, young, young/subadult, subadult/adult, and indeterminate. From the totals of unpaired and paired skeletal elements, a count of twenty-one was calculated as the minimum number of individuals.[80]

Analysis of lower and upper jaw bones revealed ancient evidence of moderate to severe dental abscesses and infections in the rat population.

Figure 5.27. Drawing of a rat skeleton showing outlines of the recovered bones. Drawing by James Hunter III. Courtesy of the Florida Department of State, Division of Historical Resources.

In several specimens the teeth had fallen out partially or entirely due to the loosening of their roots from swelling of the teeth sockets. During the examination of the rodent remains, it was noticed that six limb bones, all from very young rats, are noticeably stunted and have a distinctive, abnormal "flaring" of the end of the shaft.[81] These pathological changes typically are associated with rickets disease, caused by a lack of vitamin D. One black rat tibia exhibited numerous shallow grooves over its surface; these depressions were made by rodent incisor teeth, indicating that the specimen had been gnawed by another rat or rats. Similar markings were found on the some of the non-rodent faunal material.

Two left tibiae of the European house mouse were found among the other faunal material.[82] Armitage considered the presence of two or more mice aboard the ship as unexpected because of the large black rat population. Mice would have been preyed upon by rats, so rat infestation on ships kept mouse numbers down. However, situations in which rats can live usually provide conditions for a large population of mice.[83] In this case, perhaps we should call it the European ship mouse.

Discussion

As contemporary sources reveal, rats were commonplace on European sailing ships voyaging to the New World in the sixteenth and later centuries. In modest numbers these vermin were merely a nuisance to mariners; their greatest damage resulted when they gnawed into casks of foodstuffs and contaminated the contents with urine and feces. However, under exceptional circumstances, their depredations of the ship's provisions represented a very real danger to the well-being and even survival of the crew and passengers.[84] A rat plague besieged the returning Spanish Indies fleet of 1622, and on one vessel alone several thousand rats were caught and killed in port and during the voyage.[85]

All rat specimens from the Emanuel Point Ship have been identified as black rat. Several factors make an accurate estimate of the population size impossible. Bone remains on board account for a minimum of twenty-one individuals, probably far fewer than the total population prior to the vessel's sinking. No doubt many of the rodents tried to flee the sinking, some perhaps drowning at the site. However, the remains found on board should not be assumed to have perished as the ship went down.

Previous studies have shown that ships typically supported a population of animals that spent their entire life aboard, from birth to death, which means that some remains could have resulted from natural mortality preceding the ship's demise. Others may simply have been unlucky passengers taken aboard with provisions. However, analysis does reveal that there must have been a well-established core population of rodents on the ship, evidenced by the presence of very young, subadult, and mature individuals and both males and females. Confinement in the dark recesses of the ship's hull, away from sunlight and with a restricted diet that lacked certain minerals and vitamins essential for normal metabolism and growth, clearly took its toll on some of the rats, especially the immature individuals. This is evidenced by limb bones afflicted by rickets and poor dental health of some of the older individuals.[86] Table 6 in the appendix presents a summary of Emanuel Point identified faunal specimens.

Invertebrate Remains

Insects

We uncovered a number of chitinous fragments resembling insect wings in deposits associated with olive pits and other organic materials in the ballast above the buttresses. Samples were sent to the entomology department at Texas A&M University for identification. Horace Burke identified the most abundant insect parts as belonging to cockroaches. The remainder of the sample consisted of wing covers from a species known as the hide beetle.

To identify the specific species of cockroach, a second examination of the cockroach fragments was made at the U.S. Department of Agriculture research station in Gainesville, Florida. Analysts at that laboratory identified the wings, thoracic segments, and egg cases of the American cockroach.

In 1573 Eugenio de Salazar wrote about his voyage from Spain to Santo Domingo. In this interesting narrative, he jokingly refers to the numerous cockroaches aboard his ship as "game birds," which he called *curianas*.[87] Cockroaches are probably the world's most persistent stowaways. Aboard a ship the active, fast-running insects fed on any number of food sources while living in the darkened areas of the vessel and hiding in the many cracks and crevices. Fragments of sixteen cockroaches and five egg cases were found in five of the encrusted artifact conglomerates raised from the site of *San Estéban*, wrecked off Padre Island in 1554.[88] Articulated wings and bodies, wings, and empty oothecae (egg cases) also were found preserved between the stone cobbles of the ballast and hidden in the rope lashings of a gun carriage. Two species were present—the Oriental and the American cockroach. A single American cockroach egg case was recovered from the Spanish vessel *San Antonio* that sank off Bermuda in 1621.[89]

Despite its misleading name, the American cockroach is not endemic to the Americas. The species is believed to have originated in tropical Africa and was transported to South America, the West Indies, and the southern United States on slave ships sailing from the west coast of Africa.[90] However, evidence from the Emanuel Point Ship and other

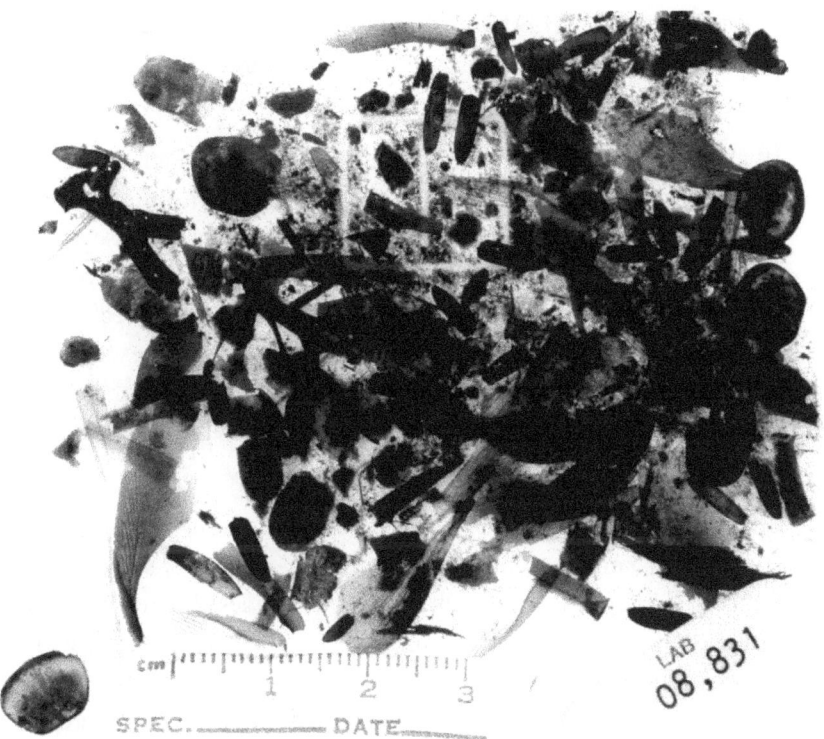

Figure 5.28. The remains of stowaways—cockroaches and hide beetles—were among the animal specimens found in the ship's bilge. Courtesy of the Florida Department of State, Division of Historical Resources.

Spanish shipwrecks demonstrates that the American cockroach had reached the Americas before the slave trade reached large proportions.

Unlike the cockroach, the hide beetle has a cosmopolitan distribution. Hide beetles produce larvae that are very active and strongly negative phototrophic, preferring the dark recesses of the ship. Full-grown beetles bore a pupal chamber into any almost compact substance. Larvae bore into hard and soft woods and have been known to damage cork, books, tobacco, tea, linen, cotton, woolens, salt, and even lead.[91] The beetle's indiscriminate boring into materials that it does not use for food has been noted frequently. Perhaps the earliest shipboard reference to this activity was associated with the last voyage of English circumnavigator

Thomas Cavendish. In 1593 one of Cavendish's ships, *Desire*, pressed for a food source, was obliged to carry some 14,000 improperly dried penguins aboard.[92] A member of the crew, John Jane, wrote . . .

> [that] after we came neere unto the sun, our dried Penguins began to corrupt, and there bred in them a most lothsome & ugly worme of an inch long. This worme did so mightily increase, and devoure our victuals, that there was in reason no hope how we should avoide famine, but be devoured of these wicked creatures: there was nothing that they did not devour, only yron excepted: our clothes, boots, shoes, hats, shirts, stockings: and for the ship they did so eat the timbers, as that we greatly feared they would undo us, by gnawing through the ships side.[93]

Both larvae and adult hide beetles feed on a variety of substances with a high protein content, including bones, carcasses, skins, meats, and cheese.[94] The presence of numerous hide beetles aboard the Emanuel Point Ship suggests that they may have been brought aboard with a cargo, possibly leather hides.

Additional insect identifications were made by UWF graduate student Jacob Shidner. His microscopic examination of bilge sediments revealed the presence of thirty-one specimens of weevil, with the possibility of at least three species.[95] They could have fed on any of the grains carried on the ship. Shidner identified the presence of a similar pest of stored grains, darkling beetle, based on its recovered prothorax.

Mollusks

We collected samples of shells during our excavations; although many of the species represented have large ranges, all of them also are native to Pensacola Bay. The bay is home to 184 native mollusk species, including ninety-six from the class Gastropoda and eighty from the class Bivalvia.[96] All of the samples in the collection come from these two classes.

By far the most common bivalve in the collection is the ubiquitous oyster. At least three species are present, including the common oyster, crested oyster, and an unidentified species, possibly coon oyster. Other bivalves include southern quahog, common cockle, disk shell, elegant disk shell, mottled chione, cross-barred chione, ponderous ark, and Vanhyning's heart cockle.[97]

Gastropods range in size from a large lightning whelk to a tiny olive nerite. Between these two extremes are the Florida rock shell, Hay's rock shell, Florida cerith, Florida auger, common eastern nassa or mottled dog whelk, and a species of *Tagelus*. All samples varied from the average to the smallest of sizes within their respective species.

Other Invertebrates

In addition to shells and insect remains, several other types of invertebrate remains were found within, or just outside, the hull remains. Eighteen pieces of coral were recovered from the dredge screen. Whitish-tan in color, the coral appears to be of one type (oculina, ivory bush or tree coral). Coral is not found growing on the site today. These remains most likely represent remnants from earlier growths, when the bay was capable of supporting coral, or they may represent fragments of coral that found their way into the ship's ballast. Wooden timbers along the outside of the hull were often found covered with numerous barnacles. Considering that these timbers often were buried under nearly a meter of sediments, the barnacles probably represent accumulations while the ship was still in service. Very minute barnacle growths also were found on the lead fragments. Their small size suggests that their growth was arrested by the effects of lead poisoning. Other small invertebrate remains include bivalve hinge parts and limpet exoskeletons that occasionally were found during dredging in most of the excavation units. Three shark teeth also were recovered.

Botanical Remains

An analysis of the botanical remains was conducted by Lee Newsom at the Center for Archaeological Investigations, Southern Illinois University at Carbondale. These remains are quite diverse and include taxa from both the Eastern and Western hemispheres as well as tropical and temperate species. Table 7 in the appendix lists the specimens and their identifications.

Plant materials from the shipwreck generally fall into six categories: ship timbers, dunnage, rope or cordage, food remains, other useful plant materials, and miscellaneous (possibly intrusive) materials from the coastal environment.

Timber Identifications

With the exception of Frame 6, which is an unidentified hardwood, all ship timbers examined to date are exclusively oak. According to Newsom, the cellular structure of the samples is consistent with the white oak anatomical group. White-type oaks are found on both sides of the Atlantic and often are difficult, if not impossible, to distinguish.[98] The use of white oak in ship construction, including sixteenth-century practices, has been well documented.

Dunnage

Interspersed in the ship's ballast we found examples of rough-hewn wood that appear to represent some of the dunnage that was used to pack and cushion cargo in the ship's lower hold atop the ballast stones. The small wooden branches occur in various lengths, and many retain a golden-colored bark. Two species of wood were identified among samples sent for identification—persimmon and hornbeam.[99]

The persimmon-type dunnage exhibits a definite ring-porous structure indicative of a temperate species. Relying on geographic range and history of cultivation, Newsom believes there are four possible candidates for the actual species match: common persimmon, Texas persimmon, Chinese persimmon, and date-plum. The latter two originated in Asia, but it is not known how long these particular species were known or cultivated by Europeans. Persimmon seeds from the wreck have dimensions that fit the range for common persimmon but are much too large for Texas persimmon. Therefore the presence of common persimmon seeds is a possible indication that the wood is from the same species.[100] If in fact this vessel was supplied with common persimmon dunnage, it probably was provisioned (or reprovisioned) in the New World prior to its voyage to Florida.

The second dunnage type, hornbeam, compares well with the ironwood or blue beech, a tree found in bottomlands, swamps, and river margins of eastern North America, including the Florida panhandle. A second possibility is European hornbeam; however, this species varies slightly from the archaeological specimens.

Rope or Cordage

Eight rope fragments were found in test pits near the bow and midships. Examination with a light microscope revealed two distinct fiber types: hemp and grass. The larger rope fragments are composed of hemp fibers worked into several threads that are right-hand laid and form three yarns. By laying these yarns left-handed, ropes were fashioned. Two other lengths of rope are composed of three interwoven strands of relatively stiff, linear fibers that are from a grass, consisting of stems and leaves.

The discovery of hemp rope fragments in the shipwreck was not unexpected; the European manufacture of hemp rope is well documented. Spanish shipyards used hemp (*cáñamo*) that was imported from France, Flanders, and sometimes Germany; however, the Iberian region of Navarre also supplied hemp for the rigging of ships.[101] The excellent preservation of the rope fragments is due in part to the presence of iron corrosion products that allowed individual fibers of the rope to remain in place. Sometimes Spanish shipyards used the grass fiber *esparto* instead of hemp, therefore discovery of a second type of cordage fashioned from grass also is not unexpected.[102]

Food Remains

The majority of botanical remains from the shipwreck consist of seeds and nuts from both tropical and temperate trees. Edible soft fruits from three American species and three European domesticates have been identified. The American taxa are common persimmon, as mentioned, sapote or *zapote*, and tentatively identified papaya. Each species has a long history of use by different Native American peoples. Similarly, sapote and papaya often were grown in neotropical home gardens for their large, edible fruits and medicinal uses. Each is found throughout the circum-Caribbean region.[103]

European fruit trees represented in the ship remains include olive, plum/prune, and cherry. More than four hundred olive pits were recovered from the wreck. Second in frequency is persimmon with twelve seeds, followed by cherry (eight seeds) and papaya (three stems). The rest of the soft fruit types—plum and sapote—are represented by single seed specimens.

Several edible nut species appear in the Emanuel Point specimens. European almond is present (four shell fragments), as is hazelnut (thirteen shell fragments). Two American nut-producing specimens are identified—hickory (four shell fragments) and oak (one acorn half, one aborted acorn). Finally, a single fragment of coconut shell was recovered. Coconut is today considered pantropical, but we do not know whether it occurred in the Atlantic Ocean and Caribbean prior to European arrival on the American continents.

Figure 5.29. This seed, identified as sapote (*zapote*), comes from a large tropical fruit found throughout the Caribbean. Courtesy of the Florida Department of State, Division of Historical Resources.

Figure 5.30. The recovery of more than four hundred olive pits demonstrates the importance of olives and olive oil to the traditional Spanish cuisine. Courtesy of the Florida Department of State, Division of Historical Resources.

UWF graduate student Colleen Lawrence examined sediment samples from the excavations and identified an unknown number of seeds from the mustard family. Tentative identifications are black mustard, brown mustard, and white mustard, all of Old World origin and possibly used as seasonings. Lawrence's use of a fine-screening technique enabled their presence aboard ship to be revealed.[104]

Other Useful Plant Materials

Two fragments of bottle gourd rind were recovered. According to Newsom, the bottle gourd is native to Africa but is known from archaeological contexts on the American continents, including Florida, as early as 7,000 years before present.[105] She suggests that the hard-shelled fruits would have been useful aboard the ship as containers or that the seeds of some varieties could have been eaten or processed into seed oil.

During excavations we recovered a mass of resinous material from the dredge screen. This substance, which since has become a loose, amorphous mass, is deep reddish in color and somewhat tacky. Newsom indicated that the resinous material is from a tree—not a coniferous species such as pine, but of a type exclusive to hardwoods, such as red mangrove. Considering the other botanicals found onboard, we suspect that the substance derives from a tropical American species and could represent glue or gum-resin sealing material in balled-up form.[106]

Alternatively, it may have been used as a medicinal and/or incense resin. For example, *Lignum vitae* ("wood of life"), a native circum-Caribbean tree, became an article of the Spanish trade by 1508.[107] One scholar of Mexican medicine, Schendel, notes that the Spaniards were amazed at Aztec knowledge and employment of medicinal herbs.[108] Evidence of this can be seen in *Santa María de Yciar*'s 1554 register, in which two medicinal substances were being shipped to Spain—*tacamahaca*, a type of gum or resin, and sarsaparilla, which Aztecs used in treating respiratory diseases.[109]

Miscellaneous Plant Remains

Five of the plant identifications probably are intrusive to the site, having washed in from adjacent coastal areas. These remains are few in number, have no value as food items, and occur throughout the Gulf Coastal Plain biogeographic region. Specimens in this group include fragments of bark (pine), seeds from two native trees (southern magnolia and swamp tupelo), probably also the aborted acorn mentioned above, several small twigs, and two leaves (red maple and oak).[110]

Pollen Analysis

To test the feasibility of recovering pollen from the shipwreck, several samples were collected from bilge debris in the pump wells, mast step mortise, and between the floors and buttresses of the ship. Four sediment samples were sent to the Palynology Laboratory at Texas A&M University for pollen processing and a presence/absence analysis. Preservation of the materials ranged from fair to good. A number of grains, and pines in particular, showed evidence of breakdown, collapse, and fragmentation. These effects indicate that pollen grains were subject to some type of mechanical stress, resulting in abrasion and grinding due to the proximity of the shipwreck to the north shore of the bay, wave action, the shallow depth of the site, and periodic high energy storm events.[111] However, each sample contained a large amount of pollen, a variety of taxa, few indeterminate grains, and high concentration values. The fossil pollen recovered in the samples was dominated by pine with lesser contributions of pecan, walnut, maple, oak, ragweed, and sunflower. These pollen samples reflect floral types that are indigenous to the areas bordering Pensacola Bay. Although pollen grains in all of the samples exhibited evidence of mechanical and biological degradation, the presence/absence analysis confirmed that sufficient quantities of identifiable pollen are preserved in the bilge sediments to warrant statistically valid counts.[112]

Discussion

The large number of olive pits found intermixed among the olive jar sherds confirms that olives were being carried aboard the ship in storage vessels. Olive remains have been a common find in Spanish shipwreck and land sites. Several olive pits were recovered from *San Estéban*, the sixteenth-century Western Ledge wreck found off Bermuda, and in sixteenth-century levels at St. Augustine and Santa Elena.[113] Olives, grapes, and products derived from them, olive oil and wine, were important elements of traditional Spanish cuisine. While survival did not depend on these products, Spaniards felt deprived if the items were absent from their daily diet. The presence of nutshells and fruit remains may represent supplements to the official rations carried aboard the vessel. Aside from fruits and vegetables, spices and condiments such as cinnamon, cloves, mustard, parsley, pepper, and saffron were used to enliven the diet. Similar botanical remains were recovered from the Western Ledge wreck: almonds, plum or cherry stones, a coconut hull fragment, European walnut shells, and the base of a pumpkin stem.[114] Food remains found on *San Estéban* included almond shells and hazelnuts.[115]

In summary, archaeobotanical analyses from the shipwreck show diverse examples of plant remains that help to establish the ship's cultural association, its original region of embarkation, and subsequent travels. European plants, such as almond, cherry, hazelnut, olive, and plum/prune are traditional Mediterranean food items. The absence of European wine grape specimens is curious, considering their presence on other early shipwrecks and frequent mention in documentary records, but wine residues or grape seeds may have been missed by our sampling. The presence among field specimens of sapote, papaya, and perhaps the coconut shell and tree resin demonstrates that the ship operated in the American tropics. Examples of native plants common to the temperate northern Gulf of Mexico or in the direct vicinity of Pensacola include common persimmon, hickory nuts, and acorns; the latter two could have served as fodder for pigs and other captive animals. Bottle gourd may have come from anywhere in the Caribbean or from Africa.

Arms and Armament

We found no artillery pieces or firearms at the wreck site. However, recovery of a variety of balls, or shot, provides clues to the types of ordnance that most likely were carried aboard the Emanuel Point Ship. Four types of shot are represented in the collection: stone, composite lead/iron, lead, and iron.

Stone

Eleven stone cannon balls, or *bolaños*, were discovered at the stern of the ship. The balls appear to have been fashioned by hand from limestone, probably with the aid of a template to guide the process of chipping the surface of the stone to a sphere of uniform size. Nine of the balls appear to have been manufactured from the same type of stone, of similar texture, color, and weight. One ball is of a much coarser stone of lighter weight, while another of similar weight and texture has a much darker color. Although several of the balls exhibit flat areas, none being truly spherical, the similarity in diameter of all the balls suggests that they may have been intended for the same weapon.[116]

Stone shot was fired from various large guns called *pedreros* (stone-throwers) or *bombardas* (lombards) and from some of smaller caliber. They required less powder than other heavier ammunition to achieve their target; upon impact, the limestone balls tended to shatter into sharp projectiles that helped to destroy rigging and injure personnel. Two large *pedreros* were raised from the Manila galleon *San Diego*, which sank off the Philippines in 1600. Both are heavy, muzzle-loading, cast-bronze cannons with four lifting rings.[117] They fired stone balls of much larger caliber than those found on the Emanuel Point Ship. Elsewhere stone

Figure 5.31. These hand-chiseled limestone cannon balls were deadly weapons because they tended to shatter into sharp projectiles on impact. Courtesy of the Florida Department of State, Division of Historical Resources.

shot varying greatly in diameter was found in association with wrought-iron lombard-type guns on the Villefranche wreck in France.[118] The smaller balls probably were ammunition for a bow-chaser, since they were found in the forward part of the ship; larger stone shot were found amidships with heavier artillery.

In the Americas similar stone cannon balls are associated with the 1554 Spanish fleet that sank off Padre Island. Five were found at the wreck site of *Espíritu Santo*, and a single stone ball was recovered from *San Estéban*.[119] Nine stone balls also were found at the sixteenth-century St. John's Bahamas wreck site.[120] A single stone shot is alleged to have been found at the early sixteenth-century Molasses Reef Wreck before the site was excavated systematically, but no record of its characteristics was made.[121]

Composite Lead/Iron

Smaller ammunition, fashioned from lead with an iron core, also was collected from the stern excavation area. Two lead balls, recovered with adhering ferrous concretions, were recognized as a type of shot characteristic of other sixteenth-century shipwrecks. Known by Spanish gunners as *bodoques*, these balls of composite construction were propelled from rapid-firing, breech-loading swivel guns called *versos*.[122] Each lead shot ball originally contained a cube of iron as a core, which has since oxidized completely, leaving a squared cavity visible through the lead shell. Similar *bodoques* were found on *Mary Rose*, Henry VIII's flagship, which sank in 1545; the 1554 Padre Island ships; a Portuguese wreck believed to date from the second half of the sixteenth century; and on the early Spanish wrecks at Highborn Cay and Molasses Reef.[123] The latter site also yielded a number of iron cubes, or "dice," cut from wrought-iron bar stock, and a bronze shot mold.

Researchers do not fully understand why shot was designed in this manner, although several hypotheses have been offered. One is that it were intended to fly apart on firing, producing multiple projectiles, or that the iron core helped to mushroom the lead on ignition, creating a tighter gas seal in the cannon barrel for increased velocity and range.[124] Another theory suggests that lead shot, as opposed to iron, created less internal wear and stress on the barrel from which they were fired.[125] Perhaps the composite makeup of the shot created a double impact that resulted in greater damage to the target; certainly the inclusion of iron in lead shot reduced the mass of the projectile and may have required less powder to propel it at the same velocity as solid lead shot.[126]

Studies of composite lead/iron shot from the Molasses Reef Wreck suggest that rather than being wrought or wrapped by hand, the balls were cast in a mold. Simmons noted that all the iron cubes in composite shot from this site and others were characteristically off-center, having migrated into one hemisphere. He reasoned that the eccentric location

Figure 5.32. Composite lead shot, known as *bodoques*, were fashioned with an iron cube in the center. In this example the cube has long since corroded away in the saltwater environment. Courtesy of the Florida Department of State, Division of Historical Resources.

of the iron cores resulted from the lighter iron "floating" on the molten lead within the mold before the shot cooled. To test this theory, he conducted an experiment using a bronze shot mold recovered from the wreck. After placing an iron cube into the mold, molten lead was added and allowed to solidify. Repeated molding of shot demonstrated that the iron cores did not float but remained at the bottom of the mold in a consistent manner. Replica shot were sectioned for comparison with sectioned examples from the wreck; the positions of the iron cores in relation to the lead shells were identical, confirming that *bodoque* shot probably were fabricated in a mold in a quick and uncomplicated manner, with little regard for the eccentric situation of the iron core.[127]

Lead

In addition to composite shot, we recovered a single example of solid lead shot. While it is heavier in weight, its diameter is quite close to those of the *bodoque* shot, suggesting that it also was intended to be fired from a *verso*-type swivel gun. *Versos* were the most common type of light artillery aboard ships of the sixteenth century. These portable, rapid-firing weapons were served by interchangeable powder chambers and could be mounted strategically in sockets along the rails of a vessel wherever they were needed. The first to be studied from an archaeological context were several examples recovered from the Padre Island wrecks.[128] *Versos* with their chambers also were found on the Highborn Cay and the Molasses Reef wrecks.[129] The latter site produced sixteen versos of three distinct types: the *verso normale*, which was the most common; the *verso doble*, a longer and heavier version; and the *verso liso*, a shorter and lighter version.

Iron

Near the other balls we found a single example of cast-iron shot, of larger caliber than the *verso* shot, suggesting that it may have been ammunition for a heavy wrought-iron gun. During the late fifteenth and early sixteenth centuries siege artillery went to sea for the purpose of bombarding enemy ships. During an age when the technology for casting large iron objects had not yet been developed, cannon tubes were hand wrought or built up from smaller, forged pieces of iron welded together to form a reinforced barrel with a corresponding powder chamber. Essentially, a series of long, flat iron staves were laid up and welded parallel around a mandrel to form a tube, open at both ends. Then a series of alternating iron sleeves and hoops were slid over the tube (barrel) and welded in place to provide reinforcement to the barrel. At least two of the hoops were fitted with lifting rings to facilitate moving the weapon and mounting it to a wooden carriage. Powder chambers that mated to the breech end of the barrel were constructed in a similar fashion; a single gun may have had several interchangeable chambers to facilitate rapid reloading.

Figure 5.33. Iron shot (*left*) and lead shot (*right*) were ammunition for common sixteenth-century wrought-iron cannons. Courtesy of the Florida Department of State, Division of Historical Resources.

The most common type of heavy built-up, wrought-iron gun found on sixteenth-century shipwrecks is called a *bombardeta*. Examples from *Mary Rose*, the Padre Island wrecks, the Highborn Cay Wreck, Molasses Reef Wreck, and the St. John's Bahamas Wreck were found with their corresponding breech chambers and solid-iron ammunition.

The single iron shot from the Emanuel Point Ship may have been intended for use in a small *bombardeta*; alternatively, it may have been intended for a shorter, smaller type of built-up, wrought-iron cannon, called a *cerbatana*. A weapon like this was noted to have been on the Molasses Reef Wreck but was removed by treasure hunters before archaeologists could study its features.[130]

Crossbow Bolt Points

Four copper crossbow points were recovered from the Emanuel Point Ship. They are similar in design to one recovered from the Hernando de Soto 1539 winter encampment in Tallahassee, Florida, eight recovered from Fort San Felipe in Georgia, a handful of copper specimens found

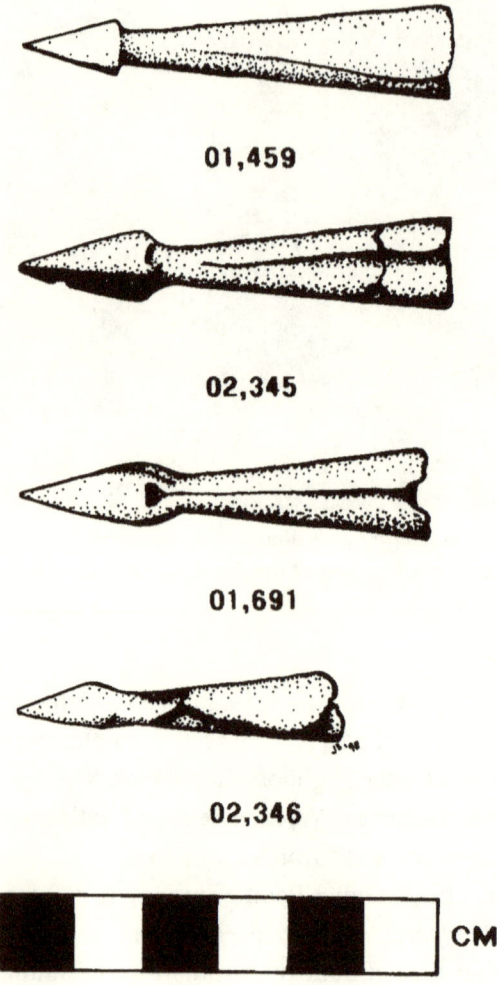

Figure 5.34. Copper crossbow points. Drawing by James Hunter III. Courtesy of the Florida Department of State, Division of Historical Resources.

at archaeological sites associated with the Coronado expedition, and two bolts on display at the U.S. Military Academy at West Point. All four exhibit a square, pyramidal tip that gradually widens into a cylindrical socket or ferule, with which the point could be connected to a wooden shaft.[131] With their square tips, such points are known as quarrels (from the French *quarel*, four-sided).

Three of the four quarrels bear a strong resemblance to a military type described in Payne-Gallwey's study of medieval crossbows.[132] The fourth, much smaller and more crudely formed, perhaps was a type used with a sporting (hunting) crossbow. Unlike the iron points used by the Soto *entrada* and the military garrison at Santa Elena, the Luna expedition quarrels likely originated in New Spain and may have been the work of Mexican Indian artisans who were ordered to manufacture projectile points for their Spanish conquerors.

By the time of the Luna expedition, popularity of the crossbow was waning, as evidenced by the growing number of *harquebusiers* (musketeers) recorded in the muster rolls of conquistadors such as Coronado and Pizarro.[133] Although crossbows were extremely powerful, their slow firing rate made them a particularly ineffective weapon against Indians, who could fire three or more arrows in the time it took a crossbowman to load and fire one bolt. However, the presence of crossbow points in the small arms assemblage from the Emanuel Point Ship seems to indicate that crossbows, while undoubtedly being superseded by *harquebuses* and other firearms, were still an important component of the Luna expedition's military arsenal.

Discussion

Evidence of the ship's artillery thus far is confined to the recovery of ammunition, examples of which indicate that the ship was armed with heavy, stone-throwing cannons, perhaps *bombardas* or *pedreros*; medium, wrought-iron ordnance, such as *bombardetas* or *cerbatanas*; and smaller swivel guns called *versos*. All examples of artillery shot were recovered from the stern of the ship, suggesting that they were stored near their respective guns, mounted in the stern. Perhaps the Emanuel Point Ship carried stern chasers, which fired through gunports in the stern transom. The Basque ship *San Juan* had one stern gunport, located on the main deck to starboard of the rudder.[134] Discovery of ammunition in the stern alternately suggests that the shot locker perhaps was located there, although other areas of the shipwreck have yet to be investigated. However, if the shot were stored in the same location as gunpowder, their location should have been farther forward in the ship, because a royal ordinance of 1552 directed that a special chamber for the powder should be constructed below deck in the bows of all Spanish ships sailing to and from the Indies.[135] On the other hand, a mid-eighteenth-century dictionary illustrating the outfitting of Spanish ships shows the powder magazine in the poop (upper stern), under the cabins.[136] The magazine was called the *rancho de Santa Barbara*, after the patron saint of gunners, who offered protection against thunderstorms, fires, and sudden death. The 1552 ordinance also listed the types of artillery, men, arms, and munitions that ships should carry, according to their respective tonnage. Ships of 100 to 170 tons were to carry two brass cannons (*sacres* and *falconetes*), six wrought-iron lombards (*bombardetas*), and twelve *versos*. Ships of between 170 and 220 tons were to carry three brass cannons (*media culebrinas*, *sacres*, and *falconetes*), eight lombards, and eighteen *versos*. And ships of between 220 and 320 tons should carry four brass cannons (*media culebrinas*), two *sacres* or *falconetes*, ten lombards, and twenty-four *versos*.[137] According to these regulations, the Emanuel Point Ship could have been quite heavily armed. However, artillery usually was loaded according to the specific mission of a ship, as were stores and provisions, rather than as an integral or permanent part of a vessel's equipment. No artillery was found at the shipwreck site, probably because its situation in shallow water close to shore offered every opportunity to salvage this expensive and essential equipment. Table 8 in the appendix is a summary of shot recovered from the Emanuel Point Ship.

Armor

The use of computerized axial tomography (CAT scanning) to examine a concreted piece of armor provides an excellent illustration of the collaboration between science and archaeology. An iron breastplate, known in Spanish as a *peto*, was discovered by Chuck Hughson adjacent to the after edge of the rudder in the starboard stern area. Heavily encrusted, the was plate carefully recorded *in situ* and removed from context for transit to the laboratory. However, due to its extreme weight and fragile condition, the plate cracked during recovery and arrived at the lab in three pieces. When we examined it, we found that almost none of the original metal remained in the heavy concretion. We also saw that the left sleeve area appeared to have been broken in antiquity.

Like most iron artifacts recovered from a marine environment, the breastplate was completely encased in a heavy coating of mineral deposits. Before any attempt was made to conserve the concreted armor, we thought it prudent to determine the original shape and extent of corrosion. Under the direction of Dr. S. Randall Hobgood, a series of high quality X-rays was taken of the breastplate at Sacred Heart Hospital in Pensacola. The CAT-scanning procedure employs a spinning X-ray head that allows viewing a human organ (or an artifact) on a computer monitor in real time. The device can rotate or slice the image in any direction or thickness. Once a desired view is obtained, the operator saves the image on film or digitally on magnetic tape. A scale can be incorporated into the image for precise measurements. In the case of the breastplate, cross sections were made across the longitudinal axis at one-centimeter intervals. Overhead views and close-ups of the arm and neck openings provided additional details about the overall construction and degree of preservation.

Not surprisingly, the X-ray images of the breastplate reveal that no original iron is left within the encrustation. They clearly show a detailed mold of the object, although cracked and broken in several places. Close examination also reveals that the armorer rolled back the sides and neck portion of the plate to blunt and strengthen the arm openings and neckline.

Information derived from the cross sections was sufficient to enable measured drawings of the breastplate to be prepared, from which a replica could be made. Although the left side of the breastplate is broken, slightly deformed, and incomplete, it was possible to reconstruct it by comparison with the almost perfectly preserved right side. According to Ian Eaves, formerly keeper of armour for the Tower of London, the principal features of the breastplate are as follows:

(1) It is of military quality and made for a man of greater than average size. (2) It is of a type intended for infantry use, lacking holes for the attachment of a cavalryman's lance rest at the right armpit. (3) It is of rounded form with no discernable medial ridge. (4) The neck and arm openings have plain, outward turns of a simple, rounded form. (5) The waistline is relatively straight. (6) The waist

flange is fairly deep and has delaminated at its center (where it has been broken and stressed), giving the false impression of two separate pieces of metal. (7) The left shoulder is pierced with a rivet hole for the attachment of a strap that would have engaged a buckle on the corresponding shoulder of the backplate. (Although a similar rivet hole cannot be discerned at the right shoulder of the breastplate, it must have existed, indicating that in common with comparable breastplates, it was furnished with shoulder straps to connect it to a backplate.) (8) The waist flange almost certainly would have been pierced with a rivet hole at either end for the attachment of a laminated skirt. Although such rivet holes cannot be discerned now, they are assumed to have existed.[138]

From these features Eaves ascertained that the breastplate was made in Italy or Spain about 1510. Similar breastplates can be found in the Royal Armouries Museum, Leeds, and the Three Ships Museum, Portsmouth, both in England. The first breastplate came from the Armoury of the Knights of St. John at Rhodes, which was overrun by the Turks in 1523, and the second came from the wreck of *Mary Rose*, which sank off Portsmouth in 1545. The Emanuel Point breastplate is the oldest breastplate discovered in America to date.

Discussion

The unexpected discovery of a breastplate at the Emanuel Point Ship offered an unusual opportunity to study one of the few surviving examples of metal body armor yet found in the Americas. Comparative examples of breastplates housed in European museums tend to represent the finest of the armorer's art, owned by royalty or nobility, but rarely used in combat. Nonetheless, this relic of the Spanish imperial *entrada* into Florida may provide clues to the identity and station of its original owner.

By the mid-sixteenth century metal body armor generally had been discarded by Spaniards in America in favor of padded cloth armor. Made of canvas and stuffed with cotton, *escaupiles*, as the padded garments were called, were patterned after those worn by Aztecs, who, the Spaniards noted, were well protected from arrows. Men of the Narváez

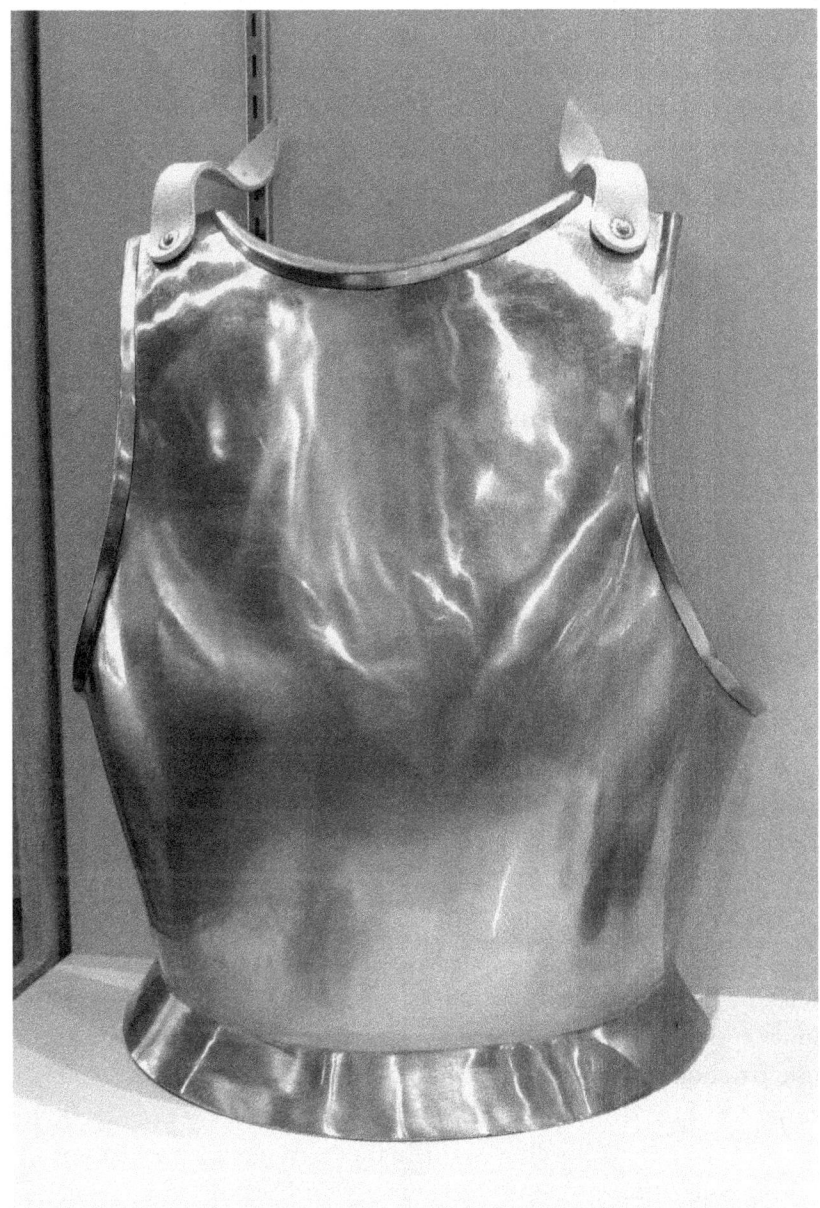

Figure 5.35. Information derived from CAT-scanned cross sections enabled measured drawings of the breastplate and allowed a replica to be prepared. Courtesy of the Florida Department of State, Division of Historical Resources.

expedition had repeatedly seen their armor pierced by Florida arrows, and by the time Soto's army arrived on the peninsula, some of the soldiers were equipped with quilted armor. Practical, lightweight, and inexpensive, padded armor became a standard issue for soldiers at Santa Elena and St. Augustine in the 1570s.[139]

OTHER MATERIALS

Obsidian

During the second field campaign we discovered in the bow of the ship two obsidian artifacts, which have been identified as prismatic blades or razors (*navajas*).[140] Both specimens are noticeably longer than they are wide and obviously were fabricated from two distinct sources of obsidian. Of Mesoamerican origin, the blades are entirely typical in their manufacture, form, size, and condition.[141] The larger of the two artifacts is typical of pieces that the Aztec hafted into wooden handles to make "swords" (*macuahuitl*). These weapons were encountered by some of Columbus's men on board a trading vessel they intercepted in the Gulf of Honduras in 1502.[142]

Both specimens are fragmentary and lack their striking platforms, which is unfortunate, since the platform is the most diagnostic feature. After AD 900 platforms were prepared by pecking and grinding. Therefore no date can be assigned, and the specimens could date to any time between 1000 BC and AD 1559. The larger blade appears to be a midsection and the smaller opaque blade an end fragment. Analysis of use wear was performed by Kenneth Hirth at Penn State University. The midsection of the larger blade is heavily striated (furrowed) as a result of use. Striations also are heavy along the right side of the dorsal (bottom) surface and the left side of the ventral (top) surface and correspond to the same activity. According to Hirth, these striations reflect cutting or sawing where the action involved drawing the blade through a material using a single directional motion—probably pulling the blade across the material toward the worker. There also are striations across the blade surface that cannot be attributed to use and probably represent post-depositional effects (e.g., sand abrasion).[143] The density of striations

Figure 5.36. Obsidian blades from central Mexico. Courtesy of the Florida Department of State, Division of Historical Resources.

and the lack of heavy micro-flaking along the edge of the blade indicate that the material being worked was fairly thick and soft—otherwise the brittle edge of the obsidian would have broken long before the striations were formed. The blade was heavily used but not to the point of complete exhaustion as a usable tool. Hirth suggests that it may have been used to cut heavy sailcloth or hemp rope.

The second blade shows evidence of light wear along the edge and micro-pitting, which are products of abrasion. Striations are short and oriented perpendicular to the cutting edge of the blade, indicating that the artifact was used for slicing or more probably for scraping. Small crescent-shaped micro-flaking is found on the dorsal side of the blade. A few longitudinal striations parallel to the edge of the artifact also were noted, which suggests the blade was also used for light cutting.[144]

Most Aztec blades from central Mexico are made from a distinctive greenish-gold obsidian from the Sierra de Pachuca, Hidalgo.[145] However, both of the Emanuel Point blades are gray or black obsidian, from other sources. Provenance was determined by Michael Glascock using an abbreviated neutron activation analysis at the Archaeometry Laboratory at Missouri University Research Reactor (MURR), which has collaborated on about two hundred archaeological research projects requesting trace element analysis.[146] More than a decade of research has produced an obsidian database containing chemical "fingerprints" for major and minor obsidian sources in Mesoamerica. Glascock's analysis of the Emanuel Point blades indicates that they came from two well-known sources at Paredón and Zaragoza, in the state of Puebla, which are the nearest sources to the coast in this region of central Mexico. These two blades apparently were used to cut different materials and may have been a part of a seaman's or colonist's personal possessions.

Coin

Jim Spirek discovered a small coin outside the hull under a piece of lead abaft the sternpost on the starboard side. Dull gray in color and highly encrusted with corrosion products, the coin is in very poor and fragmentary condition. When placed in a storage solution of sodium sesquicarbonate, it tinted the solution green, suggesting that it was made of copper. Rather than attempting to clean the piece by mechanical or electrolytic means, we decided to treat it in an airtight container with a solution of alkaline dithionite for two weeks in an attempt to reduce the corrosion products back to the parent metal. However, due to the apparent lack of core metal, the treatment was only successful in loosening the outer corrosion products from the sulfided core. Once the concretion was removed, the coin and its encrustation still retained sufficient detail to be drawn and photographed for tentative numismatic identification.

Photographs of the coin and encrustation were sent to John Kleeberg, associate curator of modern coins at the American Numismatic Society, who showed them to his colleague Alan Stahl. They identified the coin as a billon *blanca*, minted between 1471 and 1474, possibly at the Cuenca mint during the reign of Henry IV of Castile and León.[147] The term "billon" (*vellón*) refers to coinage made from an alloy of silver heavily debased with copper. *Blanca* was the lowest denomination of coins minted during this medieval monarch's reign (1454–74).

What They Left Behind: The Artifact Assemblage · 197

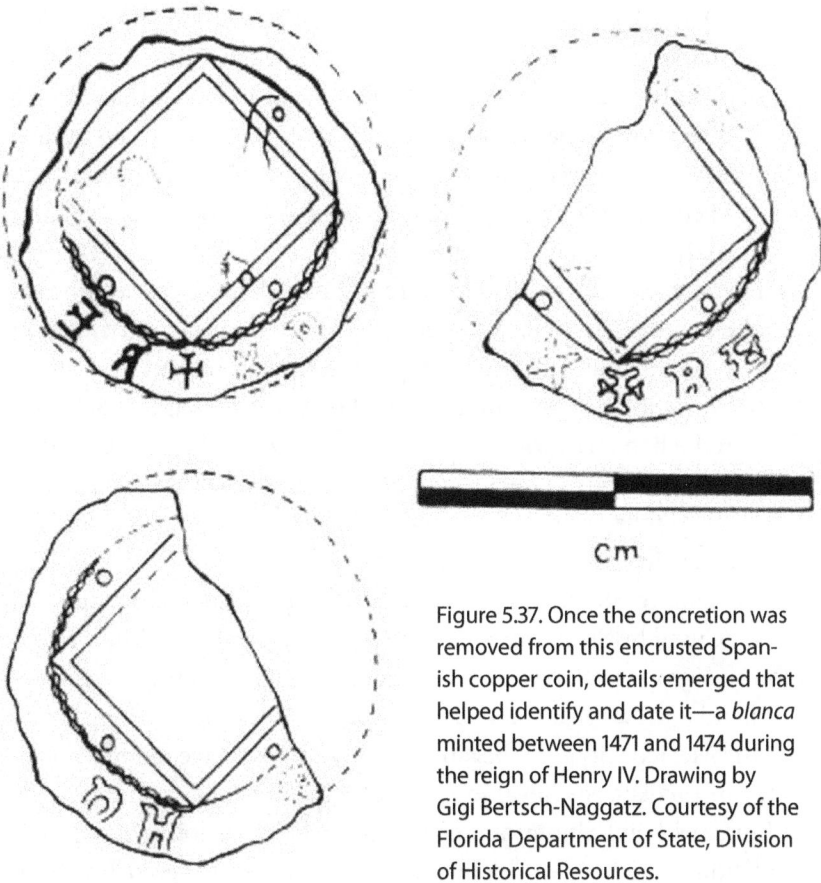

Figure 5.37. Once the concretion was removed from this encrusted Spanish copper coin, details emerged that helped identify and date it—a *blanca* minted between 1471 and 1474 during the reign of Henry IV. Drawing by Gigi Bertsch-Naggatz. Courtesy of the Florida Department of State, Division of Historical Resources.

Features discernible at the upper right quadrant on the obverse side are the edge of the castle (symbol of Castile) within a lozenge (diamond) encircled by a beaded ring. At one o'clock, the letters H E are visible, which are part of the legend HENRICUS DEI GRACIA. On the reverse side of the coin, and also visible as a mirror image on its encrustation is the rampant lion (of León) within a lozenge surrounded by a beaded ring. At the top corner of the lozenge is the Cross of Jerusalem, and at eleven o'clock the letters R E appear, which are part of the legend XPS VINCIT XPS REG (*Christ conquers, Christ reigns*).

On both sides of the coin, various annuletes (punch marks) can be discerned at the sides of the lozenges, a characteristic of Henry IV *blancas*. A similar *blanca* is described in two standard Spanish numismatic catalogs as a *dinero*.[148] However, Stahl believes this designation is incorrect; his study of medieval mint decrees indicates that *blancas* of this type replaced earlier coins in 1471 and continued to be minted until 1474, when Henry was succeeded by his half-sister, Isabella, who married Ferdinand.[149] During their reigns, no other copper-based coins were issued until the coinage reform of 1497.

Fifty-nine *blancas* of this type were unearthed during excavations at La Isabela in the Dominican Republic, the first European settlement in the New World, founded by Christopher Columbus in 1494.[150] A single Henry IV *blanca* also was found at the Long Bay site on San Salvador Island in the Bahamas, which is argued to have been the first American landfall of Columbus in 1492. Analysis by atomic absorption and emission spectography of the San Salvador coin determined that it contained 3.97 percent silver and 95.7 percent copper.[151]

According to Stahl, Henry IV *blancas* were a principal medium of exchange used by Spaniards after arriving in the Americas. Their circulation in Europe probably decreased after the 1497 minting reforms of Ferdinand and Isabella, and ended in the Americas after 1535, by which time the Mexico City mint began to have a large coinage output.[152] Discovery of this late medieval example of "small change" at the stern of the Emanuel Point Ship prompts questions about the longevity of their circulation in the New World. By the 1550s this old coin would have been of little negotiable value. Perhaps its presence aboard the sailing ship was as a keepsake or pocket-piece belonging to a passenger or crew member, or possibly it came aboard very early in the ship's career, was lost by its owner, and remained with the ship to its last port of call. Another possibility is that the coin may have been present among older ballast stones that were loaded aboard the ship at an established port, where dumps of recycled stones were available to vessels in need of additional ballast.

Apothecary Weights

We found two small brass objects in the periphery of the excavation at the bow. One is rectangular with faceted sides and has a marking similar to a fleur-de-lis stamped over a second marking resembling a starburst

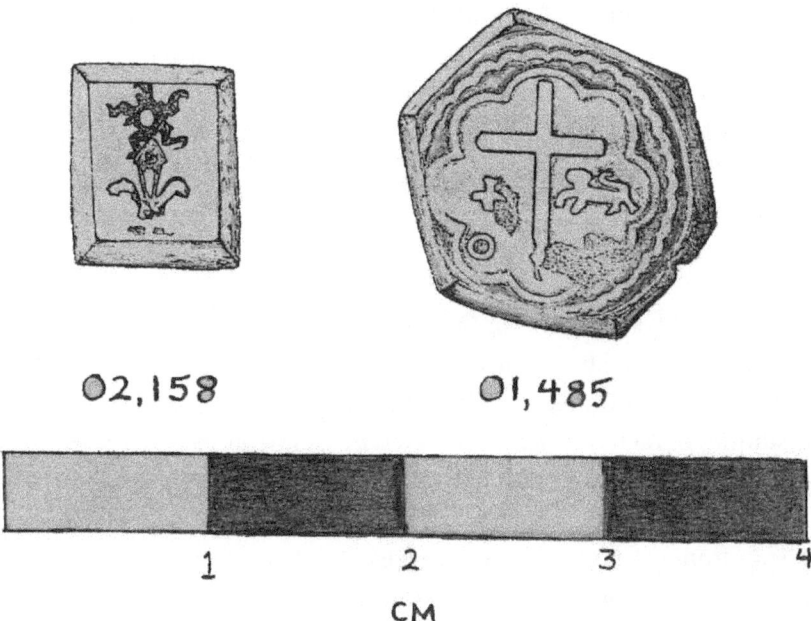

Figure 5.38. These apothecary weights probably were in a set used with a balance scale. Drawing by Gigi Bertsch-Naggatz. Courtesy of the Florida Department of State, Division of Historical Resources.

or dancing figure. The second object is six-sided and incorporates a cross surrounded by a looped circle and a rope-like circle. A small rampant lion also is present in the bottom right quadrant. The bottom left quadrant contains an image yet to be identified. Both objects are flat and unmarked on the reverse side. An excellent parallel has been made for the latter object with apothecary weights from *Mary Rose*.[153]

Glass

Two shards of thin glass were recovered from excavations amidships. One is an amber or yellowish-brown color. A single similarly amber-colored glass shard, slightly curved and badly abraded, was found on the Molasses Reef Wreck.[154] The second shard is quite thin and light greenish-gray in color. It corresponds to the pale green "lightbulb glass" found at Santa Elena, South Carolina.[155] The pieces probably were household items, from stemmed glassware. Shipboard examples of this pale green glass include the bottoms of two nearly identical pharmaceutical vials recovered at Molasses Reef.[156] These were similar to items described as containers for medicines from southern Spain that were found at the sixteenth-century offshore colony of Nueva Cádiz, Venezuela.[157]

Mercury

Tiny droplets of mercury (*azogue*) were noticed adhering to small concretions recovered first from the mast step assembly and again from the sternpost area of the site. As excavations at the stern progressed, greater quantities of mercury were discovered in sediments along the port and starboard sides and between the last three frames of the ship.

Mercury, or quicksilver, was employed in mining to separate precious metals from baser metals in crude ores. Smelted from cinnabar ore, the liquid metal formed an amalgam with nobler metals when heated in a mixture of their ores. It was then extracted through distillation for reuse. Quicksilver also was used in small quantities for medicinal purposes.[158] First transported to the New World by Columbus in 1494 to aid in the recovery of gold in the Antilles, liquid mercury was found during excavations at La Isabela, Dominican Republic, where it was collected from sediments inside the storehouse.[159] Apparently it had escaped into the soil when a container broke or rotted. Ceramic crucibles used to melt gold also were found. Quicksilver was not transported in quantity to the Spanish colonies until the mid-sixteenth century, when it was imported to Mexico under royal monopoly for the amalgamation of silver from ore by a new method called the "patio process." The process generally is credited to Bartolomé de Medina, a native of Seville, who received permission to import the metal in 1556.[160] Sources in Europe at that time were Almadén, Spain, site of one of the most extensive deposits of cinnabar, and Idria in the Austrian Alps.[161]

Mercury first came to Florida in 1559 because of Luna's expedition. Viceroy Velasco wrote to Luna that he was including in a relief voyage after the hurricane a special red stone (cinnabar) of quicksilver metal (*piedra del metal del açogue*), and another from Spain, as well as instructions on how to use them to find gold and other precious metals in the new colony.[162]

The presence of mercury in the Emanuel Point Ship bilge suggests that at some point in its career, the vessel had carried a quantity of quicksilver that leaked from containers and gravitated to the bottom of the hold. Transporting mercury was a tricky business, because the metal oxidizes very quickly, resulting in corroded containers and leakage. Moreover, it is difficult to recover, especially at sea.

Quicksilver has been found on other sixteenth-century shipwrecks, although not in the quantity recovered from the Emanuel Point Ship. Investigation of a shipwreck site in the Bay of Campechy produced brass pins with mercury adhering to them; small pools also were found in the hull of the Fuxa wreck, thought to be *Nuestra Señora de Rosario*, which sank on the northeastern coast of Cuba in 1590.[163] The largest quantity was found in the remains of two quicksilver transport vessels *Nuestra Señora de Guadalupe* and *Conde de Tolosa*, that wrecked in a hurricane on the north coast of the Dominican Republic in 1724. They were carrying 400 tons of mercury, enough to supply the mines of Mexico for a year. To carry their precious but unstable cargo, the galleons had been specially strengthened by installation of shelves in the bottom of the holds upon which boxes of mercury were stacked. The quicksilver was poured into sheepskin bags, then sealed in wooden casks. Each cask held a half-*quintal* (hundredweight) of metal; three such casks were packed into a wooden box padded with thick grass matting. Each box held 1½ quintals (about a gallon and a half) of quicksilver and was painted on the top with the royal arms of the Spanish Crown.[164]

Brass Buckle

A small brass buckle was found during excavation of the forward end of the keel. It likely was used with a strap or belt associated with clothing or shoes.

Intrusive Material

Three types of objects that apparently were deposited after the ship's wrecking were recovered during the initial testing phase. All are associated with fishing activities. Several pyramid-shaped lead fishing weights were found among the ballast stones in the central portion of the site. They are of a modern type, molded with small wire rings for attachment to fishing line.

Two encrustations were collected during examination of the ship's anchor; after electrolytic reduction, they appeared to be associated with shrimp trawling activities over the site. One encrustation consisted of several small steel chain links that were fashioned with a threaded closure fitting; the other encrustation contained a slender piece of wire rope. These modern objects may have been part of a shrimping net that became caught on the anchor's fluke.

Notes

1. Bratten, "Recent Artifact Finds."
2. Burns, "Anchor and Related Rigging Components," 72.
3. Arnold and Weddle, *Nautical Archaeology of Padre Island*, 224–27.
4. Keith, "Molasses Reef Wreck," 162–64.
5. Smith, *Vanguard of Empire*, 91.
6. Arnold and Weddle, *Nautical Archaeology of Padre Island*, 221, 236, 311; Olds, *Texas Legacy from the Gulf*, 44; Oertling, "The Concept of the Atlantic Vessel," 238.
7. Grenier, "Excavating a 400-Year-Old Basque Galleon," 68.
8. Barkham, *Spanish Basque Shipbuilding*, 29.
9. Ibid.
10. Ibid.
11. Palacio, *Instrucción Náutica*, fol. 110.
12. Lyon, "Spanish Colonial Nails," 33.
13. Keith, "Molasses Reef Wreck," 110–14.
14. Ibid.
15. South, Skowronek, and Johnson, *Spanish Artifacts from Santa Elena*, 40.
16. Pugh, "Study of Iron Fasteners," 84, 85.
17. Arnold and Weddle, *Nautical Archaeology of Padre Island*; Rosloff and Arnold, "Keel of the San Estéban"; Keith, "Molasses Reef Wreck."
18. Arnold and Weddle, *Nautical Archaeology of Padre Island*, 263.
19. Ibid., 236.
20. Palacio, *Instrucción Náutica*, 110, 126.

21. Salisbury, "Woolwich Ship," 285.
22. Rednap, "Cattewater Wreck," 47–48.
23. Arnold and Weddle, *Nautical Archaeology of Padre Island*, 261–63.
24. Keith, "Molasses Reef Wreck," 104–5.
25. Marr, "Investigation of Lead Sheathing."
26. Bancroft, "Geology of Stones."
27. Bratten, Dennis. "Preliminary Analysis of the Emanuel Point Ship's Ballast," 66–71.
28. Gifford, "Everything Is Ballast."
29. Ian MacLeod to Herb Bump, December 16, 1993.
30. Janice Carlson to J. Bratten, November 2, 1994.
31. Klein, *Graphic Worlds of Peter Bruegel the Elder*, 171.
32. Arnold and Weddle, *Nautical Archaeology of Padre Island*, 292.
33. Deagan, "Collections from La Isabela," 62.
34. Biringuccio, *Pirotechnia*, 369.
35. Palacio, *Instrucción Náutica*, 138.
36. Scappi, *The Opera of Bartolomeo Scappi*, plate 7, 932.
37. Palacio, *Instrucción Náutica*, 138.
38. Ibid., 138, 176.
39. Biringuccio, *Pirotechnia*, 368.
40. Palacio, *Instrucción Náutica*, 138.
41. Walker, *The Armada*, 168, 169.
42. Fitzgerald et al., "Basque Banded Copper Kettles," 44–57.
43. Corey Malcom, Mel Fisher Maritime Heritage Society, personal communication.
44. Rodgers, "Stale Bread and Moldy Cheese."
45. Wells, "Analysis of the Ceramic Assemblage"; Wells, "Examples of Ceramics."
46. Wells, "Analysis of the Ceramic Assemblage."
47. Goggin, "The Spanish Olive Jar."
48. Marken, *Pottery from Spanish Shipwrecks*; Avery, "Middle Style Olive Jar Rims"; Avery, "Olive Jar Production."
49. Malcom, *St. John's Bahamas Shipwreck*; Skowronek, "Ceramics and Commerce"; Marken, *Pottery from Spanish Shipwrecks*, 50–57.
50. Avery, "Pots as Packaging."
51. Martin, "Spanish Armada Pottery"; Marken, *Pottery from Spanish Shipwrecks*.
52. Skowronek, "Ceramics and Commerce," 108; Olds, *Texas Legacy from the Gulf*, 138.
53. Avery, "Middle Style Olive Jar Rims," 3; Avery, "Olive Jar Production," 4.
54. George Avery, personal communication, 1994.
55. Lister and Lister, *Andalusian Ceramics*, 132.
56. Deagan, *Artifacts of the Spanish Colonies*, 28.
57. Mullins, "More Than Just El Morro," 136.
58. Deagan, *Artifacts of the Spanish Colonies*, 62–64.
59. Noguera, *Cerámica Arqueológica de Mesoamérica*, 187.
60. Minc, "Pottery and the Potter's Craft in the Aztec Heartland," 359.
61. Barlow, "Códice de los Alfareros," 6.

62. Thomas Charlton, personal communication, 1995.
63. Arnold and Weddle, *Nautical Archaeology of Padre Island*, 259; Franklin, "Description of the Artifact Assemblage," 10; Deagan, *Artifacts of the Spanish Colonies*, 103.
64. Wells, "Examples of Ceramics."
65. Rule, *Mary Rose*, 187.
66. Grenier, "The Basque Whaling Ship," 75.
67. Bratten, "Olive Pits."
68. Breetzke, "Spanish Shoe Fragments."
69. Cliff Pequet to D. Breetzke, personal communication, April 1995.
70. June Swann to David Breetzke, personal communication, April 15, 1995.
71. June Swann to David Breetzke, personal communication, February 14, 1995.
72. Bratten, "Olive Pits."
73. Newsom, "Archaeobotanical Identifications," 4.
74. Baker, "Faunal Analysis."
75. Presley, "Analysis of Faunal Remains."
76. Baker, "Faunal Analysis."
77. Ibid.
78. Ibid.
79. Armitage, "Black Rat Bones," 5.
80. Ibid., 6, 23.
81. Ibid., 20.
82. Armitage, "Bones of House Mice"; Berry, "Town Mouse, Country Mouse," 92.
83. Berry, "Town Mouse, Country Mouse," 93, 111, 113.
84. Armitage, "Black Rat Bones," 23.
85. Phillips, *Six Galleons*, 157.
86. Armitage, "Black Rat Bones," 24.
87. Phillips, *Six Galleons*, 8.
88. Durden, "Fossil Cockroaches."
89. Roth, *American Cockroach*, 1.
90. Ibid.
91. Hinton, *Monograph of the Beetles*, 265.
92. Quinn, *Voyage of Thomas Cavendish*, 37.
93. Hakluyt, *Hakluyt Voyages*, 256.
94. Hinton, *Monograph of the Beetles*, 265.
95. Shidner, "Macro- and Microscopic Zooarchaeological Examination."
96. Cooley, *Inventory of the Estuarine Fauna*, 17.
97. Morris, *Field Guide of Shells*.
98. Newsom, "Archaeobotanical Identifications," 1.
99. Ibid., 1–2.
100. Ibid.
101. Barkham, *Spanish Basque Shipbuilding*, 47.
102. Smith, *Vanguard of Empire*, 4, 98.
103. Newsom, "Archaeobotanical Identifications," 2–3.
104. Lawrence, "Analysis of Plant Remains."

105. Newsom, "Archaeobotanical Identifications," 3.
106. Ibid., 4.
107. Record and Hess, *Timbers of the New World*, 556–58.
108. Schendel, *Medicine in Mexico*, 62–80.
109. Arnold and Weddle, *Nautical Archaeology of Padre Island*, 269–70.
110. Newsom, "Archaeobotanical Identifications," 4.
111. Weinstein, "Pollen Analysis of Samples," 4.
112. Ibid., 3.
113. Arnold and Weddle, *Nautical Archaeology of Padre Island*, 368; Franklin et al., "Preliminary Description of the Excavation," 59; Reitz and Scarry, "Reconstructing Historic Subsistence," 55.
114. Franklin et al., "Preliminary Description of the Excavation," 59.
115. Arnold and Weddle, *Nautical Archaeology of Padre Island*, 368.
116. Scott-Ireton, "Unique Artifacts."
117. Carré, Desroches, and Goddio, *Le San Diego*, 208, 209.
118. Guérout, Rieth, and Gassend, *Navire Génois de Villefranche*.
119. Olds, *Texas Legacy from the Gulf*, 250–52.
120. Malcom, *St. John's Bahamas Shipwreck*.
121. Keith, "Molasses Reef Wreck," 218.
122. Vigón, *Artillería Española*, 45.
123. Rule, *Mary Rose*; Olds, *Texas Legacy from the Gulf*; Arnold and Weddle, *Nautical Archaeology of Padre Island*; Blake and Green, "Portuguese Wreck in the Seychelles"; Peterson, "16th-Century Bahaman Shipwreck"; Keith, "Molasses Reef Wreck."
124. Keith, "Molasses Reef Wreck," 218.
125. Blake and Green, "Portuguese Wreck in the Seychelles," 13.
126. Simmons, "Fifteenth and Sixteenth-Century Ordnance," 18.
127. Ibid.
128. Olds, *Texas Legacy from the Gulf*; Arnold and Weddle, *Nautical Archaeology of Padre Island*.
129. Peterson, "16th-Century Bahaman Shipwreck"; Keith, "Molasses Reef Wreck."
130. Keith, "Molasses Reef Wreck," 182.
131. Hunter, "Analysis of Small Arms Artifacts," 147.
132. Payne-Gallwey, *The Crossbow*, 18.
133. Rhodes, "Coronado Fought Here," 46.
134. Grenier, "Basque Whalers in the New World," 80.
135. Haring, *Trade and Navigation*, 274.
136. Phillips, *Six Galleons*, 70.
137. Haring, *Trade and Navigation*, 274.
138. Eaves, *Report on the Breast Plate*.
139. Peterson, *Arms and Armor*, 125.
140. Flint, "Armas de la Tierra"; Arnold and Weddle, *Nautical Archaeology of Padre Island*, 287; López Cruz, *Naufragio en Ines de Soto*, 236.
141. William Parry, personal communication.
142. Dan Healan, personal communication, 1999.

143. Hirth, "Review of Obsidian Artifacts."
144. Bratten, "Mesoamerican Component."
145. William Parry, personal communication.
146. Glascock, "Archaeometry Laboratory at MURR."
147. Kleeberg, personal communication with Roger Smith.
148. Cayón and Castan, *Monedas Españolas*, 279.
149. Stahl, personal communication, 1995.
150. Stahl, "First Coins in the New World"; Deagan, "Collections from La Isabela."
151. Brill et al., "Artifacts Excavated on San Salvador Island."
152. Kleeberg, personal communication with Roger Smith.
153. Stuart Vine, personal communication, 1998.
154. Smith, "Glass Recovered from the Molasses Reef Wreck."
155. South, Skowronek, and Johnson, *Spanish Artifacts from Santa Elena*, 25.
156. Keith, "Molasses Reef Wreck," 255.
157. Willis, "Archaeology of 16th-Century Nueva Cádiz," 63–64, appendix 2.
158. Biringuccio, *Pirotechnia*, 81.
159. Deagan, "Collections from La Isabela," 63.
160. Haring, *Trade and Navigation*, 158.
161. Whitaker, *Mercury Mine*, 5.
162. Luís de Velasco to Luna, October 25, 1559, in Priestley (2010), 1:77.
163. Smith, "Treasure Ships of the Spanish Main," 88; Lopéz Pérez, *Estructura del Pecio de Fuxa*, 10.
164. Smith, "Treasure Ships of the Spanish Main," 104.

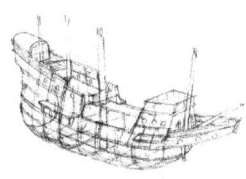

6

Archaeology in the Laboratory

Artifact Conservation

JOHN R. BRATTEN

Although many exciting discoveries happen in the field during the excavation of a shipwreck, many more occur in the lab when artifacts are reexcavated, cleaned, analyzed, and stabilized. Concretions may seem straightforward, but X-rays can reveal hidden objects or indicate completely different artifact types. For example, Emanuel Point objects that appeared to be simple spikes were determined to be several lengths of chain. What appeared to be a bolt actually consisted of a key lock bolt and two associated washers that were used to secure the bolt once the end had been struck with a hammer and flattened. The lab also is the place where details such as markings on coins are revealed. Ceramic fragments recovered in the field often are so stained that identification is nearly impossible, but cleaning in the lab can reveal glazes and patterns. Our careful cleaning of an encrusted Emanuel Point gudgeon revealed original application techniques. Not only was the iron of the gudgeon preserved beneath the concretion; a layer of pitch, a layer of burlap-like fabric, and an outer covering of sheet lead completely covered both arms of the gudgeon.

During initial test excavations of the Emanuel Point Ship, the numbers and types of artifacts recovered were small. Preliminary cleaning and stabilization of these first items were conducted at a temporary field laboratory (kitchen) in the Pensacola Shipwreck Survey headquarters at the Old School House.[1] However, by the end of the season enough artifacts had been recovered to require additional laboratory space and equipment and the services of a full-time conservator.

Courtesy of the Historic Pensacola Preservation Board, laboratory space was made available in the basement of the T. T. Wentworth Jr. Museum in Pensacola's historic district. This space previously had functioned as a dry laboratory during the excavation of a nearby British-period site and was suitable for a wet laboratory because it was equipped with a lot of counter space and running water.

After full-scale excavations resumed in 1994 the large number of concretions and other artifacts being recovered each day required the use of a second room just for storage. The two rooms were equipped with storage vats, indispensable Tupperware containers, refrigerators, an air scribe (pneumatic air chisel) and compressor, an X-ray machine, conductivity and pH meters, titration apparatus, computer, and the thousand-and-one items necessary to begin the analysis and treatment of the artifacts. Equally important was the installation of drafting and photography areas to document the objects.[2]

In addition to a conservator, the laboratory was staffed by graduate student interns, an illustrator (Gigi Bertsch-Naggatz), and a host of extremely interested and talented volunteers from the Pensacola Archaeological Society and the local community. An enthusiastic business community donated a wide variety of chemicals, equipment, and technical support.

The conservation lab quickly became a focal point for the project, where staff and volunteers assembled, students were given assignments, and the public (from school kids to the secretary of state) interfaced with the shipwreck and project staff. As noted in the acknowledgments section of this book, an impressive number of volunteers from the Pensacola Archaeological Society routinely worked in the laboratory and quickly became indispensable for completing countless tasks associated with the initial processing of artifacts, including transferring them from salt water to fresh water, doing an initial cleaning, and numbering and recording. Many volunteers became adept at monitoring the removal of salts from ceramics and faunal material or using an air scribe to process epoxy-filled concretions. These individuals donated countless hours and often acted as impromptu tour guides for the many visitors who found their way to the lab.

Often our guests were school groups, visiting archaeologists, or community clubs, but sometimes we were surprised. I remember one visitor in particular who was announced by a phone call. She had arrived at the reception area of the museum and asked whether she could see the artifacts in the lab. Because I was the only person working that day, I escorted her throughout the processing and storage areas. She peered with intense interest into each artifact container as I offered a running commentary about what she was seeing and answered an occasional question. I spent about an hour with her, and although I don't think she missed anything, she made only three or four remarks the entire time. She thanked me very nicely for her tour and left without further comment. The next day I was surprised to learn that she had dropped off a donation check for a thousand dollars to help with the project and had again offered her thanks for the impromptu tour.

The addition of an X-ray machine to our equipment was no less serendipitous. During a public presentation in 1994 I mentioned the need for an X-ray machine and explained its use for examining concreted objects recovered from marine sites. Tom Muir, a staff member at the Pensacola Historic Village, heard the talk and informed me that his museum had an X-ray machine in its collections that at one time had been exhibited with other objects from a dental office. He located the machine, and although it was an older model, it appeared to be in working condition. To be on the safe side, I looked in the phonebook and called Emerald Coast X-Ray, a local Pensacola business. After I explained our project and need, a company representative checked it and determined it was safe to use. In addition the firm donated a lead apron for our safety and provided a large supply of outdated X-ray film. Although not suitable for medical uses, the outdated film worked perfectly for our needs, and we were able to make artifact radiographs in a temporary darkroom.

However, because of the thickness of the concreted material covering some of our iron artifacts, it was not long before we "burned out" the tube head by taking too many X-rays of long duration. Once again Emerald Coast X-Ray came to our aid, providing a second machine at

Figure 6.1. Waterlogged organic artifacts such as this rope segment were often treated with the use of a freeze dryer. Courtesy of the Florida Department of State, Division of Historical Resources.

no charge. Also an older unit, it was designed for general medical use instead of just teeth. We used this machine for many years, but eventually it needed upgrading. In 2010, with financial help from the Archaeology Institute and the College of Arts and Sciences, we purchased a digital X-ray machine from Capital X-Ray, Inc.

Capital X-Ray is located in the small town of Tallassee, Alabama. I had driven by the company for many years while traveling to Lake Martin,

Alabama, for weekend getaways. One Friday afternoon I stopped at the business and discussed our X-ray needs with the company president, Terry Stiff, who suggested that we buy a veterinary model known as a Q-vet. We relied on my father-in-law's skill as a successful businessman to negotiate the price of the machine and installation to less than fifty thousand dollars. This unit has proven to be an excellent choice for our conservation laboratory; it produces radiographs rapidly and has been extremely safe and trouble free.

We also upgraded the lab's freeze-dryer to replace a rather ineffective model. An Advantage Pro manufactured by SP Scientific, the new dryer gave us the ability to pre-freeze artifacts and dry them with a computer-controlled "recipe" specific to the size of the object. This ensures a gradual ramping of applied heat that dries the artifacts with the least chance for internal collapse.

All laboratory treatment procedures generally followed standard methods for underwater sites as outlined by Hamilton and Pearson.[3] As noted later in this chapter, certain treatments and techniques were modified slightly for various artifacts due to their condition or composition.

Ceramics

Ceramics were the most numerous artifact type recovered from the Emanuel Point Ship, and well over 90 percent of the collection consisted of unglazed coarse earthenwares. Thus required conservation treatments were minimal—that is, removing soluble salts, organic stains, and some marine growth.

The most effective treatment for removing stains (tannin and/or metallic sulfides) was immersion in hydrogen peroxide or citric acid. Hamilton recommends immersion in 10–25 percent hydrogen peroxide for twenty-four to thirty-six hours.[4] In practice, however, we found that a 3 percent solution was very effective in removing organic stains in a relatively short time (one to three hours). Hydrogen peroxide of this strength is inexpensive and can be obtained at any grocery or drug store. More stubborn stains (black metallic sulfides) and some adhering marine growths required treatment in citric acid (5 percent) for anywhere from three to forty-eight hours.

Figure 6.2. Olive jar sherds. *Right*, as recovered with tannin stain. *Left*, after stain removal with hydrogen peroxide. Courtesy of the Florida Department of State, Division of Historical Resources.

A few ceramics had varying amounts of iron oxide corrosion products adhering to their surfaces. These required mechanical cleaning with dental picks and soaking in 5 percent solutions of ethylene diamine tetra-acetic acid (EDTA, di-sodium salt) or oxalic acid. The use of oxalic acid was terminated when it proved to be too effective and damaged the glaze of one fragment of tin-glazed earthenware. Fortunately, the few glazed ceramics that were recovered appeared to be less susceptible to staining and usually required only rinsing.

A number of Spanish olive jar fragments retained traces of pine resin or pitch (*pez*) on their interior surface. If we had allowed these sherds to air dry, the resin would have spalled off from the surface. Consolidation with polyvinyl acetate (PVA) or Acryloid B-72 was not an option because the resin dissolves in alcohol, acetone, or toluene solvent. Therefore the water-soluble consolidant polyvinyl alcohol (PVAL) was added to the final rinse water. A 5 percent solution of PVAL in distilled water effectively consolidated the resin to the sherd.

After cleaning the sherds we removed soluble salts by placing the ceramics in a series of distilled or deionized water baths. Rinsing continued until conductivity readings stabilized below 20 microsiemens (µS) of electrical conductance as monitored by a conductivity meter.

IRON

Hundreds of concretions were recovered from the ship. Because of the pH, depth, and mineral content of the local seawater and seafloor, the composition of the concretions is friable and sandy in texture. Consequently many of the smaller fastener concretions were found broken, possibly from storm and wave action at the site. Regardless of size, all concretions had to be handled with care, especially during transport.

Nearly all the small concretions had lost all of their original iron. Various corrosion processes had converted the iron to a black iron-sulfide slush. As is commonly the case, concretion molds were formed preserving details of the original form. A pneumatic chisel was used to inscribe a line along or around the concretions. By hitting along this line with a chisel and a hammer, the concretion was broken in a predetermined manner. Oddly shaped concretions were X-rayed, and the resulting

Figure 6.3. Charles Hughson using an air scribe (pneumatic chisel) to remove concretion from a large iron bolt. Courtesy of the Florida Department of State, Division of Historical Resources.

radiographs provided direction maps for cleaning. Corrosion residues were removed by simply washing the concretion pieces with water and/or by using dental picks and stainless steel wire. After the residue was removed, the concretion voids were filled with epoxy. When dry, the epoxy replica was easily freed from its adhering concretion with an air scribe.

A single iron shot was recovered from the wreck. Due to its compact and spherical mass, a substantial iron core was found underneath the built-up concretion. After the concretion was removed, the iron was treated successfully with a standard electrolysis process as outlined by Hamilton.[5] Similarly, one large composite concretion composed of five fasteners was found to contain both molds and corroded iron. In this case the molds were filled with epoxy first, and after the concretion was removed, the iron/epoxy artifacts were treated by electrolysis.

Larger iron objects such as gudgeons and the ship's anchor were treated by another standard electrolysis technique as outlined by Hamilton.[6] Treatment time for the anchor was two years to ensure proper chloride removal and thorough cleaning. Although smaller, the iron gudgeons required far more preparation time because of their associated strips of lead covering, fasteners, and tar-coated canvas fabric.

LEAD

During stern excavations we found more than two hundred fragments of the lead strips that had covered the ship's caulking seams. Because the corrosion products of lead are stable, conservation treatments were minimal. Selected fragments were cleaned by electrolysis or placed in a 10 percent solution of hydrochloric acid (HCl) to reveal surface details obscured by a thin layer of calcium carbonate, lead sulfide, and/or lead oxide. Electrolytic and chemical cleaning are non-abrasive and, in this case, enabled us to see surface impressions of what very likely was sail cloth.

Several lead objects, notably the *bodoques* (lead-covered iron shot), were found with adhering concretion. These pieces were easily freed of concretion with an air scribe, polished with baking soda, and sprayed with a protective coating of acrylic spray.

Cupreous Artifacts

Several copper-based artifacts were found, including a brass ring, copper pitcher, copper and silver coin, copper funnel, copper cauldrons and skillet, and a bronze mortar and pestle. Most were found in what likely was the galley area of the vessel. A shattered, riveted cauldron was recovered and was determined through analysis to have contained pitch. This cauldron likely was heated when deck caulking was required.

The brass ring, possibly associated with the ship's rigging, required a short-term cleaning in electrolysis, rinsing, and a gentle polish with baking soda. As a final stabilization step, the ring was placed in a solution

Figure 6.4. Copper funnel in sodium sesquicarbonate solution for passive treatment while on display. Courtesy of the Florida Department of State, Division of Historical Resources.

of 1 percent benzotriazole (BTA) for twenty-four hours. BTA forms an insoluble, complex compound with cupric ions and provides a barrier against moisture that could cause future corrosion, such as "bronze disease."[7] The copper pitcher and the funnel were found heavily corroded into copper sulfide. Due to their fragile nature, a long-term passive treatment in a 3 percent sodium sesquicarbonate bath was chosen. Placing the artifacts in an alkaline solution passively removed the soluble cuprous chlorides. A custom-made aquarium was used as the treatment vat, so we were able to display and treat the objects at the same time. The solution was monitored periodically for chloride counts and changed when necessary. When we determined that the chloride was at an acceptable level (below 100 ppm), the pitcher and funnel were carefully dehydrated, treated with BTA, and consolidated with acryloid B-66.

As mentioned in chapter 5, the copper coin also received passive conservation. Prior to its treatment, we did not know whether the coin was silver, copper, or an alloy of both. In this case we chose alkaline dithionite as the method most likely to preserve original details and equally suitable for either type of metal.[8] The remaining copper objects were treated with a standard electrolysis procedure followed with the application of BTA.

Faunal Materials

Bones and teeth were recovered from the wreck in very good condition except for some slight organic staining. In a few cases, bones were cleaned in 3 percent solution of hydrogen peroxide, as already outlined for ceramics. As with the ceramics, all faunal materials were rinsed in a series of deionized water baths until a conductivity reading below 20 µS was achieved. After the salts were removed, the specimens were dehydrated in a series of alcohol baths followed with acetone. Immediately afterward they were placed in a 10 percent solution of Acryloid B-72 and acetone for consolidation. This treatment procedure proved to be very effective for bones from the smallest rat vertebra to the largest cow ribs. Only very slight exfoliation or cracking was observed on some of the larger bone fragments.

BOTANICAL MATERIALS

In consultation with paleobotanist Lee Newsom, we decided that the botanical remains (olive pits, nutshells, seeds, leaves, and so forth) should be identified before any conservation treatments were applied. Therefore all specimens were stored wet. To retard fungal or bacterial decomposition, they were placed in refrigerated storage in a 20 percent solution of ethanol and deionized water. Should these materials be displayed at a future time, selected specimens will be freeze-dried or consolidated with a suitable resin, such as PVA or Acryloid B-72.

Hundreds of olive pits were recovered near the mast step of the ship. Although it was obvious that they were olive pits, Roger asked me what else we could learn about them. As a long-time lover of olives, I thought I should begin my research by buying some olives from the local grocery store. I bought a can of black olives that were sold under the Vlasic label, and a quick search provided an 800 number for Vlasic. After the company greeter answered my phone call, I explained that I was an archaeologist working on a sixteenth-century Spanish shipwreck in Pensacola, Florida, and had a question about olives. I always find that a blind phone call works very well and that the folks on the other end are intrigued by shipwreck archaeology and want to help with the research. After I restated my tale and my request for olive information, she transferred me to another company representative. Once again I repeated my story and request. The second agent was equally intrigued but told me that Vlasic is a subsidiary of Campbell's Soup and that I should contact them. I found an 800 number and called Campbell's. Undaunted, I retold my story several times to several employees and learned that Campbell's buys all its olives from the California Olive Growers Association and that the man I needed to talk with was John Daniels. Fortunately, Daniels was easy to reach and actually answered his own phone. After I provided all the relevant details, he asked one question: "Are the pits in good shape?" "Yes," I answered, and he asked me to place a handful on a photocopier with a ruler and fax him the photocopy. Within an hour, he sent a report indicating that the morphology of the pits was very evident and that we had two types of olives—the larger Gordal variety, grown for eating, and the smaller Sevillano olive, harvested for olive oil. I asked him whether the olives could have been harvested in Mexico in 1559. Daniels said no because it was too early for the trees to have been established in the New World. He was almost certain that both varieties had been harvested near Seville, Spain.

Textiles and Rope

Only one textile fragment was recovered from the ship. When a large lead fragment was removed from a gudgeon concretion, we found a small piece of textile preserved between the outer lead covering and the corroded iron arm of the gudgeon. Undoubtedly the infusion of iron corrosion products and the close proximity of the lead allowed the piece to survive. The textile fragment was cleaned in a weak solution of hydrochloric acid (10 percent) and placed in refrigerated storage pending identification.

Two types of rope or cordage—hemp and grass fiber—were recovered from the wreck. Both were found more or less covered with an orange-colored, iron-type corrosion. To measure and determine their composition accurately, we decided to place the fragments in a 5 percent solution of EDTA (di-sodium salt) for cleaning. In the case of the hemp fibers the treatment was effective and left the rope intact with its more natural lighter color. Unfortunately, we discovered that the grass fibers had been fashioned from short sections of linear fibers (probably sisal), which quickly disconnected from their original form and separated into hundreds of short segments after the iron corrosion was removed.

Insects

We had recovered a small deposit of what looked like insect parts from the ship's bilge but were unsure about just what they were. We decided to call the department of entomology and nematology, an extension of the U.S. Department of Agriculture, at the University of Florida in Gainesville. A husky voice answered the phone, "House of Insects." We explained that we had found some insect parts buried underwater in a shipwreck in Pensacola, and he clearly indicated that he thought this was a prank call. Eventually we got through to the entomology professor and department head and assured him we were not joking and needed some professional help identifying our specimens. He seemed quite intrigued by our story and agreed to look at the insect parts, so we planned a trip to visit his laboratory. When we arrived, we were met by an excited gathering of graduate students eager to see what we had brought. They put our specimens under a microscope and impatiently took turns viewing them. Meanwhile, we described our project to the department head and explained how we had retrieved the well-preserved organic remains from the bilge of the shipwreck. The students quickly identified the specimens as cockroach parts, singling out a wing, pronotum (a plate-like structure that covers all or part of the dorsal surface of the thorax), and ootheca (egg case). The professor took a quick look and said they were from the American cockroach (*Periplaneta americana*). "Where is my copy of *The Cockroach, Volume One*?" he asked the students. When it was produced, he turned to the section on *americana* and read to us that this insect originally came from Africa, disseminating throughout the New World with the slave trade in the 1700s. He frowned and noted dryly that since we had recovered evidence of *americana* on a ship of the 1500s, *The Cockroach, Volume One* might have to be revised.

Noting our newfound interest in cockroach parts, he said, "To be sure, let's go to the reading room"—or at least we thought that was what he said. But he meant "breeding room." Inside were numerous large Plexiglas containers of insects, each marked with a species name; the professor opened the one marked *americana* and removed a single roach, which he dispatched in a vacuum chamber. We now had a contemporary specimen to examine microscopically and compare with ours. At one point, Roger quietly asked the professor about the lab's function as a resource for pest eradication in Florida and inquired about his recommendation for getting rid of roaches. The expert entomologist raised his eyebrows and answered, "Why, I just step on them." I later asked him what they fed the roaches, and he replied, "Dogfood."

Because the insect samples appeared to be extremely fragile, the only conservation treatment we applied was to place them in 100 percent ethanol for storage. Study specimens were obtained by placing selected examples on microscope slides and sealing the insect remains between the glass slide and a cover slip with a thin solution of PVA glue.

Stone

Stone artifacts such as the shot required only a small amount of mechanical cleaning with an air scribe or dental pick to remove small amounts of concretion or shell. A few small spots of black surface discoloration were removed by spot treating with a mild solution of HCl applied with cotton swabs.

Ballast stones recovered from the ship's hull generally were covered with marine growth. Those stones chosen for identification were slabbed so that their unaltered surfaces could be examined without the use of chemical treatments.

Wood and Leather

Various wood items recovered in 1993 required more elaborate conservation techniques than were available at the Pensacola Shipwreck Survey headquarters. These included two dunnage specimens, two tool handles, a galleon carving, a cork, and small timber recovered from the port pump well. These specimens were treated by freeze-drying at the South Florida Conservation Center in Pompano Beach, Florida. Prior to freeze-drying, each artifact was given a pretreatment for six weeks in polyethylene glycol (PEG; 30 percent PEG 300, 20 percent PEG 1000, and 10 percent PEG 400 in distilled water).[9] Wooden objects recovered after 1993 were treated on an individual basis depending on wood type and condition. Some were treated with a 70 percent PEG immersion, others with an acetone and rosin bulking treatment, and others by freeze-drying.

Similarly, all leather artifacts were treated by freeze-drying following a pretreatment in 15 percent glycerol for four months. The PEG and glycerol pretreatments were designed to "bulk up" the wood and leather prior to freeze-drying. The methods successfully prevented subsequent cellular collapse that could have led to extreme shrinkage and deformation.

Other Artifacts

Certain artifacts such as shell, coral, stone, and a large number of the lead fragments essentially required no treatment beyond simple washing and air drying. Approximately 250 ml of recovered mercury also required no special care other than carefully pouring off a small amount of seawater that had been retrieved with it. Because of the potential health hazards associated with mercury, we placed the very heavy liquid in a tightly sealed polyethylene bottle topped with mineral oil to retard evaporation.

Summary

Artifacts recovered during an archaeological excavation can be the most important and useful form of data for determining practically every aspect of the day-to-day existence aboard a ship as well as revealing clues about the vessel's origin, function, ports of call, and manner of destruction.[10] From the anchor to the olive pits, every item has a story to tell and

Figure 6.5. Graduate student James Hunter III catalogued many finds from the Emanuel Point shipwreck using traditional drawing techniques. Courtesy of the Florida Department of State, Division of Historical Resources.

is an essential piece of information for completing the overall puzzle. Essentially, the more data that are available for analysis, the more thorough the picture of the site becomes. Archaeological illustration of many of the artifacts was a routine part of their treatment in the laboratory, since small details or characteristics of objects often can be overlooked in photographic records.

Not surprisingly, the conservation laboratory also functioned as a teaching laboratory for students engaged in study through a conservation course, assistantship, or applied thesis research. Based on this work, several students used the experience as a springboard for employment. For example, students Jason Burns and Robin Moore were employed by the Lighthouse Archaeological Maritime Program (LAMP) in St. Augustine, Florida, to establish a conservation laboratory and serve as maritime archaeologists. Both have moved on in their professional careers, but their conservation training proved useful for initial employment. Graduate student James Hunter III utilized his skills as an artifact illustrator for the Emanuel Point Ship project to gain a position with the *Hunley* recovery project and was assigned to illustrate artifacts associated with USS *Housatonic*. Undergraduate Susanne Grieve graduated from UWF specializing in underwater archaeology and conservation and traveled to University College London to complete a master's degree in conservation. From there she accepted a position at the Mariners' Museum in Virginia, later becoming a senior conservator on the USS *Monitor* project. During that time she traveled to Antarctica for seven months to complete conservation on the early explorers' huts with the Antarctic Heritage Trust. She is now a conservation instructor, conservator, and lab coordinator for the Program in Maritime Studies in the history department at East Carolina University. Many other students utilized the same hands-on experience in the conservation lab to carry the skills to other programs and cultural resource management firms.

The majority of the Emanuel Point Ship artifacts have completed conservation, and a selection is on display at the Margaret J. Smith Archaeology Institute on the University of West Florida campus and at the T. T. Wentworth Jr. State Museum in downtown Pensacola, Florida, where the anchor is exhibited. Without question, analysis of the conserved materials will continue for years to come, and they will become even more important as their information enhances the analysis of newfound sites associated with the 1559 Spanish colonization attempt in Florida.

Notes

1. Mitchell, "Preliminary Conservation of the 1993 Emanuel Point Field Specimens"; Maseman, "Conservation Treatment Reports"; Clifford Smith, "Conservation of Cultural and Biological Remains."

2. Bratten and Hunter, "Conservation."

3. Hamilton, "Methods of Conserving Archaeological Material Culture"; Pearson, *Conservation of Marine Archaeological Objects*.

4. Hamilton, "Methods of Conserving Archaeological Material Culture," 19.

5. Hamilton, *Conservation of Metal Objects from Underwater Sites*.

6. Hamilton, "Methods of Conserving Archaeological Material Culture."

7. Ibid., 92.

8. Pearson, *Conservation of Marine Archaeological Objects*, 242; Hamilton, "Methods of Conserving Archaeological Material Culture," 100.

9. Maseman, "Conservation Treatment Reports."

10. Bratten, "Buried Secrets."

7

Pensacola's Public Participation

Outreach and Engagement

DELLA A. SCOTT-IRETON

In Pensacola the tale of the ill-fated Luna expedition is well known. The city is touted as "America's First Place City" (despite what St. Augustine may think). A statue of Tristán de Luna is on the waterfront, and the search for the settlement site—(at last identified as this book was being written, but that's a story for a different book)—excited residents for decades. School children in Escambia County learn of the failed colony through field trips to Historic Pensacola Village and other museums, gaining an understanding of our nation's past that most other students do not have.

When news broke that an early Spanish shipwreck had been discovered and that archaeologists believed it could be part of Luna's sunken fleet, the residents of Pensacola and northwest Florida were captivated. The local newspaper, the *Pensacola News Journal*, provided initial information, describing the site and the first artifacts recovered; other papers in Florida quickly picked up the story and followed the ongoing work for months.[1] Soon newspapers around the country were reporting the find based on an Associated Press story.[2] People began clamoring for news and excitedly awaited the next announcement of discovery, hoping the shipwreck was in fact one of Luna's vessels. In 1994 the *Pensacola News Journal* reported in a front-page story that evidence for this likelihood was mounting.[3] In early 1995 the Associated Press released a story that

Figure 7.1. Statue of Tristán de Luna at the Pensacola waterfront. Courtesy of the Florida Department of State, Division of Historical Resources.

ran in newspapers from Stuart to St. Petersburg to Jacksonville, suggesting that the ship may have carried some of the first immigrants to Florida.[4]

The Pensacola Shipwreck Survey team, having shifted gears from survey to excavation to determine the origin of this early Spanish vessel, was determined to involve the public as much as possible in the investigations. We considered the people of Pensacola to be stakeholders in the project; they had supported the survey phase by hosting presentations, providing in-kind services and materials, and assisting with diving operations. We wanted to ensure their continued support and involvement by enabling participation in the excavation phase in whatever ways they wanted. Some people were content to participate by keeping apprised of progress through the newspaper or by attending a lecture. Others wanted to get wet in the field or dirty in the lab, and many visited a display of artifacts and information. In the days before websites—remember, this was the early 1990s—we used conventional tools to engage the local community and others in our work.

From the earliest days of the Pensacola Shipwreck Survey, volunteers helped to drive the progress. I first participated as a volunteer, fresh out of the University of West Florida's first maritime archaeology field school in summer 1989. After being hired as the field supervisor and dive safety officer during the second Pensacola Shipwreck Survey field season, I was determined to ensure that others could gain experience by volunteering. Roger Smith, Jim Spirek, Chuck Hughson, and John Bratten also were eager to have volunteers to help with the work load. Once the Emanuel Point excavation commenced and word got around that we had an early and very important wreck, we were fortunate to have many dedicated volunteers to assist our efforts. Archaeology is a collaborative discipline involving specialists in many fields, some of whom are professional and some are avocational. Archaeology also is unique among the disciplines in that volunteers can, do, and should make significant impacts, enabling work to progress through enthusiastic labor and providing important links to the community. Archaeological projects often rely on volunteer assistance, and avocational archaeologists make lasting contributions to the research.

Of course, we could not just turn people loose on the site without training, so potential volunteers were screened to make sure they had the time and attention to help the project in meaningful ways. This resulted in a cadre of the most devoted, enthusiastic, and committed volunteers I've ever had the pleasure to work with. Among them were Harv Dickey, who at this writing still volunteers his time and expertise with UWF's maritime archaeology program; the late Gigi Bertsch-Naggatz, who turned up in 1989 at UWF's first maritime archaeology field school and went on to become John's invaluable assistant in the conservation lab at the Wentworth Museum; David Pugh, who started as a volunteer, continued as an academic intern, and eventually was hired as staff; Terry Voss, who traveled from his home in south Florida to stay in Pensacola for several weeks to work with us; and Connie Franklin, who did not dive but was instrumental in raising local awareness and support. And

Pensacola's Public Participation: Outreach and Engagement · 227

Figure 7.2. Gigi Bertsch-Naggatz hosting school children on a laboratory tour. Courtesy of the Florida Department of State, Division of Historical Resources.

so many others! A look at the acknowledgments in this volume reveals just how many people donated time, energy, experience, and goodwill to make the Emanuel Point investigations successful. In many ways they enabled work at the Emanuel Point Ship to continue as long as it did. One thing I remember vividly about the excavation project is how we limped along on a shoestring budget, always worried about losing funding, which finally occurred in 1995. State of Florida grants, cash donations, and in-kind contributions of materials and supplies helped us stretch the budget into three years of investigations, and the volunteers in the field and the lab enabled a vast amount of work to be completed.

And it was not just individuals who provided resources. Pensacola companies, organizations, and businesses gave materials, products, services, and cash to support the excavation. In particular Pensacola's diving community assisted our work; Gulf Coast Dive Pros and Scuba Shack gave air fills, emergency gear repairs, and diving operation advice as well as promoting the project among their clients by showing excavation videos and hosting lectures. The Pensacola Maritime Preservation

Society, an organization of local people dedicated to preserving and promoting the community's maritime past, provided support to continue conservation laboratory operations in 1995, after the field project funding ended. The City of Pensacola funded researchers and paleographers to travel to Spanish repositories to conduct archival research and collect copies of documents related to the Luna expedition. Sacred Heart Hospital provided X-rays and CAT scans of artifacts such as the encrusted breastplate, allowing John to formulate the best conservation plan for the objects. Licon Inc., a Pensacola-based company that specialized in design and construction of evaporation equipment, allowed us to collect distilled water when they tested new equipment, providing hundreds of gallons for the conservation lab. Brown Marine Service Inc., a long-time Pensacola boat yard operated by generations of local watermen, supported the project in numerous ways, from hosting fund-raising breakfasts aboard their historic cement houseboat to providing maintenance for our boats. Brown Marine gave us a pontoon boat hull and helped us turn it into a floating platform for screening sediments. Soule Marine gave us an elderly barge to serve as our first dedicated excavation platform; it often sank on top of the site, but we got experience in raising sunken vessels! Local companies looked for ways to help. Subway Sandwiches & Salads gave us empty pickle buckets to use for hauling dredge spoil. T-Square Reprographics searched successfully for increasingly hard-to-find rolls and sheets of Mylar drafting film. Killinger Marine rushed boat engine repair jobs so that we could get back on the water. Pensacola Rubber and Gasket Company gave us industry pricing breaks even though our needs were not technically "industrial." These are just a few of the local businesses that helped us in so many ways. The entire complement is listed in the acknowledgments.

For those people who wanted to be involved but did not have time to volunteer actively, attending presentations and lectures fulfilled their desire to be engaged. Archaeologists are used to giving presentations about their work; we routinely share information with colleagues at professional conferences before publications can be produced. However, the most fun and rewarding presentations are to public audiences such as civic groups, community organizations, youth clubs, schools, and heritage societies. When word got out that one of Luna's ships had been identified, we fielded dozens of calls for lectures. We spoke to elementary schools, historical societies, church congregations, the Pensacola Yacht Club (several times), gardeners, veterans, Rotarians, Civitans, Sertomas, Lions, Oddfellows (where Jim fit right in), Colonial Dames, Elks, and Shriners. If they asked, we spoke to them. We viewed presentations as a way to announce the latest discoveries, generate and sustain interest in the project, and offer opportunities to get involved.

The individual presentations were so popular that we organized several lecture series over the course of the excavation. To appeal to audiences who did not have easy access to our programs for clubs, the lecture series were advertised widely and held in public venues. The Fiesta of Five Flags Association, a local organization that celebrates the founding of Pensacola in 1559, was a strong partner and ally in promoting the shipwreck research. Fiesta provided funding for guest lecturers for the Colonial Shipwreck Lecture Series in the summer of 1993. Intended to update the public on the shipwreck investigation, the free series featured Carl Clausen, former state underwater archaeologist of Florida; J. Barto Arnold III, state marine archaeologist of Texas; James Dunbar, underwater archaeologist with the Florida Bureau of Archaeological Research; and Christopher Amer, state underwater archaeologist of South Carolina. The Fiesta of Five Flags 1994 speaker series included Denise Lakey, an archivist specializing in sixteenth-century Spanish voyages to the Americas; Joe Simmons Jr., a researcher of sixteenth-century shipboard lifeways; and Donald Keith, director of Ships of Discovery. The Fiesta of Five Flags Shipwreck Lecture Series, held in 1997 and hosted by Cordova Mall, featured Denise Lakey speaking on new archival documents from the Luna expedition; Corey Malcom, who excavated the St. John's shipwreck in the Bahamas; and Abraham López, who worked on the Fuxa wreck in Cuba. The Northwest Florida Maritime History Symposium was held in September 1997 after the University of West Florida resumed excavations on the Emanuel Point Ship. The all-day event featured lectures by the Pensacola Shipwreck Survey team and other scholars and researchers in local and maritime history and underwater archaeology. Held at the Holiday Inn in Gulf Breeze and open to the public,

Figure 7.3. Fiesta of Five Flags 1994 banner. Courtesy of the Florida Department of State, Division of Historical Resources.

the symposium was sponsored by the City of Gulf Breeze, Gulf Breeze Historical Society, and South Santa Rosa County Tourist Development Council.

For the archaeological community who was following the shipwreck investigations closely, the annual conference of the Society for Historical Archaeology was the logical venue to share our findings. Roger organized and chaired a symposium, "The Emanuel Point Ship: A Florida Experiment in Research, Development, and Management," at the 1995

Conference on Historical and Underwater Archaeology, held in Washington, D.C. Papers featured discussion of the ship's architecture, organic remains, ceramic assemblage, and the many unusual and unique artifacts that had turned up, which we called "things that make you go 'ooohhhhh'!"[5] Another symposium was held in 1998 at the conference in Atlanta, Georgia, titled "The Emanuel Point Ship: The Second Field Campaign on a Vessel from Tristán de Luna's 1559 Fleet." Again organized by Roger, the session included papers about artifacts, hull structure, and the makeup of the fleet as well as about the local partnerships developed for research and preservation and an educational packet developed for teachers. Five of the six papers were published in the conference proceedings.[6]

Exhibits and displays of artifacts are another way to share findings with a large segment of the public, and the Historic Pensacola Village museums, already heavily visited by locals and tourists, were eager to host Luna artifacts. The T. T. Wentworth, Jr. Florida State Museum, then operated by the Historic Pensacola Preservation Board (now the UWF Historic Trust), was the first to mount an exhibit. Long a supporter of local archaeology, the Historic Pensacola Preservation Board was an early partner in the excavation project, providing space in the basement of the Wentworth for the first laboratory dedicated to the conservation of waterlogged artifacts. As items were deemed stable and ready for display, John added them to the exhibit along with interpretive text to describe their origin and use. People visited and revisited the museum to see artifacts they had read about in the newspaper. The Archaeology Institute on the campus of UWF also included Emanuel Point Ship artifacts in displays of local university projects. Located on shore within view of the Emanuel Point wreck, the Pensacola Visitor Center often was the first place where out-of-town tourists learned of the excavation. A telescope set up inside the center enabled people to see the excavation barge and activities, while a large poster provided information about the history of the Luna expedition, discovery of the shipwreck, and artifacts recovered. The poster, updated regularly, still hangs there for all to see. A Florida historical marker, placed on the visitor center grounds in 2016, officially commemorates the first multiyear European colony in Florida. Today visitors can see current displays of information about the Emanuel Point research at these facilities, which continue to promote Pensacola's fascinating archaeological discoveries.

In addition to becoming a local celebrity, the Emanuel Point Ship also drew international dignitaries. In the spring of 1998, the Spanish Honorary Vice-Consul María Davis invited Queen Sofía and the commanding officer of the Spanish Navy to participate in the 300th anniversary celebration of the second Spanish settlement at Pensacola, Santa María de Galve, established in 1698. On June 9 Spain's four-masted training ship *Juan Sebastián de Elcano* sailed into Pensacola Bay to commemorate the occasion. The next day the president and prime minister of Spain, José María Aznar, and a delegation of dignitaries, who included a living descendant of Tristán de Luna, arrived in Pensacola and were met by Florida Governor Lawton Chiles and a number of public officials aboard the Spanish training ship.[7] During the ceremony Roger was formally introduced to President Aznar and presented him with a copy of the Emanuel Point Ship report. A small armada of local boats motored out to the site of the shipwreck, and *Elcano*'s captain softly recited an old Spanish naval prayer before laying a wreath of greenery into the water.[8]

Vice-Consul Davis also arranged a visit by Spanish royalty, King Juan Carlos I and Queen Sofía, who arrived in Pensacola on February 19, 2009, to commemorate the 450th anniversary of the Tristán de Luna colony. They were met by Governor Charlie Crist and a large flag-waving crowd in Plaza Ferdinand. The king gathered several red carnations from a group of children, politely saying, "Gracias," as one of the girls shouted, "We love you!" Queen Sofía was handed yellow roses and other flowers. As they entered the T. T. Wentworth Jr. Florida State Museum, the queen said to Crist, "Very, very nice people." He responded, "They love you, they love you." At the museum the royal couple were shown artifacts from the Emanuel Point Ship. The king pointed out rat bones in a display case and the queen asked about the *blanca* coin dated 1471. "Who's on it?" she asked. She was told Spain's King Enrique IV. "Oh my goodness! Fantastic."[9] These visits were avidly covered by the Pensacola media, which by then had been reporting on the discovery and investigation of the shipwreck for years.

From the very beginning of the Pensacola Shipwreck Survey project, even before discovery of the Luna shipwreck, local media featured stories

Figure 7.4. King Juan Carlos I (*left*), Queen Sofía, and Governor Charlie Crist visiting the shipwreck artifact exhibit. Copyrighted photo used with permission, *Pensacola News Journal*/pnj.com

and updates. The *Pensacola News Journal* was our most reliable media friend, and we got to know several reporters quite well, including *PNJ*'s Dave Goodwin and Bill Kaczor of the Associated Press. Press conferences always were well attended by local media outlets, such as the one on July 25, 1995, held by the Pensacola Maritime Preservation Society to reveal the newly recovered *blanca* coin, breastplate, and Aztec ceramics. The event concluded with a tour of the conservation lab in the basement of the T. T. Wentworth Museum. Pensacola television and radio stations, including WEAR TV3, BLABB public access, and WUWF radio, featured staff and students for talk shows and public interest stories, reaching thousands of viewers and listeners. National television crews turned up too—recall our experience with FX's *Breakfast Time*. The best part of that was watching celebrated and respected archaeologists Judy Bense and Roger Smith jazzercising on the 17th Street boat ramp!

News about the ongoing investigations also was featured farther afield. For example, the fall 1995 issue of the Society for Historical Archaeology

Newsletter included a discussion about the first phase of excavations concluded that year.[10] At the time, only 20 percent of the site was estimated to have been investigated. A story on the shipwreck appeared in *EFE News*, a Spanish-language news service, on August 28, 1996.[11] The monthly digest *Sea History Gazette*, published by the National Maritime Historical Society, featured the story, "Archaeologists Studying the Emanuel Point Shipwreck," promoting the news to maritime historians throughout the country and around the world.[12] *Archaeology* Magazine, produced by the Archaeological Institute of America and one of the most widely read popular sources of archaeological information worldwide, included a story about the shipwreck and Luna's settlement attempt.[13] Even the Neiman Marcus magazine *Entrée* got in on the excitement, with an article titled "Luna's Lost Galleon."[14] In Lisbon, Portugal, the Emanuel Point Ship was featured at an international symposium on Iberian-Atlantic shipping.[15] Years later the project continued to generate enough interest for stories to be featured in such magazines as *Humanities*, produced by the National Endowment for the Humanities, and the Florida Department of State's *Florida History & the Arts*.[16]

The story of the Emanuel Point Ship's discovery and investigation would not be complete without including the engagement and support of the Pensacola community in general, and especially the contributions of dedicated volunteers who assisted in the field and the laboratory. The involvement and lasting interest of the people of Pensacola inspired and encouraged us, even as funding dwindled. At this writing, as work continues on the second Emanuel Point vessel and investigation of the Luna settlement land site begins to reveal clues, Pensacola remains a proud partner in archaeology.

Notes

1. Goodwin, "Wreck Could Be De Luna's"; Kaczor, "Divers Hail Shipwreck Discovery"; Kaczor, "Spanish Shipwreck Dates to 16th Century."
2. Associated Press, "Carving of Galleon Found in Shipwreck"; Associated Press, "Tiny Copy of Spanish Ship."
3. Goodwin, "Experts: Ship Might Be Luna's."
4. Kaczor, "Wreck Believed to Be Immigrants' Galleon."
5. Smith, "Emanuel Point Ship: A Florida."

6. Smith, "Discovery, Development, and Interpretation of Florida's Earliest Shipwreck."
7. Bense, "Spanish President Visits Site of First Pensacola."
8. Associated Press, "Spanish Sailing Ship Captain Pays Homage at Shipwreck."
9. Associated Press, "Spanish King and Queen Visit Florida."
10. Smith, "Florida."
11. Malone, "Primer Establecimiento Europeo Puede."
12. *Sea History Gazette*, "Archaeologists Studying the Emanuel Point Shipwreck."
13. Smith, "Ill-Fated Galleon."
14. Brown, "Luna's Lost Galleon."
15. Smith, "Emanuel Point Ship: A 16th-century Vessel of Spanish Colonization."
16. James Williford, "Underwater Cities"; Scott-Ireton, "Secrets in the Sea."

8

What We Learned

Conclusions

JOHN R. BRATTEN, JOSEPH COZZI,
DELLA A. SCOTT-IRETON, ROGER C. SMITH,
JAMES D. SPIREK, AND JOHN E. WORTH

In the shallow waters off Emanuel Point, the lower hull of what once was a large wooden sailing ship, weighed down by ballast stones, gradually settled into the seabed and became entombed for centuries by layers of sediments and shells. A violent storm had caused the ship to strike the outer edge of a sand bar, and repeated pounding of the hull as it lay on its port side caused planks and frames to break open, dooming the vessel. Grounded in less than three *brazas* (fathoms) of water at Bahía de Santa María de Filipina, in the Mar del Norte, the ship had reached its last port of call. Fortunately, after the storm abated, some of the vessel's equipment and cargo were accessible below decks and could be salvaged by the survivors. However, as archaeologists, we know that people do not clean up after themselves very well.

The ship's keel (*quilla*) was laid some years earlier in a Spanish shipyard; its shipwrights and carpenters followed the traditional methods of building blue-water vessels for transatlantic voyaging. They chose seasoned timbers of white oak, tested over centuries of seafaring for soundness and durability. According to the construction contract, they were to build a ship of some 400 *toneladas*, equipped for safety with two pumps instead of one. Prefabricated frames, shaped to templates, were erected at primary stations along the keel to give the hull its general form. Secondary frames, each carefully carved to follow the hull's gradual rising and narrowing body, then were inserted between the principal frames from bow to stern. Those at the stern, where the hull narrowed to meet the straight sternpost and rudder, were notched out to fit over the keel. The last few tail frames also needed to fit over a long, curved knee that braced the sternpost to the keel. Frames in the bow were notched to fit over the keel but angled slightly forward as they approached the stempost (*roda*), a curved timber joined to the forward end of the keel.

A heavy keelson (*contraquilla*), notched along the bottom at the prescribed intervals, was set into place over the frames and bolted to the keel. The thickest part of the keelson was fashioned with a large recessed mortise to hold the heel of the ship's mainmast. At the bottom of the mortise, a shipwright chiseled a cross, perhaps to mark the location of the main frame at the widest part of the hull. Just behind the mortise, carpenters had cut out concavities for a pump shaft on either side of the keelson. Once in place, the mast step area of the keelson was supported on each side by four small transverse buttresses to prevent lateral shifting of the assembly under the stress of sail. Between the buttresses, carpenters fashioned thin boards that covered the open spaces to the bottom of the hull, but could be lifted to inspect the area for trash that might clog the bilge. As this work progressed, one of the men left behind a small gimlet or auger; we can imagine him wondering what had become of it.

Other workmen laid internal planking inside the hull, fastening it to the frames below. Strakes of ceiling planks, above and below a thick footwale, would help to protect the frames and outer hull planking from shifting cargo and ballast stones. Some had to be custom fit, especially around the buttresses and pump sumps. To isolate the sumps from ballast and cargo that might interfere with the pumps, carpenters constructed a box to enclose the area. As this job was being completed, scraps of wood wound up in the pump well, one of them whittled into the silhouette of sailing ship much like the one being built.

Meanwhile, a team of men on the outside of the hull bent long strakes of planking (*tablazón*) to the frames and pinned them in place with hundreds of wrought-iron nails. After each was fastened securely, the caulkers began their work. Seams between planks were scraped and scored to allow the insertion of tarred oakum (*estopa*), which was pounded home with irons and mallets. At the stern, wrought-iron rudder gudgeons were bolted to the sternpost. They had been made to fit the hull by blacksmiths, who bent and welded straps of bar stock over forged rings to serve as hinges for the rudder, which was being fitted with corresponding pintles. The pintles similarly were forged, but with a pin instead of a ring. Above the ceiling planks inside the hull, beams for the lower deck were laid athwartships, perpendicular to the keelson. The ends of each deck beam rested on a thick shelf clamp (*contradurmiente*) running along each side of the hull and were supported by L-shaped hanging knees (*curvas*). Planking of the lower deck was nailed to the deck beams, completing the basic structure of the hull.

After the ship had been framed, decked, and planked, it was ready to be launched into the water and fitted with masts, rigging, and superstructure. Before launching, the hull was partially filled with fixed stone ballast (*lastre*) culled from cartloads of stones delivered to the shipyard by ballast mongers. The mongers collected stones where they could—from rock quarries, river banks, beaches, and ballast dumps. Dense, water-worn stones were placed at the bottom of the hold; smaller cobbles and pebbles were spread between them to form the initial layer of ballast that would keep the ship upright while its fitting out was completed dockside.

Shipowners and shipwrights knew from sorry experience that vessels entering the Indies trade were soon besieged by worms (*broma*) that bored their way into the wood below the waterline and consumed it. Warm waters of American ports, where a merchantman might lie idle between ladings, accelerated the shipworms' inevitable attack; prevention was less expensive than remedy. Worms entered the hull at the vulnerable open-grain ends of the planks and at the seams between them. While the newly built ship was still on the ways, sheets of lead were unrolled and cut into long strips; barrels of flat-headed, wrought-iron tacks were brought from the yard storehouse; old sailcloth was collected, and tar buckets made ready. Workers set about laying up tarred cloth along planking seams below the anticipated waterline of the hull. Next, they nailed the strips of lead over vertical and horizontal seams, taking care to pound an additional row of tacks directly into the oakum-filled seams. The sheathing not only covered the seams but also served to prevent their caulking from coming loose as the ship's hull worked at sea. As an added measure of protection, the arms of the gudgeons also were covered with sheathing because the fasteners to these fittings tended to become stressed at sea and eventually provide an opportunity for worm infestation in this critical area.

When the expensive and labor-intensive task of sheathing was completed, the ship was launched and its rudder (*timón*) installed. Made of two heavy balks of straight timber let into each other, joined on edge and through-bolted, the rudder, like the ship it would serve, was a marvel of craftsmanship. Designed to capture water currents delivered to it by the narrowing of the hull below the waterline, the rudder was just wide enough to serve as a foil, but not so wide as to become unwieldy to operate. Custom-fitted with pintles and straps that wrapped around the entire structure, the rudder was hung into gudgeons at the sternpost. The task of hanging the rudder involved careful alignment and coordinated engineering because the rudder's forward face had been crafted with recessed slots at each pintle that would only allow the pins to fit into their respective gudgeon rings when the rudder was inserted into place from the port side of the ship. This clever arrangement allowed a close fit with little play in the hinges and maximized the juxtaposition of wood surfaces between the sternpost and rudder.

Masts were inserted into the hull and made fast with standing rigging made of hemp (*cáñamo*) and Spanish *esparto* grass; the rigging was fine-tuned then tarred to make it weatherproof. Spars to carry sails were fixed to the masts and rove with the tackle of running rigging that would allow yards and sails to be adjusted while under way at sea. At the same time, carpenters finished their tasks of installing internal bulkheads—taking care to strengthen the gunpowder storeroom (*rancho de Santa Barbara*)—and building the superstructure above the main deck. The forecastle (*tilla*) rose above the heavy beak (*espolón*) that projected from the stempost. On top, an open platform (*castillo*) surrounded with a low bulwark and rail offered a strategic location for mariners to work the rigging of the foresail and spritsail and to deploy weapons during a sea battle. The sterncastle (*tolda*) consisted of a half deck that served as an open bridge, from which the captain and officers commanded the vessel and the mariners worked the running rigging. Below was a partially enclosed area for the rudder tiller and navigational apparatus. Above the *tolda* was the quarter deck (*cuadra cubierta*), the highest part of the superstructure, which was used for conning the ship. Below it was an enclosed roundhouse (*chupeta*), where the ship's commander had his private cabin. The quarter deck and the roundhouse made up the *toldilla*, which encompassed the after portion of the half deck, immediately above the steering station on the main deck.

To complete fitting out of the ship, hemp cables (*guindalesas*) for mooring, anchoring, and docking were taken aboard, as were wrought-iron anchors ranging in size from the large sheet anchor (*ancla de salvación*) to a small grappling hook (*cloque*). In the waist of the ship on the main deck was a metal firebox (*fogón*) filled with sand. Pans (*galletas*), copper cauldrons (*calderas*), and cooking pots (*ollas*) on hooks were used to prepare food in the "island of pots," which was used primarily in clear weather. The ship was now ready for its first voyage. A universe of other items—including arms, artillery, ammunition, spare nautical equipment and utensils, and medical supplies—would be added to the ship's complement, as would crew, cargo, passengers, and provisions, according to the purpose and destination of the new vessel.

The ship's sailing career took it to Spanish American waters, where it delivered European goods and products needed in the colonies. One product, quicksilver, was delivered to the port of Veracruz to be used in the silver mines of New Spain. Difficult to transport, the liquid mercury (*azogue*) had to be loaded at the last minute in Spain because its corrosive nature tended to rot its packing and cause leakage. Poured into sheepskin bags bound with hemp rope, the mercury was placed in a small, oak cask that was nailed shut. Three such casks fit into a rectangular wooden chest with a tightly nailed lid. Because mercury was a strictly controlled royal monopoly, the king's coat of arms was painted on a linen cloth attached to each chest. Bound with heavy rope, each chest was wrapped in coarse matting and bound again. Nonetheless, before the voyage was over, some of the king's mercury managed to escape and work its way to the bottom of the ship, from where it could not be recovered.

On another voyage the ship carried New World products back to Spain. One of these products may have been cowhides (*cueros*), loaded either in New Spain or on the island of Hispaniola, where cattle industries thrived. Accompanying this cargo were hungry beetles of a species that feeds on stored leather goods and other substances with a high protein content. Several of these hide beetles remained with the ship after the cargo reached its destination; their wing covers migrated down into the bilge.

Passengers and crew on Spanish vessels in the sixteenth century subsisted on sea rations that consisted of wine, salted pork and fish, beans and peas, oil, vinegar, garlic, rice, and sometimes cheese or beef. Evidence of these staples aboard the ship includes the bones of domestic pig, cow, sheep or goat, and chicken. Several specimens exhibit butchering marks, suggesting that they were part of standard provisions prepared before the voyage by boiling and salting. Chickens may have come aboard live to be consumed by their passenger owners. Although fish probably was among the staple foodstuffs on the ship, fish elements found among the materials at the bottom of the hold are typical of Gulf of Mexico varieties and probably were deposited in the ship after it wrecked.

Supplementary to sea rations, edible fruits and nuts were consumed aboard the ship during its sailing career. Traditional Mediterranean food items, such as olives, plums or prunes, cherries, and hazelnuts, are represented by dietary remains found in the bilge. Other fruits and nuts, including papaya, sapote, coconut, hickory, and acorn, reflect the ship's operation in the tropical Caribbean and temperate northern Gulf of Mexico. Although the hickory and acorn may be intrusive to the shipwreck, they also may have been carried as fodder for live animals such as pigs.

Inevitably, unwelcome stowaways boarded the ship along with provisions. Their eggs, perhaps borne in hampers of sea biscuit (*bizcocho*) from the bakers, hatched in the darkness of the bread locker below deck. Despite every effort to rid the vessel of the uninvited pests, cockroaches (*curianas*) multiplied in the dim and humid recesses of the hold, taking over stored provisions at night. Jokingly called "game birds" by a mariner of the time, they competed for sustenance at sea with larger stowaways—rodents. Black wharf rats (*ratones*) colonized the ship's bilges, constantly gnawing into foodstuffs that became partially consumed and contaminated during the voyage. Apart from being a nuisance, the rats also carried disease, and for this reason they periodically were hunted down by the ship's crew under direction of the boatswain. Compared with the "game birds," these larger "game" had a harsher existence aboard the ship. Their remains exhibit evidence of rickets (a growth-stunting condition caused by lack of essential vitamins), poor dental health, and cannibalism. Aside from cockroaches and rats, the ship was occupied by common house mice, remains of which also were present in the bilge. This discovery, in light of the more numerous rat population, suggests that mice had developed their own niche in the floating ecosystem and perhaps should be called ship mice rather than house mice.

As with most wooden sailing vessels, the Emanuel Point Ship required constant maintenance and repairs during its career at sea. Many larger ports along the Spanish American trade route offered facilities and manpower with which to clean ships' bottoms and to patch or replace worm-eaten and leaking planks. In an emergency some leaks could be stopped at sea by divers, who descended carrying tarred lead patches that they quickly nailed to the hull while the ship lay off the wind. More permanent repairs could be effected between voyages in the safety of a harbor. The ship was tied broadside to a wharf in shallow water, and its ballast was laboriously offloaded by hand to lighten the hull. The vessel then was hauled over with winches and tackle to expose the hull below the waterline. During this careening operation, marine growth of barnacles and weeds was scraped away by gangs of local laborers, who also applied fire with torches passed over bare planks in an attempt to kill shipworms by heat and smoke. Worn lead sheathing was removed and replaced; the old lead probably was recycled at the repair yard or sold as scrap to the lead mongers. Planks that were beyond repair were replaced by others, custom-fit into place, then caulked and tarred. When one side of the hull had been cleaned and repaired, the tackle was relieved to allow the hull to come back on an even keel and rotated 180 degrees. The same process then was repeated on the opposite side of the hull.

Although accumulations of rotting marine organisms, fouled wood and caulking, and hot tar made these tasks unpleasant, especially in tropical ports, the concurrent job of clearing the hold of slimy ballast stones could become unbearable, even with all the hatches opened. Stenches from the bilge, rotting trash, and the panic of scurrying pests conspired to discourage even the most hardened workers in the darkness of the lower hold. Once cleared, the bilges were doused with diluted vinegar in an attempt to offset the effects of their rank recesses on the repairmen, who began to inspect waterways, pumps, and internal framing. When structural elements of the hull were discovered to be rotten or damaged, the workmen took the opportunity to repair or replace them. Careening and repairs completed, the ship was reballasted. Depending on its next mission, the amount of stones was adjusted accordingly. Although the hull required a standard amount of "permanent" ballast to offset the effects of wind and waves, a heavy complement of artillery and ammunition or a cargo of quicksilver in the hold required less additional ballast than a consignment of leather goods and dyestuffs aboard a lightly armed merchantman. With most of the larger stones in place, "filler" stones from the ballast dump were brought aboard and distributed in the hold until the attitude of the hull in the water was gauged appropriate for its anticipated load. Perhaps it was at this point that a small copper coin, out of circulation for years, made its way into the ship along with recycled ballast that had served a previous succession of ships.

On its last voyage, the Emanuel Point Ship appears to have been lightly ballasted, as would have been appropriate for an armed ship carrying heavy cargo. Judging from the overall extent and depth of stones present on the shipwreck site, the ballast alone would not have been sufficient to stabilize the vessel adequately under sail. Although no artillery was found at the wreck site, a variety of ammunition recovered from the ship's stern indicates that the ship carried a battery of heavy shipboard artillery and lighter, rapid-firing swivel guns (*versos*) that undoubtedly were high priority salvage items after the hurricane.

The Emanuel Point Ship grounded violently on a shallow sand bar, far inside a normally placid and protected bay. The force with which she pounded caused the hull to break apart longitudinally; the port side separated from the ship, and she filled with water. Her back broken and frames sheared apart, the sunken wreck came to rest heeling slightly to the wounded port side. Below decks, everything was thrown forward by the impact; pots and pans were toppled, tablewares cascaded toward the bow, and barrels and jars of provisions released their contents as they broke open. At some point the galleon's rudder became unshipped from

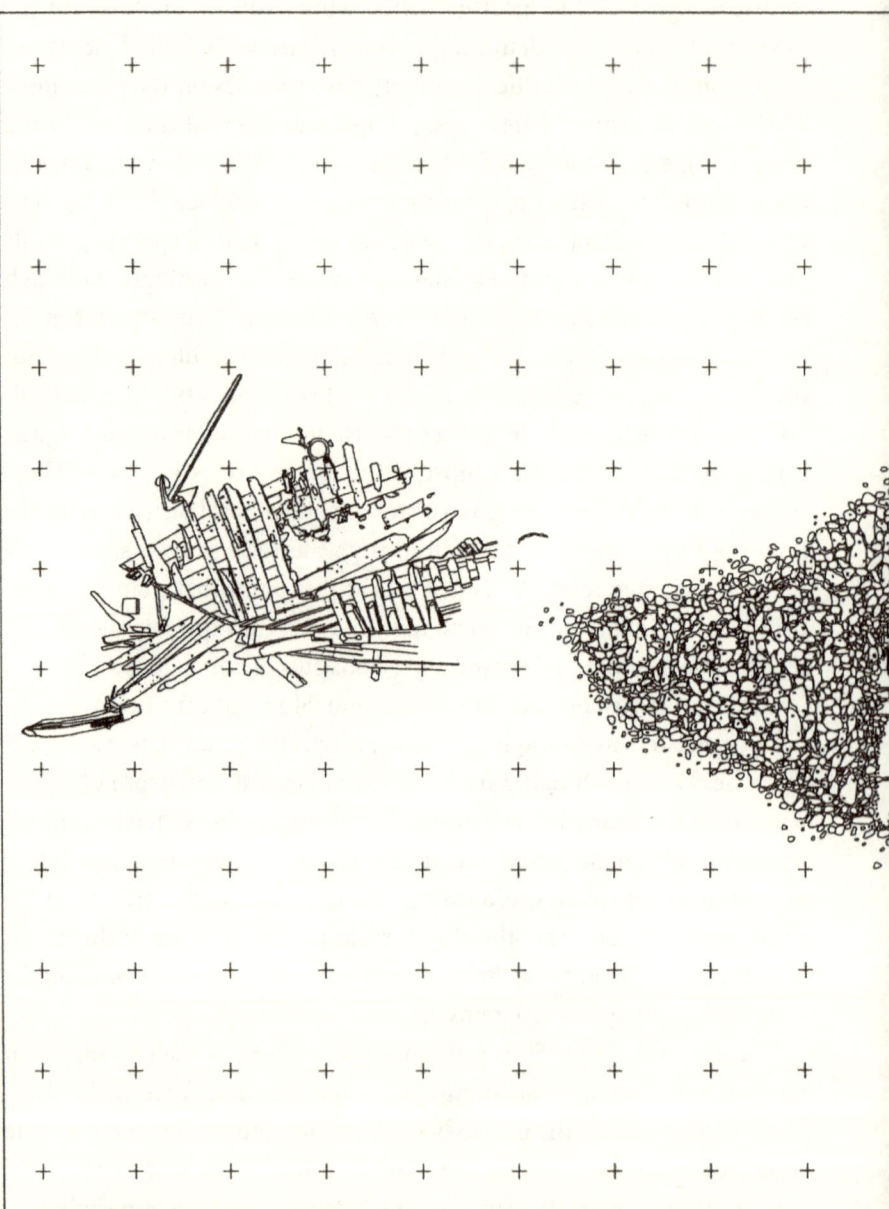

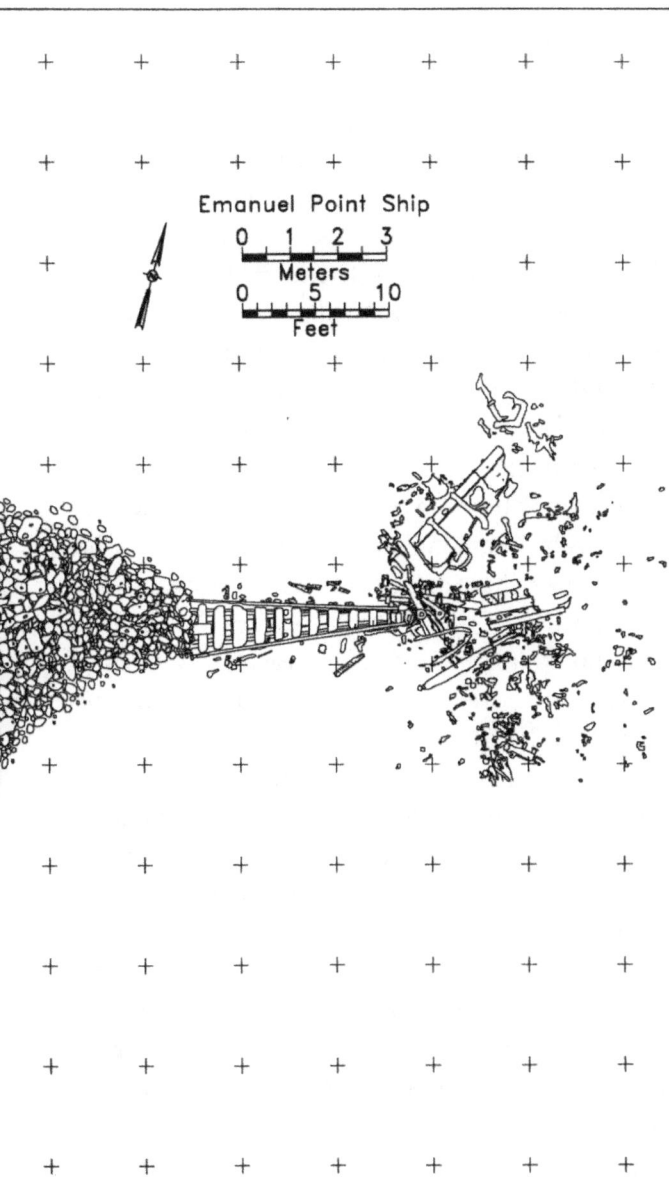

Figure 8.1. Final site plan of the Emanuel Point Ship, showing excavation trenches amidships and exposed areas of the stern and bow. Site plan by "Coz" Cozzi, James Spirek, and Lee McKenzie. Courtesy of the Florida Department of State, Division of Historical Resources.

its hinges and landed flat on the sand bar next to the stern. In addition, the upper side of the starboard bow collapsed, falling outward and away from the stem to which it had been attached, perhaps under the weight of the ship's anchor. As sand and silt drifted into the breached lower hull, its contents gradually became buried as a time-frozen tableau of turmoil. The collapsed starboard bow, with its anchor at deck level, rapidly sank into the sands to be preserved for posterity. Above decks, the timbers, planks, and spars that were not carried away deteriorated slowly into the elements and vanished from the site. As an artificial reef, the wreckage became home to opportunistic marine life seeking shelter and sustenance on the barren sand bar. For generations, shellfish lived and died in their seasonal cycles, depositing growing layers of shell that capped the galleon's grave, protecting it from the world above.

Two campaigns of fieldwork between 1992 and 1998, accompanied by jellyfish, unwelcome visits by migrating birds and crabs, unwieldy ballast stones, innumerable razor-sharp oysters, and often murky and chilly water, exposed a large portion of this sixteenth-century shipwreck for careful study and collection. With the unlocking of each excavation unit, wonderful things appeared in the sediments, resurrected after more than four centuries of sleep. At each turn, progress temporarily was halted by the discovery of yet another curious artifact emerging from the wreckage. From inside and outside the hull, thousands of objects and specimens were collected, including European and Native American ceramics, Old World and New World botanical and faunal remains, wooden tools, stone and lead ammunition, copper galley wares, and the remains of insects and rodents that inhabited the bilge during the sailing career of the vessel. Archaeology continued (and still continues) in the laboratory, where recovered materials are stabilized and studied, compared with finds from other archaeological sites, and used by graduate students to research and write master's theses. Years of analysis and consultation with experts in several professional fields have given us many clues about the life and death of this early Spanish ship.

Among the many discoveries was the realization that the Emanuel Point Ship was a larger vessel than we had anticipated. With a keel length of more than 20 m, its hull length is estimated to have been more than 34 m (100 feet). It must have been one of the capital ships of each convoy in which it sailed and probably carried its fair share of passengers and merchandise to the colonies, returning to Spain with substantially profitable cargoes. Its role in the fleet of Tristán de Luna most likely was that of a larger cargo vessel transporting people and their equipment to a new destination, rather like a moving van. In proportion to the overall size of the wrecked ship's hull, a relatively small amount of ballast was found on its central timbers, indicating that it had been heavily loaded on its last voyage and required only light ballasting prior to lading. Analysis of ballast samples indicates that the stones are diverse in size and type, and some may have been stowed in the hold while the ship was docked at a New World port.

By the time of its last voyage, the galleon was a veteran of ocean transport, its bottom full of the cracks and leaks of old age. European-built with craftsmanship and economy, perhaps in the Basque country of northern Spain, it must have completed several voyages to the Americas before steering northward toward Florida, its last port of call. Inevitably, the stress of seafaring and the worms of warmer waters took their toll on its hull. At least one major repair—replacement of an aging tail frame in the stern and the substitution of American for European oak in several parts of the hull—took place in a competent shipyard between Atlantic cargo runs. Rotten and worm-eaten wood was removed, and custom-carved new pieces were put into place. However, sea-worn seams between planks below the waterline still wanted to throw their caulking out, so they were shielded with strips of lead carefully tacked to the hull. Other persistent leaks were patched with larger pieces of lead, especially in places where iron hardware had been fastened, including the arms of the rudder gudgeons. Forestalling the inevitable last voyage, its owners had kept the ship afloat and from the scrapping yard; the vessel had long since paid for itself, and each additional assignment at sea meant more profit. But these measures were meaningless in the face of a hurricane.

After the storm, the wrecked ship and its contents were accessible to survivors on the nearby shore, who undoubtedly saved what they could from the broken hull. When discovered centuries later by archaeologists, the site contained no evidence of cargo above the bay floor or atop the ballast, where it would have been stowed. The salvors may have contributed to the collapse of the hull in attempts to fish up sunken cargo or dismantle wood for use on shore. We found a broken olive jar, iron cask hoop, and two port covers trapped below the starboard side, all of which appear to have fallen to the bay floor early in the ship's deformation process. Curiously, the associated anchor, discovered in its appropriate location for catting to the bow but buried fluke-down in the sand bar, was found to have been broken. Its ring and the top of its shank, where a wooden stock would have been attached, were twisted and sheared from the main portion of the anchor. The ring was not found. That the anchor was broken is not surprising; Spanish anchors were notoriously weak and have been found deformed and broken on other sixteenth-century shipwrecks. What is not clear is how and when the anchor was broken. It may have failed during the wrecking event, or possibly it was broken in a subsequent attempt to retrieve it after it had become embedded in the sand.

However accessible the wreckage was from shore or how persistent the salvors were, many of their things were left behind for archaeologists later to ponder. A collection of copper utensils found forward of the ballast in the narrow confines of the bow opens a new avenue for comparative studies of early European provisioning and food preparation at sea. Along with fragments of ceramic jars and tablewares, the remains of stored meat, olives, and other foodstuffs offer a glimpse of the cultural fares of immigrants en route to a new colony. The cupreous wares—cauldrons for cooking, a cauldron for melting tar, pans, a funnel, and tin-plated containers—are precisely the items listed by at least one contemporary author as being essential shipboard galley implements. The mortar and pestle are kitchen utensils still in use today. However, excavations in the ship's bow revealed no evidence of a galley stove or any brick or tile structure below decks, suggesting that cooking was accomplished on an open hearth on deck.

Ceramic storage containers and glazed tablewares also are to be expected on Spanish colonial sites, whether maritime or terrestrial. Recent studies of olive jars from dated Spanish shipwrecks have refined their typology and chronology, allowing those that we found to be recognized as a mid-sixteenth-century Early Middle Style. Fragments were situated throughout the site, some coated internally with pitch or glaze for carrying liquids. Glazed tablewares were found in a greater frequency at the bow of the ship, associated with the galley utensils. Lead-glazed El Morro plate and bowl fragments and tin-enameled majolica varieties Columbia Plain, Yayal Blue on White, Seville Blue on Blue, and Isabela Polychrome were represented aboard the ship. An intact plate of the latter variety was found beneath the crown of the ship's anchor. The greater frequency of El Morro and Columbia Plain fragments, as opposed to Isabela Polychrome, reveals that more common rather than high-class tablewares were in use on board. Similarly, a tally of animal bones found in association with broken containers in the bow shows a predominance of beef ribs, which would have been provisioning elements of a common fare, rather than choicer cuts of meat.

Compared with other sixteenth-century shipwrecks, recoveries of military-related artifacts were sparse, undoubtedly due to subsequent salvage activities that likely placed great emphasis on retrieving arms and ordnance. However, examples of artillery shot made of stone, iron, lead, and a composite of iron and lead provide clues to the ordnance once carried on the ship. Small lead shot for shoulder arms and copper crossbow bolt heads demonstrate that these weapons also were on board. At the time, the arquebus had replaced the crossbow on most European battlefields, but in the New World crossbows were still useful. Finally, discovery of body armor—an encrusted breastplate—in the stern suggests that at least a few persons on board were prepared for personal combat at sea or ashore. The presence of a breastplate that was old-fashioned for the time points to a mid-sixteenth-century colonial transition in military technology that is reflected in the entire collection of arms-related objects from the site. Recovery of obsidian blades, also found on two other contemporary shipwrecks, may reflect an unusual facet of this transition as it applied to New Spain, where use of the blades may have continued despite modern European weapons.

Clues to the Emanuel Point Ship's final port of embarkation consist of sherds found in the stern from at least three different pots identified as a post-classic native Aztec style made in the Central Valley of Mexico. The presence of these unusual ceramics has not been reported on colonial shipwreck sites, suggesting that they probably were not cargo. Rather, the native pottery may have belonged to a person, or persons, on board the ship, perhaps the Aztec Indian contingent of the expedition.

The pottery style—especially the burnished and painted, molded facial design—is indicative of a ceremonial rather than utilitarian vessel that would have been used on special occasions by persons of special status. This personal connection with the Aztec (and subsequent Spanish) capital of Mexico suggests that the ship embarked from the principal Mexican port of San Juan de Ulúa (Veracruz). Documents confirm that this was the port from which the fleet of Tristán de Luna sailed.

Other archaeological clues provide us with a general date for the ship's sinking. The earliest datable artifact is the Henry IV coin, minted in Spain between 1471 and 1474. This find provides an absolute, if eccentric, *terminus post quem* (date after which) for the ship's arrival in Pensacola. This Old World coin was replaced in the colonies by large numbers of coins that began to be minted at Mexico City in 1535. A more realistic, if general, earliest date after which the voyage occurred is provided by the presence of mercury in the shipwreck. Although small quantities were found during excavations at La Isabela in the Dominican Republic (1493–ca. 1498), quicksilver was not imported in quantity to the New World until 1556, when it was required for a new silver amalgamation process. As for a *terminus ante quem* (date before which) for the ship's last voyage, examples of ceramics offer the best clues. The Aztec pottery sherds, if actually associated with Cuauhtitlán potters, would have been from pots made prior to 1576, when a plague epidemic caused a sudden decline in production. More significantly, the larger collection of Spanish olive jar fragments recovered from the site consists predominantly of a type that was superseded by another style by 1580. A smaller number of lead-glazed sherds of the Melado variety are dated from colonial Spanish sites inhabited between 1492 and 1550. These preliminary clues suggest that the ship embarked on its last voyage sometime between the 1550s and 1570s—a time frame that encompasses the Luna colonization episode at Pensacola.

A chronological chart was developed to illustrate the relationship between artifacts recovered from the Emanuel Point Ship and the 1559 expedition of Tristán de Luna. General beginning and ending dates for the occurrences of similar materials on archaeological sites were plotted along a timeline for visual reference. Three important time markers—1492, the date after which European artifacts appear in the

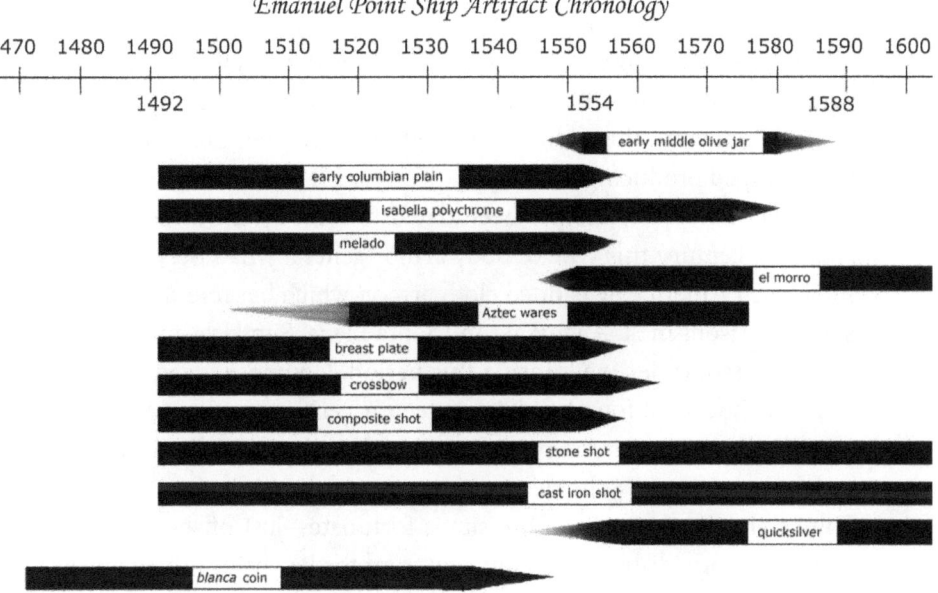

Figure 8.2. Chronological chart of the Emanuel Point Ship artifacts. Courtesy of the Florida Department of State, Division of Historical Resources.

Americas; 1554, the date of shipwreck materials from the Padre Island fleet; and 1588, the date of shipwreck materials from the Spanish Armada—have been used to place the Pensacola shipwreck into a chronological perspective.

For example, Emanuel Point olive jar sherds are of a recently recognized transitional form between Early and Middle styles. By the 1580s this form had disappeared; the 1588 Spanish Armada carried true Middle Style olive jars, as characterized by a different rim shape. Columbia Plain majolica found on the shipwreck is of the early variety, dating to the first half of the sixteenth century. Similarly, Isabela Polychrome majolica, also prevalent on most early Spanish sites in the Americas, declines in frequency after 1550 but still has been found in excavations at the early Spanish colonies of St. Augustine, Florida, and Santa Elena, South Carolina. Because lead-glazed Melado earthenware found on the shipwreck are time markers for the early sixteenth century, they are absent from St. Augustine and Santa Elena. However, El Morro earthenware occupies a later context on Spanish sites, beginning in the middle of the sixteenth century and continuing until the eighteenth century. Less understood are the Aztec ceramics found at the stern of the shipwreck. A native Mexican redware tradition that apparently was influenced by colonial Spanish demands, this pottery is thought to have been made by potters who stopped producing in 1576.

While the breastplate has been dated to 1510, by the middle of the sixteenth century this type of body armor generally had been replaced in Spanish America by padded cloth armor, which became standard issue at garrisons in St. Augustine and Santa Elena. Similarly, military use of the crossbow declined during this period. Composite lead and iron artillery shot is not found on later sixteenth-century sites, but the use of stone and cast-iron ammunition continues into the seventeenth century.

We learned many other lessons from our exploration of the Emanuel Point Ship. The location of the site is fortunate—just offshore of Pensacola's historic district, in plain view from the bay bridge that conveys thousands of commuters and visitors daily. Because the shipwreck is a publicly owned resource of significance to Pensacola and to Florida, its location was marked with a prominent buoy, and members of the public were invited to become participants in its investigation, development, and interpretation. A partnership was formed with the Historic Pensacola Preservation Board and the University of West Florida toward those ends. For an exercise in public shipwreck archaeology and historic preservation, Florida is an appropriate proving ground, given the state's legacy of treasure hunting and commercial salvage. During the course of field and laboratory work, the site was opened up to a wider world. The partnership gradually expanded to include local historical and archaeological societies, scores of businesses and civic groups, and an army of volunteers of all ages. Two field schools and a program of graduate student internships brought students from as far away as California and Canada. Local sponsorship allowed other professionals to visit the project and assess its progress in return for sharing their own discoveries during evening public lectures. As the site revealed its secrets, the Emanuel Point Ship received national and international attention, helping to foster local pride among Pensacola's residents.

Another important lesson learned was that we did not need to excavate this shipwreck in its entirety to discern its secrets and interpret its role in history. With the completion of the second campaign of excavations, less than 40 percent of the site had been opened for examination, yet a substantial portion of the ship's architecture was recorded, and a remarkable collection of its contents was recovered for analysis, conservation, and display. Sometime in the future, if additional research questions emerge that only this shipwreck can answer, perhaps further excavation of this important and well-preserved cultural resource could be planned. In the meantime, there are other ships of the Tristán de Luna fleet at the bottom of Pensacola Bay waiting to be investigated and understood.

9

New Discoveries

Epilogue

GREGORY D. COOK, JOHN R. BRATTEN, AND
JOHN E. WORTH

Discovery of the Emanuel Point Ship played a key role in the development of a maritime archaeology focus for the University of West Florida's Division of Anthropology and Archaeology. By the summer of 2006 UWF's field methods course was filled to capacity with nearly twenty students eager to learn the basics of maritime archaeology. Archaeological field schools in general are fun and challenging, and the UWF field school is no exception. Students begin by reviewing essential diving skills in the university pool, then training in archaeological methods that they need to master in an underwater environment, often in low visibility. Underwater navigation, dredge setup, knot tying, and measuring and recording are all capabilities that students learn, first on land, then in the pool, and finally in the murky waters of Pensacola Bay. These skills are supplemented by lectures about local underwater sites, ship construction, dive safety, safe boating practices, and principles of remote sensing survey. Due to the large class size and limited boat space, daily operations often involve multiple activities on a variety of sites. During summer 2006, students were involved in recording a nineteenth-century paddlewheel steamboat, searching for a potential submerged prehistoric site in East Bay, mapping a lumber schooner, and surveying around the Emanuel Point Ship.

The latter activity involved towing remote sensing devices—in this case a magnetometer and side-scan sonar—along parallel survey lines to cover a survey area systematically. Seasoned surveyors call this "mowing the lawn," because a full day of running survey lines at slow speeds can become rather mundane. Conversations begin to take strange turns as hour after hour passes, with the steady hum of the boat engine and the repetitive orders of the boat driver informing the computer operator, "start of line, begin logging" and "end of line, stop logging," to record remote sensing data. This is a crucial phase in the search for new sites, and every maritime archaeologist must know how to gather, interpret, and analyze remote sensing data. Basically, one is looking for anomalies, or anything that stands out from the natural environment. In the case of sonar data, an acoustic image of the seafloor can indicate objects lying on the bottom, and magnetometers provide a numerical reading of the local magnetic field in units called nanoteslas, which can indicate the presence of anomalous ferrous metal.

While some students find surveying fascinating, to most it is among the least exciting aspects of maritime archaeology. But everyone's pulse quickens at the next phase of investigation—diver ground-truthing of survey anomalies. This phase of the search requires divers to suit up in SCUBA gear and actually investigate magnetometer and sonar anomalies to determine what caused them. In the murky waters of Pensacola Bay, this often takes the form of dive teams conducting circle-searches, using weighted buoys to mark target locations and tape reels to swim search patterns while looking at, probing, and/or feeling the bottom to find the source of the anomaly. Nine times out of ten, the anomaly turns out to be something archaeologically insignificant; some of our finds have included a pizza oven, modern fiberglass boats, and even a car. Occasionally, those long hours of survey pay off with the discovery of a new archaeological site. During summer 2006 we found just such a site.

Earlier that year the UWF maritime archaeology faculty was awarded a grant from Florida's Division of Historical Resources to search around the Emanuel Point Ship site to determine whether previously undiscovered portions of the wreck, or a debris field of artifacts from the wrecking event, might exist in the vicinity. The possibility also existed that other vessels from the 1559 fleet might turn up. With this funding support we purchased a new magnetometer, which was considerably more sensitive than the instrument used in the discovery of the Emanuel Point Ship. With this new survey tool, staff and students began conducting surveys in spring 2006, and these continued into the summer field season. A considerable list of anomalies soon was compiled, and we prioritized them based on the size of the anomaly (its magnitude), the type of anomaly (monopole, dipole, complex), and the duration (its overall size or area).

In August, during the last week of the field school, students investigating the seventeenth magnetic anomaly on that list (Target 17) reported the presence of a few basketball-sized stones on the seafloor. As part of their training, students learn that for much of the age of sail, ships were ballasted with round river cobbles to counteract the force of the wind on sails, in effect stabilizing the vessel. Thus any time stone cobbles are found on an underwater anomaly, further investigation is warranted. The divers that day, graduate supervisor Kendra Kennedy and maritime archaeology student Maija Glasier-Lawson, reported their finds to topside supervisor Jim Collis. He in turn conferred with John Bratten, who was on another boat conducting survey operations, and they decided to send additional dive crews down to investigate the site. Other clues began to appear. Probing indicated that the area of buried stones extended over at least five square meters. One diver brought up a modern-looking glass bottle, while another diver noted what he thought might be wood fragments. By the end of the day the crew's excitement was growing. Glasier-Lawson's field notebook captured that moment, as she wrote: "What a glorious day! One stone turned to many, and it is looking more and more interesting. I cannot wait to come out again!"

Later in the week we returned to Target 17 and discovered additional evidence. One diver said he thought he felt buried wooden timbers but wasn't sure. Another diver recovered a piece of encrusted lead; the Emanuel Point Ship had lead sheathing attached to its hull. Divers scanning the site with a metal detector noted the presence of several "hits" during their search. These constituted the final dives on the site during the summer maritime archaeology course, but the entire field crew felt rising anticipation about test excavations planned for later in the year.

Figure 9.1. UWF archaeology students entering the water at the site of the second Emanuel Point ship. Courtesy of UWF Division of Anthropology and Archaeology.

After a short break, we returned to the site in the fall, laid a 1 × 1 m excavation grid on the site, and began using a water induction dredge, carefully removing sediments and ballast stones. Soon fragments of olive jar and majolica pottery sherds were found, suggesting a sixteenth-century date for the site. Additional pieces of lead sheathing were exposed. Finally, after several days of excavation, the ends of two wooden frames appeared, with the space between them capped by a "filler piece," a construction element found on many sixteenth-century Iberian shipwrecks, including the Emanuel Point Ship. With the discovery of articulated hull beneath the ballast pile, and additional finds such as stone cannonballs and more sixteenth-century pottery, we could finally announce that a second ship from the Luna fleet had been found. It was dubbed Emanuel Point II.

Any new scientific discovery is exciting, but archaeological finds seem to resonate particularly strongly with the public. An official press release announced the discovery of a second Luna shipwreck, and Roger

Figure 9.2. Secretary of State Kurt Browning (*left*) and Greg Cook completing an inspection dive on the Emanuel Point II Ship. Courtesy of the Florida Department of State, Division of Historical Resources.

summed up what we all were feeling when he began his comments with the statement, "What a great day for Florida archaeology!" During the next few weeks various newspapers and cable news channels covered the story. One of the most thrilling events occurred when Secretary of State Kurt Browning visited the site and conducted a dive tour of the remains.

Since then UWF staff and students have continued careful excavation of the site as part of our summer field schools. Portions of the bow, stern, and midships have been exposed, and with the awarding of a second research grant from the Florida Division of Historical Resources, year-round excavations have allowed the exposure of the mast step, pump well, and sternpost areas of the vessel. Although we know that most of the vessels were unloaded prior to the hurricane, more than six thousand artifacts have been recovered from Emanuel Point II at the time of this writing. These include ceramics, fragments of staves from barrels that would have held supplies, crossbow bolt shafts, shoe soles, the wheel of a gun carriage, and even an ivory manicure set. From documentary evidence we know that different types of vessels were used in the Luna fleet, including an *urca, galeones, naos, barcas*, and a single *caravela* and *fragata*. The study of two shipwrecks from the same fleet will allow side-to-side comparisons for an incredible opportunity to learn about these ships and voyages of colonization in general. Moreover, in 2015 the site of Luna's terrestrial settlement on the Emanuel Point bluff finally was identified. Ongoing excavations there are permitting glimpses into the colonial supplies and equipment offloaded before the hurricane struck and into the lives of the colonists who struggled to survive afterward. More recently, students in the Combined Archaeological Field Methods course detected a magnetic anomaly near the first two Emanuel Point shipwreck sites and the Luna settlement land site. When we investigated this anomaly during summer 2016, we encountered ballast stones, an iron concretion, sixteenth-century Spanish ceramic fragments, and articulated frames and planking. This evidence confirmed that we had found a third Luna ship, designated as Emanuel Point III.

Many exciting discoveries await as we continue our investigations, and we also are surveying for other potential wrecks from the fleet. The dark waters of Pensacola Bay are slowly divulging their secrets, providing an opportunity to examine the mute testimony of items left behind more than 450 years ago from Tristán de Luna's doomed attempt to colonize Florida.

APPENDIX

Table 1. Hull Scantling Measurements from the Emanuel Point Ship (est. = estimated)

Hull Overall

length (est.)	29.5 m
beam (est.)	9.48 m
depth of hold (est.)	4.55 m
length to beam ratio (est.)	3.11:1
capacity (est.)	417–441 tons

Preserved Hull Measurements

length (est.)	28 m
port side breadth amidships	1.8 m
starboard breadth (est.)	2.8 m (amidships)
height of hull remains at stern (est.)	1.4 m
length of bow uncovered	6.5 m
starboard side breadth forward	2 m
height of hull remains at bow (reconstructed)	3.5 m

Keel

length (est.)	20.14 m
molded height	29 cm
sided thickness	31 cm bow, 22 cm amidships, 20 cm aft

Keelson

length (est.)	19.2 m
molded height	29 cm
sided thickness	31 cm bow, 22 cm stern and 34 cm amidships

Stem

molded height	28–31 cm
sided thickness	28–30 cm

(continued)

Table 1—*Continued*

STEMSON

length (preserved)	98 cm
molded height	22 cm
sided thickness	22 cm

MAINMAST STEP

length	+2.1 m
molded height	39 cm
sided thickness	47 cm

STEP MORTISE

length	94 cm
width	22 cm
depth	20 cm

FLOOR FRAMES (FORWARD)

molded height	14–16 cm
sided thickness	20–22 cm
average on center spacing	40 cm

FLOOR FRAMES (AMIDSHIPS)

molded height	25 cm at keel, 18 cm at wronghead
sided thickness	18–20 cm
pitch	undetermined
average on center spacing	36–38 cm

FLOOR FRAMES (AFT)

average preserved height	70–90 cm
sided thickness	10–30 cm
pitch: undetermined	
average on center spacing	32–44 cm

FIRST FUTTOCKS (BOW)

molded height	16 cm
sided thickness	19 cm
average on center spacing	41 cm
preserved length on starboard side	2.9m

FIRST FUTTOCKS (AMIDSHIPS)

molded height	19 cm
sided thickness	16–18 cm
preserved length on port side	87 cm

Buttresses

maximum molded height inboard	25 cm
minimum molded height outboard	6.5 cm
sided thickness	11.5–17 cm
length at their base	63 cm

Hull Planking (bow)

thickness	5.5 cm
width	25 cm

Hull Planking (amidships)

thickness	5–7 cm
width	14–33 cm
garboard width amidships	28.5 cm

Footwales (starboard bow)

molded height	12 cm
sided thickness	13 cm

Footwale (on port side amidships)

molded height	15–16 cm
sided thickness	18.5 cm

Ceiling (bow)

thickness	6 cm
width	19 cm

Ceiling (amidships)

thickness	5–7 cm
width	31–34 cm

Sternpost

molded height (preserved)	25 cm
sided thickness	35 cm
length (est.)	70+ cm
rake (est.)	60° from horizontal (30° aft of vertical)

Stern Knee

forward end molded height	20 cm (lower limb)
forward end sided thickness	21 cm
aft end molded height	10 cm (upper limb)
aft end sided thickness	18 cm
length overall	2.5 m
height (est.)	65 cm

Table 2. Overview of the Artifact Assemblage at the Emanuel Point Ship

EMANUEL POINT SHIP ARTIFACTS

Category	Subcategory	Count
Organic	Vertebrate	663
	Botanical	510
	Wood	430
	Invertebrate	149
	Rope	37
	Leather	21
	Resin	14
	Unknown/other	13
Ceramic	Olive Jar	1,506[1]
	El Morro Ware	152
	Majolica	74[2]
	Indet. Coarse Earthenware	56
	Melado Ware	10
	Storage Jar	9[3]
	Indet. Mexican Coarse Earthenware	6
	Aztec Ware	5
	Cologne/Rhenish Stoneware	1
Metal	Lead	338
	Copper	76
	Iron	41[4]
	Unknown	28
	Brass	7
	Wire wrapped rope	5
	Mercury	2
	Slag	1
Glass	Unknown	3
Stone	Ballast	124
	Unknown/other	122
	Coral	24
	Cannon Ball	11
	Clinkers	6
	Chipped Stone	3

Category	Subcategory	Count
	Obsidian	2
	Cut stone	1
Encrusted Object	Copper	9
	Iron	1,327
	Unknown/other	25
Total		5,811

Notes: 1. Count includes 22 Olive Jar Glazed.
2. Count is composed of 68 Columbia Plain, 2 Yayal blue on white, 2 Isabela Polychrome, and 2 Indet.
3. Count includes 3 Storage Jar Glazed.
4. Count includes 1 iron cannon ball.

Table 3. Comparison of Reconstructed Whole Fasteners from the Emanuel Point Ship with South's Spanish Nail Model

Name	Length (mm)	Quantity
Escora mayor	204–305	3
Escora	168–204	10
Meida escora	125–168	15
Alfaxia	90–125	17
Barrote	73–90	11
Media barrote	57–73	5
Quarto de barrote	Less than 57	4

Source: Adapted from South et al. (1988).

Table 4. Rock and Mineral Types Included in Emanuel Point Ship Ballast

Rock Type	Count	Percentage	Remarks
METAMORPHIC			
Quartzite	16	34.0	Fine-grained equigranular and bimodal members; strong undulatory extinction. Less than 5% matrix. Some members with sparse aligned muscovite.
Spillite	1	2.1	Pheoncrysts of plagioclase olivine and pyroxene. Also contains epidote and chlorite as accessory members.
IGNEOUS			
Extrusive			
Basalt	7	14.9	Pheoncrysts of euhedral magnetite
Porphyritic rhyolite	1	2.1	
Welded tuff	1	2.1	Pheonocrysts of plagioclase and pyronexe. Ground mass likely has similar composition, and has a feathery texture.
Crystal tuff	1	2.1	
Intrusive			
Granite	1	2.1	Equigranular
SEDIMENTARY			
Carbonate			
Calcareous mudstone	7	14.9	Buff and gray colored minerals. Thinly laminated. Thin section reveals microfossils of foraminifera and other planktonic forms.
Vuggy limestone	2	4.3	Buff colored
Micritic limestone	1	2.1	
Clastic			
Feldspathic arenite	2	4.3	Phenocrysts of quartz, feldspars, muscovite, microline and lithic grains of polycrystalline quartz.
Calcitic arenite	1	2.1	
OTHER			
Vein quartz	5	10.6	
Jasperoid	1	2.1	

Source: Data and analysis by Stephen Pollock and Dennis Bratten, Department of Geology, University of Southern Maine, July 1995.

Table 5. Ceramics Recovered from the Emanuel Point Ship

Emanuel Point 1 Ceramics

Ceramic Type	Sherd Count
Aztec ware	5
Cologne/Rhenish Stoneware	1
Columbia Plain	68
Yayal Blue on White	2
Isabela Polychrome	2
Indet. Majolica	2
El Morro Ware	152
Indet. Coarse Earthenware	56
Indet. Mexican Coarse Earthenware	6
Melado Ware	10
Olive Jar Glazed	22
Olive Jar Unglazed	1,484
Storage Jar	6
Storage Jar Glazed	3
Total Ceramics	*1,819*

Table 6. Emanuel Point Faunal Remains

Species		Number of Identified Specimens[1]	Minimum Number of Individuals
Vertebrate	Chicken (*Gallus gallus*)	9	2
	Cow (*Bos taurus*)	46	1
	Pig (*Sus scrofa*)	7	2
	Black rat (*Rattus rattus*)	228	21
	House mouse (*Mus musculus*)	2	2
	Indeterminate mammal (Class Mammalia)	168	NA
	Indeterminate bird (Class Aves)	3	NA
	Indeterminate vertebrate (Subphylum Vertebrata)	200	NA
Invertebrate	American cockroach	7[2]	4
	Hide beetle (Family Dermistidae)	14[3]	6
	Weevil (*Sitophilus* sp.)	51	31
	Darkling beetles (Family Tenebrionidae)	1	1
	Indeterminate invertebrates	76	NA

Notes: 1. Fine screening was conducted using 2mm, 1mm, and 0.5mm stacking sieving screen.
2. Unknown total, 7 mouthparts found from sediment samples.
3. Unknown total, 14 elytra recovered from sediment samples.

Table 7. Emanuel Point Archaeobotanical Remains

Specimen/Taxa	Count
Olive pit (*Olea europaea*)	493[1]
Oak acorn (*Quercus* sp.)	12
Hazelnut nutshell (*Coryleus* sp. *C. avellana*)	10[2]
Cherry pit (*Prunus cerasus*)	9
Persimmon seed fragments (*Diodpyros virginiana*)	9
Twigs (unidentified)	5
Miscellaneous organic (unidentified)	4
Almond Pit (*Prunus amygdalus*)	3
Hickory nutshell (*Carya* sp.)	3[3]
Papaya stems (tentatively) (sf. *Caria papaya*)	3
Peach pit (*Prunus persica*)	3
Bark fragments (unidentified)	2
Bottle gourd rind (*Lagenaria siceraria*)	2
Plum/prune pit (*Prunus domestica*)	2
Sapote seed fragment (*Pouteria* sp.)	2
Coconut nutshell fragment (*Cocos nucifera*)	1
Water or swamp tupelo (*Nyssa aquatica/N. ogeche*)	1
Southern magnolia seed (*Magnolia grandiflora*)	1
Grape seed (*Vitis vinifera*)	1
Maple leaf (red maple tentatively) (cf. *Acer* sp.)	1
Oak leaf (*Quercus* sp.)	1
Pine bark (tentatively) (cf. *Pinus* sp.)	1
Spiny seed/fruit (unidentified)	1
Hemp rope sample (*Cannabis sativa*)	± 25ml
Grass family rope sample (*Poaceae*)	± 20ml
Resinous mass (unidentified)	-
Mustard family (*Brassicaceae*)	?

Notes: 1. Count includes 442 whole pits, 32 half pits, and 19 pit fragments.
2. Count includes 1 nutshell and 9 nutshell fragments.
3. Count includes 2 nutshells and 1 nutshell fragment.

Table 8. Shot Recovered from the Emanuel Point Ship

Type	Max. Dia. (cm)	Weight (grams)
STONE SHOT		
00,090	10.86	1,808.0
00,280	11.02	1,821.8
00,299	10.71	1,709.8
00,300	10.65	1,792.1
00,549	10.88	1,854.4
00,601	10.89	1,748.2
00,775	10.98	2,078.0
00,975	10.03	1,768.1
00,983	10.85	1,710.2
00,985	10.71	1,727.8
01,000	10.51	1,540.0
LEAD/IRON SHOT		
00,611	4.12	332.8
00,784	3.96	179.0
LEAD SHOT		
00,073	4.04	395.0
IRON SHOT		
00,515	6.23	775.0

REFERENCES

Aguilar, Francisco de. Testimony regarding the expedition of Angel de Villafañe, July 10, 1561, AGI Patronato 19, Ramo 11.
Appleyard, John. *De Luna, Founder of North America's First Colony: An Historical Novel.* 1977; reprint Cocoa: Florida Historical Society Press, 2009.
Armitage, Philip L. "Report on the Black Rat Bones from the Emanuel Point Shipwreck, Pensacola Bay, Florida." Unpubl. manuscript on file, Florida Bureau of Archaeological Research, Tallahassee, 1995.
———. "Report on the Bones of House Mice from the Emanuel Point Shipwreck, Pensacola Bay, Florida." Unpubl. manuscript on file, Florida Bureau of Archaeological Research, Tallahassee, 1995.
Arnade, Charles W. "Tristan de Luna and Ochuse (Pensacola Bay) 1559." *Florida Historical Quarterly* 37, nos. 3–4 (1959): 201–22.
Arnold, J. Barto III, and Robert S. Weddle. *The Nautical Archaeology of Padre Island: The Spanish Shipwrecks of 1554.* New York: Academic Press, 1978.
Associated Press. "Carving of Galleon Found in Shipwreck Debris in Fla. Bay." *Arizona Daily Star*, September 12, 1993.
———. "Spanish King and Queen Visit Florida." *New York Daily News*, February 20, 2009.
———. "Spanish Sailing Ship Captain Pays Homage at Shipwreck." *Boca Raton* (FL) *News*, June 11, 1998.
———. "Tiny Copy of Spanish Ship Found in Wreck." *Press and Sun-Bulletin* (Binghamton, NY), September 12, 1993.
Avellaneda, Ignacio. *Los Sobrevivientes de la Florida: The Survivors of the De Soto Expedition.* Ed. Bruce S. Chappell. Research Publications of the P. K. Yonge Library of Florida History, no. 2. Gainesville: University of Florida Libraries, 1985.
Avery, George. "A Chronological Framework for the Middle Style Olive Jar Rims." Paper presented at the Florida Anthropological Society Annual Meeting, Clearwater, May 1993.
———. "Olive Jar Production (16th–18th Century): A Multidisciplinary Approach." Paper presented at the Society for Historical Archaeology Annual Meeting, Vancouver, BC, January 1994.
———. "Pots as Packaging: The Spanish Olive Jar and Andalusian Transatlantic Commercial Activity, 16th–18th Centuries." Ph.D. diss., University of Florida, 1997.
Baker, Barry W. "Emanuel Point Shipwreck Faunal Analysis." Unpubl. manuscript on file, Florida Bureau of Archaeological Research, Tallahassee, 1995.
Ballard, Robert D. *Discovery of the Titanic.* New York: Warner Books, 1989.
Bancroft, Janet. "Geology of Stones Recovered from the Emanuel Point Shipwreck Site." Student paper on file, Florida Bureau of Archaeological Research, Tallahassee, 1993.

Barkham, Michael M. *Report on 16th Century Spanish Basque Shipbuilding, c. 1550 to c. 1600.* Manuscript Report no. 422. Ottawa: Parks Canada, 1981.
Barlow, Robert H. "El Códice de los Alfareros de Cuauhtitlán." *Revista Mexicana de Estudios Antropológicos* 12 (1951): 5–8.
Baumer, David R. *Bethune Blackwater Schooner Report.* Florida Archaeological Reports 21. Tallahassee: Florida Bureau of Archaeological Research, 1990.
Bennett, Charles E. *Laudonnière and Fort Caroline: History and Documents.* 1964; repr. Tuscaloosa: University of Alabama Press, 2001.
Bense, Judith A. *Deadman's Shipwreck, Gulf Breeze, Florida: Preliminary Investigation and Evaluation.* Report of Investigations no. 18. Pensacola: Office of Cultural and Archaeological Research, University of West Florida, 1988.
———. "Spanish President Visits Site of First Pensacola for 300th Anniversary." *Society for American Archaeology Bulletin* 16, no. 4 (September 1998).
Berry, R. J. "Town Mouse, Country Mouse: Adaptation and Adaptability in *Mus domesticus* (*M. musculus domesticus*)." *Mammal Review* 11, no. 3 (1981): 91–136.
Biringuccio, Vannoccio. *Pirotechnia.* Ed. Cyril Stanley Smith and Martha Teach Gnudi. Cambridge: Massachusetts Institute of Technology Press, 1966.
Blake, W., and Jeremy N. Green. "A Mid-XVI Century Portuguese Wreck in the Seychelles." *International Journal of Nautical Archaeology and Underwater Exploration* 15, no. 1 (1986): 1–23.
Bratten, Dennis. "Preliminary Analysis of the Emanuel Point Ship's Ballast." See Smith et al., eds., *The Emanuel Point Ship: Archaeological Investigations 1997–1998*, 66–71.
Bratten, John R. "Buried Secrets: Analyses in the Emanuel Point Ship Laboratory." *Gulf South Historical Review* 14, no. 1 (1998): 31–45.
———. "Olive Pits, Rat Bones, and Leather Shoe Soles: A Preliminary Report on the Organic Remains from the Emanuel Point Shipwreck, Pensacola, Florida." In *Underwater Archaeology Proceedings from the Society for Historical Archaeology Conference*, ed. Paul F. Johnston, 49–53. Washington, DC: Society for Historical Archaeology, 1995.
———. "Mesoamerican Component of the Emanuel Point Ships: Obsidian, Ceramics, and Projectile Points." *Florida Anthropologist* 62, nos. 3–4 (September–December 2009): 109–14.
———. "Recent Artifact Finds from the Emanuel Point Ship." In *Underwater Archaeology Proceedings from the Society for Historical Archaeology Conference*, ed. Lawrence Babbits, Catherine Fach, and Ryan Harris, 38–44. Atlanta: Society for Historical Archaeology, 1998.
Bratten, John R., and James W. Hunter III. "Conservation." See Smith et al., eds., *The Emanuel Point Ship: Archaeological Investigations 1997–1998*, 158–63.
Breetzke, David. "The History, Archaeology, and Conservation of 16th-century Spanish Shoe Fragments." Unpubl. manuscript on file, Florida Bureau of Archaeological Research, Tallahassee, 1995.
Brill, Robert H., I. L. Barnes. S.S.C. Tong, Emile C. Joel, and M. J. Murtagh. "Laboratory Studies of Some European Artifacts Excavated on San Salvador Island." In *Columbus and His World: Proceedings of the First Annual San Salvador Conference*, ed. Donald

T. Gerace, 247–67. Fort Lauderdale: College of the Finger Lakes Bahamian Field Station, 1986.

Brown, Ben. "Luna's Lost Galleon." *Entrée Magazine*, Fall 1998, 64–69.

Burns, Jason M. "The Anchor and Related Rigging Components." See Smith et al., eds., *The Emanuel Point Ship: Archaeological Investigations 1997–1998*, 72–87.

Carré, Dominique, Jean-Paul Desroches, and Franck Goddio. *Le San Diego: Un trésor sous la mer*. Paris: Réunion des Musées Nationaux, 1994.

Casado Soto, José Luis. "Atlantic Shipping in Sixteenth-Century Spain and the 1588 Armada." In *England, Spain and the Gran Armada: 1585–1604: Essays from the Anglo-Spanish Conferences, London and Madrid, 1988*, ed. Maria José Rodriguez-Salgado and Simon Adams, 95–133. Savage, MD: Barnes & Noble Books, 1991.

Cayón, Juan R., and Carlos Castan. *Monedas Españolas*. Tenth edition. Madrid: Privately printed, 1991.

Charlton, Thomas. Personal communication with Roger C. Smith, March 12, 1996.

Chaunu, Huguette, and Pierre Chaunu. *Seville et l'Atlantique (1504–1650)*. 8 vols. Paris: Libraire Armand Colin, 1955.

Childers, R. Wayne. Translation of Pedro de Yebra Account Audit by Hortuño de Ybarra, 1564, AGI Contaduría 877, Archivo General de Indias, Seville, Spain. Unpubl. manuscript on file, University of West Florida Archaeology Institute, Pensacola, September 1999.

———. Translation of Alonso Ortíz de Urrutia Account Audit by Martín de Yugoyen, 1569, AGI Contaduría 877, Archivo General de Indias, Seville, Spain. Unpubl. manuscript on file, University of West Florida Archaeology Institute, Pensacola, October 1999.

Clayton, Lawrence A., Vernon James Knight Jr., and Edward C. Moore, eds. *The De Soto Chronicles: The Expedition of Hernando de Soto to North America in 1539–1543*. 2 vols. Tuscaloosa: University of Alabama Press, 1993.

Cooley, Percy A. *An Inventory of the Estuarine Fauna in the Vicinity of Pensacola, Florida*. St. Petersburg: Florida Department of Natural Resources, Marine Research Laboratory, 1978.

Collis, James. "Empire's Reach: A Structural and Historical Analysis of the Emanuel Point Shipwreck." Master's thesis, University of West Florida, 2008.

Cozzi, J. "Hull Remains of the Emanuel Point Ship." In *Underwater Archaeology Proceedings from the Society for Historical Archaeology Conference*, ed. Lawrence Babits, Catherine Fach, and Ryan Harris, 31–37. Atlanta: Society for Historical Archaeology, 1998.

———. "Ship's Architecture." See Smith et al., eds., *The Emanuel Point Ship: Archaeological Investigations 1997–1998*, 28–65.

———. "Techniques on the Emanuel Point Ship Excavation." Paper presented at the Society for Historical Archaeology Conference on Historical and Underwater Archaeology, Atlanta, GA, January 1998.

Davis, T. Frederick. "The History of Juan Ponce de León's Voyages to Florida." *Florida Historical Quarterly* 14, no. 1 (July 1935): 1–70.

Deagan, Kathleen. *Artifacts of the Spanish Colonies of Florida and the Caribbean, 1550–1800*, vol. 1. Washington, DC: Smithsonian Institution Press, 1987.

———. "Preliminary Report on Laboratory Analysis of Archaeological Collections from La Isabela, Dominican Republic, 1989–1992." Unpubl. manuscript on file, Florida Museum of Natural History, Gainesville, 1992.

DiPaulo, Bill, and Christopher Clausen. "Cannon Brought Ashore as More Artifacts Found." *Pensacola News Journal*, March 2, 1990.

Dotson, John E. "Treatises on Shipbuilding before 1650." In *Cogs, Caravels, and Galleons: The Sailing Ship, 1000–1650*, ed. Robert Gardiner and Richard Unger, 160–68. Annapolis: Naval Institute Press, 1994.

Durden, Christopher J. "Fossil Cockroaches from a 1554 Spanish Shipwreck." In *The Nautical Archaeology of Padre Island: The Spanish Shipwrecks of 1554*, ed. J. Barto Arnold III and Robert Weddle, 407–16. New York: Academic Press, 1978.

Eaves, Ian. "Report on the Breast Plate Found in Pensacola, Florida." Unpubl. manuscript on file, Florida Bureau of Archaeological Research, Tallahassee, 1995.

Finegold, Robert J. "The Deadman's Island Sloop: Excavation of a Colonial Careenage." Master's thesis, University of St. Andrews, Fife, Scotland, 1990.

Fitzgerald, William, L. Turgeon, R. H. Whitehead, and J. W. Bradley. "Late Sixteenth-Century Basque Banded Copper Kettles." *Historical Archaeology* 27, no. 1 (1993): 44–57.

Florida Bureau of Archaeological Research. "A Proposal to Establish USS *Massachusetts* as a State Underwater Archaeological Preserve." Unpubl. manuscript on file, Florida Bureau of Archaeological Research, Tallahassee, 1992.

Flint, Richard. "Armas de la Tierra: The Mexican Indian Component of Coronado Expedition Material Culture." In *The Coronado Expedition to Tierra Nueva: The 1540–1542 Route across the Southwest*, ed. Richard Flint and Shirley Cushing Flint, 47–57. Niwot: University Press of Colorado, 1997.

Franklin, Marianne. "A Description of the Artifact Assemblage Archaeologically Recovered from the Western Ledge Reef Wreck, Bermuda." *Bermuda Journal of Archaeology and Maritime History* 5 (1993): 70–83.

Franklin, Marianne, John W. Morris III, and Roger C. Smith. *Submerged Historical Resources of Pensacola Bay, Florida*. Florida Archaeological Reports 27. Tallahassee: Florida Bureau of Archaeological Research, 1992.

Franklin, Marianne, John W. Morris III, John Broadwater, and Gordon P. Watts Jr. "A Preliminary Description of the Excavation, Timber Recording, Hull Construction, and Cultural Material Analysis of a Sixteenth-Century Vessel Wrecked on Western Ledge Reef, Bermuda." In *Underwater Archaeology Proceedings from the Society for Historical Archaeology Conference*, ed. Robyn P. Woodward and Charles D. Moore, 47–62. Vancouver, BC: Society for Historical Archaeology, 1994.

Friel, Ian. "The Carrack: The Advent of the Full-Rigged Ship." In *Cogs, Caravels, and Galleons: The Sailing Ship, 1000–1650*, ed. Robert Gardiner and Richard Unger, 77–90. Annapolis: Naval Institute Press, 1994.

Galloway, Patricia. *Choctaw Genesis, 1500–1700*. Lincoln: University of Nebraska Press, 1995.

Gayón, Gonzalo. Petition and service record, 1567, AGI Santo Domingo 11, no. 41.
Gifford, Matthew J. "Everything Is Ballast: An Examination of Ballast Related Practices and Ballast Stones from the Emanuel Point Shipwrecks." Master's thesis, University of West Florida, 2014.
Glascock, Michael D. "Archaeometry Laboratory at MURR." Electronic document, http://archaeometry.missouri.edu/.
Goggin, John M. "The Spanish Olive Jar: An Introductory Study." In *Papers in Caribbean Anthropology, nos. 57–64*, compiled by Sidney W. Mintz. New Haven: Yale University Publications in Anthropology, 1960.
Goodwin, Dave. "Wreck Could Be De Luna's. Clues Don't Refute, Confirm Possibility." *Pensacola News Journal*, March 3, 1993.
———. "Experts: Ship Might Be Luna's." *Pensacola News Journal*, June 18, 1994.
———. "Treasures from the Deep, Shipwreck Lab Looks for Clues to Local History." *Pensacola News Journal*, October 14, 1994.
Grenier, Robert. "Basque Whalers in the New World: The Red Bay Wrecks." In *Ships and Shipwrecks of the Americas*, ed. George F. Bass, 69–84. London: Thames and Hudson, 1988.
———. "The Basque Whaling Ship from Red Bay, Labrador: A Treasure Trove of Data on Iberian Atlantic Shipbuilding Design and Techniques in the Mid–16th Century." In *Proceedings, International Symposium on Archaeology of Medieval and Modern Ships of the Iberian-Atlantic Tradition: Hull Remains, Manuscripts, and Ethnographic Sources, A Comparative Approach*, ed. Francisco Alves, 269–93. Lisbon: Academia de Marinha, 1998.
———. "Excavating a 400-Year-Old Basque Galleon." *National Geographic* 168, no. 1 (July 1985): 58–68.
Grenier, Robert, Marc-André Bernier, and Willis Stevens, eds. *The Underwater Archaeology of Red Bay: Basque Shipbuilding and Whaling in the 16th Century*. 5 vols., French and English editions. Ottawa: Parks Canada Publishing and Depository Services, 2007.
Guérout, Max, Eric Rieth, and Jean-Marie Gassend. *Le Navire Génois de Villefranche: Un naufrage de 1516?* Archaeonautica 9. Paris: Centre National de la Recherche Scientifique, 1989.
Hakluyt, Richard. *Hakluyt Voyages: A Selection of the Principal Voyages, Traffiques and Discoveries of the English Nation by Richard Hakluyt, 1552–1616, Set Out with Many Embellishments and a Preface*. Ed. Laurence Irving. New York: Alfred A. Knopf, 1927.
Hamilton, Donny L. *Conservation of Metal Objects from Underwater Sites: A Study in Methods*. Austin: Texas Memorial Museum and the Texas Antiquities Committee, 1976.
———. "Methods of Conserving Archaeological Material Culture." Unpubl. manuscript on file, Department of Anthropology, Texas A&M University, College Station, 1994.
Hann, John. "Report on Contaduría 877. Documents on the Luna Expedition." Unpubl. manuscript on file, Florida Bureau of Archaeological Research, Tallahassee, 1993.
———. "Report on Trip to Gainesville, September 12–15, 1993." Unpubl. report on file, Florida Bureau of Archaeological Research, Tallahassee, 1993.

———. "Summary on Research for Luna Project." Unpubl. report on file, Florida Bureau of Archaeological Research, Tallahassee, September 2, 1993.
Haring, Clarence Henry. *Trade and Navigation between Spain and the Indies in the Time of the Hapsburgs*. 1918; repr. Gloucester, MA: Peter Smith, 1964.
Hinton, Howard Everest. *A Monograph of the Beetles Associated with Stored Products, Vol. 1*. 1945; repr. New York: Johnson Reprint Corporation, 1963.
Hirth, Kenneth. "Review of Obsidian Artifacts from the Emanuel Point Shipwreck." Unpubl. report on file, University of West Florida Archaeology Institute, Pensacola, 1999.
Hoffman, Paul E. "Lúcas Vázquez de Ayllón." In *Columbus and the Land of Ayllon: The Exploration and Settlement of the Southeast*, ed. Jeannine Cook, 27–49. Darien, GA: Lower Altamaha Historical Society, 1992.
———. "Narváez and Cabeza de Vaca in Florida." In *The Forgotten Centuries: Indians and Europeans in the American South, 1521–1704*, ed. Charles M. Hudson and Carmen Chaves Tesser, 50–73. Athens: University of Georgia Press, 1994.
———. *A New Andalucia and a Way to the Orient: The American Southeast during the Sixteenth Century*. Baton Rouge: Louisiana State University Press, 1990.
———. "A New Voyage of North American Discovery: Pedro de Salazar's Visit to the 'Island of Giants.'" *Florida Historical Quarterly* 58, no. 4 (April 1980): 415–26.
Hudson, Charles. *The Juan Pardo Expeditions: Exploration of the Carolinas and Tennessee, 1566–1568*. Washington, DC: Smithsonian Institution Press, 1990.
———. *Knights of Spain, Warriors of the Sun: Hernando de Soto and the South's Ancient Chiefdom*. Athens: University of Georgia Press, 1997.
———."A Spanish-Coosa Alliance in Sixteenth-Century North Georgia." *Georgia Historical Quarterly* 72, no. 4 (1988): 599–626.
Hudson, Charles, Marvin T. Smith, Chester B. DePratter, and Emilia Kelley. "The Tristán de Luna Expedition, 1559–1561." *Southeastern Archaeology* 8, no. 1 (1989): 31–45.
———. "The Tristán de Luna Expedition, 1559–1561." In *First Encounters: Spanish Explorations in the Caribbean and the United States, 1492–1570*, ed. Jerald T. Milanich and Susan Milbrath, 119–34. Gainesville: University of Florida Press, 1989.
Hughson, Charles E. "Remote Sensing in Pensacola Bay, Florida, on a Sixteenth-Century Spanish Shipwreck." Paper presented at the Society for Historical Archaeology Conference on Historical and Underwater Archaeology, Washington, DC, 1995.
Hunter, James W. III. "Analysis of Small Arms Artifacts from the Emanuel Point Ship." See Smith et al., eds., *The Emanuel Point Ship: Archaeological Investigations 1997–1998*, 146–55.
———. "A Broken Lifeline of Commerce, Trade and Defense on the Colonial Frontier: Historical Archaeology of the Santa Rosa Island Wreck, an Early Eighteenth-Century Spanish Shipwreck in Pensacola Bay, Florida." Master's thesis, University of West Florida, 2001.
Hunter, James W. III, John Bratten, and J. Cozzi. *Underwater Field Investigations, 1999: The Santa Rosa Island Wreck and Hamilton's Shipwreck*. Report of Investigations no. 81. Pensacola: University of West Florida, 1999.
Janowski, Davis D. "Clues to the Past." *Pensacola News Journal*, May 21, 1995.

Kaczor, Bill. "Divers Hail Shipwreck Discovery." *Tampa Tribune-Times*, March 7, 1993.
———. "Spanish Shipwreck Dates to 16th Century." *Gainesville Sun*, September 11, 1993.
———. "Wreck Believed to Be Immigrants' Galleon: Ship May Link to Colonists." *Florida Times Union*, February 21, 1995; *St. Petersburg Times*, February 21, 1995; and *Stuart News*, February 21, 1995.
Keith, Donald. "The Molasses Reef Wreck." Ph.D. dissertation, Texas A&M University, College Station, 1987.
Kleeberg, John M. Personal communication with Roger C. Smith, July 6, 1995.
Klein, H. Arthur. *Graphic Worlds of Peter Bruegel the Elder*. New York: Dover Publications, 1963.
Lakey, Denise C. "Don Tristán de Luna y Arellano, the Expedition to Florida: A Catalog of Documentary Sources." Unpubl. report on file at the John C. Pace Library, University of West Florida; P. K. Yonge Library, University of Florida; and State Library and Archives of Florida, Tallahassee, 1996.
———. "Don Tristán de Luna y Arellano: Addendum to the Catalog of Documentary Sources." Unpubl. report on file at the John C. Pace Library, University of West Florida; P. K. Yonge Library, University of Florida; and State Library and Archives of Florida, Tallahassee, 1996.
Lane, Frederic C. "Venetian Naval Architecture about 1550." *Mariner's Mirror* 20, no. 4 (1934): 24–49.
Laudonnière, René. *Three Voyages*. Transl. and ed. Charles E. Bennett. 1964; repr. Tuscaloosa: University of Alabama Press, 2001.
Lavanha, João Baptista. *Livro Primeiro da Architectura Naval*. 1615; facsimile repr. Lisbon: Academia de Marinha, 1996.
Lawrence, Colleen Reese. "An Analysis of Plant Remains from the Emanuel Point Shipwrecks." Master's thesis, University of West Florida, 2010.
Lawson, Edward W. *The Discovery of Florida and Its Discoverer Juan Ponce de León*. St. Augustine, FL: Published by the author, 1946.
Lenihan, Daniel. "Preliminary Archeological Survey of the Offshore Lands of Gulf Islands National Seashore." In *Underwater Archeology in the National Park Service*. Santa Fe: National Park Service, 1974: 34–40.
L'Hour, Michel. Personal communication with Roger C. Smith, 1995.
Lister, Florence C., and Robert H. Lister. *Andalusian Ceramics in Spain and New Spain: A Cultural Register from the Third Century B.C. to 1700*. Tucson: University of Arizona Press, 1987.
López Cruz, Abraham. *Naufragio en Ines de Soto: Un hallazgo de cuatro siglos*. Havana: Carisub, 1997.
Lopéz Pérez, Alessandro. "Sobre el Maderamen de la Estructura del Pecio de Fuxa." Departamento de Arqueología Carisub, Havana, Cuba, 1993.
Lowery, Woodbury. *The Spanish Settlements within the Present Limits of the United States, 1513–1561*. 1905; repr. New York: G. P. Putnam's Sons, 1911.
Luna, Christóbal de. Declaration regarding service of Luis de Soto, February 1, 1575, AGI Mexico 213, no. 1, ff. 1r–v.

Lyon, Eugene. "Abstracts and Translations: Luna Fleet Documents." Unpubl. report on file, Florida Bureau of Archaeological Research, March 20, 2002.

———. *The Enterprise of Florida: Pedro Menéndez de Avilés and the Spanish Conquest of 1565–1568.* Gainesville: University of Florida Press, 1976.

———. "Toward a Topology of Spanish Colonial Nails." In *Spanish Artifacts from Santa Elena.* Ed. Stanley South, Russell Skowronek, and Richard Johnson. 1979; repr. Anthropological Studies 7, Columbia: South Carolina Institute of Archaeology and Anthropology, 1988.

Malcom, Corey. *St. John's Bahamas Shipwreck Project, Interim Report I: The Excavation and Artifacts, 1991–1995.* Key West, FL: Mel Fisher Maritime Heritage Society, 1996.

Malone, Michael. "Primer Establecimiento Europeo Puede Ser Antes de San Agustin." *EFE News,* August 28, 1996.

Marken, Mitchell W. *Pottery from Spanish Shipwrecks, 1500–1800.* Gainesville: University Presses of Florida, 1994.

Marr, Andrew. "An Investigation of Lead Sheathing Recovered from Two 16th-Century Iberian Shipwrecks Located in Pensacola Bay." Master's thesis, University of West Florida, 2012.

Martin, Colin J. M. "Spanish Armada Pottery." *International Journal of Nautical Archaeology and Underwater Exploration* 8, no. 4 (1979): 279–302.

Maseman, John. "Conservation Treatment Reports: Emanuel Point Shipwreck Site." Unpubl. manuscript on file, Florida Bureau of Archaeological Research, Tallahassee, 1994.

McGrail, Sean. *Ancient Boats in N.W. Europe: The Archaeology of Water Transport in AD 1500.* London: Longman, 1987.

Meyer, Erica. "The Spanish Olive Jar." See Smith et al., eds., *The Emanuel Point Ship: Archaeological Investigations 1997–1998,* 123–34.

Minc, Leah D. "Pottery and the Potter's Craft in the Aztec Heartland." In *The Oxford Handbook of the Aztecs,* ed. Deborah L. Nichols and Enrique Rodríguez-Alegría, 355–74. New York: Oxford University Press, 2017.

Mitchell, Amy. "Preliminary Conservation of the 1993 Emanuel Point Field Specimens." Unpubl. manuscript on file, Florida Bureau of Archaeological Research, Tallahassee, 1993.

Mistovich, Tim S., Brina Agranat, and Stephen R. James Jr. *Brodie's Wharf: Maritime Archaeological Investigation of an Early Nineteenth Century Sunken Caisson at the Pensacola Naval Air Station, Florida.* Tuscaloosa: Pan American Consultants, 1991.

Moore, Robin. "The Emanuel Point Galley Ware." See Smith et al., eds., *The Emanuel Point Ship: Archaeological Investigations 1997–1998,* 88–107.

Morris, John William III. "The Preliminary Analysis of the 16th Century Vessel Remains Recovered from the Western Ledge Reef Wreck, Bermuda." *Bermuda Journal of Archaeology and Maritime History* 5 (1993): 58–69.

Morris, Percy A. *A Field Guide of Shells of the Atlantic and Gulf Coasts and the West Indies.* Boston: Houghton Mifflin, 1975.

Mullins, Deborah. "More Than Just El Morro." See Smith et al., eds., *The Emanuel Point Ship: Archaeological Investigations 1997–1998,* 135–39.

Newsom, Lee. "Archaeobotanical Identifications from Emanuel Point Shipwreck Site." Unpubl. manuscript on file, Florida Bureau of Archaeological Research, Tallahassee, 1995.

Noguera, Eduardo. *La Cerámica Arqueológica de Mesoamérica*. Mexico City: Universidad Nacional Autónoma de Mexico, Instituto de Investigaciones Antropológicas, 1975.

Nuttall, Zelia. "Royal Ordinances Concerning the Laying out of New Towns." *Hispanic American Historical Review* 4, no. 4 (1921): 743–53.

Oertling, Thomas J. "The Concept of the Atlantic Vessel." In *Proceedings, International Symposium on Archaeology of Medieval and Modern Ships of the Iberian-Atlantic Tradition: Hull Remains, Manuscripts, and Ethnographic Sources: A Comparative Approach*, ed. Francisco Alves, 233–40. Lisbon: Academia de Marinha, 1998.

———. "The Few Remaining Clues." In *Underwater Archaeology Proceedings from the Society for Historical Archaeology Conference*, ed. J. Barto Arnold III, 100–3. Pleasant Hill, CA: Society for Historical Archaeology, 1989.

———. "The Highborn Cay Wreck: The 1986 Field Season." *International Journal of Nautical Archaeology* 18, no. 3 (1989): 244–53.

———. "The Molasses Reef Wreck Hull Analysis: Final Report." *International Journal of Nautical Archaeology* 18, no. 3 (1989): 229–43.

Oertling, Thomas J., ed. "The Highborn Cay Wreck: Limited Excavations, September 1-19, 1986." Unpubl. report submitted to Bahamas Ministry of Transport by the Institute of Nautical Archaeology, Texas A&M University, College Station, 1987.

Olds, Doris. *Texas Legacy from the Gulf: A Report on Sixteenth-Century Shipwreck Materials Recovered from the Texas Tidelands*. Austin: Texas Antiquities Committee Publication no. 2, 1976.

Oliveira, Fernando. *Livro da Fabrica das Naos—The Book of Shipbuilding*. Facsimile reprint of 1580 edition, translated by F. Contente Domingues and R. A. Barker. Lisbon: Academia de Marinha, 1991.

Padilla, Augustín Dávila. *Historia de la Fundación y Discurso de la Provincia de Santiago de México de la Orden de Predicadores, por las vidas de sus varones insignes y casos Notables de Nueva España*. 2nd edition. Brussels: Juan de Meerbeque, 1625.

Palacio, Diego García de. *Instrucción Náutica Para Navegar*. Facsimile reprint of 1587 edition. Madrid: Ediciones Cultura Hispánica, 1944.

Patel, Samir S. "Sunken Dreams: A 16th-Century Shipwreck Marks Spain's Last Chance to Claim the American South." *Archaeology* 63, no. 6 (November–December 2010): 30–35.

Parks Canada staff. Personal communication with Roger C. Smith, 1995.

Payne-Gallwey, Ralph. *The Crossbow: Medieval and Modern, Military and Sporting; Its Construction, History, and Management*. New York: Bramhall House, 1958.

Pearson, Colin. *Conservation of Marine Archaeological Objects*. London: Butterworths, 1987.

Peck, Douglas T. "Reconstruction and Analysis of the 1513 Discovery Voyage of Juan Ponce de León." *Florida Historical Quarterly* 71, no. 2 (October 1992): 133–54.

Pensacola News Journal. "Fort, Shipwreck Bring Past Alive." *Pensacola News Journal Opinion*, April 30, 1993.

———. "Shipwreck Gets Research Reprieve." *Pensacola News Journal Opinion*, June 5, 1995.

———. "Ship's Excavation a Gold Mine Chance." *Pensacola News Journal Opinion*, June 3, 1997.

Peterson, Harold L. *Arms and Armor in Colonial America, 1526–1783*. New York: Bramhill House, 1956.

Peterson, Mendel. "Exploration of a 16th-Century Bahaman Shipwreck." In *National Geographic Research Reports, 1967 Projects*, ed. Paul H. Oehser, 231–42. Washington, DC: National Geographic Society, 1974.

Phillips, Carla R. "The Evolution of Spanish Ship Design from the Fifteenth to the Eighteenth Century." *American Neptune* 53, no. 4 (Fall 1993): 229–38.

———. "Iberian Ships and Shipbuilding in the Age of Discovery." In *Maritime History, Volume I: The Age of Discovery*, ed. John B. Hattendorf, 215–38. Malabar, FL: Krieger Publishing Company, 1996.

———. *Los Tres Reyes 1628–1634: The Short Life of an Unlucky Spanish Galleon*. Minneapolis: University of Minnesota Press, 1990.

———. *Six Galleons for the King of Spain: Imperial Defense in the Early Seventeenth Century*. Baltimore: Johns Hopkins University Press, 1986.

———. "Sizes and Configurations of Spanish Ships in the Age of Discovery." In *Columbus and His World: Proceedings of the First Annual San Salvador Conference*, ed. Donald T. Gerace, 69–98. Fort Lauderdale: College of the Finger Lakes Bahamian Field Station, 1987.

———. "Spanish Ship Measurements Reconsidered: The Instruccion Nautica of Diego Garcia de Palacio (1587)." *Mariners Mirror* 73 (1987): 293–96.

Plaskett, Keith. "Logistics and Equipment." See Smith et al., eds., *The Emanuel Point Ship: Archaeological Investigations 1997–1998*, 10–15.

Presley, Anna Lee. "Analysis of Faunal Remains from the Emanuel Point Shipwreck." Unpubl. manuscript on file, Florida Bureau of Archaeological Research, Tallahassee, 1995.

Priestley, Herbert Ingram. *The Luna Papers*. 2 vols. Deland: Florida State Historical Society, 1928.

———. *The Luna Papers 1559–1561: Volumes I & II*. Ed. John E. Worth. Tuscaloosa: University of Alabama Press, 2010.

———. *Tristán de Luna, Conquistador of the Old South: A Study of Spanish Imperial Strategy*. Glendale, CA: Arthur H. Clark Company, 1936.

Pugh, David. "A Study of Iron Fasteners from the Emanuel Point Ship." Master's research paper, University of West Florida, 2001.

Quinn, David Beers. *The Last Voyage of Thomas Cavendish, 1591–1592: The Autograph Manuscript of his Own Account of the Voyage Written Shortly Before his Death*. Chicago: University of Chicago Press, 1975.

Rhodes, Diane Lee. "Coronado Fought Here: Crossbow Boltheads as Possible Indicators of the 1540–1542 Expedition." In *The Coronado Expedition to Tierra Nueva: The*

1540–1542 Route Across the Southwest, ed. Richard Flint and Shirley Cushing Flint, 37–46. Niwot: University Press of Colorado, 1997.

Record, Samuel J., and Robert W. Hess. *Timbers of the New World*. New Haven: Yale University Press, 1943.

Rednap, Mark. "The Cattewater Wreck: The Investigation of an Armed Vessel of the Early Sixteenth Century." Archaeological Series no. 8. Greenwich, UK: National Maritime Museum, 1984.

Reitz, Elizabeth J., and C. Margaret Scarry. *Reconstructing Historic Subsistence with an Example from Sixteenth-Century Spanish Florida*. Special Publication Series no. 3. Tucson: Society for Historical Archaeology, 1985.

Rodgers, Ree Rebecca. "Stale Bread and Moldy Cheese: A Historical and Archaeological Study of Sixteenth-Century Foodways at Sea Using Evidence Collected from the Emanuel Point Shipwreck." Master's thesis, University of West Florida, 2003.

Rosloff, Jay, and J. Barto Arnold III. "The Keel of the San Estéban (1554): Continued Analysis." *International Journal of Nautical Archaeology and Underwater Exploration* 13, no. 4 (1984): 287–96.

Roth, Louis M. *The American Cockroach*. Ed. William J. Bell and K. G. Adiyodi. New York: Chapman and Hall, 1981.

Rule, Margaret. *The Mary Rose: The Excavation and Raising of Henry VIII's Flagship*. Greenwich, UK: Conway Maritime Press, 1981.

Salisbury, W. "The Woolwich Ship." *Mariner's Mirror* 47, no. 2 (1961): 281–90.

Scappi, Bartolomeo. *The Opera of Bartolomeo Scappi (1570): L'arte et prudenza d'un maestro cuoco*. Getty Research Institute, https://archive.org/details/operavenetiascap-00scap.

Schendel, Gordon. *Medicine in Mexico*. Austin: University of Texas Press, 1968.

Scott-Ireton, Della. "An Analysis of Spanish Colonization Fleets in the Age of Exploration Based on the Historical and Archaeological Investigation of the Emanuel Point Shipwreck in Pensacola Bay, Florida." Master's thesis, University of West Florida. 1998.

———. "The Role of Historic Preservation and Public Interpretation in Shipwreck Management: The Pensacola Partnership." In *Underwater Archaeology Proceedings from the Society for Historical Archaeology Conference*, ed. Stephen R. James and Camille Stanley, 29–34. Cincinnati: Society for Historical Archaeology, 1996.

———. "Secrets in the Sea: The Emanuel Point Shipwreck." *Florida History & The Arts Magazine*, Florida Department of State (Fall 2000): 18–19.

———. "Unique Artifacts from the Emanuel Point Shipwreck." In *Underwater Archaeology Proceedings from the Society for Historical Archaeology Conference*, ed. Paul F. Johnston, 60–63. Washington, DC: Society for Historical Archaeology, 1995.

Sea History Gazette. "Archaeologists Studying the Emanuel Point Shipwreck," vol. X, no. 10 (October 1995): 3.

Shidner, Jacob Daniel. "A Macro- and Microscopic Zooarchaeological Examination of Living Conditions Aboard the Emanuel Point Wrecks." Master's thesis, University of West Florida, 2011.

Simmons, Joe J. III. "Replicating Fifteenth- and Sixteenth-Century Ordnance." *Historical Archaeology* 26, no. 1 (1992): 14–20.

Skowronek, Russell K. "Ceramics and Commerce: The 1554 *flota* Revisited." *Historical Archaeology* 21, no. 2 (1987): 101–1.

Smith, Clifford E. "Preliminary Analysis of the Site-Formation Process of the Emanuel Point Shipwreck." Unpubl. manuscript on file, Florida Bureau of Archaeological Research, Tallahassee, 1994.

———. "Conservation of Cultural and Biological Remains: An Integral Part of the Archaeological Process Required to Preserve and Protect the Cultural Resources from the Emanuel Point Shipwreck." Master's thesis, University of South Florida, 1995.

Smith, Marvin T. *Coosa: The Rise and Fall of a Southeastern Mississippian Chiefdom*. Gainesville: University Press of Florida. 2000.

Smith, Roger C. "Discovery, Development, and Interpretation of Florida's Earliest Shipwreck: A Partnership in Research and Historic Preservation." In *Underwater Archaeology Proceedings from the Society for Historical Archaeology Conference*, ed. Lawrence Babbits, Catherine Fach, and Ryan Harris, 115–21. Atlanta: Society for Historical Archaeology, 1998.

———. "Early Spanish Shipping in Pensacola." In *The Columbus Legacy in Pensacola*, ed. Virginia Parks, 46–57. Pensacola: Pensacola Historical Society, 1992.

———. "The Emanuel Point Ship: A Florida Experiment in Research, Development, and Management." In *Underwater Archaeology Proceedings from the Society for Historical Archaeology Conference*, ed. Paul F. Johnston, 40–42. Washington, DC: Society for Historical Archaeology, 1995.

———. "The Emanuel Point Ship: A 16th-Century Vessel of Spanish Colonization." In *Proceedings of the International Symposium on the Archaeology of Medieval and Modern Ships of Iberian-Atlantic Tradition*, 295–300. 1998; repr. Lisbon: Instituto Português de Arqueologia Trabalhos de Arqueologia 18, 2001.

———. "Florida." Society for Historical Archaeology *Newsletter*, Fall 1995.

———. "Florida's Underwater Archaeological Preserves." In *Underwater Archaeology Proceedings from the Society for Historical Archaeology*, ed. John D. Broadwater, 43–46. Richmond: Society for Historical Archaeology, 1991.

———. "Glass Recovered from the Molasses Reef Wreck, Turks and Caicos Islands, B.W.I." Unpubl. manuscript on file, Institute of Nautical Archaeology, Texas A&M University, College Station, 1986.

———. "Ill-Fated Galleon." *Archaeology* 51, no. 1 (1998): 42–46.

———. "Luna's Fleet and the Discovery of the First Emanuel Point Shipwreck." *Florida Anthropologist* 62, nos. 3–4 (September–December 2009): 79–81.

———. "Marine Archaeology Comes of Age in Florida: Excavation of Deadman's Shipwreck, a Careened British Warship in Pensacola Bay." In *Underwater Archaeology Proceedings from the Society for Historical Archaeology Conference*, ed. Toni L. Carrell, 110–16. Tucson: Society for Historical Archaeology, 1990.

———. "Pensacola's Colonial Maritime Resources." In *Archaeology of Colonial Pensacola*, ed. Judith A. Bense, 91–120. Gainesville: University Press of Florida, 1999.

———. "The Ship at Emanuel Point: An Examination of Florida's Earliest Shipwreck."

In *Underwater Archaeology Proceedings from the Society for Historical Archaeology Conference*, ed. Robyn P. Woodward and Charles D. Moore, 14–18. Vancouver, BC: Society for Historical Archaeology, 1994.

———. "Ships in the Exploration of La Florida." *Gulf Coast Historical Review* 8, no. 1 (1992): 18–29.

———. "Treasure Ships of the Spanish Main: The Iberian-American Maritime Empires." In *Ships and Shipwrecks of the Americas*, ed. George F. Bass, 85–106. New York: Thames and Hudson, 1988.

———. *Vanguard of Empire: Ships of Exploration in the Age of Columbus*. New York: Oxford University Press, 1993.

Smith, Roger C., Donald Keith, and Denise Lakey. "The Highborn Cay Wreck: Further Exploration of a 16th-Century Bahaman Shipwreck." *International Journal of Nautical Archaeology and Underwater Exploration* 14, no. 1 (1985): 63–72.

Smith, Roger C., James Spirek, John Bratten, and Della Scott-Ireton. *The Emanuel Point Ship: Archaeological Investigations 1992-1995*. Tallahassee: Bureau of Archaeological Research, Division of Historical Resources, Florida Department of State, 1995.

Smith, Roger C., John R. Bratten, J. "Coz" Cozzi, and Keith Plaskett. *The Emanuel Point Ship: Archaeological Investigations 1997-1998*. Report of Investigations no. 68. Pensacola and Tallahassee: Archaeology Institute, University of West Florida, and Bureau of Archaeological Research, Division of Historical Resources, Florida Department of State, 1998.

South, Stanley, Russell K. Skowronek, and Richard E. Johnson. *Spanish Artifacts from Santa Elena*. Anthropological Studies 7. Columbia: South Carolina Institute of Archaeology and Anthropology, 1988.

Spanish Crown. Asiento with Hernando de Soto, April 20, 1537, AGI Indiferente General 415, Libro 1, ff. 41r–45r.

Spirek, James. "Pinned to the Bottom: Emanuel Point Hull Remains." In *Underwater Archaeology Proceedings from the Society for Historical Archaeology Conference*, ed. Paul F. Johnston, 43–48. Washington, DC: Society for Historical Archaeology, 1995.

———. "Ship's Architecture." In *The Emanuel Point Ship: Archaeological Investigations 1992-1995*, ed. Roger C. Smith, James Spirek, John Bratten, and Della Scott-Ireton, 24–51. Tallahassee: Bureau of Archaeological Research, Division of Historical Resources, Florida Department of State, 1995.

Spirek, James, Della Scott, Charles Hughson, Mike Williamson, and Roger C. Smith. "Submerged Historical Resources of Pensacola Bay, Florida, Phase Two." Unpubl. report on file, Florida Bureau of Archaeological Research, Tallahassee, 1993.

Stahl, Alan M. "The First Coins in the New World." *Numismatist* 105, no. 10 (1992): 1399–1402.

———. Personal communication with Roger C. Smith, 1995.

Steffy, J. Richard. *Wooden Shipbuilding and the Interpretation of Shipwrecks*. College Station: Texas A&M University Press, 1994.

Stevens, Willis, ed. *Underwater Research at Red Bay, Labrador: A Summary of the 1981 Field Season*. Ottawa: Parks Canada Research Bulletin 194, 1983.

Swanton, John R. *Early History of the Creek Indians and Their Neighbors.* Washington, DC: Government Printing Office, 1922.

———. *Final Report of the United States De Soto Expedition Commission.* Washington DC: Government Printing Office, 1939.

Tesar, Louis D. "Archaeological Survey and Testing of Gulf Islands National Seashore. Part 1: Florida." Ed. Hale G. Smith. Tallahassee: Florida State University Department of Anthropology, 1973.

Tidewater Atlantic Research. "Underwater Archaeological Investigations: Gulf of Mexico and Pensacola Bay, Florida." Unpubl. report on file, Florida Bureau of Archaeological Research, Tallahassee, 1987.

US Army Corps of Engineers. "Underwater Archaeological Investigation. Pensacola Harbor Entrance Channel." Unpubl. report on file, Florida Bureau of Archaeological Research, 1990.

———. "Underwater Remote Sensing Survey, US Navy Homeport Site, Pensacola, Florida." Unpubl. report on file, Florida Bureau of Archaeological Research, 1986.

Vigón, Jorge. *Historia de la Artillería Española.* 2 vols. Madrid: Instituto Jeronimo Zurita, 1947.

Waddell, P.J.A. "The Pump and Pump Well of a 16th-Century Galleon." *International Journal of Nautical Archaeology and Underwater Exploration* 14, no. 3 (1985): 243–59.

Walker, Bryce. *The Armada* (The Seafarers). Alexandria, VA: Time Life Books, 1981.

Watts, Gordon P. Jr. "The Western Ledge Reef Wreck: A Preliminary Report on Investigations of the Remains of a 16th-Century Shipwreck in Bermuda." *International Journal of Nautical Archaeology and Underwater Exploration* 22, no. 2 (1993): 103–24.

Watts, Gordon P. Jr., John Broadwater, John W. Morris, and Marianne Franklin. "Final Report on IMHA-3: A Sixteenth-Century Spanish Wreck off Bermuda." In *Underwater Archaeology Proceedings from the Society for Historical Archaeology Conference,* ed. Robyn P. Woodward and Charles D. Moore, 47–62. Vancouver, BC: Society for Historical Archaeology, 1994.

Weinstein, Eri. "Pollen Analysis of Samples Recovered from the Emanuel Point Shipwreck, Pensacola Bay, Florida." Unpubl. manuscript on file, Florida Bureau of Archaeological Research, Tallahassee, 1994.

Weddle, Robert S. *Spanish Sea: The Gulf of Mexico in North America Discovery 1500–1685.* College Station: Texas A&M University Press, 1985.

Wells, Debra J. "Analysis of the Ceramic Assemblage: 8ES1980, Emanuel Point Wreck." Unpubl. manuscript on file, Florida Bureau of Archaeological Research, Tallahassee, Florida, 1994.

———. "Examples of Ceramics from the Emanuel Point Shipwreck." In *Underwater Archaeology Proceedings from the Society for Historical Archaeology Conference,* ed. Paul F. Johnston, 55–59. Washington, DC: Society for Historical Archaeology, 1995.

Whitaker, Arthur P. *The Huancavelica Mercury Mine.* Cambridge, MA: Harvard University Press, 1941.

Williams, Carrie. "Analysis of Tin-glazed Ceramics from the Emanuel Point Shipwreck Second Campaign." See Smith et al., eds., *The Emanuel Point Ship: Archaeological Investigations 1997–1998,* 140–45.

Williamson, Michael H., ed. "Jack's Wreck, Gulf Islands National Seashore, Perdido Key, Florida." Unpubl. manuscript on file, Department of Sociology and Anthropology, University of West Florida, Pensacola, 1991.

Williford, James. "Underwater Clues." *Humanities* 33, no. 3 (May–June 2012): 6.

Willis, Raymond. "The Archaeology of 16th-Century Nueva Cádiz." Master's thesis, University of Florida, Gainesville, 1976.

Winsor, Justin. *Narrative and Critical History of America*. Boston: Houghton, Mifflin, and Company, 1884–89.

Worth, John E. *Discovering Florida: First Contact Narratives from Spanish Expeditions along the Lower Gulf Coast*. Gainesville: University Press of Florida, 2014.

———. "Documenting Tristán de Luna's Fleet, and the Storm That Destroyed It." *Florida Anthropologist* 62, nos. 3–4 (September–December 2009): 83–92.

———. "Preliminary Observations on the Archaeological Assemblage of the 1559–1561 Tristán de Luna Settlement." Paper presented at the 49th Annual Conference of the Society for Historical Archaeology, Washington, DC, January 9, 2016.

Worth, John E., and John R. Bratten. "The Materials of Colonization: Archaeological and Documentary Traces of Tristán de Luna's Colonial Fleet." Paper presented at the 79th Annual Meeting of the Society for American Archaeology, Austin, April 26, 2014.

CONTRIBUTORS

Dr. Elizabeth D. Benchley is director of the University of West Florida Archaeology Institute and the Division of Anthropology and Archaeology. She manages the institute's resources to support UWF maritime and terrestrial field schools, students, and grant funded projects. She has directed numerous archaeological projects in the Midwest and northwest Florida over her forty-year career and currently specializes in the colonial archaeology of downtown Pensacola. She also teaches cultural resource management and works tirelessly to promote historic preservation in archaeology.

Dr. John R. Bratten is chair and associate professor of University of West Florida's Department of Anthropology. Since 1994 he has developed state and university laboratories to conserve artifacts from the Emanuel Point ships and has directed related research theses of a number of graduate students. Bratten is the author of *The Gondola* Philadelphia *and the Battle of Lake Champlain*.

Dr. Gregory D. Cook is assistant professor in the University of West Florida Department of Anthropology and co-principal investigator (with Bratten) of excavations at the Emanuel Point II Ship. He received his doctoral degree from Syracuse University with extensive experience working on colonial-period shipwrecks and serves as field director for continued work on Pensacola shipwrecks, supporting students in research and thesis work.

Dr. Joseph Cozzi is a research associate with New College of Florida and works as an independent marine archaeological consultant. He served as assistant project director on the excavation of La Salle's ship, *La Belle*, for the Texas Historical Commission, before coming to Florida to supervise excavations during the second field campaign on the Emanuel Point Ship. He became a research associate for the University of West Florida Archaeology Institute and later managed a nautical archaeology program at Mote Marine Laboratory.

Dr. Della A. Scott-Ireton is associate director of the Florida Public Archaeology Network. She is a veteran of Pensacola's shipwreck research, having served as a principal member of the team that discovered the Emanuel Point Ship. As a tireless proponent of public outreach and participation in archaeology, Scott-Ireton is co-editor of *Submerged Cultural Resource Management, Preserving and Interpreting Our Maritime Heritage*, and *Out of the Blue: Public Interpretation of Maritime Cultural Resources* and is editor of *Between the Devil and the Deep: Meeting Challenges in the Public Interpretation of Maritime Cultural Heritage*.

KC Smith coordinated educational programs in Tallahassee at Mission San Luis Historic and Archaeological Site, the Florida Historic Capitol, and the Museum of Florida History, where she served as curator of education. She also administered the Florida History Fair, a National History Day affiliate, for fourteen years. Smith is an accomplished writer and editor and is the author of three children's books: *Ancient Shipwrecks*, *Shipwrecks of the Explorers*, and *Exploring for Shipwrecks*. Smith copy-edited the manuscript before this book went to press.

Dr. Roger C. Smith served as state underwater archaeologist for the Florida Bureau of Archaeological Research for three decades. He is the author of *Vanguard of Empire: Ships of Exploration in the Age of Columbus* and *The Maritime Heritage of the Cayman Islands*, coauthor of *An Atlas of Maritime Florida*, and editor of *Submerged History: Underwater Archaeology in Florida*.

James D. Spirek works as the state underwater archaeologist for the South Carolina Institute of Archaeology and Anthropology, University of South Carolina. He served as field director of the Pensacola Shipwreck Survey, which resulted in the discovery of the Emanuel Point Ship. He directed excavations on this site for more than two years. His meticulous recording of the ship's hull allowed an accurate determination of its shape, size, and construction details. Spirek is co-editor of *Submerged Cultural Resource Management: Preserving and Interpreting Our Maritime Heritage*.

Dr. John E. Worth, an associate professor in the University of West Florida Department of Anthropology, has extensive experience with archaeological fieldwork and archival research. He is the author of three books: *The Timucuan Chiefdoms of Spanish Florida, Vols. I and II*, *The Struggle for the Georgia Coast*, and *Discovering Florida: First-Contact Narratives of Spanish Expeditions along the Lower Gulf Coast*.

INDEX

Illustrations are shown by page numbers in *italics*. Tables are shown by page numbers in *italics* followed by a "*t*."

Acuña, Pedro de, 57, 58
Alabama River (Río de Piachi), 52
Alvarez de Pineda, Alonso, 36
Amer, Christopher F., 33n37, 74–75, 229
American cockroach, 172–73, 219
American Indian slaves, 36–37
Ammunition. *See* Arms and armaments
Anchor, 4, 15, 18, 19, 30, 31, 73–74, *73*, 94, 103, 109, 110, 122, 123, *124*, 125, 214, 222, 246, 248
Andonasgui, Pedro, 117, 118
Animal remains, 84, 166–75; barnacles, 82, 110, 175, 242; bones, 167–71, *168*, *170*, 216; coral, 175, 221; insects, 172–74, *173*, 218–19; laboratory conservation of, 216; mollusks, 174–75; overview, *264t*, *268t*; rats and mice, 169–70, *170*, 241–42, *268t*. *See also* Faunal remains
Anunciación, Domingo de la, 50
Apica, 53
Apothecary weights, 198–99, *199*
Appleyard, John, 32n16
Archaeology (magazine), 234
Archivo General de Indias (Seville), 35, 40
Arias Dávila, Gómez, 38
Armitage, Philip L., 169, 170
Armor. *See* Body armor
Arms and armaments, 182–90, 249; artillery, 189–90; cannons, 190; cast-iron ammunition, 252; composite lead/iron shot, 184–85, *185*, 214, 249, 252, *270*; crossbow bolt points, 187–89, *188*; iron shot, 22, 85, 186–87, *187*, 214, 249, 252; lead shot, 186, *187*, 214, 249, *270t*; overview, *270t*; stone shot, 22, 85, 109, 182–84, *183*, 257, *264t*, *270t*
Arnold, J. Barto, 33n37, 229
Artifact conservation. *See* Laboratory conservation
Artifacts (Emanuel Point Ship), 19–22, 23, 25, 28, 29–30, 84, 109–10, 122–202, 175–82, *178*, *179*, 246, 248–50, *264t–270t*; ammunition, 22, 85, 109; anchor, 4, 15, 18, 19, 30, 31, 73–74, *73*, 94, 103, 109, 110, 122, 123, *124*, 125, 214, 222, 246, 248; animal remains, 84, 166–75, *168*, *170*, 216, *264t*, *268t*; apothecary weights, 198–99, *199*; armor, 23, *23*, 85, 190–92, *193*, 194, 233, 249, 252; artillery, 189–90; Aztec ceramics, 25, 156–57, *157*, *158*, 159, 233, 249, 250, 252, *264t*, *267t*; ballast, 1, 3–4, 13, 14–15, 18, 22, 41, 68, 69, 70, 73–74, 75, 79, 80, 81, 85, 91, 97, 110, 119, 119–20, 133–34, 159, 163, 167, 172, 175, 176, 198, 202, 220, 236, 237, 238, 242, 243, 246, 247, 248, 256, 257, 259, *264t*, *266t*; blades and razors, 194–96, *195*, 249; bones, 167–71, *168*, *170*, 216; botanical remains, 84, 175–82, *178*, *179*, *264t*, *269t*; brass buckle, 201; brass ring, 137, 215–16; breastplate, 23, *23*, 85, 190–92, *193*, 194, 233, 249, 252; bronze mortar and pestle, 146–47, *146*; cannons, 190; categories of, 122–23; ceramics, 25, 30, 70, 74–75, 85, 109, 150–59, 211–13, *212*, 248–52, *264t*, *267t*; chronological chart of, 250–51, *251*; cockroach parts, 75–76, 172–73, *173*, 219, 241; coins, 85, 196–98, *197*, 232, 233, 243, 250; collection techniques, 20; composite lead/iron shot, 184–85, *185*, 214, 249, 252, *270t*; concretions, 213–14, *213*; cooking vessels, 29, 30; copper cauldrons, 22, 29–30, 31, 84, 94, 137–41, *138*, *139*, *142*, *143*, 144, 149, 215; copper pitcher, 134–37, *135*, *136*, 215; coral, 175, 221, *264t*; corks, 160, *161*; crossbow bolt points, 187–89, *188*; dunnage, 176–77, 220; encrustations, 202; faunal remains, 84, 166–71, *168*, *170*, *173*; fishing weights, 202; food remains, 177–79, *178*, *179*, 181; freeze-drying, *210*, 211, 220; funnel, 147–48, *147*, *215*; glass, 199–200; gudgeons, 22, 125–28, *127*, 131, 207, 214; handling and logging of, 96, *96*, 122–23; insect remains, 172–74, *173*, 218–19;

Artifacts—*continued*
iron breastplate, 23, *23*, 85, 190–92, *193*, 194, 233, 249, 252; iron fastenings, 103, 128–32, *129*, *265t*; iron shot, 22, 85, 186–87, *187*, 214, 249, 252, *270t*; laboratory conservation of, 207–23; lead-glazed earthenwares, 154, 249; lead sheathing, 130–33, *131*; lead shot, 186, *187*, 214, 249, *270t*; leather, 164–66, *165*, *166*, 220, *264t*, *269t*; mercury (quicksilver), 25, 85, 200–201, 221, 240, 250; metal pitcher, 22, 29, 83, 94; mollusks, 174–75; obsidian, 194–96, *195*, 249, *265t*; olive jars, 74–75, *75*, 109, 123, 150, *151*, 152–54, *152*, 160, 212–13, *212*, 250, 251, *264t*, *267t*; organic debris, 84, 160–66; overview, *264t–270t*; pollen, 180–81; rat and mouse bones, 169–70, *170*, 216; rope or cordage, 177, 218, *264t*, *269t*; rudder, 8, 9, 22, 23, *23*, 29, 74, 84, 88–91, *89*, 117, 125–26, 137, 239, 240, 243, 247; rudder fittings, 125–28, *127*, 133; sauce pan (cup), 144–45, *145*; seeds, 84, 175, 177–79, *178*, *179*; ship silhouette carving, 163, *164*; shoes, 164–66, *165*, *166*; shot, 22, 85, 182–87, 214, 249, 252, *264t*, *270t*; skillet, 144, 215; stabilization and conservation of, 91; stone artifacts, 220, *264t*, *266t*; stone shot, 22, 85, 109, 182–84, *183*, *264t*, *270t*; teeth, 167, 216; textiles, 218; timbers, 74, 98–99, 108, 109, 111, 176, 236; tin enamelwares, 154–56, *155*; wooden implements, 162–63, *162*, 220
Artillery. *See* Arms and armaments
Avery, George, 153
Ayllón, Lúcas Vázquez de, 37, 39
Aznar, José María, 232
Aztec blades, 195, 196, 249
Aztec ceramics, 25, 156–57, *157*, *158*, 159, 233, 249, 250, 252, *264t*, *267t*
Aztec Indians, 44–45, 249

Bahía Filipina. *See* Mobile Bay
Baker, Barry W., 167
Ballast *(lastre)*, 1, 3–4, 13, 14–15, 18, 22, 41, 68, 69, 70, 73–74, 75, 79, 80, 81, 85, 91, 97, 110, 119, 119–20, 133–34, 159, 163, 167, 172, 175, 176, 198, 202, 220, 236, 237, 238, 242, 243, 246, 247, 248, 256, 257, 259, *264t*, *266t*
Bancroft, Janet, 32n22, 133
BAR. *See* Bureau of Archaeological Research

Barkley, Jane, 32n7
Barlow, Robert H., 156, 157
Barnacles, 82, 110, 175, 242
Baumer, David, 9
Bay of Campechy shipwreck, 201
Beetles, 173–74, *173*, 241, *268t*
Bendig, Charles, 62n29
Bense, Judith, 7, 9, 31, 33n38, 92, 233
Benzotriazole (BTA), 216
Bertsch-Naggatz, Gigi, v, 22, 32n7, 33n43, 208, 226, *227*
Beteta, Gregorio de, 55
Biedma, Diego de, 55, 59
Bilge boards *(tablas de la canal)*, 79, *80*, 83, 162
Biringuccio, Vannocchio, 148
Bivalves, 174–75
Blackwater schooner, 9
Blades and razors, 194–96, *195*
Blue on Blue majolica, 156
Body armor: iron breastplate, 23, *23*, 85, 190–92, *193*, 194, 233, 249, 252; padded cloth armor, 192, 194, 252
Bones, 167–71, *168*, *170*, 216
Boquín, Felipe, 49
Botanical remains, 84, 175–82, *178*, *179*; dunnage, 176–77, 220; food remains, 177–79, *178*, *179*, 181; laboratory conservation of, 217–18; overview, *264t*, *269t*; pollen, 180–81; rope or cordage, 177, 218, *269t*; seeds, 84, 175, 177–79, *178*, *179*
Bow architecture (Emanuel Point Ship), 95, 97–99, *100*, 101–2
Bow area (Emanuel Point Ship), 29, 30, 83
Bowden, Earle, 33n38
Brass buckle, 201
Brass ring, 137, 215–16
Bratten, Dennis, 133
Bratten, John R., 5, 6, 22, 25, *27*, 28, *29*, 31, 41, 84, 92, 122, *147*, 207, 236, 254, 256
Breastplate, 23, *23*, 85, 190–92, *193*, 194, 233, 252
Breetzke, David, 164
Broussard, Larry, 7, 8, 32n7
Brown, Ted, 33nn38,39
Browning, Kurt, 258, *258*
Brown Marine Services Inc., 31, 228
BTA. *See* Benzotriazole
Bud (bulldog), 9, 10

Bureau of Archaeological Research (BAR), 11, 26, 27
Burns, Jason, 33n42, 222
Buttresses (ship component), 79–80, *80*, *263t*

Cabeza de Vaca, Álvar Núñez, 38
Caldwell, Miller, 33n38
Cancer de Barbastro, Luís, 38, 39, 40
Cannonballs (stone shot), 22, 85, 109, 182–84, *183*, *264t*, *270t*
Cannons, 190
Cape Hatteras, 59
Cape of Trafalgar, 59
Capital X-Ray, Inc., 210–11
Carolina (dredge vessel), 9
Cattewater shipwreck, 132
Cauldrons. *See* Copper cauldrons
Cavendish, Thomas, 174
Caxiti, 53
Ceier, Scott, 32n7
Ceiling planks (*amuradas*), 70, 80–83, 98, 102–3, 237–38, *263t*
Ceramics, 25, 30, 70, 74–75, 85, 109, 150–59, 248–50; Aztec ceramics, 25, 156–57, *157*, *158*, 159, 233, 249, 250, 252, *264t*, *267t*; Cologne stoneware, 159; conservation in the laboratory, 211–13, *212*; lead-glazed earthenwares, 154, 249; majolica, 154–56, *155*, 249, 251, *264t*, *267t*; olive jars, 74–75, *75*, 109, 123, 150, *151*, 152–54, *152*, 160, 212–13, *212*, 250, 251, *264t*, *267t*; overview, *264t*, *267t*; tin enamelwares, 154–56, *155*
Cerón Saavedra, Jorge, 52, 54, 55, 56, 57, 58
Charlesfort Settlement (South Carolina), 59
Chiles, Lawton, 232
Christie House, 95
Clausen, Carl, 33n37, 229
Cockroaches, 75–76, 172–73, *173*, 219, 241
Coins, 85, 196–98, *197*, 215, 216, 232, 233, 243, 250
Collis, James D., 116, 117, 118, 256
Cologne/Rhenish stoneware, 159, *264t*, *267t*
Columbia Plain majolica, 155–56, 249, 251, *267t*
Composite lead/iron shot, 184–85, *185*, 214, 249, 252, *270t*
Concretions, 213–14, *213*
Conde de Tolosa (shipwreck), 201

Conference on Historical and Underwater Archaeology (1995), 230–31
Conservation in the laboratory. *See* Laboratory conservation
Convoy (shipwreck), 8
Cook, Gregory D., 6, 41, 254
Cooking vessels, 29, 30. *See also* Galley wares
Coosa, 53, 54, 56, 60, 65n82
Copper artifacts, 215, 248; laboratory conservation of, 215–16, *215*
Copper cauldrons, 22, 29–30, 31, 84, 94, 137–41, *138*, *139*, *142*, *143*, 144, 149, 215, 248
Copper crossbow points, 187–88
Copper pitcher, 29, 83, 94, 134–37, *135*, *136*, 215
Copper sauce pan (cup), 144–45, *145*
Coral, 175, 221
Cordage, 177, 218, *264t*, *269t*
Corks, 160, *161*
Corpus Christi (bark), 43, 48, 49
Cortés, Hernan, 36
Couch, Peg, 33n38
Cozzi, Joseph "Coz," 5, 28, *29*, 31, 68, 92, 236
Crossbow bolt points, 187–89, *188*
Crossbows, 188–89, 252
Cuba, 36, 37, 38, 43, 50, 55, 56, 58, 59, 83, 201, 229
Cubit (*codo*), 113–16
Curren, Caleb, 7

Daniels, John, 17, 33n38, 217–18
D'Asaro, Pat, 33n38
Dávila Padilla, Agustín, 45, 60n14, 63n47, 64n61
Davis, María, 232
Daza, Luis, 44, 48
Deadman's Island shipwreck, 8–9
Deadrise, 81
Deagan, Kathleen, 72
De Bry, John, 159
Delft ceramics, 154
De Luna, Founder of North America's First Colony (Appleyard), 32n16
Depth of hold (*puntal*), 114–15, *261t*
Derrow, Stuart, 32n22, 33n36
Desire (Cavendish's ship), 174
de Soto, Hernando. *See* Soto, Hernando de
Dickey, Harv, 33n43, 226
Doelker, Richard, 92

Doz, Martín, 55
Dramont "H" (shipwreck), 90
Drouin, Alan, 12
Duke, Cullan, 33n43
Dunbar, James, 229
Dunnage, 176–77, 220, *269t*
Dye, Rick, 33n38

Earthenware artifacts. *See* Ceramics
Eaves, Ian, 191–92
EDTA. *See* Ethylene diamine tetra-acetic acid
El Francesillo (ship), 50
El Marién (Cuba), 55
El Morro ware, 154, 249, 251, *264t*
Emanuel Point II shipwreck, 41, 256–59, *257, 258*
"Emanuel Point Ship, The: A Florida Experiment in Research, Development, and Management" (symposium, 1995), 230–31
"Emanuel Point Ship, The: The Second Field Campaign on a Vessel from Tristán de Luna's 1559 Fleet" (symposium, 1998), 231
Emanuel Point Ship, 68–120; about, xiii–xiv, 4, 40, 70–71, 91, 106, 108–20, 236–53; ballast, 1, 3–4, 13, 14–15, 18, 22, 41, 68, 69, 70, 73–74, 75, 79, 80, 81, 85, 91, 97, 110, 119, 119–20, 133–34, 159, 163, 167, 172, 175, 176, 198, 202, 220, 236, 237, 238, 242, 243, 246, 247, 248, 256, 257, 259, *264t, 266t*; bilge, 241, 243; bilge boards, 79; bow architecture, 95, 97–99, *100*, 101–2; bow area, 29, 30, 83; buttresses, 79–80, *80, 263t*; cargo carried by, 240–41; ceiling planks, 80, 102, *263t*; construction of, 108, 236–39; decomposition of, 110–11; dimensions of, 28–29, 30, 108–9, 111, 112–17, 246–47, *261t–263t*; fasteners, 103, 129–30, *129, 265t*; filling pieces, 102–3; floors, 81, *262t*; foodstores on, 241; footwales, 70, *263t*; frames, 81, 87–88, 90, 99, 101, 237, *262t*; futtocks, 81, 101–2, *262t*; galley, 17, 25, 29, 30, 84, 94, 134, 138, 146, 147, 150, 215, 248; "hogging," 102; hull measurements, *261t*; hull planking, 102–3, *263t*; hull timbers, 98–99, 108, 109, 111, 176, 236; identifying the wreck, 118–19; keel measurements, *261t*; keelson, 77, 237, *261t*; knees, 104–5, *104*, 238, *263t*; lead sheathing, 130–33, *131*; length of, 30; main frame, 81; mainmast, 77, 81–82, *82*; mainmast step, 77–78, *78, 262t*; maintenance and repair at sea, 242–43; mast, 239; media coverage of, 23–24, 224–25, 232–34; midships architecture, 77–84, *78, 80, 80*; National Register of Historic Places, 27; planking, 80, 89, 102–3, 237–38; point of embarcation, 250; port covers, 105, *106, 107*; pump sumps, 78–79; pump well, 79; repairs on, 242, 247; rudder, 8, 9, 22, 23, *23*, 29, 74, 84, 88–91, *89*, 117, 125–26, 137, 239, 240, 243, 247; rudder fittings, 125–28, *127*, 133; sea rations, 241; sheathing, 238–39; shipworms, 110, 130–31, 238–39; sinking of, 109, 243, 246, 250; stemson, 98, *262t*; stern architecture, 84–85, *86*, 87–91; sternpost, 87, *263*; tail section, 85, 87; wreckage summary, 248–49. *See also* Artifacts (Emanuel Point Ship); Emanuel Point Ship excavation
Emanuel Point Ship excavation, 68–120, 246; about, 105, 236–53; anomalies, 4, 14, 15, 30, 68, 69, 71, 74, 255, 256, 259; archaeological tools used, 19; ballast, 1, 3–4, 13, 14–15, 18, 22, 41, 68, 69, 70, 73–74, 75, 79, 80, 81, 85, 91, 97, 110, 119, 119–20, 133–34, 159, 163, 167, 172, 175, 176, 198, 202, 220, 236, 237, 238, 242, 243, 246, 247, 248, 256, 257, 259, *264t, 266t*; barge (original wooden barge), 76, 92; conferences and symposia on, 230–32; dignitaries visiting, 232, *233*; diving suits used, 30; exploratory efforts, 68–72; first excavation campaign, 18–28, *19, 23, 25, 27*, 42–91; grid system and shrimpers, 20–21; initial excavation, 14–15, *16*; location marked, 252; marine life at excavation site, 96–97, 246; media coverage of, 23–24, 224–25, 232–34; *Nautilus* (barge/work platform), 21, 91–94; Pensacola's public participation, 224–34; pontoon, 76–77; recent visits to by Spanish royalty, 232, *233*; second excavation campaign, 28–31, *29*, 91–97, *95, 96*; site plan for, *244–45*; sponsorship of, 26, 210–11, 228, 252; student internships, 26, 28, 33n36, 222; Target 17, 256–57; volunteers, 208–9, 226–27, *227*, 252. *See also* Artifacts (Emanuel Point Ship); Emanuel Point II shipwreck; Emanuel Point Ship

Emerald Coast X-Ray, 209–10
Erreguerena, Pilar Luna, 156
Escambia River Valley, 48
Espíritu Santo (shipwreck), 183
Ethylene diamine tetra-acetic acid (EDTA), 212

Faience ceramics, 154
Fastenings, 103, 128–32, *129*, 265t
Faunal remains, 84; invertebrates, 172–75, 264t, 268t; laboratory conservation of, 216; overview, 264t, 268t; vertebrates, 166–71, *168*, *170*, 264t, 268t. *See also* Animal remains
Feria, Pedro de, 55
Fiesta of Five Flags Association, 17, 26, 229, *230*
Filipina. *See* Mobile Bay
Finegold, Robert, 9
First Spanish Period, 12, 14
Fish vertebra, 167
Floral remains. *See* Botanical remains
Florida Bureau of Archaeological Research. *See* Bureau of Archaeological Research
Florida history, 34–60; early expeditions to, 34–38; French colonization of, 59; slave expeditions, 36, 37. *See also* Luna expedition; Luna settlement
Food remains, 177–79, *178*, *179*, 181
Footwales (ship component), 70, 80, 81, 83, 98, 102, 237, *263t*
Forelock bolts (*pernos de chaveta*), 128
Fort Caroline (Florida), 59
Fossum, Andrea, 33n42
Frames (ship component), 22, 25, 70, 77, 78, 80, 81, 82–85, 87–88, 90, 98–99, 101–3, 106, 108, 114, 117, 125, 176, 236, 237, 243, 247, 257, *262t*
"Francisco de Chicorano," 37
Franklin, Connie, 33n43, 226
Franklin, Marianne, 9, 11
Frigate (*fragata*), 14, 43, 45, 46, 48, 51, 55, 58, 59, 62n29, 63–64n60
Fruchey, Cecily, 32n7
Fulford, Corey, 33n43
Funnel, 147–48, *147*, *215*, 248
Futtocks (ship component), 80–81, 83, 98, 99, 101–3, 108, *262t*
Fuxa (Cuba) shipwreck, 83, 201

Galley wares, 134–37; brass ring, 137, 215–16; bronze mortar and pestle, 146–47, *146*; copper cauldrons, 22, 29–30, 31, 84, 94, 137–41, *138*, *139*, *142*, *143*, 144, 149, 215; copper pitcher, 134–37, *135*, *136*, 215; funnel, 147–48, *147*, *215*; metal pitcher, 22, 29, 83, 94; sauce pan (cup), 144–45, *145*; skillet, 144, 215
Galloway, Patricia, 65n84
Garay, Francisco de, 36, 37
García de Palacio, Diego, 111, 114, 115, 116, 128, 145, 148
Gastropods, 174–75
Gayón, Gonzalo, 43
Gibbens, Dorothy, 9
Glascock, Michael, 195, 196
Glasier-Lawson, Maija, 256
Glass, 199–200
Goggin, John, 152, 153
Goniometer, 19
Goodwin, Dave, 233
Gordillo, Francisco, 37
Grant, Ruth, 32n7
Grieve, Susanne, 222
Gudgeons (ship component), 22, 74, 84–85, 117, 119, 125–28, *127*, 131, 133, 207, 214, 218, 238, 239, 247
Gulf Breeze, City of, 8, 9
Gulf Breeze Community Center, 9
Gulf Coast Dive Pros, 227
Gulf Islands National Seashore, 8

Hamilton, Donny L., 214
Harris, Norma, 33n43
Hatteras, Cape, 59
Havana (Cuba), 37, 38, 43, 50, 55, 56, 58, 59
Henry IV *blancas*, 85, 197–98, 232, 233, 250
Heywood, Keene, 32n7
Hide beetles, 173–74, *173*, 241, *268t*
Highborn Cay (Bahamas) shipwreck, 15, 83, 106, 112, 184, 186, 187
Himour, Brad, 33n36
Hirth, Kenneth, 194
Hispaniola, 59
Historic Pensacola Inc., 26
Historic Pensacola Preservation Board, 4, 11, 17, 27, 208, 231, 252
Historic Pensacola Village, 224, 231

Hobgood, S. Randall, 191
"Hogging," 102
Hudson, Charles, 35, 41, 65n82
Hughson, Charles (Chuck), 3, 12, 13, 14, 22, 68, 71, *213*
Hull, measurements, *261t*
Hull planking, 70, 80–84, 87, 88, 97–99, 101–3, 108, 119, 126, 130–33, 237, 247, *263t*
Hunter, James, 33nn42,43, *221*, 222

Insect remains, 75–76, 172–74, *173*, 218–19
Instrucción Náutica Para Navegar (García de Palacio), 111, 148
Invertebrate remains, 172–75, *264t*, *268t*
Iron artifacts, laboratory conservation of, 213–14, *213*
Iron breastplate, 23, *23*, 85, 190–92, *193*, 194, 233, 249, 252
Iron fastenings, 103, 128–30, *129*, *265t*
Iron shot, 22, 85, 186–87, *187*, 214, 249, 252, *270t*
Isabela Polychrome ceramics, 249, 251, *267t*

Jane, John, 174
J. Earle Bowden Building, 28
Jesús (urca), 43, 49, 118, 119
Johnson, Bob, 33n43
Johnson, Sandra, 32n22
Juan Carlos I (King of Spain), 232, *233*
Juan Sebastián de Elcano (Spanish training ship), 232
Judah (shipwreck), 7

Kaczor, Bill, 233
Keel (*quilla*), 29, 30, 70, 77, 98, 99, 101, 106, 112, 114–16, 236–37, 246, *261t*
Keelson (*contraquilla*), 1, 15, 70, *71*, 77–79, *82*, 85, 87, 98, 108, 237, 238, *261t*
Keith, Donald, *27*, 33n37, 229
Kennedy, Kendra, 256
Kennedy, Sheryl, 32n22
Keoghan, Phil, 24, 33n32
Kerr, Bill, 32n22
Killinger Marine, 228
Kirkland, Ann, 33n43
Kitchen wares. *See* Galley wares
Kleeberg, John, 196

Knees (ship component), 104–5, *104*, 238, *263t*
Konstantinou, Hera, 33n43

Laboratory conservation, 207–23; archaeological illustration, *221*, 222; benzotriazole (BTA), 216; of botanical remains, 217–18; of ceramics, 211–13, *212*; of copper artifacts, 215–16, *215*; ethylene diamine tetra-acetic acid (EDTA), 212; of faunal materials, 216; freeze-drying, *210*, 211, 220; of insects, 218–19; of iron artifacts, 213–14, *213*; of lead artifacts, 214; oxalic acid, 212; passive conservation, 216; pneumatic chisel, 213, *213*; of stone artifacts, 220; students, 222; of textiles and rope, 218; volunteers, 208–9; of wood and leather, 220; X-ray machines, 209–11
Lacsohe (Indian woman), 48
La Isabela (Dominican Republic), 137, 198, 250
Lakey, Denise, 33n37, 229
LAMP. *See* Lighthouse Archaeological Maritime Program
LaSalle Shipwreck Project, 92
La Salvadora (bark), 43, 49
Lavanha, João Baptista, 111
Lavezaris, Guido de, 42, 43
Lawrence, Colleen, 179
Lawton, Michael, 33n43
Lead artifacts, laboratory conservation of, 214
Lead-covered iron shot, 184–85, *185*, 214, 249, 252, *270t*
Lead-glazed earthenwares, 154, 249
Lead sheathing, 84, 98, 108, 127, 130–33, *131*, 238, 239, 242, 256, 257
Lead shot, 186, *187*, 214, 249, *270t*
Leather, 164–66, *165*, *166*, 220, *264t*, *269t*
Licon Inc., 228
Lighthouse Archaeological Maritime Program (LAMP), 222
Lignum vitae, 180
Livro da Fabrica das Naos (Oliveira), 111
Livro Primeiro da Architectura Naval (Lavanha), 111
Lockwood, Jeffrey, 17, 72
Long Bay site (Bahamas), 198
López, Abraham, *27*, 33n37, 229
López, Diego, 49
Los Alacranes (Mexico), 42, 61n26

Luna, Christóbal de, 65n84
Luna, Tristán de. *See* Luna y Arellano, Tristán de
Luna expedition, 25, 34, 40; archival documents, 27–28, 40–41; equipment and supplies, 45; expedition members, 44–45; first reconnaissance expedition, 42–43; fleet, 43–44, 117–18; hurricane, 48–49, 63–64n60, 117–18; Nanipacana, 49–50, 51–57; objectives of, 34; painting of landing, *46;* relief expedition for, 50; routes (actual), *54;* routes (planned), *51;* second reconnaissance expedition, 43; start of, 42
Luna expedition ships, 12; first excavation campaign, 18–28, *19, 23, 25, 27;* second excavation campaign, 28–31, *29. See also* Emanuel Point Ship
Luna Papers, The (Priestley), 40
Luna settlement: about, xiii–xiv; layout for, 47–48
Luna y Arellano, Tristán de, xvii, 4–5, 32n16, 46–47, 48, 49, 51, 52, 54, 55, 58, 59, 110, 117, 224, *225*

MacDonald, "Mac," 33n43
Magnetometer, 12, 254–55
Main frame (*quaderna maestre*), 81, 84, 114
Mainmast (ship component), 1, 15, 70, 74, 77, 81–82, *82,* 83
Mainmast step (*carlinga*), 1, 4, 15, 21, 29, 69, 70, 77–83, *78, 82,* 237, *262t*
Majolica ceramics, 154–56, *155,* 249, 251, *264t, 267t*
Malcom, Corey, *27,* 33n37, 229
Maldonado, Francisco de, 38
Marcus, Harold, 33n38
Marcus, Pat, 33n38
Margaret J. Smith Archaeology Institute (University of West Florida), 222, 231
Mariél (Cuba), 55
Marine archaeology: illustrations, *221, 222;* laboratory techniques and artifact conservation, 207–23; media coverage of, 23–24, 224–25, 232–34; Pensacola's public participation, 224–34; surveying, 254–55; University of West Florida program, 31, 41, 254–56. *See also* Artifacts (Emanuel Point Ship); Emanuel Point Ship excavation; Pensacola marine archaeology
Marr, Andrew, 133
Marsh, David, 12
Martire d'Anghiera, Pietro (Peter Martyr), 37
Marx, Morris, 26, 31
Mary Rose (Henry VIII's flagship), 90, 184, 187, 192
Massachusetts, USS (battleship), 12
Mast (ship component), 1, 51, 77, 78, 109, 117, 238, 239
Matheos, Bartolomé, 49
McDaniel, Josh, 32n7
McLean, Shea, 32n22
McMahon, Don, 33nn38,39
Media coverage, 23–24, 224–25, 232–34
Meide, Chuck, 33n43
Melado ceramics, 154, 251–52, *267t*
Menéndez de Avilés, Pedro, 58–59, 60
Mercury (quicksilver), 25, 85, 141, 200–201, 221, 240, 250, *264t*
Metal artifacts, overview, *264t*
Mice, bones, 169, 170, 242, *268t*
Midships architecture (Emanuel Point Architecture), 77–84, *78,* 80, *80*
Miller, Jim, 7, 17
Miruelo, Diego de, 36
Missouri University Research Reactor (MURR), 196
Mitchell, Amy, 17, 32n7, 72
Mitchell, Philip, 33n36
Mobile Bay (Bahía Filipina), 42, 43, 45, 54
Molasses Reef Wreck, 106, 112, 123, 125, 127, 129, 130, 131, 133, 183, 184, 187, 199, 200
Mollusks, 174–75
Monte Cristi (Hispaniola), 59
Moore, Robin, 222
Morris, John "Billy Ray," 11
Mortar and pestle, 146–47, *146*
Mueller, Kyle, 32n22
Muir, Tom, 209
MURR. *See* Missouri University Research Reactor

Nanipacana settlement, 49–50, 51–57
Nanoteslas, 255
Napochín (Napochies), 53

Narváez, Pánfilo de, 37, 39
National Maritime Historical Society, 234
National Park Service, 8
Nautilus (barge/work platform), 21, 91–94
Newsom, Lee, 175, 217
Nicolò, Theodoro de, 111
Nieto, Alvaro, 44
No Opportunity Wasted (Keoghan), 33n32
Northwest Florida Maritime History Symposium (1997), 229–30
Nuestra Señora de Atocha (shipwreck), 149
Nuestra Señora de Guadalupe (shipwreck), 201
Nuestra Señora de Rosario. *See* Fuxa (Cuba) shipwreck
Nypacana. *See* Nanipacana settlement

Obsidian, 194–96, *195*, 249, *265t*
Ochuse. *See* Pensacola Bay
Ochuse settlement (Santa María de Ochuse), 46–48, 50, 52, 56
Old Christ Church Parish School House, 12
Oliveira, Fernando, 111, 115
Olive jars, 74–75, *75*, 109, 123, 150, *151*, 152–54, *152*, 160, 212–13, *212*, 250, 251, *264t*, *267t*
Olmos, Andrés de, 42
Onachiqui, 53
Organic debris, 84, 160–66; corks, 160, *161;* faunal remains, 84, 166–71, *168*, *170*, *173;* leather, 164–66, *165*, *166*, 220, *269t;* overview, *269t;* ship silhouette carving, 163, *164;* shoes, 164–66, *165*, *166;* wooden implements, 162–63, *162*, 220
Oxalic acid, 212

Padgett, Beth, 32n22
Padilla, Agustín Dávila, 45, 60n14, 63n47, 64n61
Padre Island shipwrecks, 94, 123, 127, 131, 137, 153, 159, 172, 183, 184, 186, 187
Palacio, Diego García de, 111, 114, 115, 116, 128, 145, 148
Panamerican Consultants Inc., 11
Pardo, Juan, 60
Parmelee, Rich, 32n7
Pensacola (Florida): outreach and engagement with Emanuel Point excavation, 224–34; recent visit by Spanish royalty, 232, *233*

Pensacola Archaeological Society, 208
Pensacola Bay (Ochuse), 60; early expeditions to, 38, 42, 45, 46
Pensacola marine archaeology, 7–31; 1990 pilot study, 11–12; 1993 joint project, 17–18, 32n22; development of investigative plan, 14–15, 17; early discoveries, 8–11; first excavation campaign, 18–28, *19*, *23*, *25*, *27;* second excavation campaign, 28–31, *29;* sponsors of, 26, 210–11, 228, 252. *See also* Emanuel Point Ship; Luna expedition ships
Pensacola Maritime Preservation Society, 27, 33n39, 227–28, 234
Pensacola Naval Air Station, 8
Pensacola News Journal, 16, 23, 24, 224, 233
Pensacola Rubber and Gasket Co., 228
Pensacola Shipwreck Survey, 2–4, 11–12, 72, 225, 226
Pensacola Visitor Center, 231
Percy, George, 17
Phillip II (King of Spain), 34, 40, 83
Phillips, Carla R., 113, 115
Pintles (ship component), 88, 125, 126
Pitt Slip Marina, 76, 95
P.K. Yonge Library of Florida History, 35
Planking, 15, 69, 78, 80, 89, 102–3, 106, 108, 115, 131, 237–38, 242, 246, 259
Plant material. *See* Botanical remains
Plaskett, Keith, 28, *29*, 31, 92, *96*
Pneumatic chisel, 213, *213*
Pollen, 180–81
Pollock, Stephen, 133
Polonça. *See* Pensacola Bay
Polyvinyl acetate (PVA), 212
Polyvinyl alcohol (PVAL), 212
Ponce de León, Juan, 36, 39
Porras, Juan de, 53, 54, 57
Port covers (ship component), 105, *106*, *107*
Presley, Anna Lee, 167
Priestley, Herbert, 40, 63n59
Pugh, David, 28, *29*, 33n36, 92, 130, 226
Pump, ship's, 1, 8, 78, 79, 83, 101, 102, 166, 236, 243; well (sump), 1, 2, 15, 21, 74, 78–80, 81, *82*, 83, 220, 237, 258; shaft, 1, 70, *71*, 78, 79, 237
Punta de Santa Elena, 42, 55, 59, 199
PVA. *See* Polyvinyl acetate
PVAL. *See* Polyvinyl alcohol

Quarrels (points), 187–89
Quejo, Pedro de, 37
Quicksilver. *See* Mercury

Ramírez de Arellano, Christóbal, 53, 56
Rangel, Rodrigo, 42
Rats, bones, 169–70, *170*, 216, 241–42, *268t*
Red Bay (Labrador) shipwreck, 83, 90, 106, 108, 112, 127, 163, 164, 166, 189
Rentería, Juan de, 43
Rentz, Lucy, 33n38
Ribault, Jean, 59
Río de Piachi. *See* Alabama River
Río Tome. *See* Tombigbee River
Rock and mineral artifacts. *See* Stone artifacts
Rodgers, Ree, 149
Roose, Deana, 33n43
Rope. *See* Cordage
Rudder (*timón*), 22, 23, *23*, 29, 51, 74, 84, 87–91, *89*, 117, 125–26, 137, 239, 240, 243
Rudder fittings (*machefemeas*), 74, 84, 88, 125–28, *127*, 131, 133, 238, 247
Rudeen, Herbert, *46*

Sacred Heart Hospital, 228
Salazar, Domingo de, 50
Salazar, Eugenio de, 172
Salazar, Pedro de, 36, 37
San Amaro (cargo ship), 43
San Andrés (cargo ship), 43, 118, 119
San Antón (ship), 50
San Antonio (shipwreck), 172
San Diego (shipwreck), 90, 114, 182
San Estéban (shipwreck), 94, 131, 132, 133, 137, 181, 183
San Juan (Basque whaler shipwreck), 83, 90, 106, 108, 112, 127, 164, 166, 189
San Juan (caravel), 59
San Juan (frigate), 59
San Juan (patache), 59
San Juan de Ulúa (galleon of Andonasgui), 43, 49, 117, 118, 119
San Juan de Ulúa (Mexico), 43, 250
San Juan de Ulúa (new galleon), 43, 48, 50, 55, 56, 58, 59, 118
San Luis Aragón (bark), 43, 48, 50
San Marcos (caravel), 58
San Miguel de Gualdape (colony), 37

San Salvador Island (Bahamas), 198
Santa Clara (shipwreck), 149
Santa Cruz de Nanipacana. *See* Nanipacana settlement
Santa Elena. *See* Punta de Santa Elena
Santa María de Ayuda (cargo ship), 43, 128
Santa María de la Rosa (shipwreck), 148–49
Santa María de Ochuse (Florida). *See* Ochuse settlement
Santa María de Yciar (ship), 180
Santa Rosa Island, 14
Santiago (patache), 55, 56, 57
Santi Espiritu (caravel), 43, 48, 50, 64n61
Santi Espiritu (cargo ship), 43
Sarsaparilla, 180
Sauce pan (cup), 144–45, *145*
Sauz, Mateo del, 50, 53, 57
Scafuri, David, 33n36
Scantlings, 111, *261t–263t*
Scappi, Bartolomeo, 141, *143*, 144, 149
Scarf, 81, 98, 101, 108
Scott-Ireton, Della, 3, 5, 12, 13, 14, 25, 32n7, 68, 69, 72, 84, 224, 236
Seale, Ty, 33n36
Sea rations, 241
Second Spanish Period, 12
Seeds, 84, 175, 177–79, *178*, *179*
Sevilla Blue on White majolica, 156, 249
Shells, 174–75, 221
Sherer, Dianne, 33n43
Shidner, Jacob, 174
Shipbuilding techniques: calculating dimensions, 111, 112–17; fastenings, 128–30; tonnage, 113; treatises on, 111–12; units of measurement, 113
Ship's hardware, 123–34. *See also* Anchor; Ballast; Fastenings; Lead sheathing
Ship silhouette carving (artifact), 2, *3*, 163, *164*
Shipworms (*Teredo navalis*), 110, 130–31, 238–39
Shipwrecks (16th-century Spanish shipwrecks). *See* Bay of Campechy shipwreck; *Conde de Tolosa*; Dramont "H" (shipwreck); *Espíritu Santo*; Fuxa (Cuba) shipwreck; Highborn Cay (Bahamas) shipwreck; *Mary Rose*; Molasses Reef Wreck; Padre Island shipwrecks; Red Bay (Labrador) shipwreck; *San Antonio*; *San Diego*; *San Estéban*; *San Juan*

Shipwrecks—*continued*
(Basque whaler shipwreck); *Santa Clara; Santa María de la Rosa*; St. John's Bahamas shipwreck; Villefranche shipwreck; Western Ledge Reef Wreck; Woolwich shipwreck
Shoes, 164–66, *165, 166*
Shot: composite lead/iron shot, 184–85, *185*, 214, 249, 252, *270t*; iron shot, 22, 85, 186–87, *187*, 214, 249, 252, *270t*; lead shot, 186, *187*, 214, 249, *270t*; overview, *270t*; stone shot, 22, 85, 109, 182–84, *183, 264t, 270t*
Simmons, Joe, Jr., 33n37, 229
Simons, Norman, 7, 8, 11
Skillet, 144, 215
Slave expeditions, Florida history, 36, 37
Smalley, Jinkey, 33n36
Smith, Clifford, 33n36
Smith, Peg, 32n7
Smith, Roger C., xiii, xiv, 1, 7, *29*, 33n38, 35, 40–41, 71, 72, 74, 92, 94, 217, 219, 226, 230, 231, 232, 233, 236, 257
Society for Historical Archaeology, 230, 233–34
Sofía (Queen of Spain), 232, *233*
Sommer, Monti, 32n22
Soto, Casado, 113
Soto, Hernando de, 38, 39–40, 42, 45, 187, 189
Soule, John, 33nn38,39
Soule Marine, 228
South, Stanley, 130
South Carolina, 59
South Florida Conservation Center, 220
Spalding, Lucas, 33n42
Spanish shipbuilding. *See* Shipbuilding techniques
Spanish shipwrecks. *See* Emanuel Point Ship; Emanuel Point Ship excavation; *individual shipwrecks*
Spirek, James, 3, 5, 12, 14, 25, *25*, 68, 69, 196, 226, 229, 236
Stahl, Alan, 196, 198
Stark, Teri, 32n7
St. Augustine (Florida), 60
Stem (ship component), 29, 98, 99, 101, 103, 108, 115, 246, *261t*
Stempost (*roda*), 30, 115, 237, 239

Stemson (ship component), 98, 108, *262t*
Stern architecture (Emanuel Point Ship), 84–85, *86*, 87–91
Sternpost (*codaste*), 22, 29, 74, 84–85, 87–90, 94, 125–27, *127, 131*, 132, 237–39, *263t*
St. John's Bahamas shipwreck, 149, 153, 183, 187
Stone artifacts: laboratory conservation of, 220; overview, *264t, 266t. See also* Ballast; Stone shot
Stone crabs, at excavation site, 97
Stone shot, 22, 85, 109, 182–84, *183, 264t, 270t*
Strategic Homeporting Project, 8, 9
Stringfield, Margo, 33n38
Student internship program, 26, 28, 33n36
Subway Sandwiches & Salads, 228
Swann, Brenda, 33n42
Swann, June, 165

Tacks (*estoperoles*), 129, 131–32
Tail section (Emanuel Point Ship), 85–87, *86*
Tatem, Juliet, 33n36, 92
Teeth, animal, 167, 216
Temple, John Joseph, 156
Textile remains, 218
Tidewater Atlantic Research, 8
Tin enamelwares, 154–56, *155*, 249
Tivoli High House, 11
Tombigbee River (Río Tome), 53
Tonnage (of ship), 111–13, 115–19, *115–18*, 190
Townsend, Greg, 32n22
Treenail (*cabilla de palo*), 70, 87, 88, 103, 108, 129
Trinidad (frigate), 59, 64n60
T-Square Reprographics, 228
T.T. Wentworth Jr. Florida State Museum, 10, 22, 84, 208, 222, 226, 231, 232, 233
Tumblehome, 117

Underwater Archaeological Preserves, 12
University of West Florida (UWF), xiv, 4, 17, 252; Archaeology Steering Committee, 26–27; Margaret J. Smith Archaeology Institute, 222, 231; maritime archaeology program, 31, 41, 254–56
Upiache, Province of, 52
UWF Historic Trust, 4

Van Epps, Nancy, 33n43
Vázquez, Rodrigo, 44
Velasco, Luís de (Viceroy), 34, 42, 49, 50, 58, 110, 200
Velázquez, Alonso, 50
Velázquez del Cuellar, Diego, 36
Vera, Juan, *27*, 33n37
Vertebrate remains, 166–71, *168*, *170*, *264t*, *268t*
Villafañe, Angel de, 58, 59, 64n60, 67n111
Villefranche shipwreck (France), 183
Vizsla, Rudy, *29*
Volunteers, 208–9, 226–27, *227*, 252
Voss, Terry, 226

Wahrhaftig, Solomon, 33n36, 92
Watts, Jenna, 33n36
Weathers, Suzanne, 33n43
Weeks, Warren, 8
Wells, Debra, 32n22, 33n36, 150
Wentworth State Museum. *See* T.T. Wentworth Jr. Florida State Museum
Western Ledge Reef Wreck, 106, 112, 159
Williams, Randy, 33n38
Williams, Sean, 33n42
Williamson, Mike, 3, 10, 12, 32n7, 33n43
Windham, Sandra, 33n38
Wood dunnage, 176–77, 220, *264t*, *269t*
Wooden implements, 162–63, *162*
Woolwich shipwreck, 132
Worth, John E., 4, 5, 6, 34, 118, 236, 254

Xaramillo, Juan, 50
X-ray machines, 209–11

Yayal Blue on White majolica, 156, 249, *267t*
Ypacana. *See* Nanipacana settlement

www.ingramcontent.com/pod-product-compliance
Lightning Source LLC
Chambersburg PA
CBHW020830160426
43192CB00007B/589